The Lantern-Bearers
and Other Essays

The Lantern-Bearers
and Other Essays

Robert Louis Stevenson

Edited by Jeremy Treglown

Cooper Square Press

Copyright © 1988 by Jeremy Treglown

First Cooper Square Press edition 1999

This Cooper Square Press paperback edition of *The Lantern-Bearers and Other Essays* is an unabridged republication of the edition published in New York in 1988. It is reprinted by arrangement with Farrar, Straus & Giroux.

Published by Cooper Square Press,
An Imprint of Rowman & Littlefield Publishers, Inc.
150 Fifth Avenue, Suite 911
New York, New York 10011

Distributed by National Book Network

Library of Congress Cataloging-in-Publication Data

Stevenson, Robert Louis, 1850–1894.
  The lantern-bearers and other essays / Robert Louis Stevenson ; selected
with an introduction by Jeremy Treglown.—1st Cooper Square Press ed.
    p.   cm.
  Includes index.
  ISBN 0-8154-1012-3 (pbk.: alk. paper)
  I. Treglown, Jeremy. II. Title. III. Title: Lantern-bearers.
PR5488.L18   1999
824'.8—dc21   99-33329
                                                   CIP

⊖™ The paper used in this publication meets the minimum requirements of American National Standard for Information Sciences—Permanence of Paper for Printed Library Materials, ANSI/NISO Z39.48–1992.
Manufactured in the United States of America.

CONTENTS

INTRODUCTION

Robert Louis Stevenson's work has paid the critical price of being both very popular and, on the face of things, quite simple. The simplicity is deceptive: his essays make clear how much painstaking art went into his stories. But it is a kind of art which twentieth-century criticism, with its preference for complexities of psychology and tone over mastery of form and narrative handling, has not been much interested in understanding. To be sure, he has always had a good number of vocal admirers, but it is interesting that, like Kipling's, they have until recently, and with some notable exceptions, tended to come from outside the academy: G. K. Chesterton, Edwin Muir, Janet Adam Smith, Graham Greene, Jorge Luis Borges, Alasdair Gray, Angela Carter. For good and ill, scholars have paid far less attention to him than to his contemporaries (and admirers) James and Conrad, and his work has not been properly edited. The texts of even his most famous books are unreliable, and much of what he wrote, including his essays, has long been out of print: a complete new edition is needed. In its absence, though, it is important to put back into circulation the best of what has been missing. As far as the essays are concerned, that is the object of this selection.

Part of the appeal of the nineteenth-century periodical essay is precisely, of course, its *un*academicness. With the help of Lamb and Hazlitt, the form had succeeded in keeping the humour and informality which characterised it in the eighteenth century and earlier, while taking on some of the new seriousness that entered British cultural life, largely under German influence, in the Romantic period. And although that influence would ultimately encourage the growth of academic specialisation, the fissiparousness of modern scholarship was far off. These generalisations are fallible: there was plenty of crabbed learning in Victorian Scotland and England, and there are writers today who can be compared to the Victorian essayists. But it is broadly true that there was then, as there is not now, a live popular tradition of essay-writing whose many practitioners applied themselves with both flair and, where it was appropriate, authority, to a large range of subjects, trivial and grave. As a reviewer of Stevenson's first collection, *Virginibus Puerisque*, wrote in the *Pall Mall Gazette* in April 1881,

Essays and discursive reflections on morals and society form so considerable a part of current newspaper and magazine literature in England, and are written in many quarters with so fair a measure of shrewdness and competence, that when exceptional excellence in this kind of writing occurs its recognition is apt to be less prompt and certain than would be the case in times relatively of dearth.

Critical recognition of Stevenson's excellence in this field was neither instantaneous nor unanimous, but he was widely admired, particularly for the fresh observation and imaginative sympathy the aspiring novelist and poet brought to the form, and for his stylistic *brio*. Like the young Shakespeare, Stevenson wrote effectively in the manner of many different authors he liked, while always making it his own. He famously said that he 'played the sedulous ape to Hazlitt, to Lamb, to Wordsworth, to Sir Thomas Browne, to Defoe, to Hawthorne, to Montaigne . . .', and we could add many more to the list. Although some contemporary critics were severe about this stylistic adaptability, everyone saw that Stevenson was a virtuoso. And the *Pall Mall* reviewer rightly went on to say that Stevenson has a 'fundamental . . . and formal originality'. Between the high rigour of Carlyle and Macaulay, and the brilliant but ultimately arid playfulness of Wilde, a unique voice is heard in Stevenson, both moral and irreverent, subjective and socially aware, keen to draw conclusions yet always conscious of relativism and the unreliability of dogma; and in all this, light in tone, and vividly concrete:

If youth is not quite right in its opinions, there is a strong probability that age is not much more so. Undying hope is co-ruler of the human bosom with infallible credulity. A man finds he has been wrong at every preceding stage of his career, only to deduce the astonishing conclusion that he is at last entirely right. Mankind, after centuries of failure, are still upon the eve of a thoroughly constitutional millennium. Since we have explored the maze so long without result, it follows, for poor human reason, that we cannot have to explore much longer; close by must be the centre, with a champagne luncheon and a piece of ornamental water. How if there were no centre at all, but just one alley after another, and the whole world a labyrinth without end or issue?

While Stevenson practised the techniques of writing like a painter copying old masters, he also continually developed his own imaginative response to subjects he found for himself in history, in literature, in the lives of members of his family, in the world through which he prowled observantly as an undergraduate truant, drinker and lover in Edinburgh, and more widely as, both before and after his marriage to Fanny Osbourne in San Francisco in 1880, he travelled in Europe and America. He wrote essays, like fiction, all his adult life, from a history of the Pentland Rising printed at his father's expense in 1866, before he was sixteen, to some reminiscences begun in the year he died, 1894. The best of them come from the period between 1873, when he was still reading for the bar at Edinburgh, and his setting off with his wife and family for Polynesia in 1888, after which they were partly superseded by lengthier non-fictional work on the politics and social anthropology of the South Sea Islands. In all, he wrote well over 100 essays (including the reflective topographical pieces that make up *Edinburgh: Picturesque Notes*, but excluding serialised episodes of travel books designed as continuous narratives). Not all of them were published: 'Confessions of a Unionist', made available to the general reader for the first time here, was rejected at proof stage (presumably because it would have offended American public sentiment about Ireland) by *Scribner's Magazine*; and 'Authors and Publishers', in which Stevenson contributes judiciously and amusingly to the vehement debate over publishers' commercial practices provoked by Walter Besant and the new Society of Authors in the late 1880s, has had to wait almost a hundred years to be seen in print. Many more, of course, went no further than notes, or ideas mentioned to friends. But most of the finished pieces (between a quarter and a third of which are included in this book) appeared in one or other of a large number of periodicals: in the early days, principally the *Portfolio* (which paid him his first literary fee, £3. 8s., for 'Roads' after it had been turned down by the *Saturday Review*), *Macmillan's Magazine, London, The Academy* and, most importantly for Stevenson, the *Cornhill Magazine*, whose editor, Leslie Stephen, was to be a severe and encouraging influence and to commission many of his best essays – so many, indeed, that it was said that the initials 'R.L.S.' in the *Cornhill* stood for 'the Real Leslie Stephen'. By 1881–2, just into his thirties, Stevenson was in demand as a contributor to many magazines, particularly new ones, and the publication of his first two collections of essays, *Virginibus Puerisque* and *Familiar Studies of Men and Books*, followed by the popular success of *Treasure Island* and *Dr Jekyll and Mr Hyde*, brought yet more outlets. By the time he returned to New York in 1887, newspaper editors were fighting each other for pieces by him. S. S. McClure wanted Stevenson for the New York *World*, in the words of

McClure's biographer, 'exactly as Sam Goldwyn wanted Maeterlinck', though *Scribner's Magazine* won the contest with a smaller but also less demanding offer: $3,500 a year for a dozen monthly essays, rather than $10,000 for a weekly column. 'I am sure it will do me harm to do it,' wrote Stevenson (who handled the negotiations extremely badly), 'but the sum was irresistible . . . I am like to be a millionaire if this goes on.'

The number and variety of periodicals he wrote for reflect not only the quality but the imaginative scope of his work. The fact that he was a writer of fiction had important effects on his essays: on their subject-matter and their intellectual cast. Superficially, it is true, he fits well into the non-fictional line he admired: Montaigne, Browne, Hazlitt. In that tradition, he often – and more and more as he grew older – used the essay as a form of autobiography, describing his Scottish childhood, his upbringing in a family of eminent marine engineers, and the increasing independence of his own career as he worked both at his desk and, literally, in his dreams, to become a professional story-teller. Even a selection of these pieces, with its inevitable omissions, draws the outlines of his life: his adolescent bohemianism; his early travels, partly for the sake of his health, partly for adventure; his falling in love in France with the already married Fanny Osbourne, and coming to terms with the complications and jealousies of their situation; his period in California, where he and Fanny married, and his formative encounter in Monterey with the visible ebb and flow of civilisations, a subject which would come to preoccupy him; and as well as all this the sheer practicalities of his writing: how he began *Treasure Island* and *Dr Jekyll and Mr Hyde*; his views on the best relations between authors and publishers. But of course the essays are more than simply narrative memoirs, and he uses the form in ·many different ways: as a descriptive sketchbook; as a contemplative exercise in which he could explore moral and aesthetic questions; as a vehicle for critical biography (here he had learnt most from Johnson, Carlyle and Macaulay), as a polemical mode and particularly as an educational one. Stevenson is not often teacherly, but he was a conscientious teacher of his step-family, and his 'Letter to a Young Gentleman who Proposes to Embrace the Career of Art' is full of useful practical advice. Few of his essays, however light, are uninstructive.

To a fictional writer, though, an idea, however educative, may be not so much an intellectual unit as part of an imaginative game. He accepted the playfulness intrinsic in a certain kind of essay and brought to it the forensic skills he learnt as a law student and in the Edinburgh University Debating Society. Shouldn't the possession of an umbrella entitle one to vote, he asked in a student magazine? Inactivity is good of itself, he asserted in 'An Apology for Idlers' in 1876; then, five years later in 'Talk and Talkers', denied it: 'restfulness is a quality for cattle; the virtues are all active'. These pieces are particularly noticeable for the characteristics that can be found to some degree in almost all of Stevenson's essays: humour, and a kind of gently taboo-busting common sense. 'An Apology for Idlers' baits adherents to the work-ethic (one of his favourite targets), and goes on to mock any kind of aspiration, including the literary: from the unimportance of whether an author 'should publish three or thirty articles a year' to how little the world would have been changed if Shakespeare had never been born. All this, of course, goes beyond whimsy and paradox, enjoyably as he uses them. 'An Apology for Idlers' has important things to say against mere 'busyness', and is valuable in imagining a different set of values from those practised by most of its readers, then and now. Stevenson was a relativist: he liked situations which lent a new perspective to conventional morality. This is partly why he travelled. But he said that all writing was a form of travel, and his best essays tend to be those in which he taxes his imagination as much as his experience: where he asks himself what it would have been like to have been John Knox, or one of Knox's women; or what it must be like to be a dog.

In the process of such imagining, he sometimes bends facts, or gets them wrong; perhaps nowhere more revealingly than in his arguments for truancy, when he claims that the open street was the 'favourite school' of Dickens, as if Dickens had not been desperate for the formal educational chances Stevenson could afford to neglect. Both the errors and the inconsistencies were, he claimed, justifiable. In the preface to *Virginibus Puerisque* he explained (in a way very reminiscent of Montaigne) that it was inevitable that he had changed his mind since several of the essays were first published. And in one of those essays, 'Crabbed Age and Youth', he proclaims that 'All error . . . is a strong way of stating that the current truth is incomplete'. Some contemporary critics were suspicious of this playful – or youthful – attitude to ideas, attacking what they took as shallowness, sophistry, posing and (in William Archer's phrase) 'happy-go-lucky-ism'. In the *Academy*, Edmund Purcell wanted to know whether Stevenson's essays were 'in the strict sense genuine' – 'are they, as they profess to be, the spontaneous, careless pastime of a philosopher, or the studied, artificial, practised work of a man of letters?' – and concluded,

His pen is well worthy . . . to describe the heaving tints of a sunset river, or the transient emotions of an artistic soul; but a philosopher or moralist we cannot allow him to be.

J. A. Symonds, too, wondered how much 'solid mental stuff' Stevenson had. These critics admired Stevenson. The context of their remarks is the over-praise from which he has often suffered, and their cooler assessments are worth pondering.

Much of what could seem like posturing was genuine unorthodoxy. Henry James soon came to see this. He had not taken to Stevenson when they first met, but was impressed by the seriousness of 'A Humble Remonstrance', his reply to James's 'The Art of Fiction', and from then on they argued and corresponded on literary as well as personal subjects until Stevenson's death ten years later. James, perhaps unpredictably, admired Stevenson's fictions: the catholic taste which enabled each of these very different writers to like the other's work was one of the qualities they shared. In particular, they both read voraciously among foreign authors. Stevenson wrote about Villon, Hugo, Balzac, Tolstoy. Like others in the then *avant-garde*, he became interested in Japanese history and art; and he was among the first and most discerning of British critics of Whitman and Thoreau. Again, he and James together consciously pioneered the analytical and theoretical study of prose fiction. These interests were not well calculated to attract middle-brow English sympathy; and as far as the Scots were concerned, Stevenson offended with a harsh verdict on Burns, and a heterodox reappraisal of John Knox, written when he was twenty-three.

These Scottish pieces have often been dismissed as juvenilia. But with their mixture of vigour, solid (though far from infallible) knowledge and independent judgement, they deserve to put Stevenson, alongside Leslie Stephen, in the front rank of Victorian biographical essayists. They also, along with a remarkable passage in 'A Chapter on Dreams', suggest how well he might have written in fiction about relations between the sexes. Everyone – including Stevenson himself – has commented on this absence in his work, and there have been various explanations, most interestingly G. K. Chesterton's, that in reacting against the artistic limitations and moral dangers of Decadence by seeking out an alternative in the innocent optimism of childhood, Stevenson cut himself off from some contemporary adult concerns. (Chesterton may have taken his cue from James's essay on Stevenson: 'The idea of making believe appeals to him much more than the idea of making love . . . He has given to the world the romance of boyhood.') Whatever the truth of this, it is clear from some of his essays, as well as from his mature fictions 'The Beach of Falesá' and *Weir of Hermiston*, that Stevenson was drawn to, and emotionally capable of, writing about sexual passion. And it is tantalising to see the imaginative potentiality he found in what might appear the unrewarding world of John Knox: in the first essay (which there has not been room for here), how skilfully he reconstructs the historical context that led Knox to write the *First Blast Against the Monstrous Regiment of Women*; and how sympathetically, in 'Private Life', he reconciles its author with the man who, he shows, so loved and was loved by women. Many readers may feel that Stevenson goes too far towards Knox in all this, and exaggerates what Mrs Mackgil, Mrs Bowes and her daughter, Mrs Barron, Mrs Locke, Mrs Adamson and the others stood to gain from him, but it is a remarkable and far from uncritical (or unfunny) piece of pleading, which puts the story before us in a new way without compromising Stevenson's then very modern premise, the equality of the sexes: a subject he returns to with amusing, though not unequivocal, sharpness in the second part of a little-known piece, 'The Latin Quarter', about a women's art studio in Paris.

His father – no male chauvinist, but in religion not far from Knox – called the Knox essays dull, which is so off-target as to suggest that he may have been embarrassed to read his son in this vein. Undeterred, Stevenson published them in *Macmillan's Magazine*, and immediately started work on Burns. Again, hostile critics would find the interpretation perverse (so much so that the *Encyclopaedia Britannica*, for which an earlier version was written, turned it down, and it was not salvaged until Stephen commissioned it as a review for the *Cornhill* five years later, in 1879). But again the perversity is that of an author obliged, in pursuit of the truth, to overturn some previous assumptions that stand in his way.

The obstacle in the case of Burns was Carlyle's magnificent but erratic essay, with its large claims for the poetry (subsequently put into an international perspective, as Stevenson probably knew, by Whitman), and its apparent incomprehension of the life. Three things must have sharpened Stevenson's interest in Carlyle's article: first, the extent to which its disdainful tolerance of a misspent youth ('a kind of mud-bath, in which the youth is, as it were, necessitated to steep, and, we suppose, cleanse himself, before the real toga of Manhood can be laid on him') might apply to himself; second, Carlyle's passing over the fact that Burns, unlike the newly reforming Stevenson, went on misspending his youth until he died: died, Stevenson says, not of drink but of being Robert Burns; and third, the gap between what Burns did in his poetry with the vernacular, and the austere grandeur of the language in which Carlyle contrived to write about him.

Stevenson's essay attends, by contrast, not only to Burns's sexual vagaries and emotional cruelty, but also to his pretensions (Burns called himself an old hawk as a seducer; Stevenson says the style of his letters 'is more suggestive of a Bird of Paradise'). He is very good on the poetry, by which his own was much influenced, while pointing out that the best of it was produced within a period of six months. In all this, to the extent that he is answering Carlyle, he distorts matters. But as with Knox and in all his biographical articles – especially the famous essay on Pepys – what best characterise him are firmness of judgement, a desire to get at the truth, and a conviction (this was something he knew he shared with Burns) that in doing so, imaginative intuition is as important as learning.

Most of Stevenson's best essays were written not in Scotland, but at the various temporary homes abroad – the Côte d'Azur, Paris, Fontainebleau, California, the Alps, Saranac Lake in New York State – to which he was taken by illness, restlessness and, after they met at Grez in 1876, love of Fanny Osbourne. He describes many of these places and his reactions to them in some of his topographical pieces, which, with their concern for subjective impressionism, are more volatile than the biographies, but kept in focus by a painterly kind of external observation. Stevenson read Ruskin, and it may have been from him, as much as from his artist friends, that he learnt to use the essay as the verbal equivalent of a painter's sketch: certainly in his more disenchanted (often very funny) pieces on the Alps he seems to stand in the same relationship to Ruskin, of influence and independence, as in the Burns piece he does to Carlyle. (His many enthusiastic references to trains may also have been prompted in part by a reaction against Ruskin's fastidiousness about modern means of travel.) These pieces, like the longer travel writings, manage scenic description with a combination of virtuosity and calm attentiveness that – along with Stevenson's usual good humour – steadies the more excitable responses of the invalid, the lover and the late-Victorian Bohemian.

For Stevenson was prey not only to the moods of his condition (and of his genetic inheritance), but to a despairing aestheticism fashionable among his generation. Much of what he had to say in his more personal and general essays of the 1870s – particularly those collected in *Virginibus Puerisque* – was owed to the cultural climate that Oscar Wilde would define. At their best, these pieces, among them some of his most widely known, such as 'Ordered South', 'Walking Tours', and 'Crabbed Age and Youth', manage a new description of the interplay between the observing artist and the world he is part of that anticipates the young Joyce and Virginia Woolf, much as the Barbizon School does the painting of the Impressionists. But it comes at a price. There is the sometimes extravagantly plush style, the weakness for effect, the indulgence with which, having given us a beautiful picture for its own sake – 'a group of washerwomen relieved, on a spit of shingle, against the blue sea' – he goes on tautologously to justify it by saying it justifies itself, that we may allow ourselves 'the satisfaction by which we tell each other that we are the richer by one more beautiful experience'. This has its glamour. In making a selection, though, I have preferred to emphasise other qualities, omitting 'Ordered South', for example, in favour of a more robust, very little known piece, 'The Misgivings of Convalescence'. It has not been difficult to do so, for Stevenson rarely, for all his occasional solipsism, goes along with art-for-art's sake, or the-artist-for-the-artist's-sake, to a point where contact is lost with everyday humanity. In certain respects he was a prototypical Bloomsburyite, not only in the way that he saw the artist, but in his paramount concern with personal relationships. Not art, but the individual, is the true subject of the essays in *Virginibus Puerisque* (and many of Stevenson's other pieces of their kind): individuals in love, marrying to the bafflement of their friends, growing old and facing death; individuals wanting to be alone, delighted not to be alone any more, struggling to tell each other the truth.

How much truth Stevenson himself manages to tell in his essays, with their in some ways greater freedom than the fictions, can be gauged by the extent to which passages from them have entered the language: 'Marriage is a step so grave and decisive that it attracts light-headed, variable men by its very awfulness'; 'It is better to be a fool than dead'; 'Politics is perhaps the only profession for which no preparation is thought necessary'; 'To travel hopefully is a better thing than to arrive'. Indeed, to those who collected his work after he died, there sometimes seemed too little dishonesty in what he wrote. 'The Misgivings of Convalescence', published in the *Pall Mall Gazette* when he was thirty, asks rational questions about the desirability or otherwise of an invalid's life, and lightly ironises the supposed benefits of the Alps: at least if you are going to die, he says, they will kill you more quickly. Until now, the piece has never been reprinted.

One of the most interesting aspects of Stevenson's work is the point of contact between morals and aesthetics over truth-telling, in his negotiation between a belief that literature is essentially abstract – a drawing-out of pleasing patterns from the confusion and ugliness of life – and an equally strong conviction of the overwhelming pre-eminence of life itself. Again, it was (as it always is) a current concern. Ruskin pointed out that while a painting of a bird's nest would fetch a better price than the original nest, this was no argument against birds' nests. Henry James and Oscar Wilde were less sure, and the most vigorous passage in Stevenson's 'A Humble Remonstrance', one of the best passages, indeed, in all his essays, is his onslaught on James's claim that art should compete with life – that life, Stevenson says, 'whose sun we cannot look upon, whose passions and diseases waste and slay us'. How art is to express life, though, and whether there is a clear choice to be made between points on the formal spectrum that we think of as abstract on the one hand and realistic on the other, remain for him uncertain questions. If objections against Stevenson's inconsistency are to find much purchase, it is in his statements on this subject.

In those essays which overtly deal with the matter, his views of the role and aims of the artist seem to show no clear development. A writer may be unsuccessful if judged by purely aesthetic standards, he argues in 1878 about Whitman, yet his work may still be of importance. What is 'importance', though, if we are talking about art, he asks ten years later in his 'Letter to a Young Gentleman who Proposes to Embrace the Career of Art'? Artists rank with 'dancing girls and billiard-markers', and the responsibility of feeding a family comes higher than any abstract duty in aesthetics. Yet in 'The Morality of the Profession of Letters', in 1881, he had made strong claims for certain duties in literature, among them 'truth to the fact': even though he was doubtful elsewhere about what that meant, recognising the subjectivity of truth, and the rival merits of a kind of writing that sets out – as he puts it in 'A Gossip on a Novel of Dumas's' (1887) – 'not to be true merely, but to be lovable: not simply to convince, but to enchant'. Truthfulness for its own sake, he sometimes feared, could grow rancid: he gives Zola as an example.

One should take account, here, of Stevenson's scepticism: his belief, which (like so much else) he shared with Montaigne, that inconsistency and contrariety are among the most consistent, incontrovertible facts about human beings, and that it is more truthful to disagree with oneself than to promulgate a dogma. It is also relevant that, as we have seen, he was eclectic as a writer, putting on styles like theatrical costumes and throwing himself mentally into the attitudes to which they might be appropriate. Assuming roles is, after all, part of an imaginative writer's job. And one of the things that make all these essays about writing (as well as about specific authors) fascinating, and more unified than they appear from their ostensible arguments, is their unfailing practical interest in how literature works: how it is written – its practical origins in experience, whether 'actual' or in the unconscious, the interplay of setting and event, the manipulation of narrative tension, the achievement of economy – how it affects readers, and, as in 'Letter to a Young Gentleman' and 'Authors and Publishers', the economic realities that help to make it what it is. But within the bounds of Stevenson's self-contradiction it is anyway easy to find certain common themes and assumptions about literature, particularly if we look outside the critical-theoretical pieces, both to essays on other subjects and to the rest of his work. Like any artist's, his responses to art in general were at bottom practical and predatory, concerned more with what he could use than with developing some overarching theory about it. And the various and apparently incompatible qualities he at different times praises and analyses are in practice readily worked together in his best stories – 'The Merry Men', say, or *Jekyll and Hyde* – which are highly artificial, yet also shockingly real; and which helped to feed his family without compromising the high artistic duty in which we cannot doubt that he believed.

For all their avoidance of any developmental, dogmatic programme, however, some of his essays inevitably reflect what was, within a wide stylistic range, a clear shift as he got older (and particularly as, with his move to the South Seas, he grew healthier and stronger) towards documentary truth-telling and political activism. From 1887, he began to write fewer essays, and those sometimes less well. Much of Stevenson's best non-fictional writing in his last years – indeed, simply much of his best writing – is to be found in his ambitious but uncompleted book of travels and social anthropology, *In the South Seas*, and his polemical account of recent events in Western Samoa, *A Footnote to History*. One might go further and say that much of his best work there was not written, but done: his settlement at Vailima and his care of his wife, her family, and his mother; and his participation in the political and domestic affairs of Samoa.

Certainly Stevenson saw things this way; and for all his doubts and regrets about the departure, Henry James conceded the point and defended it against the criticisms of their mutual London friends: 'how can one grudge his really *living* – with such an apparent plenitude of physical life, no matter how the literature suffers?' It is a development clearly foreshadowed in the essays, yet we have heard little from his critics about the political Stevenson: the Stevenson who in 'Crabbed Age and Youth' describes his loss of faith in socialism, and in 'The Day After To-morrow' prophesies the stagnancy of totalitarian communism. Without doubt, some of the political articles are hasty, they suffer from distortion and incompleteness. One may respond from the armchair to Stevenson's claims for individualism, uncertainty and danger in 'The Day After To-morrow', but the argument begs too many questions, particularly about the helpless. And a similar impulsiveness mars 'Confessions of a Unionist': it is one thing to sympathise with Stevenson's call for an end to terrorism in Ireland as a precondition of constitutional change (which he supports); another to find in this article any real sense either of the complexity of the local situation, whose factions he lumps together, or of how the extirpation of violence is to be brought about in practice.

Yet these pieces are of considerable interest, both in themselves and for what they reveal about their author. 'The Day After Tomorrow' more than hints at Orwell, with its vision of a land crawling with inspectors and darkened by control of the press. And 'Confessions of a Unionist' has telling points to make against American ignorance of the Irish situation, and about the double standard by which Americans condemned without consideration the kind of measures in Ireland which they had unhesitatingly and successfully dealt out to Irishmen in San Francisco. Chesterton pointed out that in Stevenson's Highland stories he is intellectually on the side of the Whigs, but morally on the side of the Jacobites. The political essays provide valuable insights into the ambivalent moral world of the historical fictions, as well as into Stevenson's attempts to defend the independent, in some ways liberal, but autocratic and rule-bound society he found in Polynesia. To omit them would be to misrepresent him.

What is most missed in 'Confessions of a Unionist' is an account of the human situation that fired Stevenson's interest in Ireland. On November 13, 1885, a Kerry farmer, John O'Connell Curtin, had surprised a group of nationalist 'Moonlighters' in the act of burgling his house for arms. They fired on him; he replied, killing one of them, and was in turn killed. Curtin was not a landlord, or in any way a direct enemy of the raiders. His family, though, were now to become a target because they would not protect his murderers. When two of the gang were brought to trial, the prosecution case depended heavily on the Curtins' identifying them – which they did, knowing the risks. The ensuing threats to, and boycott of, the family were widely reported in the British press, and lent support to the hard line on Ireland of the new Conservative government under Lord Salisbury.

Stevenson's gallantry was stirred by reading reports in *The Times* of the sufferings and courage of Norah Curtin, the dead man's sister; and he seriously contemplated going to stay with her, in the hope of getting himself martyred. (He had recently been excited by Gordon's death at Khartoum.) Nothing, of course, came of his quixotic plans, and the Curtins proved well able to look after themselves. But this imagined adventure is what lies behind Stevenson's onslaught on Irish terrorism. It is a pity that he did not tell the story, using the narrative and polemical skills and the righteous vituperativeness he displays at their best at close quarters in 'Father Damien', with its exultantly (and in some factual respects unfair) attack on a detractor of the priest and of his activities at the leper colony. For although Stevenson's work was to follow more than one new direction, the best qualities of his essays remain those of a novelist: the sheer inventiveness of his satirical portrayal of Dr Hyde, in this essay; his earlier watchful attention to the moods of lovers, or the social behaviour of dogs; the professional discipline with which, so eloquently, he governs what he has to say about his beloved father, soon after his death; the minute details of his description, twenty years after it happened, of his descent in a diving suit in Wick harbour, and the technical assurance which leads him to colour that experience with another, seemingly irrelevant but equally symbolic of his own situation: his encounter with a couple of Italian children who appear from nowhere on the shores of the Pentland Firth, 'one with a hurdy-gurdy, the other with a cage of mice . . . as though a bird of paradise had risen from the heather, or an albatross come fishing in the bay of Wick'.

Stevenson confesses in 'The Old Pacific Capital' that in the midst of a forest fire in California he set a tree alight, to watch how it caught. In his essays, he wrote as he lived, not to prove a point, but to find out, sometimes recklessly, how things were. Like most writers of fiction, he preferred to begin with something concrete and, it might be, incidental, as he did, he tells us, with the map that started him writing *Treasure Island*, or as he does in his essay 'The Lantern-Bearers', with the lamps he and other boys kept concealed under their coats, for a game.

Toward the end of September, when schooltime was drawing near and the nights were already black, we would begin to sally from our respective villas, each equipped with a tin bull's-eye lantern. The thing was so well known that it had worn a rut in the commerce of Great Britain; and the grocers, about the due time, began to garnish their windows with our particular brand of luminary. We wore them buckled to the waist upon a cricket belt, and over them, such was the rigour of the game, a buttoned top-coat. They smelled noisomely of blistered tin; they never burned aright, though they would always burn our fingers; their use was naught; the pleasure of them merely fanciful; and yet a boy with a bull's-eye under his top-coat asked for nothing more. The fishermen used lanterns about their boats, and it was from them, I suppose, that we had got the hint; but theirs were not bull's-eyes, nor did we ever play at being fishermen. The police carried them at their belts, and we had plainly copied them in that; yet we did not pretend to be policemen. Burglars, indeed, we may have had some haunting thoughts of; and we had certainly an eye to past ages when lanterns were more common, and to certain story-books in which we had found them to figure very largely. But take it for all in all, the pleasure of the thing was substantive; and to be a boy with a bull's-eye under his top-coat was good enough for us.

The lamp serves him as a metaphor for the secret imaginative life, but however he makes use of it, it is remembered by the reader, as by the author, chiefly for its own sake: 'the pleasure of the thing was substantive'. This is the point of 'An Apology for Idlers', of 'Walking Tours', and it is what makes all his essays cohere, in their wonderful readability and their neglected scope and substance: that they so fully convey the substantiveness of anything he writes about.

A NOTE ON THE TEXT

There is no textually reliable edition of Stevenson's complete works, and both the essays and much else have for some years been out of print. It is not the job of a selection, as distinct from a complete edition, to establish an ideal text, but I hope this book will encourage such a project.

What is provided here, with a few exceptions, is the text of each essay as it last appeared in print in Stevenson's lifetime, either in a magazine or in a later collection such as *Familiar Studies of Men and Books* or the second edition (1887) of *Virginibus Puerisque*, which was set from his corrected version of the first edition. The chief exceptions are two pieces which he did not see published, 'Confessions of a Unionist', taken here from G. P. Winship's privately printed edition (1921) of the corrected proofs in the Houghton Library at Harvard; and 'Authors and Publishers', taken from the holograph draft in the Beinecke Library at Yale, by kind permission of the Librarian. 'My First Book' was printed more reliably in the United States in *McClure's Magazine* than in England in *The Idler*: it is reprinted here from the Tusitala edition, which follows the American version.

The essays appear in order of composition (so far as it is known), not of publication. Obvious printer's errors have been corrected but the original spelling and punctuation (with the exception of quotation marks and hyphenation, which have been made consistent) are followed in every case except that of the draft 'Authors and Publishers', which has been lightly corrected and punctuated in the style of the finished essays. Each piece is printed in full. It should be noted, however, that the essay on John Knox's 'Private Life' is the second of a pair of articles, the first of which is entitled 'The Controversy over Female Rule', that 'Idle Hours' is an individual essay within a group published together under the title 'Forest Notes', and that 'Edinburgh' is the introduction to Stevenson's book of essays about the city, most of them first published as magazine articles.

Full details of the copy-texts are given below. I am very grateful for the generous, full and expert advice of Mr Ernest Mehew. I have also benefited from Roger G. Swearingen's *The Prose Writings of Robert Louis Stevenson: A Guide* (1980).

TEXTS FOLLOWED

'The Philosophy of Umbrellas': Edinburgh Edition, 21 (1896)

'John Knox and his Relations to Women': *Familiar Studies of Men and Books* (1882)

'Forest Notes: Idle Hours': *Cornhill Magazine*, May 1876, 545–52

'Walking Tours', 'An Apology for Idlers', 'On Falling in Love': *Virginibus Puerisque*, ed. cit.

'In the Latin Quarter': *London*, February 10 and 17, 1877

'Crabbed Age and Youth': *Virginibus Puerisque*, ed. cit.

'Walt Whitman': *Familiar Studies*, ed. cit.

'Edinburgh': *Edinburgh: Picturesque Notes* (1879)

'Truth of Intercourse': *Virginibus Puerisque*, ed. cit.

'Some Aspects of Robert Burns', 'The Old Pacific Capital': *Across the Plains* (1892)

'Samuel Pepys': *Familiar Studies*, ed. cit.

'Davos in Winter': *Pall Mall Gazette*, February 21, 1881, 689–70

'The Misgivings of Convalescence': *ibid.*, March 17, 1881, 10

'The Foreigner at Home', 'A Gossip on Romance', 'The Character of Dogs', 'A Humble Remonstrance': *Memories and Portraits* (1887)

'The Day After Tomorrow': *The Contemporary Review*, April 1887, 472–9

'Thomas Stevenson, Civil Engineer': *Memories and Portraits*, ed. cit.

'A Chapter on Dreams', 'The Lantern-Bearers': *Across the Plains*, ed. cit.

'Confessions of a Unionist': *Confessions of a Unionist: An Unpublished 'Talk on Things Current'*, ed. G. P. Winship, Cambridge, Massachusetts, 1921

'Letter to a Young Gentleman who Proposes to Embrace the Career of Art', 'The Education of an Engineer': *Across the Plains*, ed. cit.

'Authors and Publishers': Yale University, Beinecke Library MS 5997

'Father Damien': *Father Damien: An Open Letter to the Reverend Dr Hyde of Honolulu* (1890)

'My First Book – *Treasure Island*': Tusitala Edition, 2 (1924)

ACKNOWLEDGEMENTS

Various people have helped with this book, by their knowledge, encouragement or practical advice. I am particularly grateful to Rosemary Ashton, Alan Bell, Richard Brain, Holly Eley, Roy Foster, Jonathan Galassi, Hermione Lee, Ernest Mehew, Janet Adam Smith, Ben Sonnenberg, Susan Sontag and Jennifer Uglow, as well as to Douglas Matthews, who prepared the index.

Librarians at the following institutions assisted by answering enquiries or supplying photocopies: the Beinecke Library at Yale, the Bodleian Library, the British Library, the English Faculty Library at Oxford, the Houghton Library at Harvard, the Huntington Library, the Library of Congress, the London Library and the National Library of Scotland.

Two other institutions were exceptionally helpful: All Souls College, Oxford, where I was a Visiting Fellow for the term in which the book was completed, and one of whose secretaries, Humaira Erfan Ahmed, did the typing; and Times Newspapers Limited, which gave me leave from *The Times Literary Supplement* in order to go there. As always, the staff of the *TLS*, and particularly the Deputy Editor, Alan Hollinghurst, were both encouraging and forbearing.

Jeremy Treglown, All Souls College, Oxford, December 1986

THE ESSAYS

THE PHILOSOPHY OF
UMBRELLAS[1]

It is wonderful to think what a turn has been given to our whole Society by the fact that we live under the sign of Aquarius, – that our climate is essentially wet. A mere arbitrary distinction, like the walking-swords of yore, might have remained the symbol of foresight and respectability, had not the raw mists and dropping showers of our island pointed the inclination of Society to another exponent of those virtues. A ribbon of the Legion of Honour or a string of medals may prove a person's courage; a title may prove his birth; a professorial chair his study and acquirement; but it is the habitual carriage of the umbrella that is the stamp of Respectability. The umbrella has become the acknowledged index of social position.

Robinson Crusoe presents us with a touching instance of the hankering after them inherent in the civilised and educated mind. To the superficial, the hot suns of Juan Fernandez may sufficiently account for his quaint choice of a luxury; but surely one who had borne the hard labour of a seaman under the tropics for all these years could have supported an excursion after goats or a peaceful *constitutional* arm in arm with the nude Friday. No, it was not this: the memory of a vanished respectability called for some outward manifestation, and the result was – an umbrella. A pious castaway might have rigged up a belfry and solaced his Sunday mornings with the mimicry of church-bells; but Crusoe was rather a moralist than a pietist, and his leaf-umbrella is as fine an example of the civilised mind striving to express itself under adverse circumstances as we have ever met with.

It is not for nothing, either, that the umbrella has become the very foremost badge of modern civilisation – the Urim and Thummim of respectability. Its pregnant symbolism has taken its rise in the most natural manner. Consider, for a moment, when umbrellas were first introduced into this country, what manner of men would use them, and

---

[1]'This paper was written in collaboration with James Walter Ferrier, and if reprinted this is to be stated, though his principal collaboration was to lie back in an easy-chair and laugh.' – R.L.S., Oct. 25, 1894.

what class would adhere to the useless but ornamental cane. The first, without doubt, would be the hypochrondriacal, out of solicitude for their health, or the frugal, out of care for their raiment; the second, it is equally plain, would include the fop, the fool, and the Bobadil. Anyone acquainted with the growth of Society, and knowing out of what small seeds of cause are produced great revolutions, and wholly new conditions of intercourse, sees from this simple thought how the carriage of an umbrella came to indicate frugality, judicious regard for bodily welfare, and scorn for mere outward adornment, and, in one word, all those homely and solid virtues implied in the term RESPECT-ABILITY. Not that the umbrella's costliness has nothing to do with its great influence. Its possession, besides symbolising (as we have already indicated) the change from wild Esau to plain Jacob dwelling in tents, implies a certain comfortable provision of fortune. It is not every one that can expose twenty-six shillings' worth of property to so many chances of loss and theft. So strongly do we feel on this point, indeed, that we are almost inclined to consider all who possess really well-conditioned umbrellas as worthy of the Franchise. They have a qualification standing in their lobbies; they carry a sufficient stake in the common-weal below their arm. One who bears with him an umbrella – such a complicated structure of whalebone, of silk, and of cane, that it becomes a very microcosm of modern industry – is necessarily a man of peace. A half-crown cane may be applied to an offender's head on a very moderate provocation; but a six-and-twenty shilling silk is a possession too precious to be adventured in the shock of war.

These are but a few glances at how umbrellas (in the general) came to their present high estate. But the true Umbrella-philosopher meets with far stranger applications as he goes about the streets.

Umbrellas, like faces, acquire a certain sympathy with the individual who carries them: indeed, they are far more capable of betraying his trust; for whereas a face is given to us so far ready made, and all our power over it is in frowning, and laughing, and grimacing, during the first three or four decades of life, each umbrella is selected from a whole shopful, as being most consonant to the purchaser's disposition. An undoubted power of diagnosis rests with the practised Umbrella-philosopher. O you who lisp, and amble, and change the fashion of your countenances – you who conceal all these, how little do you think that you left a proof of your weakness in our umbrella-stand – that even now, as you shake out the folds to meet the thickening snow, we read in its

[4]

ivory handle the outward and visible sign of your snobbery, or from the exposed gingham of its cover detect, through coat and waistcoat, the hidden hypocrisy of the '*dickey*'! But alas! even the umbrella is no certain criterion. The falsity and the folly of the human race have degraded that graceful symbol to the ends of dishonesty; and while some umbrellas, from carelessness in selection, are not strikingly character-istic (for it is only in what a man loves that he displays his real nature), others, from certain prudential motives, are chosen directly opposite to the person's disposition. A mendacious umbrella is a sign of great moral degradation. Hypocrisy naturally shelters itself below a silk; while the fast youth goes to visit his religious friends armed with the decent and reputable gingham. May it not be said of the bearers of these inappropriate umbrellas that they go about the streets 'with a lie in their right hand'?

The kings of Siam, as we read, besides having a graduated social scale of umbrellas (which was a good thing), prevented the great bulk of their subjects from having any at all, which was certainly a bad thing. We should be sorry to believe that this Eastern legislator was a fool – the idea of an aristocracy of umbrellas is too philosophic to have originated in a nobody – and we have accordingly taken exceeding pains to find out the reason of this harsh restriction. We think we have succeeded; but, while admiring the principle at which he aimed, and while cordially recognising in the Siamese potentate the only man before ourselves who had taken a real grasp of the umbrella, we must be allowed to point out how unphilosophically the great man acted in this particular. His object, plainly, was to prevent any unworthy persons from bearing the sacred symbol of domestic virtues. We cannot excuse his limiting these virtues to the circle of his court. We must only remember that such was the feeling of the age in which he lived. Liberalism had not yet raised the war-cry of the working classes. But here was his mistake: it was a needless regulation. Except in a very few cases of hypocrisy joined to a powerful intellect, men, not by nature *umbrellarians*, have tried again and again to become so by art, and yet have failed – have expended their patrimony in the purchase of umbrella after umbrella, and yet have systematically lost them, and have finally, with contrite spirits and shrunken purses, given up their vain struggle, and relied on theft and borrowing for the remainder of their lives. This is the most remarkable fact that we have had occasion to notice; and yet we challenge the candid reader to call it in question. Now, as there cannot be any *moral selection* in a mere dead piece of furniture – as the umbrella cannot be supposed to have an affinity for individual men equal and reciprocal to that which men certainly feel toward individual umbrellas, – we took the trouble of consulting a scientific friend as to whether there was any possible physical explanation of the phenomenon. He was unable to supply a plausible theory, or even hypothesis; but we extract from his letter the following interesting passage relative to the physical peculiarities of umbrellas: 'Not the least important, and by far the most curious property of the umbrella, is the energy which it displays in affecting the atmospheric strata. There is no fact in meteorology better established – indeed, it is almost the only one on which meteorologists are agreed – than that the carriage of an umbrella produces desiccation of the air; while if it be left at home, aqueous vapour is largely produced, and is soon deposited in the form of rain. No theory,' my friend continues, 'competent to explain this hygrometric law has yet been given (as far as I am aware) by Herschel, Dove, Glaisher, Tait, Buchan, or any other writer; nor do I pretend to supply the defect. I venture, however, to throw out the conjecture that it will be ultimately found to belong to the same class of natural laws as that agreeable to which a slice of toast always descends with the buttered surface downwards.'

But it is time to draw to a close. We could expatiate much longer upon this topic, but want of space constrains us to leave unfinished these few desultory remarks – slender contributions towards a subject which has fallen sadly backward, and which, we grieve to say, was better understood by the king of Siam in 1686 than by all the philosophers of today. If, however, we have awakened in any rational mind an interest in the symbolism of umbrellas – in any generous heart a more complete sympathy with the dumb companion of his daily walk, – or in any grasping spirit a pure notion of respectability strong enough to make him expend his six-and-twenty shillings – we shall have deserved well of the world, to say nothing of the many industrious persons employed in the manufacture of the article.

JOHN KNOX
AND HIS RELATIONS TO WOMEN
Private Life

To those who know Knox by hearsay only, I believe the matter of this paper will be somewhat astonishing. For the hard energy of the man in all public matters has possessed the imagination of the world; he remains for posterity in certain traditional phrases, browbeating Queen Mary, or breaking beautiful carved work in abbeys and cathedrals, that had long smoked themselves out and were no more than sorry ruins, while he was still quietly teaching children in a country gentleman's family. It does not consist with the common acceptation of his character to fancy him much moved, except with anger. And yet the language of passion came to his pen as readily, whether it was a passion of denunciation against some of the abuses that vexed his righteous spirit, or of yearning for the society of an absent friend. He was vehement in affection, as in doctrine. I will not deny that there may have been, along with his vehemence, something shifty, and for the moment only; that, like many men, and many Scotchmen, he saw the world and his own heart, not so much under any very steady, equable light, as by extreme flashes of passion, true for the moment, but not true in the long run. There does seem to me to be something of this traceable in the Reformer's utterances: precipitation and repentance, hardy speech and action somewhat circumspect, a strong tendency to see himself in a heroic light and to place a ready belief in the disposition of the moment. Withal he had considerable confidence in himself, and in the uprightness of his own disciplined emotions, underlying much sincere aspiration after spiritual humility. And it is this confidence that makes his intercourse with women so interesting to a modern. It would be easy, of course, to make fun of the whole affair, to picture him strutting vaingloriously among these inferior creatures, or compare a religious friendship in the sixteenth century with what was called, I think, a literary friendship in the eighteenth. But it is more just and profitable to recognise what there is sterling and human underneath all his theoretical affectations of superiority. Women, he has said in his 'First Blast,' are 'weak, frail, impatient, feeble, and foolish;' and yet it does not appear that he was himself any less dependent than other men upon the sympathy and affection of these weak, frail, impatient, feeble, and foolish creatures; it seems even as if he had been rather more dependent than most.

Of those who are to act influentially on their fellows, we should expect always something large and public in their way of life, something more or less urbane and comprehensive in their sentiment for others. We should not expect to see them spend their sympathy in idylls, however beautiful. We should not seek them among those who, if they have but a wife to their bosom, ask no more of womankind, just as they ask no more of their own sex, if they can find a friend or two for their immediate need. They will be quick to feel all the pleasures of our association – not the great ones alone, but all. They will know not love only, but all those other ways in which man and woman mutually make each other happy – by sympathy, by admiration, by the atmosphere they bear about them – down to the mere impersonal pleasure of passing happy faces in the street. For, through all this gradation, the difference of sex makes itself pleasurably felt. Down to the most lukewarm courtesies of life, there is a special chivalry due and a special pleasure received, when the two sexes are brought ever so lightly into contact. We love our mothers otherwise than we love our fathers; a sister is not as a brother to us; and friendship between man and woman, be it never so unalloyed and innocent, is not the same as friendship between man and man. Such friendship is not even possible for all. To conjoin tenderness for a woman that is not far short of passionate with such disinterestedness and beautiful gratuity of affection as there is between friends of the same sex, requires no ordinary disposition in the man. For either it would presuppose quite womanly delicacy of perception, and, as it were, a curiosity in shades of differing sentiment; or it would mean that he had accepted the large, simple divisions of society: a strong and positive spirit robustly virtuous, who has chosen a better part coarsely, and holds to it steadfastly, with all its consequences of pain to himself and others; as one who should go straight before him on a journey, neither tempted by wayside flowers nor very scrupulous of small lives under foot. It was in virtue of this latter disposition that Knox was capable of those intimacies with women that embellished his life; and we find him preserved for us in old letters as a man of many women friends; a man of some expansion toward the other sex; a man ever ready to comfort weeping women, and to weep along with them.

[8]

Of such scraps and fragments of evidence as to his private life and more intimate thoughts as have survived to us from all the perils that environ written paper, an astonishingly large proportion is in the shape of letters to women of his familiarity. He was twice married, but that is not greatly to the purpose; for the Turk, who thinks even more meanly of women than John Knox, is none the less given to marrying. What is really significant is quite apart from marriage. For the man Knox was a true man, and woman, the *ewig-weibliche*, was as necessary to him, in spite of all low theories, as ever she was to Goethe. He came to her in a certain halo of his own, as the minister of truth, just as Goethe came to her in a glory of art; he made himself necessary to troubled hearts and minds exercised in the painful complications that naturally result from all changes in the world's way of thinking; and those whom he had thus helped became dear to him, and were made the chosen companions of his leisure if they were at hand, or encouraged and comforted by letter if they were afar.

It must not be forgotten that Knox had been a presbyter of the old Church, and that the many women whom we shall see gathering around him, as he goes through life, had probably been accustomed, while still in the communion of Rome, to rely much upon some chosen spiritual director, so that the intimacies of which I propose to offer some account, while testifying to a good heart in the Reformer, testify also to a certain survival of the spirit of the confessional in the Reformed Church, and are not properly to be judged without this idea. There is no friendship so noble, but it is the product of the time; and a world of little finical observances, and little frail proprieties and fashions of the hour, go to make or to mar, to stint or to perfect, the union of spirits the most loving and the most intolerant of such interference. The trick of the country and the age steps in even between the mother and her child, counts out their caresses upon niggardly fingers, and says, in the voice of authority, that this one thing shall be a matter of confidence between them, and this other thing shall not. And thus it is that we must take into reckoning whatever tended to modify the social atmosphere in which Knox and his women friends met, and loved and trusted each other. To the man who had been their priest and was now their minister, women would be able to speak with a confidence quite impossible in these latter days; the women would be able to speak, and the man to hear. It was a beaten road just then; and I daresay we should be no less scandalised at their plain speech than they, if they could come back to earth, would be

[9]

offended at our waltzes and worldly fashions. This, then, was the footing on which Knox stood with his many women friends. The reader will see, as he goes on, how much of warmth, of interest, and of that happy mutual dependence which is the very gist of friendship, he contrived to ingraft upon this somewhat dry relationship of penitent and confessor.

It must be understood that we know nothing of his intercourse with women (as indeed we know little at all about his life) until he came to Berwick in 1549, when he was already in the forty-fifth year of his age. At the same time it is just possible that some of a little group at Edinburgh, with whom he corresponded during his last absence, may have been friends of an older standing. Certainly they were, of all his female correspondents, the least personally favoured. He treats them throughout in a comprehensive sort of spirit that must at times have been a little wounding. Thus, he remits one of them to his former letters, 'which I trust be common betwixt you and the rest of our sisters, for to me ye are all equal in Christ.'[1] Another letter is a gem in this way. 'Albeit' it begins, 'albeit I have no particular matter to write unto you, beloved sister, yet I could not refrain to write these few lines to you in declaration of my remembrance of you. True it is that I have many whom I bear in equal remembrance before God with you, to whom at present I write nothing, either for that I esteem them stronger than you, and therefore they need the less my rude labours, or else because they have not provoked me by their writing to recompense their remembrance.'[2] His 'sisters in Edinburgh' had evidently to 'provoke' his attention pretty constantly; nearly all his letters are, on the face of them, answers to questions, and the answers are given with a certain crudity that I do not find repeated when he writes to those he really cares for. So when they consult him about women's apparel (a subject on which his opinion may be pretty correctly imagined by the ingenious reader for himself) he takes occasion to anticipate some of the most offensive matter of the 'First Blast' in a style of real brutality.[3] It is not merely that he tells them 'the garments of women do declare their weakness and inability to execute the office of man,' though that in itself is neither very wise nor very opportune in such a correspondence one would think; but if the reader will take the trouble to wade through the long, tedious sermon for himself, he will see proof enough that Knox neither loved,

[1]Works, iv. 244.   [2]Ibid. iv. 246.   [3]Ibid. iv. 225.

nor very deeply respected, the women he was then addressing. In very truth, I believe these Edinburgh sisters simply bored him. He had a certain interest in them as his children in the Lord; they were continually 'provoking him by their writing;' and, if they handed his letters about, writing to them was as good a form of publication as was then open to him in Scotland. There is one letter, however, in this budget, addressed to the wife of Clerk-Register Mackgil, which is worthy of some further mention. The Clerk-Register had not opened his heart, it would appear, to the preaching of the Gospel, and Mrs Mackgil has written, seeking the Reformer's prayers in his behalf. 'Your husband,' he answers, 'is dear to me for that he is a man indued with some good gifts, but more dear for that he is your husband. Charity moveth me to thirst his illumination, both for his comfort and for the trouble which you sustain by his coldness, which justly may be called infidelity.' He wishes her, however, not to hope too much; he can promise that his prayers will be earnest, but not that they will be effectual; it is possible that this is to be her 'cross' in life; that 'her head, appointed by God for her comfort, should be her enemy.' And if this be so, well, there is nothing for it; 'with patience she must abide God's merciful deliverance,' taking heed only that she does not 'obey manifest iniquity for the pleasure of any mortal man.'[1] I conceive this epistle would have given a very modified sort of pleasure to the Clerk-Register, had it chanced to fall into his hands. Compare its tenor – the dry resignation not without a hope of merciful deliverance therein recommended – with these words from another letter, written but the year before to two married women of London: 'Call first for grace by Jesus, and thereafter communicate with your faithful husbands, and then shall God, I doubt not, conduct your footsteps, and direct your counsels to His glory.'[2] Here the husbands are put in a very high place; we can recognise here the same hand that has written for our instruction how the man is set above the woman, even as God above the angels. But the point of the distinction is plain. For Clerk-Register Mackgil was not a faithful husband; displayed, indeed, towards religion a 'coldness which justly might be called infidelity.' We shall see in more notable instances how much Knox's conception of the duty of wives varies according to the zeal and orthodoxy of the husband.

As I have said, he may possibly have made the acquaintance of Mrs

[1]*Works,* iv. 245. [2]*Ibid.* iv. 221.

Mackgil, Mrs Guthrie, or some other, or all, of these Edinburgh friends while he was still Douglas of Longniddry's private tutor. But our certain knowledge begins in 1549. He was then but newly escaped from his captivity in France, after pulling an oar for nineteen months on the benches of the galley *Nostre Dame*; now up the rivers, holding stealthy intercourse with other Scottish prisoners in the castle of Rouen; now out in the North Sea, raising his sick head to catch a glimpse of the far-off steeples of St Andrews. And now he was sent down by the English Privy Council as a preacher to Berwick-upon-Tweed; somewhat shaken in health by all his hardships, full of pains and agues, and tormented by gravel, that sorrow of great men; altogether, what with his romantic story, his weak health, and his great faculty of eloquence, a very natural object for the sympathy of devout women. At this happy juncture he fell into the company of a Mrs Elizabeth Bowes, wife of Richard Bowes, of Aske, in Yorkshire, to whom she had borne twelve children. She was a religious hypochondriac, a very weariful woman, full of doubts and scruples, and giving no rest on earth either to herself or to those whom she honoured with her confidence. From the first time she heard Knox preach she formed a high opinion of him, and was solicitous ever after of his society.[1] Nor was Knox unresponsive. 'I have always delighted in your company,' he writes, 'and when labours would permit, you know I have not spared hours to talk and commune with you.' Often when they had met in depression he reminds her, 'God hath sent great comfort unto both.'[2] We can gather from such letters as are yet extant how close and continuous was their intercourse. 'I think it best you remain till the morrow,' he writes once, 'and so shall we commune at large at afternoon. This day you know to be the day of my study and prayer unto God; yet if your trouble be intolerable, or if you think my presence may release your pain, do as the Spirit shall move you ... Your messenger found me in bed, after a sore trouble and most dolorous night, and so dolour may complain to dolour when we two meet ... And this is more plain than ever I spoke, to let you know you have a companion in trouble.'[3] Once we have the curtain raised for a moment, and can look at the two together for the length of a phrase. 'After the writing of this preceding,' writes Knox, 'your brother and mine, Harrie Wycliffe, did advertise me by writing, that your adversary

[1]Works, vi. 514.   [2]*Ibid.* iii. 338.   [3]*Ibid.* iii. 352, 353.

(the devil) took occasion to trouble you because that *I did start back from you rehearsing your infirmities. I remember myself so to have done, and that is my common consuetude when anything pierceth or toucheth my heart. Call to your mind what I did standing at the cupboard at Alnwick.* In very deed I thought that no creature had been tempted as I was; and when I heard proceed from your mouth the very same words that he troubles me with, I did wonder and from my heart lament your sore trouble, knowing in myself the dolour thereof.'[1] Now intercourse of so very close a description, whether it be religious intercourse or not, is apt to displease and disquiet a husband; and we know incidentally from Knox himself that there was some little scandal about his intimacy with Mrs Bowes. 'The slander and fear of men,' he writes, 'has impeded me to exercise my pen so oft as I would; *yea, very shame hath holden me from your company, when I was most surely persuaded that God had appointed me at that time to comfort and feed your hungry and afflicted soul. God in His infinite mercy,'* he goes on, '*remove not only from me all fear that tendeth not to godliness, but from others suspicion to judge of me otherwise than it becometh one member to judge of another.'*[2] And the scandal, such as it was, would not be allayed by the dissension in which Mrs Bowes seems to have lived with her family upon the matter of religion, and the countenance shown by Knox to her resistance. Talking of these conflicts, and her courage against 'her own flesh and most inward affections, yea, against some of her most natural friends,' he writes it, 'to the praise of God, he has wondered at the bold constancy which he has found in her when his own heart was faint.'[3]

Now, perhaps in order to stop scandalous mouths, perhaps out of a desire to bind the much-loved evangelist nearer to her in the only manner possible, Mrs Bowes conceived the scheme of marrying him to her fifth daughter, Marjorie; and the Reformer seems to have fallen in with it readily enough. It seems to have been believed in the family that the whole matter had been originally made up between these two, with no very spontaneous inclination on the part of the bride.[4] Knox's idea of marriage, as I have said, was not the same for all men; but on the whole, it was not lofty. We have a curious letter of his, written at the request of Queen Mary, to the Earl of Argyle, on very delicate household matters; which, as he tells us, 'was not well accepted of the said Earl.'[5] We may

---

[1]Works, iii. 350. [2]*Ibid.* iii. 390, 391. [3]*Ibid.* iii. 142.
[4]*Ibid.* iii. 378. [5]*Ibid.* ii. 379.

suppose, however, that his own home was regulated in a similar spirit. I can fancy that for such a man, emotional, and with a need, now and again, to exercise parsimony in emotions not strictly needful, something a little mechanical, something hard and fast and clearly understood, would enter into his ideal of a home. There were storms enough without, and equability was to be desired at the fireside even at a sacrifice of deeper pleasures. So, from a wife, of all women, he would not ask much. One letter to her which has come down to us is, I had almost said, conspicuous for coldness.[1] He calls her, as he called other female correspondents, 'dearly beloved sister;' the epistle is doctrinal, and nearly the half of it bears, not upon her own case, but upon that of her mother. However, we know what Heine wrote in his wife's album; and there is, after all, one passage that may be held to intimate some tenderness, although even that admits of an amusingly opposite construction. 'I think,' he says, 'I *think* this be the first letter I ever wrote to you.' This, if we are to take it literally, may pair off with the 'two *or three* children' whom Montaigne mentions having lost at nurse; the one is as eccentric in a lover as the other in a parent. Nevertheless, he displayed more energy in the course of his troubled wooing than might have been expected. The whole Bowes family, angry enough already at the influence he had obtained over the mother, set their faces obdurately against the match. And I daresay the opposition quickened his inclination. I find him writing to Mrs Bowes that she need no further trouble herself about the marriage; it should now be his business altogether; it behoved him now to jeopard his life 'for the comfort of his own flesh, both fear and friendship of all earthly creature laid aside.'[2] This is a wonderfully chivalrous utterance for a Reformer forty-eight years old; and it compares well with the leaden coquetries of Calvin, not much over thirty, taking this and that into consideration, weighing together dowries and religious qualifications and the instancy of friends, and exhibiting what M. Bungener calls 'an honourable and Christian difficulty' of choice, in frigid indecisions and insincere proposals. But Knox's next letter is in a humbler tone; he has not found the negotiation so easy as he fancied; he despairs of the marriage altogether, and talks of leaving England — regards not 'what country consumes his wicked carcass.' 'You shall understand,' he says, 'that this sixth of November, I spoke with Sir Robert Bowes' (the head of the family, his bride's uncle)

[1] Works, iii. 394.   [2] *Ibid.* iii. 376.

'in the matter you know, according to your request; whose disdainful, yea, despiteful, words hath so pierced my heart that my life is bitter to me. I bear a good countenance with a sore troubled heart, because he that ought to consider matters with a deep judgement is become not only a despiser, but also a taunter of God's messengers – God be merciful unto him! Amongst others his most unpleasing words, while that I was about to have declared my heart in the whole matter, he said, "Away with your rhetorical reasons! for I will not be persuaded with them." God knows I did use no rhetoric nor coloured speech; but would have spoken the truth, and that in most simple manner. I am not a good orator in my own cause; but what he would not be content to hear of me, God shall declare to him one day to his displeasure, unless he repent.'[1] Poor Knox, you see, is quite commoved. It has been a very unpleasant interview. And as it is the only sample that we have of how things went with him during his courtship, we may infer that the period was not as agreeable for Knox as it has been for some others.

However, when once they were married, I imagine he and Marjorie Bowes hit it off together comfortably enough. The little we know of it may be brought together in a very short space. She bore him two sons. He seems to have kept her pretty busy, and depended on her to some degree in his work; so that when she fell ill, his papers got at once into disorder.[2] Certainly she sometimes wrote to his dictation; and, in this capacity, he calls her 'his left hand.'[3] In June 1559, at the headiest moment of the Reformation in Scotland, he writes regretting the absence of his helpful colleague, Goodman, 'whose presence' (this is the not very grammatical form of his lament) 'whose presence I more thirst, than she that is my own flesh.'[4] And this, considering the source and the circumstances, may be held as evidence of a very tender sentiment. He tells us himself in his history, on the occasion of a certain meeting at the Kirk of Field, that 'he was in no small heaviness by reason of the late death of his dear bedfellow, Marjorie Bowes.'[5] Calvin, condoling with him, speaks of her as 'a wife whose like is not to be found everywhere' (that is very like Calvin), and again, as 'the most delightful of wives.' We know what Calvin thought desirable in a wife, 'good humour, chastity, thrift, patience, and solicitude for her husband's health,' and so we may suppose that the first Mrs Knox fell not far short of this ideal.

[1]Works, iii. 378. [2]Ibid. vi. 104. [3]Ibid. v. 5.
[4]Ibid. vi. 27. [5]Ibid. ii. 138.

The actual date of the marriage is uncertain; but by September 1556, at the latest, the Reformer was settled in Geneva with his wife. There is no fear either that he will be dull; even if the chaste, thrifty, patient Marjorie should not altogether occupy his mind, he need not go out of the house to seek more female sympathy; for behold! Mrs Bowes is duly domesticated with the young couple. Dr M'Crie imagined that Richard Bowes was now dead, and his widow, consequently, free to live where she would; and where could she go more naturally than to the house of a married daughter? This, however, is not the case. Richard Bowes did not die till at least two years later. It is impossible to believe that he approved of his wife's desertion, after so many years of marriage, after twelve children had been born to them; and accordingly we find in his will, dated 1558, no mention either of her or of Knox's wife.[1] This is plain sailing. It is easy enough to understand the anger of Bowes against this interloper, who had come into a quiet family, married the daughter in spite of the father's opposition, alienated the wife from the husband and the husband's religion, supported her in a long course of resistance and rebellion, and, after years of intimacy, already too close and tender for any jealous spirit to behold without resentment, carried her away with him at last into a foreign land. But it is not quite easy to understand how, except out of sheer weariness and disgust, he was ever brought to agree to the arrangement. Nor is it easy to square the Reformer's conduct with his public teaching. We have, for instance, a letter addressed by him, Craig, and Spottiswood, to the Archbishops of Canterbury and York, anent 'a wicked and rebellious woman,' one Anne Good, spouse to 'John Barron, a minister of Christ Jesus his evangel,' who, 'after great rebellion shown unto him, and divers admonitions given, as well by himself as by others in his name, that she should in no wise depart from this realm, nor from his house without his license, hath not the less stubbornly and rebelliously departed, separated herself from his society, left his house, and withdrawn herself from this realm.'[2] Perhaps some sort of license was extorted, as I have said, from Richard Bowes, weary with years of domestic dissension; but setting that aside, the words employed with so much righteous indignation by Knox, Craig, and Spottiswood, to describe the conduct of that wicked and rebellious woman, Mrs Barron, would describe nearly as exactly the conduct of the religious Mrs Bowes. It is a little bewildering, until we recollect the

[1] Mr Laing's preface to the sixth volume of Knox's Works, p. lxii.
[2] Works, vi. 534.

distinction between faithful and unfaithful husbands; for Barron was 'a minister of Christ Jesus his evangel,' while Richard Bowes, besides being own brother to a despiser and taunter of God's messengers, is shrewdly suspected to have been 'a bigoted adherent of the Roman Catholic faith,' or, as Knox himself would have expressed it, 'a rotten Papist.'

You would have thought that Knox was now pretty well supplied with female society. But we are not yet at the end of the roll. The last year of his sojourn in England had been spent principally in London, where he was resident as one of the chaplains of Edward the Sixth; and here he boasts, although a stranger, he had, by God's grace, found favour before many.[1] The godly women of the metropolis made much of him; once he writes to Mrs Bowes that her last letter had found him closeted with three, and he and the three women were all in tears.[2] Out of all, however, he had chosen two. '*God*,' he writes to them, '*brought us in such familiar acquaintance, that your hearts were incensed and kindled with a special care over me, as a mother useth to be over her natural child*; and my heart was opened and compelled in your presence to be more plain than ever I was to any.'[3] And out of the two even he had chosen one, Mrs Anne Locke, wife to Mr Harry Locke, merchant, nigh to Bow Kirk, Cheapside, in London, as the address runs. If one may venture to judge upon such imperfect evidence, this was the woman he loved best. I have a difficulty in quite forming to myself an idea of her character. She may have been one of the three tearful visitors before alluded to; she may even have been that one of them who was so profoundly moved by some passages of Mrs Bowes's letter, which the Reformer opened, and read aloud to them before they went. 'O would to God,' cried this impressionable matron, 'would to God that I might speak with that person, for I perceive there are more tempted than I.'[4] This *may* have been Mrs Locke, as I say; but even if it were, we must not conclude from this one fact that she was such another as Mrs Bowes. All the evidence tends the other way. She was a woman of understanding, plainly, who followed political events with interest, and to whom Knox thought it worth while to write, in detail, the history of his trials and successes. She was religious, but without that morbid perversity of spirit that made religion so heavy a burden for the poor-hearted Mrs Bowes. More of her I do not find, save testimony to the profound affection that united her to the Reformer. So we find him writing to her from Geneva,

---

[1]Works, iv. 220.　　[2]*Ibid*. iii. 380.　　[3]*Ibid*. iv. 220.　　[4]*Ibid*. iii. 380.

in such terms as these: – 'You write that your desire is earnest to see me. *Dear sister, if I should express the thirst and languor which I have had for your presence, I should appear to pass measure . . . Yea, I weep and rejoice in remembrance of you;* but that would evanish by the comfort of your presence, which I assure you is so dear to me, that if the charge of this little flock here, gathered together in Christ's name, did not impede me, my coming should prevent my letter.'[1] I say that this was written from Geneva; and yet you will observe that it is no consideration for his wife or mother-in-law, only the charge of his little flock, that keeps him from setting out forthwith for London, to comfort himself with the dear presence of Mrs Locke. Remember that there was a certain plausible enough pretext for Mrs Locke to come to Geneva – 'the most perfect school of Christ that ever was on earth since the days of the Apostles' – for we are now under the reign of that 'horrible monster Jezebel of England,' when a lady of good orthodox sentiments was better out of London. It was doubtful, however, whether this was to be. She was detained in England, partly by circumstances unknown, 'partly by empire of her head,' Mr Harry Locke, the Cheapside merchant. It is somewhat humorous to see Knox struggling for resignation, now that he has to do with a faithful husband (for Mr Harry Locke was faithful). Had it been otherwise, 'in my heart,' he says, 'I could have wished – yea,' here he breaks out, 'yea, and cannot cease to wish – that God would guide you to this place.'[2] And after all, he had not long to wait, for, whether Mr Harry Locke died in the interval, or was wearied, he too, into giving permission, five months after the date of the letter last quoted, 'Mrs Anne Locke, Harry her son, and Anne her daughter, and Katharine her maid,' arrived in that perfect school of Christ, the Presbyterian paradise, Geneva. So now, and for the next two years, the cup of Knox's happiness was surely full. Of an afternoon, when the bells rang out for the sermon, the shops closed, and the good folk gathered to the churches, psalm-book in hand, we can imagine him drawing near to the English chapel in quite patriarchal fashion, with Mrs Knox and Mrs Bowes and Mrs Locke, James his servant, Patrick his pupil, and a due following of children and maids. He might be alone at work all morning in his study, for he wrote much during these two years; but at night, you may be sure there was a circle of admiring women, eager to hear the new paragraph, and not sparing of applause. And what work, among others,

[1]Works, iv. 238.   [2]*Ibid*. iv. 240.

was he elaborating at this time, but the notorious 'First Blast'? So that he may have rolled out in his big pulpit voice, how women were weak, frail, impatient, feeble, foolish, inconstant, variable, cruel, and lacking the spirit of counsel, and how men were above them, even as God is above the angels, in the ears of his own wife, and the two dearest friends he had on earth. But he had lost the sense of incongruity, and continued to despise in theory the sex he honoured so much in practice, of whom he chose his most intimate associates, and whose courage he was compelled to wonder at, when his own heart was faint.

We may say that such a man was not worthy of his fortune; and so, as he would not learn, he was taken away from that agreeable school, and his fellowship of women was broken up, not to be reunited. Called into Scotland to take at last that strange position in history which is his best claim to commemoration, he was followed thither by his wife and his mother-in-law. The wife soon died. The death of her daughter did not altogether separate Mrs Bowes from Knox, but she seems to have come and gone between his house and England. In 1562, however, we find him characterised as 'a sole man by reason of the absence of his mother-in-law, Mrs Bowes,' and a passport is got for her, her man, a maid, and 'three horses, whereof two shall return,' as well as liberty to take all her own money with her into Scotland. This looks like a definite arrangement; but whether she died at Edinburgh, or went back to England yet again, I cannot find. With that great family of hers, unless in leaving her husband she had quarrelled with them all, there must have been frequent occasion for her presence, one would think. Knox at least survived her; and we possess his epigraph to their long intimacy, given to the world by him in an appendix to his latest publication. I have said in a former paper that Knox was not shy of personal revelations in his published works. And the trick seems to have grown on him. To this last tract, a controversial onslaught on a Scottish Jesuit, he prefixed a prayer, not very pertinent to the matter in hand, and containing references to his family which were the occasion of some wit in his adversary's answer; and appended what seems equally irrelevant, one of his devout letters to Mrs Bowes, with an explanatory preface. To say truth, I believe he had always felt uneasily that the circumstances of this intimacy were very capable of misconstruction; and now, when he was an old man, taking 'his good night of all the faithful in both realms,' and only desirous 'that without any notable sclander to the evangel of Jesus Christ, he might end his battle; for as the world was weary of him, so was he of it;' – in such a spirit it was not, perhaps, unnatural that he should return to this old story, and seek to put it right in the eyes of all men, ere he died. 'Because that God,' he says, 'because that God now in His mercy hath put an end to the battle of my dear mother, Mistress Elizabeth Bowes, before that He put an end to my wretched life, I could not cease but declare to the world what was the cause of our great familiarity and long acquaintance; which was neither flesh nor blood, but a troubled conscience upon her part, which never suffered her to rest but when she was in the company of the faithful, of whom (from the first hearing of the word at my mouth) she judged me to be one . . . Her company to me was comfortable (yea, honourable and profitable, for she was to me and mine a mother), but yet it was not without some cross; for besides trouble and fashery of body sustained for her, my mind was seldom quiet, for doing somewhat for the comfort of her troubled conscience.'[1] He had written to her years before, from his first exile in Dieppe, that 'only God's hand' could withhold him from once more speaking with her face to face; and now, when God's hand has indeed interposed, when there lies between them, instead of the voyageable straits, that great gulf over which no man can pass, this is the spirit in which he can look back upon their long acquaintance. She was a religious hypochondriac, it appears, whom, not without some cross and fashery of mind and body, he was good enough to tend. He might have given a truer character of their friendship, had he thought less of his own standing in public estimation, and more of the dead woman. But he was in all things, as Burke said of his son in that ever memorable passage, a public creature. He wished that even into this private place of his affections posterity should follow him with a complete approval; and he was willing, in order that this might be so, to exhibit the defects of his lost friend, and tell the world what weariness he had sustained through her unhappy disposition. There is something here that reminds one of Rousseau.

I do not think he ever saw Mrs Locke after he left Geneva; but his correspondence with her continued for three years. It may have continued longer, of course, but I think the last letters we possess read like the last that would be written. Perhaps Mrs Locke was then remarried, for there is much obscurity over her subsequent history. For as long as their intimacy was kept up, at least, the human element

[1]Works, vi. 513, 514.

remains in the Reformer's life. Here is one passage, for example, the most likeable utterance of Knox's that I can quote: — Mrs Locke has been upbraiding him as a bad correspondent. 'My remembrance of you,' he answers, 'is not so dead, but I trust it shall be fresh enough, albeit it be renewed by no outward token for one year. *Of nature, I am churlish; yet one thing I ashame not to affirm, that familiarity once thoroughly contracted was never yet broken on my default. The cause may be that I have rather need of all, than that any have need of me.* However it (*that*) be, it cannot be, as I say, the corporal absence of one year or two that can quench in my heart that familiar acquaintance in Christ Jesus, which half a year did engender, and almost two years did nourish and confirm. And therefore, whether I write or no, be assuredly persuaded that I have you in such memory as becometh the faithful to have of the faithful.'[1] This is the truest touch of personal humility that I can remember to have seen in all the five volumes of the Reformer's collected works: it is no small honour to Mrs Locke that his affection for her should have brought home to him this unwonted feeling of dependence upon others. Everything else in the course of the correspondence testifies to a good, sound, downright sort of friendship between the two, less ecstatic than it was at first, perhaps, but serviceable and very equal. He gives her ample details as to the progress of the work of reformation; sends her the sheets of the *Confession of Faith*, 'in quairs,' as he calls it; asks her to assist him with her prayers, to collect money for the good cause in Scotland, and to send him books for himself — books by Calvin especially, one on Isaiah, and a new revised edition of the 'Institutes.' 'I must be bold on your liberality,' he writes, 'not only in that, but in greater things as I shall need.'[2] On her part she applies to him for spiritual advice, not after the manner of the drooping Mrs Bowes, but in a more positive spirit, — advice as to practical points, advice as to the Church of England, for instance, whose ritual he condemns as a 'mingle- mangle.'[3] Just at the end she ceases to write, sends him 'a token, without writing.' 'I understand your impediment,' he answers, 'and therefore I cannot complain. Yet if you understood the variety of my temptations, I doubt not but you would have written somewhat.'[4] One letter more, and then silence.

And I think the best of the Reformer died out with that correspondence. It is after this, of course, that he wrote that ungenerous

[1]Works, vi. 11.   [2]*Ibid.* vi. pp. 21, 101, 108, 130.
[3]*Ibid.* vi. 83.   [4]*Ibid.* vi. 129.

description of his intercourse with Mrs Bowes. It is after this, also, that we come to the unlovely episode of his second marriage. He had been left a widower at the age of fifty-five. Three years after, it occurred apparently to yet another pious parent to sacrifice a child upon the altar of his respect for the Reformer. In January 1563, Randolph writes to Cecil: 'Your Honour will take it for a great wonder when I shall write unto you that Mr Knox shall marry a very near kinswoman of the Duke's, a Lord's daughter, a young lass not above sixteen years of age.'[1] He adds that he fears he will be laughed at for reporting so mad a story. And yet it was true; and on Palm Sunday, 1564, Margaret Stewart, daughter of Andrew Lord Stewart of Ochiltree, aged seventeen, was duly united to John Knox, Minister of St Giles's Kirk, Edinburgh, aged fifty-nine – to the great disgust of Queen Mary from family pride, and I would fain hope of many others for more humane considerations. 'In this,' as Randolph says, 'I wish he had done otherwise.' The Consistory of Geneva, 'that most perfect school of Christ that ever was on earth since the days of the Apostles,' were wont to forbid marriages on the ground of too great a disproportion in age. I cannot help wondering whether the old Reformer's conscience did not uneasily remind him, now and again, of this good custom of his religious metropolis, as he thought of the two-and-forty years that separated him from his poor bride. Fitly enough, we hear nothing of the second Mrs Knox until she appears at her husband's deathbed, eight years after. She bore him three daughters in the interval; and I suppose the poor child's martyrdom was made as easy for her as might be. She was 'extremely attentive to him' at the end, we read; and he seems to have spoken to her with some confidence. Moreover, and this is very characteristic, he had copied out for her use a little volume of his own devotional letters to other women.

This is the end of the roll, unless we add to it Mrs Adamson, who had delighted much in his company 'by reason that she had a troubled conscience,' and whose deathbed is commemorated at some length in the pages of his history.[2]

And now, looking back, it cannot be said that Knox's intercourse with women was quite of the highest sort. It is characteristic that we find him more alarmed for his own reputation than for the reputation of the women with whom he was familiar. There was a fatal preponderance of self in all his intimacies: many women came to learn from him, but he

[1]Works, vi. 532.   [2]Ibid. i. 246.

never condescended to become a learner in his turn. And so there is not anything idyllic in these intimacies of his; and they were never so renovating to his spirit as they might have been. But I believe they were good enough for the women. I fancy the women knew what they were about when so many of them followed after Knox. It is not simply because a man is always fully persuaded that he knows the right from the wrong and sees his way plainly through the maze of life, great qualities as these are, that people will love and follow him, and write him letters full of their 'earnest desire for him' when he is absent. It is not over a man, whose one characteristic is grim fixity of purpose, that the hearts of women are 'incensed and kindled with a special care,' as it were over their natural children. In the strong quiet patience of all his letters to the weariful Mrs Bowes, we may perhaps see one cause of the fascination he possessed for these religious women. Here was one whom you could besiege all the year round with inconsistent scruples and complaints; you might write to him on Thursday that you were so elated it was plain the devil was deceiving you, and again on Friday that you were so depressed it was plain God had cast you off for ever; and he would read all this patiently and sympathetically, and give you an answer in the most reassuring polysyllables, and all divided into heads – who knows? – like a treatise on divinity. And then, those easy tears of his. There are some women who like to see men crying; and here was this great-voiced, bearded man of God, who might be seen beating the solid pulpit every Sunday, and casting abroad his clamorous denunciations to the terror of all, and who on the Monday would sit in their parlours by the hour, and weep with them over their manifold trials and temptations. Nowadays, he would have to drink a dish of tea with all these penitents . . . It sounds a little vulgar, as the past will do, if we look into it too closely. We could not let these great folk of old into our drawing-rooms. Queen Elizabeth would positively not be eligible for a housemaid. The old manners and the old customs go sinking from grade to grade, until, if some mighty emperor revisited the glimpses of the moon, he would not find anyone of his way of thinking, anyone he could strike hands with and talk to freely and without offence, save perhaps the porter at the end of the street, or the fellow with his elbows out who loafs all day before the public-house. So that this little note of vulgarity is not a thing to be dwelt upon; it is to be put away from us, as we recall the fashion of these old intimacies; so that we may only remember Knox as one who was very long-suffering with women, kind to them in his own way, loving them in his own way –

and that not the worst way, if it was not the best — and once at least, if not twice, moved to his heart of hearts by a woman, and giving expression to the yearning he had for her society in words that none of us need be ashamed to borrow.

And let us bear in mind always that the period I have gone over in this essay begins when the Reformer was already beyond the middle age, and already broken in bodily health: it has been the story of an old man's friendships. This it is that makes Knox enviable. Unknown until past forty, he had then before him five-and-thirty years of splendid and influential life, passed through uncommon hardships to an uncommon degree of power, lived in his own country as a sort of king, and did what he would with the sound of his voice out of the pulpit. And besides all this, such a following of faithful women! One would take the first forty years gladly, if one could be sure of the last thirty. Most of us, even if, by reason of great strength and the dignity of gray hairs, we retain some degree of public respect in the latter days of our existence, will find a falling away of friends, and a solitude making itself round about us day by day, until we are left alone with the hired sick-nurse. For the attraction of a man's character is apt to be outlived, like the attraction of his body; and the power to love grows feeble in its turn, as well as the power to inspire love in others. It is only with a few rare natures that friendship is added to friendship, love to love, and the man keeps growing richer in affection — richer, I mean, as a bank may be said to grow richer, both giving and receiving more — after his head is white and his back weary, and he prepares to go down into the dust of death.

FOREST NOTES: IDLE HOURS

The woods by night, in all their uncanny effect, are not rightly to be understood until you can compare them with the woods by day. The stillness of the medium, the floor of glittering sand, these trees that go streaming up like monstrous sea-weeds and waver in the moving winds like the weeds in submarine currents, all these set the mind working on the thought of what you may have seen off a foreland or over the side of a boat, and make you feel like a diver, down in the quiet water, fathoms below the tumbling, transitory surface of the sea. And yet in itself, as I say, the strangeness of these nocturnal solitudes is not to be felt fully without the sense of contrast. You must have risen in the morning and seen the woods as they are by day, kindled and coloured in the sun's light; you must have felt the odour of innumerable trees at even, the unsparing heat along the forest roads and the coolness of the groves.

And on the first morning, you will doubtless rise betimes. If you have not been wakened before by the visit of some adventurous pigeon, you will be wakened as soon as the sun can reach your window – for there are no blinds or shutters to keep him out – and the room, with its bare wood floor and bare whitewashed walls, shines all round you in a sort of glory of reflected lights. You may doze a while longer by snatches, or lie awake to study the charcoal-men and dogs and horses with which former occupants have defiled the partitions; Thiers, with wily profile; local celebrities, pipe in hand; or maybe a romantic landscape, splashed in oil. Meanwhile artist after artist drops into the *salle-à-manger* for coffee, and then shoulders easel, sunshade, stool, and paint-box, bound into a faggot, and sets off for what he calls his 'motive'. And artist after artist, as he goes out of the village, carries with him a little following of dogs. For the dogs, who belong only nominally to any special master, hang about the gate of the forest all day long, and whenever anyone goes by, who hits their fancy, profit by his escort, and go forth with him to play an hour or two at hunting. They would like to be under the trees all day. But they cannot go alone. They require a pretext. And so they take the passing artist as an excuse to go into the woods, as they might take a walking-stick as an excuse to bathe. With quick ears, long spines, and bandy legs, or perhaps as tall as a greyhound and with a bulldog's head, this company of mongrels will trot by your side all day and come home with you at night, still showing white teeth and wagging stunted tail. Their good humour is not to be exhausted. You may pelt them with stones, if you please, and all they will do is to give you a wider berth. If once they come out with you, to you they will remain faithful, and with you return; although if you meet them next morning in the street, it is as like as not they will cut you with a countenance of brass.

The forest – a strange thing for an Englishman – is very destitute of birds. This is no country where every patch of wood among the meadows gives up an incense of song, and every valley, wandered through by a streamlet, rings and reverberates from side to side with a profusion of clear notes. And this rarity of birds is not to be regretted on its own account only. For the insects prosper in their absence, and become as one of the plagues of Egypt. Ants swarm in the hot sand; mosquitoes drone their nasal drone; wherever the sun finds a hole in the roof of the forest you see a myriad transparent creatures coming and going in the shaft of light; and even between whiles, even where there is no incursion of sun-rays into the dark arcade of the wood, you are conscious of a continual drift of insects, an ebb and flow of infinitesimal living things between the trees. Nor are insects the only evil creatures that haunt the forest. For you may plump into a cave among the rocks, and find yourself face to face with a wild boar; or see a crooked viper slither across the road.

Perhaps you may set yourself down in the bay between two spreading beech-roots with a book on your lap, and be awakened all of a sudden by a friend: 'I say, just keep where you are, will you? You make the jolliest motive.' And you reply: 'Well, I don't mind, if I may smoke.' And thereafter the hours go idly by. Your friend at the easel labours doggedly, a little way off, in the wide shadow of the tree; and yet farther, across a strait of glaring sunshine, you see another painter, encamped in the shadow of another tree, and up to his waist in the fern. You cannot watch your own effigy growing out of the white trunk, and the trunk beginning to stand forth from the rest of the wood, and the whole picture getting dappled over with the flecks of sun, that slip through the leaves overhead, and as a wind goes by and sets the trees a-talking, flicker hither and thither like butterflies of light. But you know it is going forward; and, out of emulation with the painter, get ready your own palette and lay out the colour for a woodland scene in words.

Your tree stands in a hollow paved with fern and heather, set in a basin of low hills, and scattered over with rocks and junipers. All the open is steeped in pitiless sunlight. Everything stands out as though it were cut in cardboard, every colour is strained into its highest key. The boulders are some of them upright and dead like monolithic castles, some of them prone like sleeping cattle. The junipers – looking, in their soiled and ragged mourning, like some funeral procession that has gone seeking the place of sepulture three hundred years and more in wind and rain – are daubed in, forcibly, against the glowing ferns and heather. Every tassel of their rusty foliage is defined with pre-Raphaelite minuteness. And a sorry figure they make out there in the sun, like misbegotten yew-trees! The scene is all pitched in a key of colour so peculiar, and lit up with such a discharge of violent sunlight as a man might live fifty years in England and not see.

Meanwhile at your elbow someone tunes up a song, words of Ronsard to a pathetic tremulous air, of how the poet loved his mistress long ago, and pressed on her the flight of time, and told her how white and quiet the dead lay under the stones, and how the boat dipped and pitched as the shades embarked for the passionless land. Yet a little while, sang the poet, and there shall be no more love; only to sit, and remember loves that might have been. There is a falling flourish in the air that remains in the memory and comes back in incongruous places, on the seat of hansoms or in the warm bed at night, with something of a forest savour.

'You can get up now,' says the painter; 'I'm at the background.'

And so up you get, stretching yourself, and go your way into the wood, the daylight becoming richer and more golden, and the shadows stretching further into the open. A cool air comes along the highways, and the scents awaken. The fir-trees breathe abroad their ozone. Out of unknown thickets comes forth the soft, secret, aromatic odour of the woods, not like a smell of the free heaven, but as though court ladies, who had known these paths in ages long gone by, still walked in the summer evenings, and shed, from their brocades, a breath of musk or bergamot upon the woodland winds. One side of the long avenues is still kindled with the sun, the other is plunged in transparent shadow. Over the trees, the west begins to burn like a furnace; and the painters gather up their chattels, and go down, by avenue or footpath, to the plain.

WALKING TOURS

It must not be imagined that a walking tour, as some would have us fancy, is merely a better or worse way of seeing the country. There are many ways of seeing landscape quite as good; and none more vivid, in spite of canting dilettantes, than from a railway train. But landscape on a walking tour is quite accessory. He who is indeed of the brotherhood does not voyage in quest of the picturesque, but of certain jolly humours – of the hope and spirit with which the march begins at morning, and the peace and spiritual repletion of the evening's rest. He cannot tell whether he puts his knapsack on, or takes it off, with more delight. The excitement of the departure puts him in key for that of the arrival. Whatever he does is not only a reward in itself, but will be further rewarded in the sequel; and so pleasure leads on to pleasure in an endless chain. It is this that so few can understand; they will either be always lounging or always at five miles an hour; they do not play off the one against the other, prepare all day for the evening, and all evening for the next day. And, above all, it is here that your overwalker fails of comprehension. His heart rises against those who drink their curaçao in liqueur glasses, when he himself can swill it in a brown john. He will not believe that the flavour is more delicate in the smaller dose. He will not believe that to walk this unconscionable distance is merely to stupefy and brutalise himself, and come to his inn, at night, with a sort of frost on his five wits, and a starless night of darkness in his spirit. Not for him the mild luminous evening of the temperate walker! He has nothing left of man but a physical need for bedtime and a double nightcap; and even his pipe, if he be a smoker, will be savourless and disenchanted. It is the fate of such an one to take twice as much trouble as is needed to obtain happiness, and miss the happiness in the end; he is the man of the proverb, in short, who goes further and fares worse.

Now, to be properly enjoyed, a walking tour should be gone upon alone. If you go in a company, or even in pairs, it is no longer a walking tour in anything but name; it is something else and more in the nature of a picnic. A walking tour should be gone upon alone, because freedom is of the essence; because you should be able to stop and go on, and follow this way or that, as the freak takes you; and because you must have your own pace, and neither trot alongside a champion walker, nor mince in time with a girl. And then you must be open to all impressions and let your thoughts take colour from what you see. You should be as a pipe for any wind to play upon. 'I cannot see the wit,' says Hazlitt, 'of walking and talking at the same time. When I am in the country I wish to vegetate like the country,' – which is the gist of all that can be said upon the matter. There should be no cackle of voices at your elbow, to jar on the meditative silence of the morning. And so long as a man is reasoning he cannot surrender himself to that fine intoxication that comes of much motion in the open air, that begins in a sort of dazzle and sluggishness of the brain, and ends in a peace that passes comprehension.

During the first day or so of any tour there are moments of bitterness, when the traveller feels more than coldly towards his knapsack, when he is half in a mind to throw it bodily over the hedge and, like Christian on a similar occasion, 'give three leaps and go on singing.' And yet it soon acquires a property of easiness. It becomes magnetic; the spirit of the journey enters into it. And no sooner have you passed the straps over your shoulder than the lees of sleep are cleared from you, you pull yourself together with a shake, and fall at once into your stride. And surely, of all possible moods, this, in which a man takes the road, is the best. Of course, if he *will* keep thinking of his anxieties, if he *will* open the merchant Abudah's chest and walk arm-in-arm with the hag – why, wherever he is, and whether he walk fast or slow, the chances are that he will not be happy. And so much the more shame to himself! There are perhaps thirty men setting forth at that same hour, and I would lay a large wager there is not another dull face among the thirty. It would be a fine thing to follow, in a coat of darkness, one after another of these wayfarers, some summer morning, for the first few miles upon the road. This one, who walks fast, with a keen look in his eyes, is all concentrated in his own mind; he is up at his loom, weaving and weaving, to set the landscape to words. This one peers about, as he goes, among the grasses; he waits by the canal to watch the dragon-flies; he leans on the gate of the pasture, and cannot look enough upon the complacent kine. And here comes another, talking, laughing, and gesticulating to himself. His face changes from time to time, as indignation flashes from his eyes or anger clouds his forehead. He is composing articles, delivering orations, and conducting the most impassioned interviews, by the way. A little farther on, and it is as like as not he will begin to sing. And well for him, supposing him to be no great master in that art, if he stumble across no stolid peasant at a corner; for on such an occasion, I scarcely know which is the more troubled, or whether it is worse to suffer the confusion of your troubadour, or the unfeigned alarm of your clown. A sedentary population, accustomed, besides, to the strange mechanical bearing of the common tramp, can in no wise explain to itself the gaiety of these passers-by. I knew one man who was arrested as a runaway lunatic, because, although a full-grown person with a red beard, he skipped as he went like a child. And you would be astonished if I were to tell you all the grave and learned heads who have confessed to me that, when on walking tours, they sang – and sang very ill – and had a pair of red ears when, as described above, the inauspicious peasant plumped into their arms from round a corner. And here, lest you should think I am exaggerating, is Hazlitt's own confession, from his essay *On Going a Journey*, which is so good that there should be a tax levied on all who have not read it: –

'Give me the clear blue sky over my head,' says he, 'and the green turf beneath my feet, a winding road before me, and a three hours' march to dinner – and then to thinking! It is hard if I cannot start some game on these lone heaths. I laugh, I run, I leap, I sing for joy.'

Bravo! After that adventure of my friend with the policeman, you would not have cared, would you, to publish that in the first person? But we have no bravery nowadays, and, even in books, must all pretend to be as dull and foolish as our neighbours. It was not so with Hazlitt. And notice how learned he is (as, indeed, throughout the essay) in the theory of walking tours. He is none of your athletic men in purple stockings, who walk their fifty miles a day: three hours' march is his ideal. And then he must have a winding road, the epicure!

Yet there is one thing I object to in these words of his, one thing in the great master's practice that seems to me not wholly wise. I do not approve of that leaping and running. Both of these hurry the respiration; they both shake up the brain out of its glorious open-air confusion; and they both break the pace. Uneven walking is not so agreeable to the body, and it distracts and irritates the mind. Whereas, when once you have fallen into an equable stride, it requires no conscious thought from you to keep it up, and yet it prevents you from thinking earnestly of anything else. Like knitting, like the work of a copying clerk, it gradually neutralises and sets to sleep the serious activity of the mind. We can think of this or that, lightly and laughingly, as a child thinks, or as we think in a morning dose; we can make puns or puzzle out acrostics, and trifle in a thousand ways with words and rhymes; but when it comes to honest work, when we come to gather ourselves together for an effort, we may sound the trumpet as loud and long as we please; the great barons of the mind will not rally to the standard, but sit, each one, at home, warming his hands over his own fire and brooding on his own private thought!

In the course of a day's walk, you see, there is much variance in the mood. From the exhilaration of the start, to the happy phlegm of the arrival, the change is certainly great. As the day goes on, the traveller moves from the one extreme towards the other. He becomes more and more incorporated with the material landscape, and the open-air drunkenness grows upon him with great strides, until he posts along the road, and sees everything about him, as in a cheerful dream. The first is certainly brighter, but the second stage is the more peaceful. A man does not make so many articles towards the end, nor does he laugh aloud; but the purely animal pleasures, the sense of physical wellbeing, the delight of every inhalation, of every time the muscles tighten down the thigh, console him for the absence of the others, and bring him to his destination still content.

Nor must I forget to say a word on bivouacs. You come to a milestone on a hill, or some place where deep ways meet under trees; and off goes the knapsack, and down you sit to smoke a pipe in the shade. You sink into yourself, and the birds come round and look at you; and your smoke dissipates upon the afternoon under the blue dome of heaven; and the sun lies warm upon your feet, and the cool air visits your neck and turns aside your open shirt. If you are not happy, you must have an evil conscience. You may dally as long as you like by the roadside. It is almost as if the millennium were arrived, when we shall throw our clocks and watches over the housetop, and remember time and seasons no more. Not to keep hours for a lifetime is, I was going to say, to live for ever. You have no idea, unless you have tried it, how endlessly long is a summer's day, that you measure out only by hunger, and bring to an end only when you are drowsy. I know a village where there are hardly any clocks, where no one knows more of the days of the week than by a sort of instinct for the fête on Sundays, and where only one person can tell you the day of the month, and she is generally wrong; and if people were

aware how slow Time journeyed in that village, and what armfuls of
spare hours he gives, over and above the bargain, to its wise inhabitants,
I believe there would be a stampede out of London, Liverpool, Paris, and
a variety of large towns, where the clocks lose their heads, and shake the
hours out each one faster than the other, as though they were all in a
wager. And all these foolish pilgrims would each bring his own misery
along with him, in a watch-pocket! It is to be noticed, there were no
clocks and watches in the much-vaunted days before the flood. It
follows, of course, there were no appointments, and punctuality was not
yet thought upon. 'Though ye take from a covetous man all his treasure,'
says Milton, 'he has yet one jewel left; ye cannot deprive him of his
covetousness.' And so I would say of a modern man of business, you
may do what you will for him, put him in Eden, give him the elixir of life
– he has still a flaw at heart, he still has his business habits. Now, there is
no time when business habits are more mitigated than on a walking tour.
And so during these halts, as I say, you will feel almost free.

But it is at night, and after dinner, that the best hour comes. There are
no such pipes to be smoked as those that follow a good day's march; the
flavour of the tobacco is a thing to be remembered, it is so dry and
aromatic, so full and so fine. If you wind up the evening with grog, you
will own there was never such grog; at every sip a jocund tranquillity
spreads about your limbs, and sits easily in your heart. If you read a
book – and you will never do so save by fits and starts – you find the
language strangely racy and harmonious; words take a new meaning;
single sentences possess the ear for half an hour together; and the writer
endears himself to you, at every page, by the nicest coincidence of
sentiment. It seems as if it were a book you had written yourself in a
dream. To all we have read on such occasions we look back with special
favour. 'It was on the 10th of April, 1798,' says Hazlitt, with amorous
precision, 'that I sat down to a volume of the new *Héloïse*, at the Inn at
Llangollen, over a bottle of sherry and a cold chicken.' I should wish to
quote more, for though we are mighty fine fellows nowadays, we cannot
write like Hazlitt. And, talking of that, a volume of Hazlitt's essays
would be a capital pocket-book on such a journey; so would a volume of
Heine's songs; and for *Tristram Shandy* I can pledge a fair experience.

If the evening be fine and warm, there is nothing better in life than to
lounge before the inn door in the sunset, or lean over the parapet of the
bridge, to watch the weeds and the quick fishes. It is then, if ever, that
you taste Joviality to the full significance of that audacious word. Your

muscles are so agreeably slack, you feel so clean and so strong and so idle, that whether you move or sit still, whatever you do is done with pride and a kingly sort of pleasure. You fall in talk with anyone, wise or foolish, drunk or sober. And it seems as if a hot walk purged you, more than of anything else, of all narrowness and pride, and left curiosity to play its part freely, as in a child or a man of science. You lay aside all your own hobbies, to watch provincial humours develop themselves before you, now as a laughable farce, and now grave and beautiful like an old tale.

Or perhaps you are left to your own company for the night, and surly weather imprisons you by the fire. You may remember how Burns, numbering past pleasures, dwells upon the hours when he has been 'happy thinking.' It is a phrase that may well perplex a poor modern, girt about on every side by clocks and chimes, and haunted, even at night, by flaming dial-plates. For we are all so busy, and have so many far-off projects to realise, and castles in the fire to turn into solid habitable mansions on a gravel soil, that we can find no time for pleasure trips into the Land of Thought and among the Hills of Vanity. Changed times, indeed, when we must sit all night, beside the fire, with folded hands; and a changed world for most of us, when we find we can pass the hours without discontent, and be happy thinking. We are in such haste to be doing, to be writing, to be gathering gear, to make our voice audible a moment in the derisive silence of eternity, that we forget that one thing, of which these are but the parts – namely, to live. We fall in love, we drink hard, we run to and fro upon the earth like frightened sheep. And now you are to ask yourself if, when all is done, you would not have been better to sit by the fire at home, and be happy thinking. To sit still and contemplate, – to remember the faces of women without desire, to be pleased by the great deeds of men without envy, to be everything and everywhere in sympathy, and yet content to remain where and what you are – is not this to know both wisdom and virtue, and to dwell with happiness? After all, it is not they who carry flags, but they who look upon it from a private chamber, who have the fun of the procession. And once you are at that, you are in the very humour of all social heresy. It is no time for shuffling, or for big, empty words. If you ask yourself what you mean by fame, riches, or learning, the answer is far to seek; and you go back into that kingdom of light imaginations, which seem so vain in the eyes of Philistines perspiring after wealth, and so momentous to those who are stricken with the disproportions of the world, and, in the face of the gigantic stars, cannot stop to split differences between two degrees of the infinitesimally small, such as a tobacco pipe or the Roman Empire, a million of money or a fiddlestick's end.

You lean from the window, your last pipe reeking whitely into the darkness, your body full of delicious pains, your mind enthroned in the seventh circle of content; when suddenly the mood changes, the weather-cock goes about, and you ask yourself one question more: whether, for the interval, you have been the wisest philosopher or the most egregious of donkeys? Human experience is not yet able to reply; but at least you have had a fine moment, and looked down upon all the kingdoms of the earth. And whether it was wise or foolish, tomorrow's travel will carry you, body and mind, into some different parish of the infinite.

AN APOLOGY FOR IDLERS

BOSWELL: We grow weary when idle.
JOHNSON: That is, sir, because others being busy, we want company; but if we were idle, there would be no growing weary; we should all entertain one another.

Just now, when everyone is bound, under pain of a decree in absence convicting them of *lèse*-respectability, to enter on some lucrative profession, and labour therein with something not far short of enthusiasm, a cry from the opposite party who are content when they have enough, and like to look on and enjoy in the meanwhile, savours a little of bravado and gasconade. And yet this should not be. Idleness so called, which does not consist in doing nothing, but in doing a great deal not recognised in the dogmatic formularies of the ruling class, has as good a right to state its position as industry itself. It is admitted that the presence of people who refuse to enter in the great handicap race for sixpenny pieces, is at once an insult and a disenchantment for those who do. A fine fellow (as we see so many) takes his determination, votes for the sixpences, and in the emphatic Americanism, 'goes for' them. And while such an one is ploughing distressfully up the road, it is not hard to understand his resentment, when he perceives cool persons in the meadows by the wayside, lying with a handkerchief over their ears and a glass at their elbow. Alexander is touched in a very delicate place by the disregard of Diogenes. Where was the glory of having taken Rome for these tumultuous barbarians, who poured into the Senate house, and found the Fathers sitting silent and unmoved by their success? It is a sore thing to have laboured along and scaled the arduous hilltops, and when all is done, find humanity indifferent to your achievement. Hence physicists condemn the unphysical; financiers have only a superficial toleration for those who know little of stocks; literary persons despise the unlettered; and people of all pursuits combine to disparage those who have none.

But though this is one difficulty of the subject, it is not the greatest. You could not be put in prison for speaking against industry, but you can be sent to Coventry for speaking like a fool. The greatest difficulty with most subjects is to do them well; therefore, please to remember this is an apology. It is certain that much may be judiciously argued in favour of diligence; only there is something to be said against it, and that is what, on the present occasion, I have to say. To state one argument is not necessarily to be deaf to all others, and that a man has written a book of travels in Montenegro, is no reason why he should never have been to Richmond.

It is surely beyond a doubt that people should be a good deal idle in youth. For though here and there a Lord Macaulay may escape from school honours with all his wits about him, most boys pay so dear for their medals that they never afterwards have a shot in their locker, and begin the world bankrupt. And the same holds true during all the time a lad is educating himself, or suffering others to educate him. It must have been a very foolish old gentleman who addressed Johnson at Oxford in these words: 'Young man, ply your book diligently now, and acquire a stock of knowledge; for when years come upon you, you will find that poring upon books will be but an irksome task.' The old gentleman seems to have been unaware that many other things besides reading grow irksome, and not a few become impossible, by the time a man has to use spectacles and cannot walk without a stick. Books are good enough in their own way, but they are a mighty bloodless substitute for life. It seems a pity to sit, like the Lady of Shalott, peering into a mirror, with your back turned on all the bustle and glamour of reality. And if a man reads very hard, as the old anecdote reminds us, he will have little time for thought.

If you look back on your own education, I am sure it will not be the full, vivid, instructive hours of truantry that you regret; you would rather cancel some lack-lustre periods between sleep and waking in the class. For my own part, I have attended a good many lectures in my time. I still remember that the spinning of a top is a case of Kinetic Stability. I still remember that Emphyteusis is not a disease, nor Stillicide a crime. But though I would not willingly part with such scraps of science, I do not set the same store by them as by certain other odds and ends that I came by in the open street while I was playing truant. This is not the moment to dilate on that mighty place of education, which was the favourite school of Dickens and of Balzac, and turns out yearly many inglorious masters in the Science of the Aspects of Life. Suffice it to say this: if a lad does not learn in the streets, it is because he has no faculty of learning. Nor is the truant always in the streets, for if he prefers, he may go out by the gardened suburbs into the country. He may pitch on some tuft of lilacs over a burn, and smoke innumerable pipes to the tune of the water on the stones. A bird will sing in the thicket. And there he may fall into a vein of kindly thought, and see things in a new perspective. Why, if this be not education, what is? We may conceive Mr Worldly Wiseman accosting such an one, and the conversation that should thereupon ensue: —

'How now, young fellow, what dost thou here?'

'Truly, sir, I take mine ease.'

'Is not this the hour of the class? and should'st thou not be plying thy Book with diligence, to the end thou mayest obtain knowledge?'

'Nay, but thus also I follow after Learning, by your leave.'

'Learning, quotha! After what fashion, I pray thee? Is it mathematics?'

'No, to be sure.'

'Is it metaphysics?'

'Nor that.'

'Is it some language?'

'Nay, it is no language.'

'Is it a trade?'

'Nor a trade neither.'

'Why, then, what is't?'

'Indeed, sir, as a time may soon come for me to go upon Pilgrimage, I am desirous to note what is commonly done by persons in my case, and where are the ugliest Sloughs and Thickets on the Road; as also, what manner of Staff is of the best service. Moreover, I lie here, by this water, to learn by root-of-heart a lesson which my master teaches me to call Peace, or Contentment.'

Hereupon Mr Worldly Wiseman was much commoved with passion, and shaking his cane with a very threatful countenance, broke forth upon this wise: 'Learning, quotha!' said he; 'I would have all such rogues scourged by the Hangman!'

And so he would go his way, ruffling out his cravat with a crackle of starch, like a turkey when it spread its feathers.

Now this, of Mr Wiseman's, is the common opinion. A fact is not called a fact, but a piece of gossip, if it does not fall into one of your scholastic categories. An inquiry must be in some acknowledged direction, with a name to go by; or else you are not inquiring at all, only lounging; and the workhouse is too good for you. It is supposed that all knowledge is at the bottom of a well, or the far end of a telescope. Sainte-Beuve, as he grew older, came to regard all experience as a single great book, in which to study for a few years ere we go hence; and it seemed all one to him whether you should read in Chapter xx, which is the differential calculus, or in Chapter xxxix, which is hearing the band play in the gardens. As a matter of fact, an intelligent person, looking out of his eyes and hearkening in his ears, with a smile on his face all the time, will get more true education than many another in a life of heroic vigils. There is certainly some chill and arid knowledge to be found upon the summits of formal and laborious science; but it is all round about you, and for the trouble of looking, that you will acquire the warm and palpitating facts of life. While others are filling their memory with a lumber of words, one-half of which they will forget before the week be out, your truant may learn some really useful art: to play the fiddle, to know a good cigar, or to speak with ease and opportunity to all varieties of men. Many who have 'plied their book diligently,' and know all about some one branch or another of accepted lore, come out of the study with an ancient and owl-like demeanour, and prove dry, stockish, and dyspeptic in all the better and brighter parts of life. Many make a large fortune, who remain underbred and pathetically stupid to the last. And meantime there goes the idler, who began life along with them – by your leave, a different picture. He has had time to take care of his health and his spirits; he has been a great deal in the open air, which is the most salutary of all things for both body and mind; and if he has never read the great Book in very recondite places, he has dipped into it and skimmed it over to excellent purpose. Might not the student afford some Hebrew roots, and the business man some of his half-crowns, for a share of the idler's knowledge of life at large, and Art of Living? Nay, and the idler has another and more important quality than these. I mean his wisdom. He who has much looked on at the childish satisfaction of other people in their hobbies, will regard his own with only a very ironical indulgence. He will not be heard among the dogmatists. He will have a great and cool allowance for all sorts of people and opinions. If he finds no out-of-the-way truths, he will identify himself with no very burning falsehood. His way takes him along a by-road, not much frequented, but very even and pleasant, which is called Commonplace Lane, and leads to the Belvedere of Commonsense. Thence he shall command an agreeable, if no very noble prospect; and while others behold the East and West, the Devil and the Sunrise, he will be contentedly aware of a sort of morning hour upon all sublunary things, with an army of shadows running speedily and in many different directions into the great daylight of Eternity. The shadows and the generations, the shrill doctors and the plangent wars, go by into ultimate silence and emptiness; but underneath all this, a man may see, out of the Belvedere windows, much green and peaceful landscape; many firelit parlours; good people laughing, drinking, and making love as they did before the Flood or the French Revolution; and the old shepherd telling his tale under the hawthorn.

Extreme *busyness*, whether at school or college, kirk or market, is a symptom of deficient vitality; and a faculty for idleness implies a catholic appetite and a strong sense of personal identity. There is a sort of dead-alive, hackneyed people about, who are scarcely conscious of living except in the exercise of some conventional occupation. Bring these fellows into the country, or set them aboard ship, and you will see how they pine for their desk or their study. They have no curiosity; they cannot give themselves over to random provocations; they do not take pleasure in the exercise of their faculties for its own sake; and unless Necessity lays about them with a stick, they will even stand still. It is no good speaking to such folk: they *cannot* be idle, their nature is not generous enough; and they pass those hours in a sort of coma, which are not dedicated to furious moiling in the gold-mill. When they do not require to go to the office, when they are not hungry and have no mind to drink, the whole breathing world is a blank to them. If they have to wait an hour or so for a train, they fall into a stupid trance with their eyes open. To see them, you would suppose there was nothing to look at and no one to speak with; you would imagine they were paralysed or alienated; and yet very possibly they are hard workers in their own way, and have good eyesight for a flaw in a deed or a turn of the market. They have been to school and college, but all the time they had their eye on the medal; they have gone about in the world and mixed with clever people, but all the time they were thinking of their own affairs. As if a man's soul were not too small to begin with, they have dwarfed and narrowed theirs by a life of all work and no play; until here they are at forty, with a listless attention, a mind vacant of all material of amusement, and not one thought to rub against another, while they wait for the train. Before he was breeched, he might have clambered on the boxes; when he was twenty, he would have stared at the girls; but now the pipe is smoked out, the snuff-box empty, and my gentleman sits bolt upright upon a bench, with lamentable eyes. This does not appeal to me as being Success in Life.

But it is not only the person himself who suffers from his busy habits, but his wife and children, his friends and relations, and down to the very people he sits with in a railway carriage or an omnibus. Perpetual devotion to what a man calls his business, is only to be sustained by perpetual neglect of many other things. And it is not by any means certain that a man's business is the most important thing he has to do. To an impartial estimate it will seem clear that many of the wisest, most virtuous, and most beneficent parts that are to be played upon the Theatre of Life are filled by gratuitous performers, and pass, among the world at large, as phases of idleness. For in that Theatre, not only the walking gentlemen, singing chambermaids, and diligent fiddlers in the orchestra, but those who look on and clap their hands from the benches, do really play a part and fulfil important offices towards the general result. You are no doubt very dependent on the care of your lawyer and stockbroker, of the guards and signalmen who convey you rapidly from place to place, and the policemen who walk the streets for your protection; but is there not a thought of gratitude in your heart for certain other benefactors who set you smiling when they fall in your way, or season your dinner with good company? Colonel Newcome helped to lose his friend's money; Fred Bayham had an ugly trick of borrowing shirts; and yet they were better people to fall among than Mr Barnes. And though Falstaff was neither sober nor very honest, I think I could name one or two long-faced Barabbases whom the world could better have done without. Hazlitt mentions that he was more sensible of obligation to Northcote, who had never done him anything he could call a service, than to his whole circle of ostentatious friends; for he thought a good companion emphatically the greatest benefactor. I know there are people in the world who cannot feel grateful unless the favour has been done them at the cost of pain and difficulty. But this is a churlish disposition. A man may send you six sheets of letter-paper covered with the most entertaining gossip, or you may pass half an hour pleasantly, perhaps profitably, over an article of his; do you think the service would be greater, if he had made the manuscript in his heart's blood, like a compact with the devil? Do you really fancy you should be more beholden to your correspondent, if he had been damning you all the while for your importunity? Pleasures are more beneficial than duties because, like the quality of mercy, they are not strained, and they are twice blest. There must always be two to a kiss, and there may be a score in a jest; but wherever there is an element of sacrifice, the favour is conferred with pain, and, among generous people, received with confusion. There is no duty we so much underrate as the duty of being happy. By being happy, we sow anonymous benefits upon the world, which remain unknown even to ourselves, or when they are disclosed, surprise nobody so much as the benefactor. The other day, a ragged, barefoot boy ran down the street after a marble, with so jolly an air that he set every one he passed into a good humour; one of these persons, who had been delivered from more than usually black thoughts, stopped the little fellow and gave him some money with this remark: 'You see what sometimes comes of looking pleased.' If he had looked pleased before, he had now to look both pleased and mystified. For my part, I justify this encouragement of smiling rather than tearful children; I do not wish to pay for tears anywhere but upon the stage; but I am prepared to deal largely in the opposite commodity. A happy man or woman is a better thing to find than a five-pound note. He or she is a radiating focus of goodwill; and their entrance into a room is as though another candle had been lighted. We need not care whether they could prove the forty-seventh proposition; they do a better thing than that, they practically demonstrate the great Theorem of the Liveableness of Life. Consequently, if a person cannot be happy without remaining idle, idle he should remain. It is a revolutionary precept; but thanks to hunger and the workhouse, one not easily to be abused; and within practical limits, it is one of the most incontestable truths in the whole Body of Morality. Look at one of your industrious fellows for a moment, I beseech you. He sows hurry and reaps indigestion; he puts a vast deal of activity out to interest, and receives a large measure of nervous derangement in return. Either he absents himself entirely from all fellowship, and lives a recluse in a garret, with carpet slippers and a leaden inkpot; or he comes among people swiftly and bitterly, in a contraction of his whole nervous system, to discharge some temper before he returns to work. I do not care how much or how well he works, this fellow is an evil feature in other people's lives. They would be happier if he were dead. They could easier do without his services in the Circumlocution Office, than they can tolerate his fractious spirits. He poisons life at the well-head. It is better to be beggared out of hand by a scapegrace nephew, than daily hag-ridden by a peevish uncle.

And what, in God's name, is all this pother about? For what cause do they embitter their own and other people's lives? That a man should publish three or thirty articles a year, that he should finish or not finish his great allegorical picture, are questions of little interest to the world. The ranks of life are full; and although a thousand fall, there are always some to go into the breach. When they told Joan of Arc she should be at home minding women's work, she answered there were plenty to spin and wash. And so, even with your own rare gifts! When nature is 'so careless of the single life,' why should we coddle ourselves into the fancy that our own is of exceptional importance? Suppose Shakespeare had been knocked on the head some dark night in Sir Thomas Lucy's preserves, the world would have wagged on better or worse, the pitcher gone to the well, the scythe to the corn, and the student to his book; and no one been any the wiser of the loss. There are not many works extant, if you look the alternative all over, which are worth the price of a pound of tobacco to a man of limited means. This is a sobering reflection for the proudest of our earthly vanities. Even a tobacconist may, upon consideration, find no great cause for personal vainglory in the phrase; for although tobacco is an admirable sedative, the qualities necessary for retailing it are neither rare nor precious in themselves. Alas and alas! you may take it how you will, but the services of no single individual are indispensable. Atlas was just a gentleman with a protracted nightmare! And yet you see merchants who go and labour themselves into a great fortune and thence into the bankruptcy court; scribblers who keep scribbling at little articles until their temper is a cross to all who come about them, as though Pharaoh should set the Israelites to make a pin instead of a pyramid; and fine young men who work themselves into a decline, and are driven off in a hearse with white plumes upon it. Would you not suppose these persons had been whispered, by the Master of the Ceremonies, the promise of some momentous destiny? and that this lukewarm bullet on which they play their farces was the bull's-eye and centrepoint of all the universe? And yet it is not so. The ends for which they give away their priceless youth, for all they know, may be chimerical or hurtful; the glory and riches they expect may never come, or may find them indifferent; and they and the world they inhabit are so inconsiderable that the mind freezes at the thought.

ON FALLING IN LOVE

'Lord, what fools these mortals be!'

There is only one event in life which really astonishes a man and startles him out of his prepared opinions. Everything else befalls him very much as he expected. Event succeeds to event, with an agreeable variety indeed, but with little that is either startling or intense; they form together no more than a sort of background, or running accompaniment to the man's own reflections; and he falls naturally into a cool, curious, and smiling habit of mind, and builds himself up in a conception of life which expects tomorrow to be after the pattern of today and yesterday. He may be accustomed to the vagaries of his friends and acquaintances under the influence of love. He may sometimes look forward to it for himself with an incomprehensible expectation. But it is a subject in which neither intuition nor the behaviour of others will help the philosopher to the truth. There is probably nothing rightly thought or rightly written on this matter of love that is not a piece of the person's experience. I remember an anecdote of a well-known French theorist, who was debating a point eagerly in his *cénacle*. It was objected against him that he had never experienced love. Whereupon he arose, left the society, and made it a point not to return to it until he considered that he had supplied the defect. 'Now,' he remarked, on entering, 'now I am in a position to continue the discussion.' Perhaps he had not penetrated very deeply into the subject after all; but the story indicates right thinking, and may serve as an apologue to readers of this essay.

When at last the scales fall from his eyes, it is not without something of the nature of dismay that the man finds himself in such changed conditions. He has to deal with commanding emotions instead of the easy dislikes and preferences in which he has hitherto passed his days; and he recognises capabilities for pain and pleasure of which he had not yet suspected the existence. Falling in love is the one illogical adventure, the one thing of which we are tempted to think as supernatural, in our trite and reasonable world. The effect is out of all proportion with the cause. Two persons, neither of them, it may be, very amiable or very beautiful, meet, speak a little, and look a little into each other's eyes. That has been done a dozen or so of times in the experience of either with no great result. But on this occasion all is different. They fall at once into that state in which another person becomes to us the very gist and centrepoint of God's creation, and demolishes our laborious theories with a smile; in which our ideas are so bound up with the one master-thought that even the trivial cares of our own person become so many acts of devotion, and the love of life itself is translated into a wish to remain in the same world with so precious and desirable a fellow-creature. And all the while their acquaintances look on in stupor, and ask each other, with almost passionate emphasis, what so-and-so can see in that woman, or such-an-one in that man? I am sure, gentlemen, I cannot tell you. For my part, I cannot think what the women mean. It might be very well, if the Apollo Belvedere should suddenly glow all over into life, and step forward from the pedestal with that godlike air of his. But of the misbegotten changelings who call themselves men, and prate intolerably over dinner-tables, I never saw one who seemed worthy to inspire love – no, nor read of any, except Leonardo da Vinci, and perhaps Goethe in his youth. About women I entertain a somewhat different opinion; but there, I have the misfortune to be a man.

There are many matters in which you may waylay Destiny, and bid him stand and deliver. Hard work, high thinking, adventurous excitement, and a great deal more that forms a part of this or the other person's spiritual bill of fare, are within the reach of almost anyone who can dare a little and be patient. But it is by no means in the way of everyone to fall in love. You know the difficulty Shakespeare was put into when Queen Elizabeth asked him to show Falstaff in love. I do not believe that Henry Fielding was ever in love. Scott, if it were not for a passage or two in *Rob Roy*, would give me very much the same effect. These are great names and (what is more to the purpose) strong, healthy, high-strung, and generous natures, of whom the reverse might have been expected. As for the innumerable army of anaemic and tailorish persons who occupy the face of this planet with so much propriety, it is palpably absurd to imagine them in any such situation as a love-affair. A wet rag goes safely by the fire; and if a man is blind, he cannot expect to be much impressed by romantic scenery. Apart from all this, many lovable people miss each other in the world, or meet under some unfavourable star. There is the nice and critical moment of declaration to be got over. From timidity or lack of opportunity a good half of possible love cases never get so far, and at least another quarter do there cease and determine. A very adroit person, to be sure, manages to prepare the way and out with his declaration in the nick of time. And then there is a fine solid sort of man, who goes on from snub to snub; and if he has to declare forty times, will continue imperturbably declaring, amid the astonished consideration of men and angels, until he has a favourable answer. I daresay, if one were a woman, one would like to marry a man who was capable of doing this, but not quite one who had done so. It is just a little bit abject, and somehow just a little bit gross; and marriages in which one of the parties has been thus battered into consent scarcely form agreeable subjects for meditation. Love should run out to meet love with open arms. Indeed, the ideal story is that of two people who go into love step for step, with a fluttered consciousness, like a pair of children venturing together into a dark room. From the first moment when they see each other, with a pang of curiosity, through stage after stage of growing pleasure and embarrassment, they can read the expression of their own trouble in each other's eyes. There is here no declaration properly so called; the feeling is so plainly shared, that as soon as the man knows what it is in his own heart, he is sure of what it is in the woman's.

This simple accident of falling in love is as beneficial as it is astonishing. It arrests the petrifying influence of years, disproves cold-blooded and cynical conclusions, and awakens dormant sensibilities. Hitherto the man had found it a good policy to disbelieve the existence of any enjoyment which was out of his reach; and thus he turned his back upon the strong sunny parts of nature, and accustomed himself to look exclusively on what was common and dull. He accepted a prose ideal, let himself go blind of many sympathies by disuse; and if he were young and witty, or beautiful, wilfully forewent these advantages. He joined himself to the following of what, in the old mythology of love, was prettily called *nonchaloir*; and in an odd mixture of feelings, a fling of self-respect, a preference for selfish liberty, and a great dash of that fear with which honest people regard serious interests, kept himself back from the straightforward course of life among certain selected activities. And now, all of a sudden, he is unhorsed, like St Paul, from his infidel affectation. His heart, which has been ticking accurate seconds for the last year, gives a bound and begins to beat high and irregularly in his breast. It seems as if he had never heard or felt or seen until that moment;

and by the report of his memory, he must have lived his past life between sleep and waking, or with the preoccupied attention of a brown study. He is practically incommoded by the generosity of his feelings, smiles much when he is alone, and develops a habit of looking rather blankly upon the moon and stars. But it is not at all within the province of a prose essayist to give a picture of this hyperbolical frame of mind; and the thing has been done already, and that to admiration. In *Adelaide*, in Tennyson's *Maud*, and in some of Heine's songs, you get the absolute expression of this midsummer spirit. Romeo and Juliet were very much in love; although they tell me some German critics are of a different opinion, probably the same who would have us think Mercutio a dull fellow. Poor Antony was in love, and no mistake. That lay figure Marius, in *Les Misérables*, is also a genuine case in his own way, and worth observation. A good many of George Sand's people are thoroughly in love; and so are a good many of George Meredith's. Altogether, there is plenty to read on the subject. If the root of the matter be in him, and if he has the requisite chords to set in vibration, a young man may occasionally enter, with the key of art, into that land of Beulah which is upon the borders. of Heaven and within sight of the City of Love. There let him sit awhile to hatch delightful hopes and perilous illusions.

One thing that accompanies the passion in its first blush is certainly difficult to explain. It comes (I do not quite see how) that from having a very supreme sense of pleasure in all parts of life – in lying down to sleep, in waking, in motion, in breathing, in continuing to be – the lover begins to regard his happiness as beneficial for the rest of the world and highly meritorious in himself. Our race has never been able contentedly to suppose that the noise of its wars, conducted by a few young gentlemen in a corner of an inconsiderable star, does not re-echo among the courts of Heaven with quite a formidable effect. In much the same taste, when people find a great to-do in their own breasts, they imagine it must have some influence in their neighbourhood. The presence of the two lovers is so enchanting to each other that it seems as if it must be the best thing possible for everybody else. They are half inclined to fancy it is because of them and their love that the sky is blue and the sun shines. And certainly the weather is usually fine while people are courting . . . In point of fact, although the happy man feels very kindly towards others of his own sex, there is apt to be something too much of the magnifico in his demeanour. If people grow presuming and self-important over such matters as a dukedom or the Holy See, they will scarcely support the dizziest elevation in life without some suspicion of a strut; and the dizziest elevation is to love and be loved in return. Consequently, accepted lovers are a trifle condescending in their address to other men. An overweening sense of the passion and importance of life hardly conduces to simplicity of manner. To women, they feel very nobly, very purely, and very generously, as if they were so many Joan of Arcs; but this does not come out in their behaviour; and they treat them to Grandisonian airs marked with a suspicion of fatuity. I am not quite certain that women do not like this sort of thing; but really, after having bemused myself over *Daniel Deronda*, I have given up trying to understand what they like.

If it did nothing else, this sublime and ridiculous superstition, that the pleasure of the pair is somehow blessed to others, and everybody is made happier in their happiness, would serve at least to keep love generous and great-hearted. Nor is it quite a baseless superstition after all. Other lovers are hugely interested. They strike the nicest balance between pity and approval, when they see people aping the greatness of their own sentiments. It is an understood thing in the play, that while the young gentlefolk are courting on the terrace, a rough flirtation is being carried on, and a light, trivial sort of love is growing up, between the footman and the singing chambermaid. As people are generally cast for the leading parts in their own imaginations, the reader can apply the parallel to real life without much chance of going wrong. In short, they are quite sure this other love-affair is not so deep-seated as their own, but they like dearly to see it going forward. And love, considered as a spectacle, must have attractions for many who are not of the confraternity. The sentimental old maid is a commonplace of the novelists; and he must be rather a poor sort of human being, to be sure, who can look on at this pretty madness without indulgence and sympathy. For nature commends itself to people with a most insinuating art; the busiest is now and again arrested by a great sunset; and you may be as pacific or as cold-blooded as you will, but you cannot help some emotion when you read of well-disputed battles, or meet a pair of lovers in the lane.

Certainly, whatever it may be with regard to the world at large, this idea of beneficent pleasure is true as between the sweethearts. To do good and communicate is the lover's grand intention. It is the happiness of the other that makes his own most intense gratification. It is not possible to disentangle the different emotions, the pride, humility, pity and passion, which are excited by a look of happy love or an unexpected caress. To make one's self beautiful, to dress the hair, to excel in talk, to do anything and all things that puff out the character and attributes and make them imposing in the eyes of others, is not only to magnify one's self, but to offer the most delicate homage at the same time. And it is in this latter intention that they are done by lovers; for the essence of love is kindness; and indeed it may be best defined as passionate kindness: kindness, so to speak, run mad and become importunate and violent. Vanity in a merely personal sense exists no longer. The lover takes a perilous pleasure in privately displaying his weak points and having them, one after another, accepted and condoned. He wishes to be assured that he is not loved for this or that good quality, but for himself, or something as like himself as he can contrive to set forward. For, although it may have been a very difficult thing to paint the marriage of Cana, or write the fourth act of *Antony and Cleopatra*, there is a more difficult piece of art before everyone in this world who cares to set about explaining his own character to others. Words and acts are easily wrenched from their true significance; and they are all the language we have to come and go upon. A pitiful job we make of it, as a rule. For better or worse, people mistake our meaning and take our emotions at a wrong valuation. And generally we rest pretty content with our failures; we are content to be misapprehended by cackling flirts; but when once a man is moonstruck with this affection of love, he makes it a point of honour to clear such dubieties away. He cannot have the Best of her Sex misled upon a point of this importance; and his pride revolts at being loved in a mistake.

He discovers a great reluctance to return on former periods of his life. To all that has not been shared with her, rights and duties, bygone fortunes and dispositions, he can look back only by a difficult and repugnant effort of the will. That he should have wasted some years in ignorance of what alone was really important, that he may have entertained the thought of other women with any show of complacency, is a burthen almost too heavy for his self-respect. But it is the thought of another past that rankles in his spirit like a poisoned wound. That he himself made a fashion of being alive in the bald, beggarly days before a certain meeting, is deplorable enough in all good conscience. But that She should have permitted herself the same liberty seems inconsistent with a Divine providence.

A great many people run down jealousy, on the score that it is an artificial feeling, as well as practically inconvenient. This is scarcely fair; for the feeling on which it merely attends, like an ill-humoured courtier, is itself artificial in exactly the same sense and to the same degree. I suppose what is meant by that objection is that jealousy has not always been a character of man; formed no part of that very modest kit of sentiments with which he is supposed to have begun the world; but waited to make its appearance in better days and among richer natures. And this is equally true of love, and friendship, and love of country, and delight in what they call the beauties of nature, and most other things worth having. Love, in particular, will not endure any historical scrutiny: to all who have fallen across it, it is one of the most incontestable facts in the world; but if you begin to ask what it was in other periods and countries, in Greece for instance, the strangest doubts begin to spring up, and everything seems so vague and changing that a dream is logical in comparison. Jealousy, at any rate, is one of the consequences of love; you may like it or not, at pleasure; but there it is.

It is not exactly jealousy, however, that we feel when we reflect on the past of those we love. A bundle of letters found after years of happy union creates no sense of insecurity in the present; and yet it will pain a man sharply. The two people entertain no vulgar doubt of each other: but this pre-existence of both occurs to the mind as something indelicate. To be altogether right, they should have had twin birth together, at the same moment with the feeling that unites them. Then indeed it would be simple and perfect and without reserve or afterthought. Then they would understand each other with a fulness impossible otherwise. There would be no barrier between them of associations that cannot be imparted. They would be led into none of those comparisons that send the blood back to the heart. And they would know that there had been no time lost, and they had been together as much as was possible. For besides terror for the separation that must follow some time or other in the future, men feel anger, and something like remorse, when they think of that other separation which endured until they met. Someone has written that love makes people believe in immortality, because there seems not to be room enough in life for so great a tenderness, and it is inconceivable that the most masterful of our emotions should have no more than the spare moments of a few years. Indeed, it seems strange; but if we call to mind analogies, we can hardly regard it as impossible.

'The blind bow-boy,' who smiles upon us from the end of terraces in old Dutch gardens, laughingly hails his bird-bolts among a fleeting generation. But for as fast as ever he shoots, the game dissolves and disappears into eternity from under his falling arrows; this one is gone ere he is struck; the other has but time to make one gesture and give one passionate cry; and they are all the things of a moment. When the generation is gone, when the play is over, when the thirty years' panorama has been withdrawn in tatters from the stage of the world, we may ask what has become of these great, weighty, and undying loves, and the sweethearts who despised mortal conditions in a fine credulity; and they can only show us a few songs in a bygone taste, a few actions worth remembering, and a few children who have retained some happy stamp from the disposition of their parents.

IN THE LATIN QUARTER
I *A Ball at Mr Elsinare's*

Mr Elsinare's studio lies in a long, rambling, silent street not a hundred miles from the Boulevard Mont-Parnasse – a quarter of Paris which is cheap, airy, and free from the visitation of tourists. The house presents to the thoroughfare a modest gable, a rickety carriage-gate, and a sort of cottage on the other side of it, which looks as if it was meant for the porter. The wicket stands open as we arrive, but there is no sign of life. We venture in, as we might venture after nightfall into a farm-steading, with a kind of beware-of-the-dog feeling at heart. The court is long and narrow like a bit of a country lane; the ground descends, the pavement is of the roughest; and ladies with high heels, on their way to Mr Elsinare's, stumble in the darkness over all manner of heights and hollows, and have to pilot their drapery through many dangers.

The studio is up several pair of stairs; it has been arranged with much art for the occasion. The floor is cleaned; Elsinare and his partner, Smiler, have been rubbing it with candle-ends all the morning, until now it is as shiny and as slippery as heart could wish. Two Chinese lanterns and a couple of bronze lamps illuminate the ballroom from the rafters. There is a piano against the wall, and casts make a great figure on the shelves.

A door stands open on one side, and gives entrance into a small closet which is to do duty on the present occasion as a buttery and a lady's cloak-room. Here a French *bonne*, lent for the evening by the lady patroness, mixes glasses of syrup and water and lays out sweet biscuits for distribution. She is surrounded by cloaks and hats and great-coats, and from time to time examines her own face critically in the mirror. Even in the cloak-room, the eye is scared by unexpected and inharmonious details. An iron bedstead leaning against the wall strikes rather a homely note for the ante-chambers of a festival. One corner is occupied by a lay figure with an air of glaring immorality. From another, a death's-head, jauntily accoutred with a helmet, scowls down upon the syrup and sweet biscuits, and catches the young ladies' eyes wickedly in the mirror, as if to remind them of the vanity of balls. Truly, this

Egyptian refinement is but little in key with the mild and innocent diversions of the evening. Syrup and water is scarcely the right sort of beverage to quaff among the emblems of mortality.

The company is mixed as to nationality, and varied in attire. The chaperon is an Austrian Countess, who seems to have had all the Austria taken out of her by a prolonged sojourn in New York. There are many Americans, a sprinkling of French, a Swede, and some Britishers. Most of the men are in evening dress, and one or two in costume. Elsinare appears as Hamlet, and makes a very graceful host. Dear Smiler, the best of men, has waxed his moustaches until he is nearly off the face of the earth, and radiates welcome and good happiness as though he had six thousand a year and an island in the Ægean. The floor is just a trifle too much waxed for his free, Californian style of dancing; and, as he goes round in the last figure of the quadrille, he falls into the arms of all the ladies in succession. It makes no difference, however, for they are mostly bigger than he is, and he carries it off with a good humour that is more beautiful than grace. Shaun O'Shaughnessy also bites the dust repeatedly with true Hibernian *aplomb*. George Rowland, dressed as a Yorkshire farmer of the old school, makes his entrance in character, to the unfeigned alarm of all the French. They evidently think the scalping is going to begin. But it is just Rowland's way, and they are reassured by the laughter of the rest. Willie MacIntyre, in the national costume, brings with him a powerful atmosphere of sporran. He does not dance from motives of delicacy, and tries as far as possible to keep the sporran in unfrequented corners. A sporran, like a bag-pipe, is most agreeable in the extreme distance, and in breezy, mountainous places.

Almost all the young ladies are in costume. There are some pretty Italian dresses round the room, to say nothing of their wearers. But Belle Bird is not to be passed over among the rest. She is a Californian girl, and has spent her childhood among Bret Harte's stories, petted by miners, and gamblers, and trappers, and ranche-men, and all the *dramatis personæ* of the new romance; and, I must say, they seem to spoil people in the right direction, for Belle is frank and simple and not at all like an American miss. She looks like a Russian – a South Russian, I mean. The pleasant gentlemen, old and young, who make it their business to accost ladies on the streets of Paris, had a favourite phrase by way of endeavouring to open a friendly understanding with her: – 'Quelle jolie, gentille petite Russe!' they would remark. Belle says it was by mistake she hit one of these intelligent young men over the mouth last winter;

but, of course, we all have our own ideas; I am glad, at least, it was the intelligent young man who got the buffet, instead of you or me. For a young lady of sixteen, to employ her own idiom, you bet your sweet life she'd fetch him! Tonight she is dressed in gilt, like a stage fairy, and her hair is full of gold powder; her dark face is flushed, and her eyes shine with happiness. She and Smiler are quite the features of the evening; Smiler looks so gratified with everybody else, and she looks so pleased with herself. Upon my word, it is impossible to say which is the more becoming sentiment. You cannot set eyes on either of them without solid satisfaction. Your heart gives a bounce and a thrill; and, like the Ancient Mariner with the watersnakes, you want badly to bless them. I know I keep blessing little Smiler all night long.

George Rowland considers syrup and water an unwholesome, if not an impertinent, beverage. He eyes the tray dejectedly; and so I draw near and begin to conjure up divine drinks before his thirsty imagination. I ask him what he would think of a pint of stout? 'I should look upon it with a very friendly eye,' answers George, in a tragic voice. 'Or a bottle of the Cluny Pommard?' I go on, referring to the crack café of the Quarter. George passes his hand waterily over his mouth, and his eyes wink and look suffused. 'Or even one of Laverne's Fleury?' He begs me to stop, and we drink to each other dispiritedly in syrup and water.

Willie MacIntyre is only a passing visitor in town. He has the eccentricity to remain all winter at one of those artistic villages, which are the Brighton and Scarborough of the Latin Quarter. Hence he is an object of interest; and old frequenters of G——— draw near the sporran gingerly to hear the news. The landlord's daughter has been unwell; the captain of the *pompiers* has been exceptionally drunk. MacIntyre, being a man of means, is going to build a studio at the back of the inn, entering out of the room Reake Yetton had last summer. It is to be more of a menagerie than a studio, as is to be expected from the man in question; and he has come up to town to buy pigeons, a cat, a monkey, and another dog – Taureau, his bull terrier, having succumbed to natural laws on a diet of absinthe, vermouth, coffee, champagne, and mutton cutlets.

There is another topic of interest. Shaun O'Shaughnessy, MacIntyre, and another Scotchman, happily absent from Paris and still ignorant of his misfortune, are in a fair way to lose all their furniture for another man's debts, owing to some infamous chink in the French Code. MacIntyre looks stiff and smiles evilly when the subject is broached.

Rowland offers burlesque counsel in a graveyard tone of voice, and relapses into his character part of the Yorkshire farmer fitfully and rather feebly; for the syrup has done its work. Shaun comes into the corner between the dances, and denunciates the whole French nation in a sweeping organ-roll of brogue.

It is strange to think that almost all these good folk are daubers of canvas; even Belle has a maul-stick with which she will break your head if you are impolite; and yet, while they all diligently paint and paint by the month together, and wash their brushes with quite as knowing an air as any R.A. in England, and send really quite a considerable extent of canvas into different exhibitions – there is not one painter that ever you heard of in the party; they are all as unknown as if they were dead, and the most of them have never sold a pennyworth of their productions. You may hear of them some day for all that; and, in the meantime, I am sure they enjoy their evening rarely.

11 *A Studio of Ladies*

Students of Art in Paris are usually attached to some painter of name, in whose wake they humbly follow. The master gives them so much of his time for criticism and advice, and when he is occupied on a work of any magnitude, employs the most capable to lay it in. The pupils pay by subscription for the models and the large studio in which they work. Some learn to forge the master's touch with great nicety; others recoil to the opposite extreme, and take pleasure in producing battle-pieces under the tuition of a painter of sheep; but all, when they come to exhibit in the Salon, sign themselves as the pupil of M. Couture, or M. Gérome, or M. Carolus Duran, as the case may be. This is an arrangement honourable and useful to both parties.

In the case of lady students there is one little difference. The peculiar chivalry of the male sex comes strongly to the front. It is a question of money. Thews and sinews ruled the world of yore; it was 'none but the brave, none but the brave, none but the brave deserve the fair;' and the prize-fighter came swelling into the arena to the sound of trumpets. And in those days men had the advantage because they were strong. Now a pocketful of yellow sovereigns makes sweeter music than Joachim's fiddle; and the bald and peak-faced banker, sitting humped up in a brougham and two, is, for most practical purposes, stronger and more beautiful than Hercules or Apollo. And we still have the pull, because we carry the purse. The ball is still at our feet. But we are aware of peril; we know we must keep the money greedily to ourselves; for we are fonder of women than they are of us; we must bribe them to come to us, as we bribe a child with a sugar almond for a kiss; and if once they have all our sugar almonds, they will leave us like a pack of Satyrs, sitting in dim oak-coverts, and hearing only afar off the voices and swift feet of Artemis's maidens. Hence we cozen them by law; studiously making account of their greater longevity in the case of annuities, where it takes something out of their pocket; and slily omitting that consideration in cases of insurance, where it would put something into it. Hence, also, painters will not accept female students without mulcting them in a smart fee.

M. Concert, a heavy-shouldered French painter, with a sneering countenance, a long nose, and a most seductive deportment, had thrown open his *atelier* to ladies, and pocketed their money with great sweetness. To him flocked quite a troop of English, Americans, and French, and a knot of indefatigable Swedes.

Now, however hard the other women work, the Swedes outdo them. This Swedish cohort at M. Concert's had many things in common: there were thin Swedes and fat Swedes, the Swede who always had her jaw tied up for toothache, and the Swede who came day about in curl-papers and in curls; and yet they all had the same profile, so that you could only distinguish them from the front, and they were all the early birds on Monday morning. Monday morning is an epoch in studio existence; it is then that a new model begins a sitting, and those who arrive first have the first choice of places for the week. At Carolus Duran's, the other year, there were one or two fellows who lived in the same building with the studio. These would arise wilily at three or four on Monday morning, and, after having inscribed their names upon the board, return cozily to roost. You may imagine the discomfiture of early students from all parts of Paris, when they dropped in as soon as the studio was opened, and found a whole company of names already registered. At last the trick got wind. The porter was found to be venal; through his connivance Shaun O'Shaughnessy and the whole ruck of out-students made their entrance on Sunday evening; and when their tricksy comrades crept down before daybreak with a bit of candle and their finger to their nose, they found the tables turned, and had to inscribe themselves humbly in the fag-end of the class. The Swedes, as I said, were invariably the first of M. Concert's pupils; and not just by ones or twos, but in a body. Adventurous girls would rise very early; it would be freezing weather; the lamps would still burn along the streets of Paris, now in belated midnight, now jostling with a blink of dawn; but there would be all the Swedes – the lean and the corpulent, she with the toothache and she with the curl-papers – seated in awful guise upon the *atelier* doorstep; and there would be all the Swedish names, chalked up with shivering fingers on the jamb of the *atelier* door. This began in time to take legendary proportions; whisperers broached strange theories; and the street has a doubtful reputation in Paris to this day.

Time of work at M. Concert's was remarkable for a good deal of talk and some unlovely singularities. The conversation ran generally in two lines – those who could not paint, spoke of their conquests and admirers; those who could, discoursed exclusively upon cheap clothing. I wish it had been the other way, I am sure, and the women of talent had talked all day long about the excellence of men, only it wasn't so, and it is just another proof of our precarious situation. Oh, my brothers! let us stand back to back, and keep the women poor; raise your fees, if necessary. Already I wander in fancy upon dismal hill-tops, and my heart quivers as Dian's hunt goes by below me in the woods. I raise my streaming eyes towards the stars, and accuse the gods vainly; for I must go for ever without a mate! As I was saying, the clever ones spoke of cheap clothing, and where to buy shoes, and where a dress might be dyed and yet look like new. Mrs Nero and another talked scandal in a feminine strain, small, and false, and deadly; and a prim American girl might be overheard by her neighbours in a placid running commentary on the scandal. 'That's a lie,' she would remark, in a grave undertone. 'That's another; I ain't so. Oh, you Spanish wretch!' On the whole, a capital American girl.

I have spoken of unlovely singularities among M. Concert's lady pupils; these were connected with the models, whom they used disgracefully. Women generally prefer to *pose* to men, and men to women; but in this studio, where they treated all badly, they treated the men like brutes. It may be as well to explain to the mercantile British mind that there is no such thing as delicacy about a model. The Briton would have seen this for himself with stupefaction had he been an hour in Concert's. The Swedes, from where they sat in the first places, used to arrange the model's hair, and generally poke him up and make him look lively with the end of their maul-sticks. An old Frenchwoman with false hair would scuttle forward among the easels, and measure him all over with a bit of tape. In sharp wintry weather they kept one poor fellow bringing coal from a distant cellar during his intervals of repose, to save them the trouble of going into the next room and calling down a tube. He not unnaturally developed a smart catarrh, and whenever he sneezed or had to blow his nose, the Swedes and Mrs Nero would cry out upon him as if he had done it on purpose.

These were the sharpest persecutors. With the Swedes it was done in the way of business. The model should take an arduous position, because they wished to draw it; he should rest little, because they wanted as much as possible for their money; and they shoved him about with their maul-sticks, because it was the handiest way to straighten him up. There was no ill-will about these denizens of the pensive North; they merely drove their slave. Mrs Nero, on the other hand, was a pretty, curly French-American, fond of ices and flirtation; and I suspect a certain inverted element of sex prompted and intensified her cruelty to men. She did not misuse them in callousness, but out of an evil-minded sensibility. I think I can see her by Faustina's elbow, above the confusion of the amphitheatre; I think I can see the little thumb turned down, and the curly head look forth in a luxurious horror on the carnival of death.

One day a splendid, brawny Hercules of a fellow came to M. Concert's, and the Swedes, who always carried their point, decided he should pose in the attitude of the Dying Gladiator. Women models have an interval of rest every thirty minutes; men only once in the hour. An hour on end in the attitude of the Dying Gladiator is no joke, and the man soon began to give the most distressing tokens of exhaustion; his muscles quivered, great drops stood upon him; it was the spectacle of an agony. Murmurs arose among the better-natured members of the class; but as long as any one person insists on his going on, the model must finish his hour or forfeit his money, and Mrs Nero would hear of no compromise. 'It is our business to paint,' she said; 'it is his to *pose* for an hour at a time; he has been paid to do so, and I mean he shall.' 'Don't you see the man is suffering?' they asked. She took some colour off her *palette*, and laid it on deliberately. 'I just love to see him suffer,' said she. It appears the model had a smattering of English, for he understood this remark, or perhaps the tone in which it was uttered, and, raising his head, he gave Mrs Nero a murderous stare between the eyes. With that the class broke out into revolt. Mrs Wycherley and many more would stay no longer in the room. But Mrs Nero and the Swedes – those conscientious artists – finished their hour with great deliberation.

The model would not stay out the week; it was the first time he had ever *posed* for women, he said, and he vowed horribly it would be the last.

CRABBED AGE AND YOUTH

'You know my mother now and then argues very notably;
always very warmly at least. I happen often to differ from
her; and we both think so well of our own arguments,
that we very seldom are so happy as to convince one
another. A pretty common case, I believe, in all *vehement*
debatings. She says, I am *too witty*; Anglicè, *too pert*; I,
that she is *too wise*; that is to say, being likewise put into
English, *not so young as she has been.*' – Miss Howe to
Miss Harlowe, *Clarissa*, vol. ii, Letter xiii.

There is a strong feeling in favour of cowardly and prudential
proverbs. The sentiments of a man while he is full of ardour and hope
are to be received, it is supposed, with some qualification. But when the
same person has ignominiously failed and begins to eat up his words,
he should be listened to like an oracle. Most of our pocket wisdom is
conceived for the use of mediocre people, to discourage them from
ambitious attempts, and generally console them in their mediocrity.
And since mediocre people constitute the bulk of humanity, this is no
doubt very properly so. But it does not follow that the one sort of
proposition is any less true than the other, or that Icarus is not to be
more praised, and perhaps more envied, than Mr Samuel Budgett the
Successful Merchant. The one is dead, to be sure, while the other is still
in his counting-house counting out his money; and doubtless this is a
consideration. But we have, on the other hand, some bold and
magnanimous sayings common to high races and natures, which set
forth the advantage of the losing side, and proclaim it better to be a
dead lion than a living dog. It is difficult to fancy how the mediocrities
reconcile such sayings with their proverbs. According to the latter,
every lad who goes to sea is an egregious ass; never to forget your
umbrella through a long life would seem a higher and wiser flight of
achievement than to go smiling to the stake; and so long as you are a
bit of a coward and inflexible in money matters, you fulfil the whole
duty of man.

It is a still more difficult consideration for our average men, that while all their teachers, from Solomon down to Benjamin Franklin and the ungodly Binney, have inculcated the same ideal of manners, caution, and respectability, those characters in history who have most notoriously flown in the face of such precepts are spoken of in hyperbolical terms of praise, and honoured with public monuments in the streets of our commercial centres. This is very bewildering to the moral sense. You have Joan of Arc, who left a humble but honest and reputable livelihood under the eyes of her parents, to go a-colonelling, in the company of rowdy soldiers, against the enemies of France; surely a melancholy example for one's daughters! And then you have Columbus, who may have pioneered America, but, when all is said, was a most imprudent navigator. His life is not the kind of thing one would like to put into the hands of young people; rather, one would do one's utmost to keep it from their knowledge, as a red flag of adventure and disintegrating influence in life. The time would fail me if I were to recite all the big names in history whose exploits are perfectly irrational and even shocking to the business mind. The incongruity is speaking; and I imagine it must engender among the mediocrities a very peculiar attitude towards the nobler and showier sides of national life. They will read of the Charge of Balaclava in much the same spirit as they assist at a performance of the *Lyons Mail*. Persons of substance take in the *Times* and sit composedly in pit or boxes according to the degree of their prosperity in business. As for the generals who go galloping up and down among bomb-shells in absurd cocked hats – as for the actors who raddle their faces and demean themselves for hire upon the stage – they must belong, thank God! to a different order of beings, whom we watch as we watch the clouds careering in the windy, bottomless inane, or read about like characters in ancient and rather fabulous annals. Our offspring would no more think of copying their behaviour, let us hope, than of doffing their clothes and painting themselves blue in consequence of certain admissions in the first chapter of their school history of England.

Discredited as they are in practice, the cowardly proverbs hold their own in theory; and it is another instance of the same spirit, that the opinions of old men about life have been accepted as final. All sorts of allowances are made for the illusions of youth; and none, or almost none, for the disenchantments of age. It is held to be a good taunt, and somehow or other to clinch the question logically, when an old gentleman waggles his head and says: 'Ah, so I thought when I was your age.' It is not thought an answer at all, if the young man retorts: 'My venerable sir, so I shall most probably think when I am yours.' And yet the one is as good as the other: pass for pass, tit for tat, a Roland for an Oliver.

'Opinion in good men,' says Milton, 'is but knowledge in the making.' All opinions, properly so called, are stages on the road to truth. It does not follow that a man will travel any further; but if he has really considered the world and drawn a conclusion, he has travelled as far. This does not apply to formulae got by rote, which are stages on the road to nowhere but second childhood and the grave. To have a catchword in your mouth is not the same thing as to hold an opinion; still less is it the same thing as to have made one for yourself. There are too many of these catchwords in the world for people to rap out upon you like an oath and by way of an argument. They have a currency as intellectual counters; and many respectable persons pay their way with nothing else. They seem to stand for vague bodies of theory in the background. The imputed virtue of folios full of knockdown arguments is supposed to reside in them, just as some of the majesty of the British Empire dwells in the constable's truncheon. They are used in pure superstition, as old clodhoppers spoil Latin by way of an exorcism. And yet they are vastly serviceable for checking unprofitable discussion and stopping the mouths of babes and sucklings. And when a young man comes to a certain stage of intellectual growth, the examination of these counters forms a gymnastic at once amusing and fortifying to the mind.

Because I have reached Paris, I am not ashamed of having passed through Newhaven and Dieppe. They were very good places to pass through, and I am none the less at my destination. All my old opinions were only stages on the way to the one I now hold, as itself is only a stage on the way to something else. I am no more abashed at having been a red-hot Socialist with a panacea of my own than at having been a sucking infant. Doubtless the world is quite right in a million ways; but you have to be kicked about a little to convince you of the fact. And in the meanwhile you must do something, be something, believe something. It is not possible to keep the mind in a state of accurate balance and blank; and even if you could do so, instead of coming ultimately to the right conclusion, you would be very apt to remain in a state of balance and blank to perpetuity. Even in quite intermediate stages, a dash of enthusiasm is not a thing to be ashamed of in the retrospect: if St

Paul had not been a very zealous Pharisee, he would have been a colder Christian. For my part, I look back to the time when I was a Socialist with something like regret. I have convinced myself (for the moment) that we had better leave these great changes to what we call great blind forces: their blindness being so much more perspicacious than the little, peering, partial eyesight of men. I seem to see that my own scheme would not answer; and all the other schemes I ever heard propounded would depress some elements of goodness just as much as they encouraged others. Now I know that in thus turning Conservative with years, I am going through the normal cycle of change and travelling in the common orbit of men's opinions. I submit to this, as I would submit to gout or gray hair, as a concomitant of growing age or else of failing animal heat; but I do not acknowledge that it is necessarily a change for the better – I daresay it is deplorably for the worse. I have no choice in the business, and can no more resist this tendency of my mind than I could prevent my body from beginning to totter and decay. If I am spared (as the phrase runs) I shall doubtless outlive some troublesome desires; but I am in no hurry about that; nor, when the time comes, shall I plume myself on the immunity. Just in the same way, I do not greatly pride myself on having outlived my belief in the fairy tales of Socialism. Old people have faults of their own; they tend to become cowardly, niggardly, and suspicious. Whether from the growth of experience or the decline of animal heat, I see that age leads to these and certain other faults; and it follows, of course, that while in one sense I hope I am journeying towards the truth, in another I am indubitably posting towards these forms and sources of error.

As we go catching and catching at this or that corner of knowledge, now getting a foresight of generous possibilities, now chilled with a glimpse of prudence, we may compare the headlong course of our years to a swift torrent in which a man is carried away; now he is dashed against a boulder, now he grapples for a moment to a trailing spray; at the end, he is hurled out and overwhelmed in a dark and bottomless ocean. We have no more than glimpses and touches; we are torn away from our theories; we are spun round and round and shown this or the other view of life, until only fools or knaves can hold to their opinions. We take a sight at a condition in life, and say we have studied it; our most elaborate view is no more than an impression. If we had breathing space, we should take the occasion to modify and adjust; but at this breakneck hurry, we are no sooner boys than we are adult, no sooner in love than married or jilted, no sooner one age than we begin to be another, and no sooner in the fulness of our manhood than we begin to decline towards the grave. It is in vain to seek for consistency or expect clear and stable views in a medium so perturbed and fleeting. This is no cabinet science, in which things are tested to a scruple; we theorise with a pistol to our head; we are confronted with a new set of conditions on which we have not only to pass a judgement, but to take action, before the hour is at an end. And we cannot even regard ourselves as a constant; in this flux of things, our identity itself seems in a perpetual variation; and not infrequently we find our own disguise the strangest in the masquerade. In the course of time, we grow to love things we hated and hate things we loved. Milton is not so dull as he once was, nor perhaps Ainsworth so amusing. It is decidedly harder to climb trees, and not nearly so hard to sit still. There is no use pretending; even the thrice royal game of hide and seek has somehow lost in zest. All our attributes are modified or changed; and it will be a poor account of us if our views do not modify and change in a proportion. To hold the same views at forty as we held at twenty is to have been stupefied for a score of years, and take rank, not as a prophet, but as an unteachable brat, well birched and none the wiser. It is as if a ship captain should sail to India from the Port of London; and having brought a chart of the Thames on deck at his first setting out, should obstinately use no other for the whole voyage.

And mark you, it would be no less foolish to begin at Gravesend with a chart of the Red Sea. *Si Jeunesse savait, si Vieillesse pouvait*, is a very pretty sentiment, but not necessarily right. In five cases out of ten, it is not so much that the young people do not know, as that they do not choose. There is something irreverent in the speculation, but perhaps the want of power has more to do with the wise resolutions of age than we are always willing to admit. It would be an instructive experiment to make an old man young again and leave him all his *savoir*. I scarcely think he would put his money in the Savings Bank after all; I doubt if he would be such an admirable son as we are led to expect; and as for his conduct in love, I believe firmly he would out-Herod Herod, and put the whole of his new compeers to the blush. Prudence is a wooden Juggernaut, before whom Benjamin Franklin walks with the portly air of a high priest, and after whom dances many a successful merchant in the character of Atys. But it is not a deity to cultivate in youth. If a man lives to any considerable age, it cannot be denied that he laments his imprudences, but I notice he often laments his youth a deal more bitterly and with a more genuine intonation.

It is customary to say that age should be considered, because it comes last. It seems just as much to the point, that youth comes first. And the scale fairly kicks the beam, if you go on to add that age, in a majority of cases, never comes at all. Disease and accident make short work of even the most prosperous persons; death costs nothing, and the expense of a headstone is an inconsiderable trifle to the happy heir. To be suddenly snuffed out in the middle of ambitious schemes, is tragical enough at best; but when a man has been grudging himself his own life in the meanwhile, and saving up everything for the festival that was never to be, it becomes that hysterically moving sort of tragedy which lies on the confines of farce. The victim is dead – and he has cunningly overreached himself: a combination of calamities none the less absurd for being grim. To husband a favourite claret until the batch turns sour, is not at all an artful stroke of policy; and how much more with a whole cellar – a whole bodily existence! People may lay down their lives with cheerfulness in the sure expectation of a blessed immortality; but that is a different affair from giving up youth with all its admirable pleasures, in the hope of a better quality of gruel in a more than problematical, nay, more than improbable, old age. We should not compliment a hungry man, who should refuse a whole dinner and reserve all his appetite for the dessert, before he knew whether there was to be any dessert or not. If there be such a thing as imprudence in the world, we surely have it here. We sail in leaky bottoms and on great and perilous waters; and to take a cue from the dolorous old naval ballad, we have heard the mermaidens singing, and know that we shall never see dry land any more. Old and young, we are all on our last cruise. If there is a fill of tobacco among the crew, for God's sake pass it round, and let us have a pipe before we go!

Indeed, by the report of our elders, this nervous preparation for old age is only trouble thrown away. We fall on guard, and after all it is a friend who comes to meet us. After the sun is down and the west faded, the heavens begin to fill with shining stars. So, as we grow old, a sort of equable jog-trot of feeling is substituted for the violent ups and downs of passion and disgust; the same influence that restrains our hopes, quiets our apprehensions; if the pleasures are less intense, the troubles are milder and more tolerable; and in a word, this period for which we are asked to hoard up everything as for a time of famine, is, in its own right, the richest, easiest, and happiest of life. Nay, by managing its own work and following its own happy inspiration, youth is doing the best it can to endow the leisure of age. A full, busy youth is your only prelude to a self-contained and independent age; and the muff inevitably develops into the bore. There are not many Doctor Johnsons, to set forth upon their first romantic voyage at sixty-four. If we wish to scale Mont Blanc or visit a thieves' kitchen in the East End, to go down in a diving dress or up in a balloon, we must be about it while we are still young. It will not do to delay until we are clogged with prudence and limping with rheumatism, and people begin to ask us: 'What does Gravity out of bed?' Youth is the time to go flashing from one end of the world to the other both in mind and body; to try the manners of different nations; to hear the chimes at midnight; to see sunrise in town and country; to be converted at a revival; to circumnavigate the metaphysics, write halting verses, run a mile to see a fire, and wait all day long in the theatre to applaud *Hernani*. There is some meaning in the old theory about wild oats; and a man who has not had his green-sickness and got done with it for good, is as little to be depended on as an unvaccinated infant. 'It is extraordinary,' says Lord Beaconsfield, one of the brightest and best preserved of youths up to the date of his last novel,[1] 'it is extraordinary how hourly and how violently change the feelings of an inexperienced young man.' And this mobility is a special talent entrusted to his care; a sort of indestructible virginity; a magic armour, with which he can pass unhurt through great dangers and come unbedaubed out of the miriest passages. Let him voyage, speculate, see all that he can, do all that he may; his soul has as many lives as a cat; he will live in all weathers, and never be a halfpenny the worse. Those who go to the devil in youth, with anything like a fair chance, were probably little worth saving from the first; they must have been feeble fellows – creatures made of putty and pack-thread, without steel or fire, anger or true joyfulness, in their composition; we may sympathise with their parents, but there is not much cause to go into mourning for themselves; for to be quite honest, the weak brother is the worst of mankind.

When the old man waggles his head and says, 'Ah, so I thought when I was your age,' he has proved the youth's case. Doubtless, whether from growth of experience or decline of animal heat, he thinks so no longer; but he thought so while he was young; and all men have thought so while they were young, since there was dew in the morning or hawthorn

[1]*Lothair.*

in May; and here is another young man adding his vote to those of previous generations and rivetting another link to the chain of testimony. It is as natural and as right for a young man to be imprudent and exaggerated, to live in swoops and circles, and beat about his cage like any other wild thing newly captured, as it is for old men to turn gray, or mothers to love their offspring, or heroes to die for something worthier than their lives.

By way of an apologue for the aged, when they feel more than usually tempted to offer their advice, let me recommend the following little tale. A child who had been remarkably fond of toys (and in particular of lead soldiers) found himself growing to the level of acknowledged boyhood without any abatement of this childish taste. He was thirteen; already he had been taunted for dallying overlong about the playbox; he had to blush if he was found among his lead soldiers; the shades of the prison-house were closing about him with a vengeance. There is nothing more difficult than to put the thoughts of children into the language of their elders; but this is the effect of his meditations at this juncture: 'Plainly,' he said, 'I must give up my playthings, in the meanwhile, since I am not in a position to secure myself against idle jeers. At the same time, I am sure that playthings are the very pick of life; all people give them up out of the same pusillanimous respect for those who are a little older; and if they do not return to them as soon as they can, it is only because they grow stupid and forget. I shall be wiser; I shall conform for a little to the ways of their foolish world; but so soon as I have made enough money, I shall retire and shut myself up among my playthings until the day I die.' Nay, as he was passing in the train along the Esterel mountains between Cannes and Fréjus, he remarked a pretty house in an orange garden at the angle of a bay, and decided that this should be his Happy Valley. *Astrea Redux*; childhood was to come again! The idea has an air of simple nobility to me, not unworthy of Cincinnatus. And yet, as the reader has probably anticipated, it is never likely to be carried into effect. There was a worm i' the bud, a fatal error in the premises. Childhood must pass away, and then youth, as surely as age approaches. The true wisdom is to be always seasonable, and to change with a good grace in changing circumstances. To love playthings well as a child, to lead an adventurous and honourable youth, and to settle when the time arrives, into a green and smiling age, is to be a good artist in life and deserve well of yourself and your neighbour.

You need repent none of your youthful vagaries. They may have been over the score on one side, just as those of age are probably over the score on the other. But they had a point; they not only befitted your age and expressed its attitude and passions, but they had a relation to what was outside of you, and implied criticisms on the existing state of things, which you need not allow to have been undeserved, because you now see that they were partial. All error, not merely verbal, is a strong way of stating that the current truth is incomplete. The follies of youth have a basis in sound reason, just as much as the embarrassing questions put by babes and sucklings. Their most antisocial acts indicate the defects of our society. When the torrent sweeps the man against a boulder, you must expect him to scream, and you need not be surprised if the scream is sometimes a theory. Shelley, chafing at the Church of England, discovered the cure of all evils in universal atheism. Generous lads irritated at the injustices of society, see nothing for it but the abolishment of everything and Kingdom Come of anarchy. Shelley was a young fool; so are these cocksparrow revolutionaries. But it is better to be a fool than to be dead. It is better to emit a scream in the shape of a theory than to be entirely insensible to the jars and incongruities of life and take everything as it comes in a forlorn stupidity. Some people swallow the universe like a pill; they travel on through the world, like smiling images pushed from behind. For God's sake give me the young man who has brains enough to make a fool of himself! As for the others, the irony of facts shall take it out of their hands, and make fools of them in downright earnest, ere the farce be over. There shall be such a mopping and a mowing at the last day, and such blushing and confusion of countenance for all those who have been wise in their own esteem, and have not learnt the rough lessons that youth hands on to age. If we are indeed here to perfect and complete our own natures, and grow larger, stronger, and more sympathetic against some nobler career in the future, we had all best bestir ourselves to the utmost while we have the time. To equip a dull, respectable person with wings would be but to make a parody of an angel.

In short, if youth is not quite right in its opinions, there is a strong probability that age is not much more so. Undying hope is co-ruler of the human bosom with infallible credulity. A man finds he has been wrong at every preceding stage of his career, only to deduce the astonishing conclusion that he is at last entirely right. Mankind, after centuries of failure, are still upon the eve of a thoroughly constitutional millennium. Since we have explored the maze so long without result, it follows, for poor human reason, that we cannot have to explore much longer; close by must be the centre, with a champagne luncheon and a piece of ornamental water. How if there were no centre at all, but just one alley after another, and the whole world a labyrinth without end or issue?

I overheard the other day a scrap of conversation, which I take the liberty to reproduce. 'What I advance is true,' said one. 'But not the whole truth,' answered the other. 'Sir,' returned the first (and it seemed to me there was a smack of Dr Johnson in the speech), 'Sir, there is no such thing as the whole truth!' Indeed, there is nothing so evident in life as that there are two sides to a question. History is one long illustration. The forces of nature are engaged, day by day, in cudgelling it into our backward intelligences. We never pause for a moment's consideration, but we admit it as an axiom. An enthusiast sways humanity exactly by disregarding this great truth, and dinning it into our ears that this or that question has only one possible solution; and your enthusiast is a fine florid fellow, dominates things for a while and shakes the world out of a doze; but when once he is gone, an army of quiet and uninfluential people set to work to remind us of the other side and demolish the generous imposture. While Calvin is putting everybody exactly right in his *Institutes*, and hot-headed Knox is thundering in the pulpit, Montaigne is already looking at the other side in his library in Perigord, and predicting that they will find as much to quarrel about in the Bible as they had found already in the Church. Age may have one side, but assuredly Youth has the other. There is nothing more certain than that both are right, except perhaps that both are wrong. Let them agree to differ; for who knows but what agreeing to differ may not be a form of agreement rather than a form of difference?

I suppose it is written that anyone who sets up for a bit of a philosopher, must contradict himself to his very face. For here have I fairly talked myself into thinking that we have the whole thing before us at last; that there is no answer to the mystery, except that there are as many as you please; that there is no centre to the maze because, like the famous sphere, its centre is everywhere; and that agreeing to differ with every ceremony of politeness, is the only 'one undisturbed song of pure concent' to which we are ever likely to lend our musical voices.

WALT WHITMAN

Of late years the name of Walt Whitman has been a good deal bandied about in books and magazines. It has become familiar both in good and ill repute. His works have been largely bespattered with praise by his admirers, and cruelly mauled and mangled by irreverent enemies. Now, whether his poetry is good or bad as poetry, is a matter that may admit of a difference of opinion without alienating those who differ. We could not keep the peace with a man who should put forward claims to taste and yet depreciate the choruses in *Samson Agonistes*; but, I think, we may shake hands with one who sees no more in Walt Whitman's volume, from a literary point of view, than a farrago of incompetent essays in a wrong direction. That may not be at all our own opinion. We may think that, when a work contains many unforgettable phrases, it cannot be altogether devoid of literary merit. We may even see passages of a high poetry here and there among its eccentric contents. But when all is said, Walt Whitman is neither a Milton nor a Shakespeare; to appreciate his works is not a condition necessary to salvation; and I would not disinherit a son upon the question, nor even think much the worse of a critic, for I should always have an idea what he meant.

What Whitman has to say is another affair from how he says it. It is not possible to acquit anyone of defective intelligence, or else stiff prejudice, who is not interested by Whitman's matter and the spirit it represents. Not as a poet, but as what we must call (for lack of a more exact expression) a prophet, he occupies a curious and prominent position. Whether he may greatly influence the future or not, he is a notable symptom of the present. As a sign of the times, it would be hard to find his parallel. I should hazard a large wager, for instance, that he was not unacquainted with the works of Herbert Spencer; and yet where, in all the history books, shall we lay our hands on two more incongruous contemporaries? Mr Spencer so decorous – I had almost said, so dandy – in dissent; and Whitman, like a large shaggy dog, just unchained, scouring the beaches of the world and baying at the moon. And when was an echo more curiously like a satire, than when Mr

Spencer found his Synthetic Philosophy reverberated from the other shores of the Atlantic in the 'barbaric yawp' of Whitman?

I

Whitman, it cannot be too soon explained, writes up to a system. He was a theoriser about society before he was a poet. He first perceived something wanting, and then sat down squarely to supply the want. The reader, running over his works, will find that he takes nearly as much pleasure in critically expounding his theory of poetry as in making poems. This is as far as it can be from the case of the spontaneous village minstrel dear to elegy, who has no theory whatever, although sometimes he may have fully as much poetry as Whitman. The whole of Whitman's work is deliberate and preconceived. A man born into a society comparatively new, full of conflicting elements and interests, could not fail, if he had any thoughts at all, to reflect upon the tendencies around him. He saw much good and evil on all sides, not yet settled down into some more or less unjust compromise as in older nations, but still in the act of settlement. And he could not but wonder what it would turn out; whether the compromise would be very just or very much the reverse, and give great or little scope for healthy human energies. From idle wonder to active speculation is but a step; and he seems to have been early struck with the inefficacy of literature and its extreme unsuitability to the conditions. What he calls 'Feudal Literature' could have little living action on the tumult of American democracy; what he calls the 'Literature of Woe,' meaning the whole tribe of Werther and Byron, could have no action for good in any time or place. Both propositions, if art had none but a direct moral influence, would be true enough; and as this seems to be Whitman's view, they were true enough for him. He conceived the idea of a Literature which was to inhere in the life of the present; which was to be, first, human, and next, American; which was to be brave and cheerful as per contract; to give culture in a popular and poetical presentment; and, in so doing, catch and stereotype some democratic ideal of humanity which should be equally natural to all grades of wealth and education, and suited, in one of his favourite phrases, to 'the average man.' To the formation of some such literature as this his poems are to be regarded as so many contributions, one sometimes explaining, sometimes superseding, the other: and the whole together not so much a finished work as a body of suggestive hints. He does not profess to have built the castle, but he pretends he has traced the lines of the foundation. He has not made the poetry, but he flatters himself he has done something towards making the poets.

His notion of the poetic function is ambitious, and coincides roughly with what Schopenhauer has laid down as the province of the metaphysician. The poet is to gather together for men, and set in order, the materials of their existence. He is 'The Answerer;' he is to find some way of speaking about life that shall satisfy, if only for the moment, man's enduring astonishment at his own position. And besides having an answer ready, it is he who shall provoke the question. He must shake people out of their indifference, and force them to make some election in this world, instead of sliding dully forward in a dream. Life is a business we are all apt to mismanage; either living recklessly from day to day, or suffering ourselves to be gulled out of our moments by the inanities of custom. We should despise a man who gave as little activity and forethought to the conduct of any other business. But in this, which is the one thing of all others, since it contains them all, we cannot see the forest for the trees. One brief impression obliterates another. There is something stupefying in the recurrence of unimportant things. And it is only on rare provocations that we can rise to take an outlook beyond daily concerns, and comprehend the narrow limits and great possibilities of our existence. It is the duty of the poet to induce such moments of clear sight. He is the declared enemy of all living by reflex action, of all that is done betwixt sleep and waking, of all the pleasureless pleasurings and imaginary duties in which we coin away our hearts and fritter invaluable years. He has to electrify his readers into an instant unflagging activity, founded on a wide and eager observation of the world, and make them direct their ways by a superior prudence, which has little or nothing in common with the maxims of the copy-book. That many of us lead such lives as they would heartily disown after two hours' serious reflection on the subject is, I am afraid, a true, and, I am sure, a very galling thought. The Enchanted Ground of dead-alive respectability is next, upon the map, to the Beulah of considerate virtue. But there they all slumber and take their rest in the middle of God's beautiful and wonderful universe; the drowsy heads have nodded together in the same position since first their fathers fell asleep; and not even the sound of the last trumpet can wake them to a single active thought. The poet has a hard task before him to stir up such fellows to a sense of their own and other people's principles in life.

And it happens that literature is, in some ways, but an indifferent means to such an end. Language is but a poor bull's-eye lantern wherewith to show off the vast cathedral of the world; and yet a particular thing once said in words is so definite and memorable, that it makes us forget the absence of the many which remain unexpressed; like a bright window in a distant view, which dazzles and confuses our sight of its surroundings. There are not words enough in all Shakespeare to express the merest fraction of a man's experience in an hour. The speed of the eyesight and the hearing, and the continual industry of the mind, produce, in ten minutes, what it would require a laborious volume to shadow forth by comparisons and roundabout approaches. If verbal logic were sufficient, life would be as plain sailing as a piece of Euclid. But, as a matter of fact, we make a travesty of the simplest process of thought when we put it into words; for the words are all coloured and forsworn, apply inaccurately, and bring with them, from former uses, ideas of praise and blame that have nothing to do with the question in hand. So we must always see to it nearly, that we judge by the realities of life and not by the partial terms that represent them in man's speech; and at times of choice, we must leave words upon one side, and act upon those brute convictions, unexpressed and perhaps inexpressible, which cannot be flourished in an argument, but which are truly the sum and fruit of our experience. Words are for communication, not for judgement. This is what every thoughtful man knows for himself, for only fools and silly schoolmasters push definitions over far into the domain of conduct; and the majority of women, not learned in these scholastic refinements, live all-of-a-piece and unconsciously, as a tree grows, without caring to put a name upon their acts or motives. Hence, a new difficulty for Whitman's scrupulous and argumentative poet; he must do more than waken up the sleepers to his words; he must persuade them to look over the book and at life with their own eyes.

This side of truth is very present to Whitman; it is this that he means when he tells us that 'To glance with an eye confounds the learning of all times.' But he is not unready. He is never weary of descanting on the undebatable conviction that is forced upon our minds by the presence of other men, of animals, or of inanimate things. To glance with an eye, were it only at a chair or a park railing, is by far a more persuasive process, and brings us to a far more exact conclusion, than to read the works of all the logicians extant. If both, by a large allowance, may be said to end in certainty, the certainty in the one case transcends the other to an incalculable degree. If people see a lion, they run away; if they only apprehend a deduction, they keep wandering around in an experimental humour. Now, how is the poet to convince like nature, and not like books? Is there no actual piece of nature that he can show the man to his face, as he might show him a tree if they were walking together? Yes, there is one: the man's own thoughts. In fact, if the poet is to speak efficaciously, he must say what is already in his hearer's mind. That, alone, the hearer will believe; that, alone, he will be able to apply intelligently to the facts of life. Any conviction, even if it be a whole system or a whole religion, must pass into the condition of common-place, or postulate, before it becomes fully operative. Strange excursions and high-flying theories may interest, but they cannot rule behaviour. Our faith is not the highest truth that we perceive, but the highest that we have been able to assimilate into the very texture and method of our thinking. It is not, therefore, by flashing before a man's eyes the weapons of dialectic; it is not by induction, deduction, or construction; it is not by forcing him on from one stage of reasoning to another, that the man will be effectually renewed. He cannot be made to believe anything; but he can be made to see that he has always believed it. And this is the practical canon. It is when the reader cries, 'Oh, I know!' and is, perhaps, half irritated to see how nearly the author has forestalled his own thoughts, that he is on the way to what is called in theology a Saving Faith.

Here we have the key to Whitman's attitude. To give a certain unity of ideal to the average population of America – to gather their activities about some conception of humanity that shall be central and normal, if only for the moment – the poet must portray that population as it is. Like human law, human poetry is simply declaratory. If any ideal is possible, it must be already in the thoughts of the people; and, by the same reason, in the thoughts of the poet, who is one of them. And hence Whitman's own formula: 'The poet is individual – he is complete in himself: the others are as good as he; only he sees it, and they do not.' To show them how good they are, the poet must study his fellow-countrymen and himself somewhat like a traveller on the hunt for his book of travels. There is a sense, of course, in which all true books are books of travel; and all genuine poets must run their risk of being charged with the traveller's exaggeration; for to whom are such books more surprising than to those whose own life is faithfully and smartly pictured? But this danger is all upon one side; and you may judiciously flatter the portrait without any likelihood of the sitter's disowning it for a faithful likeness. And so Whitman has reasoned: that by drawing at first hand from himself and his neighbours, accepting without shame the inconsistencies and brutalities that go to make up man, and yet treating the whole in a high, magnanimous spirit, we would make sure of belief, and at the same time encourage people forward by the means of praise.

II

We are accustomed nowadays to a great deal of puling over the circumstances in which we are placed. The great refinement of many poetical gentlemen has rendered them practically unfit for the jostling and ugliness of life, and they record their unfitness at considerable length. The bold and awful poetry of Job's complaint produces too many flimsy imitators; for there is always something consolatory in grandeur, but the symphony transposed for the piano becomes hysterically sad. This literature of woe, as Whitman calls it, this *Maladie de René*, as we like to call it in Europe, is in many ways a most humiliating and sickly phenomenon. Young gentlemen with three or four hundred a year of private means look down from a pinnacle of doleful experience on all the grown and hearty men who have dared to say a good word for life since the beginning of the world. There is no prophet but the melancholy Jacques, and the blue devils dance on all our literary wires.

It would be a poor service to spread culture, if this be its result, among the comparatively innocent and cheerful ranks of men. When our little poets have to be sent to look at the ploughman and learn wisdom, we must be careful how we tamper with our ploughmen. Where a man in not the best of circumstances preserves composure of mind, and relishes ale and tobacco, and his wife and children, in the intervals of dull and unremunerative labour; where a man in this predicament can afford a lesson by the way to what are called his intellectual superiors, there is plainly something to be lost, as well as something to be gained, by teaching him to think differently. It is better to leave him as he is than to teach him whining. It is better that he should go without the cheerful lights of culture, if cheerless doubt and paralysing sentimentalism are to be the consequence. Let us, by all means, fight against that hide-bound stolidity of sensation and sluggishness of mind which blurs and decolorises for poor natures the wonderful pageant of consciousness; let us teach people, as much as we can, to enjoy, and they will learn for themselves to sympathise; but let us see to it, above all, that we give these lessons in a brave, vivacious note, and build the man up in courage while we demolish its substitute, indifference.

Whitman is alive to all this. He sees that, if the poet is to be of any help, he must testify to the livableness of life. His poems, he tells us, are to be 'hymns of the praise of things.' They are to make for a certain high joy in living, or what he calls himself 'a brave delight fit for freedom's athletes.' And he has had no difficulty in introducing his optimism: it fitted readily enough with his system; for the average man is truly a courageous person and truly fond of living. One of Whitman's remarks upon this head is worth quotation, as he is there perfectly successful, and does precisely what he designs to do throughout: Takes ordinary and even commonplace circumstances; throws them out, by a happy turn of thinking, into significance and something like beauty; and tacks a hopeful moral lesson to the end.

'The passionate tenacity of hunters, woodmen, early risers, cultivators of gardens and orchards and fields,' he says, 'the love of healthy women for the manly form, seafaring persons, drivers of horses, the passion for light and the open air, – all is an old unvaried sign of the unfailing perception of beauty, and of a residence of the poetic in outdoor people.'

There seems to me something truly original in this choice of trite examples. You will remark how adroitly Whitman begins, hunters and woodmen being confessedly romantic. And one thing more. If he had said 'the love of healthy men for the female form,' he would have said almost a silliness; for the thing has never been dissembled out of delicacy, and is so obvious as to be a public nuisance. But by reversing it, he tells us something not unlike news; something that sounds quite freshly in words; and, if the reader be a man, gives him a moment of great self-satisfaction and spiritual aggrandisement. In many different authors you may find passages more remarkable for grammar, but few of a more ingenious turn, and none that could be more to the point in our connection. The tenacity of many ordinary people in ordinary pursuits is a sort of standing challenge to everybody else. If one man can grow absorbed in delving his garden, others may grow absorbed and happy over something else. Not to be upsides in this with any groom or gardener, is to be very meanly organised. A man should be ashamed to take his food if he has not alchemy enough in his stomach to turn some of it into intense and enjoyable occupation.

Whitman tries to reinforce this cheerfulness by keeping up a sort of outdoor atmosphere of sentiment. His book, he tells us, should be read 'among the cooling influences of external nature;' and this recommendation, like that other famous one which Hawthorne prefixed to his collected tales, is in itself a character of the work. Everyone who has been upon a walking or a boating tour, living in the open air, with the body in constant exercise and the mind in fallow, knows true ease and quiet. The irritating action of the brain is set at rest; we think in a plain, unfeverish temper; little things seem big enough, and great things no longer portentous; and the world is smilingly accepted as it is. This is the spirit that Whitman inculcates and parades. He thinks very ill of the atmosphere of parlours or libraries. Wisdom keeps school outdoors. And he has the art to recommend this attitude of mind by simply pluming himself upon it as a virtue; so that the reader, to keep the advantage over his author which most readers enjoy, is tricked into professing the same view. And this spirit, as it is his chief lesson, is the greatest charm of his work. Thence, in spite of an uneven and emphatic key of expression, something trenchant and straightforward, something simple and surprising, distinguishes his poems. He has sayings that come home to one like the Bible. We fall upon Whitman, after the works of so many men who write better, with a sense of relief from strain, with a sense of touching nature, as when one passes out of the flaring, noisy thoroughfares of a great city into what he himself has called, with unexcelled imaginative justice of language, 'the huge and thoughtful night.' And his book in consequence, whatever may be the final judgement of its merit, whatever may be its influence on the future, should be in the hands of all parents and guardians as a specific for the distressing malady of being seventeen years old. Green-sickness yields to his treatment as to a charm of magic; and the youth, after a short course of reading, ceases to carry the universe upon his shoulders.

III

Whitman is not one of those who can be deceived by familiarity. He considers it just as wonderful that there are myriads of stars, as that one man should rise from the dead. He declares 'a hair on the back of his hand just as curious as any special revelation.' His whole life is to him what it was to Sir Thomas Browne, one perpetual miracle. Everything is strange, everything unaccountable, everything beautiful; from a bug to the moon, from the sight of the eyes to the appetite for food. He makes it his business to see things as if he saw them for the first time, and professes astonishment on principle. But he has no leaning towards mythology; avows his contempt for what he calls 'unregenerate poetry;' and does not mean by nature

The smooth walks, trimmed hedges, butterflies, posies, and nightingales of the Enigsh poets, but the whole orb, with its geologic history, the Kosmos, carrying fire and snow, that rolls through the illimitable areas, light as a feather though weighing billions of tons.

Nor is this exhaustive; for in his character of idealist all impressions, all thoughts, trees and people, love and faith, astronomy, history, and religion, enter upon equal terms into his notion of the universe. He is not against religion; not, indeed, against any religion. He wishes to drag with a larger net, to make a more comprehensive synthesis, than any or than all of them put together. In feeling after the central type of man, he must embrace all eccentricities; his cosmology must subsume all cosmologies, and the feelings that gave birth to them; his statement of facts must include all religion and all irreligion, Christ and Boodha, God and the devil. The world as it is, and the whole world as it is, physical, and spiritual, and historical, with its good and bad, with its manifold inconsistencies, is what he wishes to set forth, in strong, picturesque, and popular lineaments, for the understanding of the average man. One of his favourite endeavours is to get the whole matter into a nutshell; to knock the four corners of the universe, one after another, about his reader's ears; to hurry him, in breathless phrases, hither and thither, back and forward, in time and space; to focus all this about his own momentary personality; and then, drawing the ground from under his feet, as if by some cataclysm of nature, to plunge him into the unfathomable abyss sown with enormous suns and systems, and among the inconceivable numbers and magnitudes and velocities of the heavenly bodies. So that he concludes by striking into us some sense of that disproportion of things which Shelley has illuminated by the ironical flash of these eight words: The desire of the moth for the star.

The same truth, but to what a different purpose! Whitman's moth is mightily at his ease about all the planets in heaven, and cannot think too highly of our sublunary tapers. The universe is so large that imagination flags in the effort to conceive it; but here, in the meantime, is the world under our feet, a very warm and habitable corner. 'The earth, that is sufficient; I do not want the constellations any nearer,' he remarks. And again: 'Let your soul stand cool and composed,' says he, 'before a million universes.' It is the language of a transcendental common sense, such as Thoreau held and sometimes uttered. But Whitman, who has a somewhat vulgar inclination for technical talk and the jargon of philosophy, is not content with a few pregnant hints; he must put the dots upon his i's; he must corroborate the songs of Apollo by some of the darkest talk of human metaphysic. He tells his disciples that they must be ready 'to confront the growing arrogance of Realism.' Each person is, for himself, the keystone and the occasion of this universal edifice. 'Nothing, not God,' he says, 'is greater to one than oneself is;' a statement with an irreligious smack at the first sight; but like most startling sayings, a manifest truism on a second. He will give effect to his own character without apology; he sees 'that the elementary laws never apologise.' 'I reckon,' he adds, with quaint colloquial arrogance, 'I reckon I behave no prouder than the level I plant my house by, after all.' The level follows the law of its being; so, unrelentingly, will he; everything, every person, is good in his own place and way; God is the maker of all, and all are in one design. For he believes in God, and that with a sort of blasphemous security. 'No array of terms,' quoth he, 'no array of terms can say how much at peace I am about God and about death.' There certainly never was a prophet who carried things with a higher hand; he gives us less a body of dogmas than a series of proclamations by the grace of God; and language, you will observe, positively fails him to express how far he stands above the highest human doubts and trepidations.

But next in order of truths to a person's sublime conviction of himself, comes the attraction of one person for another, and all that we mean by the word love:

The dear love of man for his comrade – the attraction of friend for friend,
Of the well-married husband and wife, of children and parents,
Of city for city and land for land.

The solitude of the most sublime idealist is broken in upon by other people's faces; he sees a look in their eyes that corresponds to something in his own heart; there comes a tone in their voices which convicts him of a startling weakness for his fellow-creatures. While he is hymning the *ego* and commercing with God and the universe, a woman goes below his window; and at the turn of her skirt or the colour of her eyes, Icarus is recalled from heaven by the run. Love is so startlingly real that it takes rank upon an equal footing of reality with the consciousness of personal existence. We are as heartily persuaded of the identity of those we love as of our own identity. And so sympathy pairs with self-assertion, the two gerents of human life on earth; and Whitman's ideal man must not only be strong, free, and self-reliant in himself, but his freedom must be bounded and his strength perfected by the most intimate, eager, and long-suffering love for others. To some extent this is taking away with the left hand what has been so generously given with the right. Morality has been ceremoniously extruded from the door only to be brought in again by the window. We are told, on one page, to do as we please; and on the next we are sharply upbraided for not having done as the author pleases. We are first assured that we are the finest fellows in the world in our own right; and then it appears that we are only fine fellows in so far as we practise a most quixotic code of morals. The disciple who saw himself in clear ether a moment before is plunged down again among the fogs and complications of duty. And this is all the more overwhelming because Whitman insists not only on love between sex and sex, and between friends of the same sex, but in the field of the less intense political sympathies; and his ideal man must not only be a generous friend but a conscientious voter into the bargain.

His method somewhat lessens the difficulty. He is not, the reader will remember, to tell us how good we ought to be, but to remind us how good we are. He is to encourage us to be free and kind, by proving that we are free and kind already. He passes our corporate life under review, to show that it is upheld by the very virtues of which he makes himself the advocate. 'There is no object so soft,' he says somewhere in his big, plain way, 'there is no object so soft but it makes a hub for the wheel'd universe.' Rightly understood, it is on the softest of all objects, the sympathetic heart, that the wheel of society turns easily and securely as on a perfect axle. There is no room, of course, for doubt or discussion, about conduct, where everyone is to follow the law of his being with exact compliance. Whitman hates doubt, deprecates discussion, and discourages to his utmost the craving, carping sensibilities of the conscience. We are to imitate, to use one of his absurd and happy phrases, 'the satisfaction and aplomb of animals.' If he preaches a sort of ranting Christianity in morals, a fit consequent to the ranting optimism of his cosmology, it is because he declares it to be the original deliverance of the human heart; or at least, for he would be honestly historical in

[79]

method, of the human heart as at present Christianised. His is a morality without a prohibition; his policy is one of encouragement all round. A man must be a born hero to come up to Whitman's standard in the practice of any of the positive virtues; but of a negative virtue, such as temperance or chastity, he has so little to say, that the reader need not be surprised if he drops a word or two upon the other side. He would lay down nothing that would be a clog; he would prescribe nothing that cannot be done ruddily, in a heat. The great point is to get people under way. To the faithful Whitmanite this would be justified by the belief that God made all, and that all was good; the prophet, in this doctrine, has only to cry 'Tally-ho,' and mankind will break into a gallop on the road to El Dorado. Perhaps, to another class of minds, it may look like the result of the somewhat cynical reflection that you will not make a kind man out of one who is unkind by any precepts under heaven; tempered by the belief that, in natural circumstances, the large majority is well disposed. Thence it would follow, that if you can only get everyone to feel more warmly and act more courageously, the balance of results will be for good.

So far, you see, the doctrine is pretty coherent as a doctrine; as a picture of man's life it is incomplete and misleading, although eminently cheerful. This he is himself the first to acknowledge; for if he is prophetic in anything, it is in his noble disregard of consistency. 'Do I contradict myself?' he asks somewhere; and then pat comes the answer, the best answer ever given in print, worthy of a sage, or rather of a woman: 'Very well, then, I contradict myself!' with this addition, not so feminine and perhaps not altogether so satisfactory: 'I am large – I contain multitudes.' Life, as a matter of fact, partakes largely of the nature of tragedy. The gospel according to Whitman, even if it be not so logical, has this advantage over the gospel according to Pangloss, that it does not utterly disregard the existence of temporal evil. Whitman accepts the fact of disease and wretchedness like an honest man; and instead of trying to qualify it in the interest of his optimism, sets himself to spur people up to be helpful. He expresses a conviction, indeed, that all will be made up to the victims in the end; that 'what is untried and afterward' will fail no one, not even 'the old man who has lived without purpose and feels it with bitterness worse than gall.' But this is not to palliate our sense of what is hard or melancholy in the present. Pangloss, smarting under one of the worst things that ever was supposed to come from America, consoled himself with the reflection that it was the price we have to pay for cochineal. And with that murderous parody, logical optimism and the praises of the best of possible worlds went irrevocably out of season, and have been no more heard of in the mouths of reasonable men. Whitman spares us all allusions to the cochineal; he treats evil and sorrow in a spirit almost as of welcome; as an old sea-dog might have welcomed the sight of the enemy's topsails off the Spanish Main. There, at least, he seems to say, is something obvious to be done. I do not know many better things in literature than the brief pictures – brief and vivid like things seen by lightning – with which he tries to stir up the world's heart upon the side of mercy. He braces us, on the one hand, with examples of heroic duty and helpfulness; on the other, he touches us with pitiful instances of people needing help. He knows how to make the heart beat at a brave story; to inflame us with just resentment over the hunted slave; to stop our mouths for shame when he tells of the drunken prostitute. For all the afflicted, all the weak, all the wicked, a good word is said in a spirit which I can only call one of ultra-Christianity; and however wild, however contradictory, it may be in parts, this at least may be said for his book, as it may be said of the Christian Gospels, that no one will read it, however respectable, but he gets a knock upon his conscience; no one however fallen, but he finds a kindly and supporting welcome.

IV

Nor has he been content with merely blowing the trumpet for the battle of well-doing; he has given to his precepts the authority of his own brave example. Naturally a grave, believing man, with little or no sense of humour, he has succeeded as well in life as in his printed performances. The spirit that was in him has come forth most eloquently in his actions. Many who have only read his poetry have been tempted to set him down as an ass, or even as a charlatan; but I never met anyone who had known him personally who did not profess a solid affection and respect for the man's character. He practises as he professes; he feels deeply that Christian love for all men, that toleration, that cheerful delight in serving others, which he often celebrates in literature with a doubtful measure of success. And perhaps, out of all his writings, the best and the most human and convincing passages are to be found in 'these soil'd and creas'd little livraisons, each composed of a sheet or two of paper, folded small to carry in the pocket, and fastened with a pin,' which he scribbled during the war by the bedsides of the wounded or in the excitement of great events. They are hardly literature in the formal meaning of the word; he has left his jottings for the most part as he made them; a homely detail, a word from the lips of a dying soldier, a business memorandum, the copy of a letter – short, straightforward to the point, with none of the trappings of composition; but they breathe a profound sentiment, they give us a vivid look at one of the sides of life, and they make us acquainted with a man whom it is an honour to love.

Whitman's intense Americanism, his unlimited belief in the future of These States (as, with reverential capitals, he loves to call them), made the war a period of great trial to his soul. The new virtue, Unionism, of which he is the sole inventor, seemed to have fallen into premature unpopularity. All that he loved, hoped, or hated, hung in the balance. And the game of war was not only momentous to him in its issues; it sublimated his spirit by its heroic displays, and tortured him intimately by the spectacle of its horrors. It was a theatre, it was a place of education, it was like a season of religious revival. He watched Lincoln going daily to his work; he studied and fraternised with young soldiery passing to the front; above all, he walked the hospitals, reading the Bible, distributing clean clothes, or apples, or tobacco; a patient, helpful, reverend man, full of kind speeches.

His memoranda of this period are almost bewildering to read. From one point of view they seem those of a district visitor; from another, they look like the formless jottings of an artist in the picturesque. More than one woman, on whom I tried the experiment, immediately claimed the writer for a fellow-woman. More than one literary purist might identify him as a shoddy newspaper correspondent without the necessary faculty of style. And yet the story touches home; and if you are of the weeping order of mankind, you will certainly find your eyes fill with tears, of which you have no reason to be ashamed. There is only one way to characterise a work of this order, and that is to quote. Here is a passage from a letter to a mother, unknown to Whitman, whose son died in hospital:

Frank, as far as I saw, had everything requisite in surgical treatment, nursing, etc. He had watches much of the time. He was so good and well-behaved, and affectionate, I myself liked him very much. I was in the habit of coming in afternoons and sitting by him, and he liked to have me – liked to put out his arm and lay his hand on my knee – would keep it so a long while. Toward the last he was more restless and flighty at night – often fancied himself with his regiment – by his talk sometimes seem'd as if his feelings were hurt by being blamed by his officers for something he was entirely innocent of – said 'I never in my life was thought capable of such a thing, and never was.' At other times he would fancy himself talking as it seem'd to children or such like, his relatives, I suppose, and giving them good advice; would talk to them a long while. All the time he was out of his head not one single bad word, or thought, or idea escaped him. It was remark'd that many a man's conversation in his senses was not half so good as Frank's delirium.

He was perfectly willing to die – he had become very weak, and had suffer'd a good deal, and was perfectly resign'd, poor boy. I do not know his past life, but I feel as if it must have been good. At any rate what I saw of him here, under the most trying circumstances, with a painful wound, and among strangers, I can say that he behaved so brave, so composed, and so sweet and affectionate, it could not be surpassed. And now, like many other noble and good men, after serving his country as a soldier, he has yielded up his young life at the very outset in her service. Such things are gloomy – yet there is a text, 'God doeth all things well,' the meaning of which, after due time, appears to the soul.

I thought perhaps a few words, though from a stranger, about your son, from one who was with him at the last, might be worth while, for I loved the young man, though I but saw him immediately to lose him.

It is easy enough to pick holes in the grammar of this letter, but what are we to say of its profound goodness and tenderness? It is written as though he had the mother's face before his eyes, and saw her wincing in the flesh at every word. And what, again, are we to say of its sober truthfulness, not exaggerating, not running to phrases, not seeking to make a hero out of what was only an ordinary but good and brave young man? Literary reticence is not Whitman's stronghold; and this reticence is not literary, but humane; it is not that of a good artist but that of a good man. He knew that what the mother wished to hear about was Frank; and he told her about her Frank as he was.

V

Something should be said of Whitman's style, for style is of the essence of thinking. And where a man is so critically deliberate as our author, and goes solemnly about his poetry for an ulterior end, every indication is worth notice. He has chosen a rough, unrhymed, lyrical verse; sometimes instinct with a fine processional movement; often so rugged and careless that it can only be described by saying that he has not taken the trouble to write prose. I believe myself that it was selected principally because it was easy to write, although not without recollections of the marching measures of some of the prose in our English Old Testament.

According to Whitman, on the other hand, 'the time has arrived to essentially break down the barriers of form between Prose and Poetry . . . for the most cogent purposes of those great inland states, and for Texas, and California, and Oregon;' – a statement which is among the happiest achievements of American humour. He calls his verses 'recitatives,' in easily followed allusion to a musical form. 'Easily-written, loose-fingered chords,' he cries, 'I feel the thrum of your climax and close.' Too often, I fear, he is the only one who can perceive the rhythm; and in spite of Mr Swinburne, a great part of his work considered as verses is poor bald stuff. Considered, not as verse, but as speech, a great part of it is full of strange and admirable merits. The right detail is seized; the right word, bold and trenchant, is thrust into its place. Whitman has small regard to literary decencies, and is totally free from literary timidities. He is neither afraid of being slangy nor of being dull; nor, let me add, of being ridiculous. The result is a most surprising compound of plain grandeur, sentimental affectation, and downright nonsense. It would be useless to follow his detractors and give instances of how bad he can be at his worst; and perhaps it would be not much wiser to give extracted specimens of how happily he can write when he is at his best. These come in to most advantage in their own place; owing something, it may be, to the offset of their curious surroundings. And one thing is certain, that no one can appreciate Whitman's excellences until he has grown accustomed to his faults. Until you are content to pick poetry out of his pages almost as you must pick it out of a Greek play in Bohn's translation, your gravity will be continually upset, your ears perpetually disappointed, and the whole book will be no more to you than a particularly flagrant production by the Poet Close.

A writer of this uncertain quality was, perhaps, unfortunate in taking for thesis the beauty of the world as it now is, not only on the hill-tops but in the factory; not only by the harbour full of stately ships, but in the magazine of the hopelessly prosaic hatter. To show beauty in common things is the work of the rarest tact. It is not to be done by the wishing. It is easy to posit as a theory, but to bring it home to men's minds is the problem of literature, and is only accomplished by rare talent, and in comparatively rare instances. To bid the whole world stand and deliver, with a dogma in one's right hand by way of pistol; to cover reams of paper in a galloping, headstrong vein; to cry louder and louder over everything as it comes up, and make no distinction in one's enthusiasm over the most incomparable matters; to prove one's entire want of sympathy for the jaded, literary palate, by calling, not a spade a spade, but a hatter a hatter, in a lyrical apostrophe; – this, in spite of all the airs of inspiration, is not the way to do it. It may be very wrong, and very wounding to a respectable branch of industry, but the word 'hatter' cannot be used seriously in emotional verse; not to understand this, is to have no literary tact; and I would, for his own sake, that this were the only inadmissible expression with which Whitman had bedecked his pages. The book teems with similar comicalities; and, to a reader who is determined to take it from that side only, presents a perfect carnival of fun.

A good deal of this is the result of theory playing its usual vile trick upon the artist. It is because he is a Democrat that Whitman must have in the hatter. If you may say Admiral, he reasons, why may you not say Hatter? One man is as good as another, and it is the business of the 'great poet' to show poetry in the life of the one as well as the other. A most incontrovertible sentiment surely, and one which nobody would think of controverting, where – and here is the point – where any beauty has been shown. But how, where that is not the case? where the hatter is simply introduced, as God made him and as his fellow-men have miscalled him, at the crisis of a high-flown rhapsody? And what are we to say, where a man of Whitman's notable capacity for putting things in a bright, picturesque, and novel way, simply gives up the attempt, and indulges, with apparent exultation, in an inventory of trades or implements, with no more colour or coherence than so many index-words out of a dictionary? I do not know that we can say anything, but that it is a prodigiously amusing exhibition for a line or so. The worst of it is, that Whitman must have known better. The man is a great critic, and, so far as I can make out, a good one; and how much criticism does it require to know that capitulation is not description, or that fingering on a dumb keyboard, with whatever show of sentiment and execution, is not at all the same thing as discoursing music? I wish I could believe he was quite honest with us; but, indeed, who was ever quite honest who wrote a book for a purpose? It is a flight beyond the reach of human magnanimity.

One other point, where his means failed him, must be touched upon, however shortly. In his desire to accept all facts loyally and simply, it fell within his programme to speak at some length and with some plainness on what is, for I really do not know what reason, the most delicate of subjects. Seeing in that one of the most serious and interesting parts of

[85]

life, he was aggrieved that it should be looked upon as ridiculous or shameful. No one speaks of maternity with his tongue in his cheek; and Whitman made a bold push to set the sanctity of fatherhood beside the sanctity of motherhood, and introduce this also among the things that can be spoken of without either a blush or a wink. But the Philistines have been too strong; and, to say truth, Whitman has rather played the fool. We may be thoroughly conscious that his end is improving; that it would be a good thing if a window were opened on these close privacies of life; that on this subject, as on all others, he now and then lets fall a pregnant saying. But we are not satisfied. We feel that he was not the man for so difficult an enterprise. He loses our sympathy in the character of a poet by attracting too much of our attention in that of a Bull in a China Shop. And where, by a little more art, we might have been solemnised ourselves, it is too often Whitman alone who is solemn in the face of an audience somewhat indecorously amused.

VI

Lastly, as most important, after all, to human beings in our disputable state, what is that higher prudence which was to be the aim and issue of these deliberate productions?

Whitman is too clever to slip into a succinct formula. If he could have adequately said his say in a single proverb, it is to be presumed he would not have put himself to the trouble of writing several volumes. It was his programme to state as much as he could of the world with all its contradictions, and leave the upshot with God who planned it. What he has made of the world and the world's meanings is to be found at large in his poems. These altogether give his answers to the problems of belief and conduct; in many ways righteous and high-spirited, in some ways loose and contradictory. And yet there are two passages from the preface to the *Leaves of Grass* which do pretty well condense his teaching on all essential points, and yet preserve a measure of his spirit.

'This is what you shall do,' he says in the one, 'love the earth, and sun, and animals, despise riches, give alms to everyone that asks, stand up for the stupid and crazy, devote your income and labour to others, hate tyrants, argue not concerning God, have patience and indulgence towards the people, take off your hat to nothing known or unknown, or to any man or number of men; go freely with powerful uneducated persons, and with the young, and mothers of families, read these leaves (his own works) in the open air every season of every year of your life; re-examine all you have been told at school or church, or in any book, and dismiss whatever insults your own soul.'

'The prudence of the greatest poet,' he adds in the other – and the greatest poet is, of course, himself – 'knows that the young man who composedly perilled his life and lost it, has done exceeding well for himself; while the man who has not perilled his life, and retains it to old age in riches and ease, has perhaps achieved nothing for himself worth mentioning; and that only that person has no great prudence to learn, who has learnt to prefer real long-lived things, and favours body and soul the same, and perceives the indirect surely following the direct, and what evil or good he does leaping onward and waiting to meet him again, and who in his spirit, in any emergency whatever, neither hurries nor avoids death.'

There is much that is Christian in these extracts, startlingly Christian. Any reader who bears in mind Whitman's own advice and 'dismisses whatever insults his own soul' will find plenty that is bracing, brightening, and chastening to reward him for a little patience at first. It seems hardly possible that any being should get evil from so healthy a book as the *Leaves of Grass*, which is simply comical wherever it falls short of nobility; but if there be any such, who cannot both take and leave, who cannot let a single opportunity pass by without some unworthy and unmanly thought, I should have as great difficulty, and neither more nor less, in recommending the works of Whitman as in lending them Shakespeare, or letting them go abroad outside of the grounds of a private asylum.

EDINBURGH

The ancient and famous metropolis of the North sits overlooking a windy estuary from the slope and summit of three hills. No situation could be more commanding for the head city of a kingdom; none better chosen for noble prospects. From her tall precipice and terraced gardens she looks far and wide on the sea and broad champaigns. To the east you may catch at sunset the spark of the May lighthouse, where the Firth expands into the German Ocean; and away to the west, over all the carse of Stirling, you can see the first snows upon Ben Ledi.

But Edinburgh pays cruelly for her high seat in one of the vilest climates under heaven. She is liable to be beaten upon by all the winds that blow, to be drenched with rain, to be buried in cold sea fogs out of the east, and powdered with the snow as it comes flying southward from the Highland hills. The weather is raw and boisterous in winter, shifty and ungenial in summer, and a downright meteorological purgatory in the spring. The delicate die early, and I, as a survivor, among bleak winds and plumping rain, have been sometimes tempted to envy them their fate. For all who love shelter and the blessings of the sun, who hate dark weather and perpetual tilting against squalls, there could scarcely be found a more unhomely and harassing place of residence. Many such aspire angrily after that Somewhere-else of the imagination, where all troubles are supposed to end. They lean over the great bridge which joins the New Town with the Old – that windiest spot, or high altar, in this northern temple of the winds – and watch the trains smoking out from under them and vanishing into the tunnel on a voyage to brighter skies. Happy the passengers who shake off the dust of Edinburgh, and have heard for the last time the cry of the east wind among her chimney-tops! And yet the place establishes an interest in people's hearts; go where they will, they find no city of the same distinction; go where they will, they take a pride in their old home.

Venice, it has been said, differs from all other cities in the sentiment which she inspires. The rest may have admirers; she only, a famous fair one, counts lovers in her train. And indeed, even by her kindest friends,

Edinburgh is not considered in a similar sense. These like her for many reasons, not any one of which is satisfactory in itself. They like her whimsically, if you will, and somewhat as a virtuoso dotes upon his cabinet. Her attraction is romantic in the narrowest meaning of the term. Beautiful as she is, she is not so much beautiful as interesting. She is pre-eminently Gothic, and all the more so since she has set herself off with some Greek airs, and erected classic temples on her crags. In a word, and above all, she is a curiosity. The Palace of Holyrood has been left aside in the growth of Edinburgh, and stands gray and silent in a workman's quarter and among breweries and gas works. It is a house of many memories. Great people of yore, kings and queens, buffoons and grave ambassadors, played their stately farce for centuries in Holyrood. Wars have been plotted, dancing has lasted deep into the night, murder has been done in its chambers. There Prince Charlie held his phantom levées, and in a very gallant manner represented a fallen dynasty for some hours. Now, all these things of clay are mingled with the dust, the king's crown itself is shown for sixpence to the vulgar; but the stone palace has outlived these changes. For fifty weeks together, it is no more than a show for tourists and a museum of old furniture; but on the fifty-first, behold the palace reawakened and mimicking its past. The Lord Commissioner, a kind of stage sovereign, sits among stage courtiers; a coach and six and clattering escort come and go before the gate; at night, the windows are lighted up, and its near neighbours, the workmen, may dance in their own houses to the palace music. And in this the palace is typical. There is a spark among the embers; from time to time the old volcano smokes. Edinburgh has but partly abdicated, and still wears, in parody, her metropolitan trappings. Half a capital and half a country town, the whole city leads a double existence; it has long trances of the one and flashes of the other; like the king of the Black Isles, it is half alive and half a monumental marble. There are armed men and cannon in the citadel overhead; you may see the troops marshalled on the high parade; and at night after the early winter evenfall, and in the morning before the laggard winter dawn, the wind carries abroad over Edinburgh the sound of drums and bugles. Grave judges sit bewigged in what was once the scene of imperial deliberations. Close by in the High Street perhaps the trumpets may sound about the stroke of noon; and you see a troop of citizens in tawdry masquerade; tabard above, heather-mixture trowser below, and the men themselves trudging in the mud among unsympathetic bystanders. The grooms of a well-appointed circus tread the streets with a better presence. And yet these are the Heralds and Pursuivants of Scotland, who are about to proclaim a new law of the United Kingdom before two score boys, and thieves, and hackney-coachmen. Meanwhile every hour the bell of the University rings out over the hum of the streets, and every hour a double tide of students, coming and going, fills the deep archways. And lastly, one night in the springtime – or say one morning rather, at the peep of day – late folk may hear the voices of many men singing a psalm in unison from a church on one side of the old High Street; and a little after, or perhaps a little before, the sound of many men singing a psalm in unison from another church on the opposite side of the way. There will be something in the words about the dew of Hermon, and how goodly it is to see brethren dwelling together in unity. And the late folk will tell themselves that all this singing denotes the conclusion of two yearly ecclesiastical parliaments – the parliaments of Churches which are brothers in many admirable virtues, but not specially like brothers in this particular of a tolerant and peaceful life.

Again, meditative people will find a charm in a certain consonancy between the aspect of the city and its odd and stirring history. Few places, if any, offer a more barbaric display of contrasts to the eye. In the very midst stands one of the most satisfactory crags in nature – a Bass Rock upon dry land, rooted in a garden, shaken by passing trains, carrying a crown of battlements and turrets, and describing its warlike shadow over the liveliest and brightest thoroughfare of the new town. From their smoky beehives, ten stories high, the unwashed look down upon the open squares and gardens of the wealthy; and gay people sunning themselves along Princes Street, with its mile of commercial palaces all beflagged upon some great occasion, see, across a gardened valley set with statues, where the washings of the old town flutter in the breeze at its high windows. And then, upon all sides, what a clashing of architecture! In this one valley, where the life of the town goes most busily forward, there may be seen, shown one above and behind another by the accidents of the ground, buildings in almost every style upon the globe. Egyptian and Greek temples, Venetian palaces and Gothic spires, are huddled one over another in a most admired disorder; while, above all, the brute mass of the Castle and the summit of Arthur's Seat look down upon these imitations with a becoming dignity, as the works of Nature may look down upon the monuments of Art. But Nature is a more indiscriminate patroness than we imagine, and in no way frightened of a strong effect. The birds roost as willingly among the

Corinthian capitals as in the crannies of the crag; the same atmosphere and daylight clothe the eternal rock and yesterday's imitation portico; and as the soft northern sunshine throws out everything into a glorified distinctness – or easterly mists, coming up with the blue evening, fuse all these incongruous features into one, and the lamps begin to glitter along the street, and faint lights to burn in the high windows across the valley – the feeling grows upon you that this also is a piece of nature in the most intimate sense; that this profusion of eccentricities, this dream in masonry and living rock, is not a drop-scene in a theatre, but a city in the world of everyday reality, connected by railway and telegraph-wire with all the capitals of Europe, and inhabited by citizens of the familiar type, who keep ledgers, and attend church, and have sold their immortal portion to a daily paper. By all the canons of romance, the place demands to be half deserted and leaning towards decay; birds we might admit in profusion, the play of the sun and winds, and a few gipsies encamped in the chief thoroughfare: but these citizens, with their cabs and tramways, their trains and posters, are altogether out of key. Chartered tourists, they make free with historic localities, and rear their young among the most picturesque sites with a grand human indifference. To see them thronging by, in their neat clothes and conscious moral rectitude, and with a little air of possession that verges on the absurd, is not the least striking feature of the place.[1]

And the story of the town is as eccentric as its appearance. For centuries it was a capital thatched with heather, and more than once, in the evil days of English invasion, it has gone up in flame to heaven, a beacon to ships at sea. It was the jousting-ground of jealous nobles, not only on Greenside or by the King's Stables, where set tournaments were fought to the sound of trumpets and under the authority of the royal presence, but in every alley where there was room to cross swords, and in the main street, where popular tumult under the Blue Blanket

---

[1]These sentences have, I hear, given offence in my native town, and a proportionable pleasure to our rivals of Glasgow. I confess the news caused me both pain and merriment. May I remark, as a balm for wounded fellow-townsmen, that there is nothing deadly in my accusations? Small blame to them if they keep ledgers: 'tis an excellent business habit. Churchgoing is not, that ever I heard, a subject of reproach; decency of linen is a mark of prosperous affairs, and conscious moral rectitude one of the tokens of good living. It is not their fault if the city calls for something more specious by way of inhabitants. A man in a frock-coat looks out of place upon an Alp or Pyramid, although he has the virtues of a Peabody and the talents of a Bentham. And let them console themselves – they do as well as anybody else; the population of (let us say) Chicago would cut quite as rueful a figure on the same romantic stage. To the Glasgow people I would say only one word, but that is of gold: *I have not yet written a book about Glasgow.*

alternated with the brawls of outlandish clansmen and retainers. Down in the palace John Knox reproved his queen in the accents of modern democracy. In the town, in one of those little shops plastered like so many swallows' nests among the buttresses of the old Cathedral, that familiar autocrat, James VI, would gladly share a bottle of wine with George Heriot the goldsmith. Up on the Pentland Hills, that so quietly look down on the Castle with the city lying in waves around it, those mad and dismal fanatics, the Sweet Singers, haggard from long exposure on the moors, sat day and night with 'tearful psalmns' to see Edinburgh consumed with fire from heaven, like another Sodom or Gomorrah. There, in the Grass-market, stiff-necked, covenanting heroes offered up the often unnecessary, but not less honourable, sacrifice of their lives, and bade eloquent farewell to sun, moon, and stars, and earthly friendships, or died silent to the roll of drums. Down by yon outlet rode Grahame of Claverhouse and his thirty dragoons, with the town beating to arms behind their horses' tails – a sorry handful thus riding for their lives, but with a man at the head who was to return in a different temper, make a dash that staggered Scotland to the heart, and die happily in the thick of fight. There Aikenhead was hanged for a piece of boyish incredulity; there, a few years afterwards, David Hume ruined Philosophy and Faith, an undisturbed and well-reputed citizen; and thither, in yet a few years more, Burns came from the plough-tail, as to an academy of gilt unbelief and artificial letters. There, when the great exodus was made across the valley, and the new town began to spread abroad its draughty parallelograms and rear its long frontage on the opposing hill, there was such a flitting, such a change of domicile and dweller, as was never excelled in the history of cities: the cobbler succeeded the earl; the beggar ensconced himself by the judge's chimney; what had been a palace was used as a pauper refuge; and great mansions were so parcelled out among the least and lowest in society, that the hearthstone of the old proprietor was thought large enough to be partitioned off into a bedroom by the new.

TRUTH OF INTERCOURSE

Among sayings that have a currency in spite of being wholly false upon the face of them for the sake of a half-truth upon another subject which is accidentally combined with the error, one of the grossest and broadest conveys the monstrous proposition that it is easy to tell the truth and hard to tell a lie. I wish heartily it were. But the truth is one; it has first to be discovered, then justly and exactly uttered. Even with instruments specially contrived for such a purpose – with a foot rule, a level, or a theodolite – it is not easy to be exact; it is easier, alas! to be inexact. From those who mark the divisions on a scale to those who measure the boundaries of empires or the distance of the heavenly stars, it is by careful method and minute, unwearying attention that men rise even to material exactness or to sure knowledge even of external and constant things. But it is easier to draw the outline of a mountain than the changing appearance of a face; and truth in human relations is of this more intangible and dubious order: hard to seize, harder to communicate. Veracity to facts in a loose, colloquial sense – not to say that I have been in Malabar when as a matter of fact I was never out of England, not to say that I have read Cervantes in the original when as a matter of fact I know not one syllable of Spanish – this, indeed, is easy and to the same degree unimportant in itself. Lies of this sort, according to circumstances, may or may not be important; in a certain sense even they may or may not be false. The habitual liar may be a very honest fellow, and live truly with his wife and friends; while another man who never told a formal falsehood in his life may yet be himself one lie – heart and face, from top to bottom. This is the kind of lie which poisons intimacy. And, *vice versâ*, veracity to sentiment, truth in a relation, truth to your own heart and your friends, never to feign or falsify emotion – that is the truth which makes love possible and mankind happy.

L'art de bien dire is but a drawing-room accomplishment unless it be pressed into the service of the truth. The difficulty of literature is not to write, but to write what you mean; not to affect your reader, but to affect him precisely as you wish. This is commonly understood in the case of books or set orations; even in making your will, or writing an explicit letter, some difficulty is admitted by the world. But one thing you can never make Philistine natures understand; one thing, which yet lies on the surface, remains as unseizable to their wits as a high flight of metaphysics – namely, that the business of life is mainly carried on by means of this difficult art of literature, and according to a man's proficiency in that art shall be the freedom and the fulness of his intercourse with other men. Anybody, it is supposed, can say what he means; and, in spite of their notorious experience to the contrary, people so continue to suppose. Now, I simply open the last book I have been reading – Mr Leland's captivating *English Gipsies*. 'It is said,' I find on p. 7, 'that those who can converse with Irish peasants in their own native tongue form far higher opinions of their appreciation of the beautiful, and of *the elements of humour and pathos in their hearts*, than do those who know their thoughts only through the medium of English. I know from my own observations that this is quite the case with the Indians of North America, and it is unquestionably so with the gipsy.' In short, where a man has not a full possession of the language, the most important, because the most amiable, qualities of his nature have to lie buried and fallow; for the pleasure of comradeship, and the intellectual part of love, rest upon these very 'elements of humour and pathos.' Here is a man opulent in both, and for lack of a medium he can put none of it out to interest in the market of affection! But what is thus made plain to our apprehensions in the case of a foreign language is partially true even with the tongue we learned in childhood. Indeed, we all speak different dialects; one shall be copious and exact, another loose and meagre; but the speech of the ideal talker shall correspond and fit upon the truth of fact – not clumsily, obscuring lineaments, like a mantle, but cleanly adhering, like an athlete's skin. And what is the result? That the one can open himself more clearly to his friends, and can enjoy more of what makes life truly valuable – intimacy with those he loves. An orator makes a false step; he employs some trivial, some absurd, some vulgar phrase; in the turn of a sentence he insults, by a side wind, those whom he is labouring to charm; in speaking to one sentiment he unconsciously ruffles another in parenthesis; and you are not surprised, for you know his task to be delicate and filled with perils. 'O frivolous mind of man, light ignorance!' As if yourself, when you seek to explain some misunderstanding or excuse some apparent fault, speaking swiftly and addressing a mind still recently incensed, were not harnessing for a more perilous adventure; as if yourself required less tact and eloquence; as if an angry friend or a suspicious lover were not more easy to offend than a meeting of indifferent politicians! Nay, and the orator treads in a beaten round; the matters he discusses have been discussed a thousand times before; language is ready-shaped to his purpose; he speaks out of a cut and dry vocabulary. But you – may it not be that your defence reposes on some subtlety of feeling, not so much as touched upon in Shakespeare, to express which, like a pioneer, you must venture forth into zones of thought still unsurveyed, and become yourself a literary innovator? For even in love there are unlovely humours; ambiguous acts, unpardonable words, may yet have sprung from a kind sentiment. If the injured one could read your heart, you may be sure that he would understand and pardon; but, alas! the heart cannot be shown – it has to be demonstrated in words. Do you think it is a hard thing to write poetry? Why, that is to write poetry, and of a high, if not the highest, order.

I should even more admire 'the lifelong and heroic literary labours' of my fellow-men, patiently clearing up in words their loves and their contentions, and speaking their autobiography daily to their wives, were it not for a circumstance which lessens their difficulty and my admiration by equal parts. For life, though largely, is not entirely carried on by literature. We are subject to physical passions and contortions; the voice breaks and changes, and speaks by unconscious and winning inflections; we have legible countenances, like an open book; things that cannot be said look eloquently through the eyes; and the soul, not locked into the body as a dungeon, dwells ever on the threshold with appealing signals. Groans and tears, looks and gestures, a flush or a paleness, are often the most clear reporters of the heart, and speak more directly to the hearts of others. The message flies by these interpreters in the least space of time, and the misunderstanding is averted in the moment of its birth. To explain in words takes time and a just and patient hearing; and in the critical epochs of a close relation, patience and justice are not qualities on which we can rely. But the look or the gesture explains things in a breath; they tell their message without ambiguity; unlike speech, they cannot stumble, by the way, on a reproach or an allusion that should steel your friend against the truth; and then they have a higher authority, for they are the direct expression of the heart, not yet transmitted through the unfaithful and sophistica-ting brain. Not long ago I wrote a letter to a friend which came near involving us in quarrel; but we met, and in personal talk I repeated the worst of what I had written, and added worse to that; and with the commentary of the body it seemed not unfriendly either to hear or say. Indeed, letters are in vain for the purposes of intimacy; an absence is a dead break in the relation; yet two who know each other fully and are bent on perpetuity in love, may so preserve the attitude of their affections that they may meet on the same terms as they had parted.

Pitiful is the case of the blind, who cannot read the face; pitiful that of the deaf, who cannot follow the changes of the voice. And there are others also to be pitied; for there are some of an inert, uneloquent nature, who have been denied all the symbols of communication, who have neither a lively play of facial expression, nor speaking gestures, nor a responsive voice, nor yet the gift of frank, explanatory speech: people truly made of clay, people tied for life into a bag which no one can undo. They are poorer than the gipsy, for their heart can speak no language under heaven. Such people we must learn slowly by the tenor of their acts, or through yea and nay communications; or we take them on trust on the strength of a general air, and now and again, when we see the spirit breaking through in a flash, correct or change our estimate. But these will be uphill intimacies, without charm or freedom, to the end; and freedom is the chief ingredient in confidence. Some minds, romantically dull, despise physical endowments. That is a doctrine for a misanthrope; to those who like their fellow-creatures it must always be meaningless; and, for my part, I can see few things more desirable, after the possession of such radical qualities as honour and humour and pathos, than to have a lively and not a stolid countenance; to have looks to correspond with every feeling; to be elegant and delightful in person, so that we shall please even in the intervals of active pleasing, and may never discredit speech with uncouth manners or become unconsciously our own burlesques. But of all unfortunates there is one creature (for I will not call him man) conspicuous in misfortune. This is he who has forfeited his birthright of expression, who has cultivated artful intonations, who has taught his face tricks, like a pet monkey, and on every side perverted or cut off his means of communication with his fellow-men. The body is a house of many windows: there we all sit, showing ourselves and crying on the passers-by to come and love us. But this fellow has filled his windows with opaque glass, elegantly coloured. His house may be admired for its design, the crowd may pause before the stained windows, but meanwhile the poor proprietor must lie languishing within, uncomforted, unchangeably alone.

Truth of intercourse is something more difficult than to refrain from open lies. It is possible to avoid falsehood and yet not tell the truth. It is not enough to answer formal questions. To reach the truth by yea and nay communications implies a questioner with a share of inspiration, such as is often found in mutual love. *Yea* and *nay* mean nothing; the meaning must have been related in the question. Many words are often necessary to convey a very simple statement; for in this sort of exercise we never hit the gold; the most that we can hope is by many arrows, more or less far off on different sides, to indicate, in the course of time, for what target we are aiming, and after an hour's talk, back and forward, to convey the purport of a single principle or a single thought. And yet while the curt, pithy speaker misses the point entirely, a wordy, prolegomenous babbler will often add three new offences in the process of excusing one. It is really a most delicate affair. The world was made before the English language, and seemingly upon a different design. Suppose we held our converse not in words, but in music; those who have a bad ear would find themselves cut off from all near commerce, and no better than foreigners in this big world. But we do not consider how many have 'a bad ear' for words, nor how often the most eloquent find nothing to reply. I hate questioners and questions; there are so few that can be spoken to without a lie. '*Do you forgive me?*' Madam and sweetheart, so far as I have gone in life I have never yet been able to discover what forgiveness means. '*Is it still the same between us?*' Why, how can it be? It is eternally different; and yet you are still the friend of my heart. '*Do you understand me?*' God knows; I should think it highly improbable.

The cruellest lies are often told in silence. A man may have sat in a room for hours and not opened his teeth, and yet come out of that room a disloyal friend or a vile calumniator. And how many loves have perished because, from pride, or spite, or diffidence, or that unmanly shame which withholds a man from daring to betray emotion, a lover, at the critical point of the relation, has but hung his head and held his tongue? And, again, a lie may be told by a truth, or a truth conveyed through a lie. Truth to facts is not always truth to sentiment; and part of the truth, as often happens in answer to a question, may be the foulest calumny. A fact may be an exception; but the feeling is the law, and it is that which you must neither garble nor belie. The whole tenor of a conversation is a part of the meaning of each separate statement; the beginning and the end define and travesty the intermediate conversation. You never speak to God; you address a fellow-man, full of his own tempers; and to tell truth, rightly understood, is not to state the true facts, but to convey a true impression; truth in spirit, not truth to letter, is the true veracity. To reconcile averted friends a Jesuitical discretion is often needful, not so much to gain a kind hearing as to communicate sober truth. Women have an ill name in this connection; yet they live in as true relations; the lie of a good woman is the true index of her heart.

'It takes,' says Thoreau, in the noblest and most useful passage I remember to have read in any modern author,[1] 'two to speak truth – one to speak and another to hear.' He must be very little experienced, or have no great zeal for truth, who does not recognise the fact. A grain of anger or a grain of suspicion produces strange acoustical effects, and makes the ear greedy to remark offence. Hence we find those who have once quarrelled carry themselves distantly, and are ever ready to break the truce. To speak truth there must be moral equality or else no respect; and hence between parent and child intercourse is apt to degenerate into a verbal fencing bout, and misapprehensions to become ingrained. And there is another side to this, for the parent begins with an imperfect notion of the child's character, formed in early years or during the equinoctial gales of youth; to this he adheres, noting only the facts which suit with his preconception; and wherever a person fancies himself unjustly judged, he at once and finally gives up the effort to speak truth. With our chosen friends, on the other hand, and still more between lovers (for mutual understanding is love's essence), the truth is easily indicated by the one and aptly comprehended by the other. A hint taken, a look understood, conveys the gist of long and delicate explanations; and where the life is known even *yea* and *nay* become luminous. In the closest of all relations – that of a love well founded and equally shared – speech is half discarded, like a roundabout, infantile process or a ceremony of formal etiquette; and the two communicate directly by their presences, and with few looks and fewer words contrive to share their good and evil and uphold each other's hearts in joy. For love rests upon a physical basis; it is a familiarity of nature's making and apart from voluntary choice. Understanding has in some sort outrun knowledge, for the affection perhaps began with the acquaintance; and as it was not made like other relations, so it is not, like them, to be perturbed or clouded. Each knows more than can be uttered; each lives

[1] *A Week on the Concord and Merrimack Rivers*, Wednesday, p. 283.

by faith, and believes by a natural compulsion; and between man and wife the language of the body is largely developed and grown strangely eloquent. The thought that prompted and was conveyed in a caress would only lose to be set down in words – ay, although Shakespeare himself should be the scribe.

Yet it is in these dear intimacies, beyond all others, that we must strive and do battle for the truth. Let but a doubt arise, and alas! all the previous intimacy and confidence is but another charge against the person doubted. '*What a monstrous dishonesty is this if I have been deceived so long and so completely!*' Let but that thought gain entrance, and you plead before a deaf tribunal. Appeal to the past; why, that is your crime! Make all clear, convince the reason; alas! speciousness is but a proof against you. '*If you can abuse me now, the more likely that you have abused me from the first.*'

For a strong affection such moments are worth supporting, and they will end well; for your advocate is in your lover's heart and speaks her own language; it is not you but she herself who can defend and clear you of the charge. But in slighter intimacies, and for a less stringent union? Indeed, is it worth while? We are all *incompris*, only more or less concerned for the mischance; all trying wrongly to do right; all fawning at each other's feet like dumb, neglected lap-dogs. Sometimes we catch an eye – this is our opportunity in the ages – and we wag our tail with a poor smile. '*Is that all?*' All? If you only knew! But how can they know? They do not love us; the more fools we to squander life on the indifferent.

But the morality of the thing, you will be glad to hear, is excellent; for it is only by trying to understand others that we can get our own hearts understood; and in matters of human feeling the clement judge is the most successful pleader.

SOME ASPECTS OF ROBERT BURNS

To write with authority about another man, we must have fellow-feeling and some common ground of experience with our subject. We may praise or blame according as we find him related to us by the best or worst in ourselves; but it is only in virtue of some relationship that we can be his judges, even to condemn. Feelings which we share and understand enter for us into the tissue of the man's character; those to which we are strangers in our own experience we are inclined to regard as blots, exceptions, inconsistencies, and excursions of the diabolic; we conceive them with repugnance, explain them with difficulty, and raise our hands to heaven in wonder when we find them in conjunction with talents that we respect or virtues that we admire. David, king of Israel, would pass a sounder judgement on a man than either Nathaniel or David Hume. Now, Principal Shairp's recent volume, although I believe no one will read it without respect and interest, has this one capital defect – that there is imperfect sympathy between the author and the subject, between the critic and the personality under criticism. Hence an inorganic, if not an incoherent, presentation of both the poems and the man. Of *Holy Willie's Prayer*, Principal Shairp remarks that 'those who have loved most what was best in Burns's poetry must have regretted that it was ever written.' To the *Jolly Beggars*, so far as my memory serves me, he refers but once; and then only to remark on the 'strange, not to say painful,' circumstance that the same hand which wrote the *Cotter's Saturday Night* should have stooped to write the *Jolly Beggars*. The *Saturday Night* may or may not be an admirable poem; but its significance is trebled, and the power and range of the poet first appears, when it is set beside the *Jolly Beggars*. To take a man's work piecemeal, except with the design of elegant extracts, is the way to avoid, and not to perform, the critic's duty. The same defect is displayed in the treatment of Burns as a man, which is broken, apologetical, and confused. The man here presented to us is not that Burns, *teres atque rotundus* – a burly figure in literature, as, from our present vantage of time, we have begun to see him. This, on the other hand, is Burns as he may have appeared to

a contemporary clergyman, whom we shall conceive to have been a kind
and indulgent but orderly and orthodox person, anxious to be pleased,
but too often hurt and disappointed by the behaviour of his red-hot
protégé, and solacing himself with the explanation that the poet was
'the most inconsistent of men.' If you are so sensibly pained by the
misconduct of your subject, and so paternally delighted with his virtues,
you will always be an excellent gentleman, but a somewhat questionable
biographer. Indeed, we can only be sorry and surprised that Principal
Shairp should have chosen a theme so uncongenial. When we find a man
writing on Burns, who likes neither *Holy Willie*, nor the *Beggars*, nor the
Ordination, nothing is adequate to the situation but the old cry of
Géronte: '*Que diable allait-il faire dans cette galère?*' And every merit
we find in the book, which is sober and candid in a degree unusual with
biographies of Burns, only leads us to regret more heartily that good
work should be so greatly thrown away.

It is far from my intention to tell over again a story that has been so
often told; but there are certainly some points in the character of Burns
that will bear to be brought out, and some chapters in his life that
demand a brief rehearsal. The unity of the man's nature, for all its
richness, has fallen somewhat out of sight in the pressure of new
information and the apologetical ceremony of biographers. Mr Carlyle
made an inimitable bust of the poet's head of gold; may I not be forgiven
if my business should have more to do with the feet, which were of clay?

YOUTH

Any view of Burns would be misleading which passed over in silence the
influences of his home and his father. That father, William Burnes, after
having been for many years a gardener, took a farm, married, and, like
an emigrant in a new country, built himself a house with his own hands.
Poverty of the most distressing sort, with sometimes the near prospect of
a gaol, embittered the remainder of his life. Chill, backward, and austere
with strangers, grave and imperious in his family, he was yet a man of
very unusual parts and of an affectionate nature. On his way through life
he had remarked much upon other men, with more result in theory than
practice; and he had reflected upon many subjects as he delved the
garden. His great delight was in solid conversation; he would leave his
work to talk with the schoolmaster Murdoch; and Robert, when he
came home late at night, not only turned aside rebuke but kept his father

two hours beside the fire by the charm of his merry and vigorous talk. Nothing is more characteristic of the class in general, and William Burnes in particular, than the pains he took to get proper schooling for his boys, and, when that was no longer possible, the sense and resolution with which he set himself to supply the deficiency by his own influence. For many years he was their chief companion; he spoke with them seriously on all subjects as if they had been grown men; at night, when work was over, he taught them arithmetic; he borrowed books for them on history, science, and theology; and he felt it his duty to supplement this last – the trait is laughably Scottish – by a dialogue of his own composition, where his own private shade of orthodoxy was exactly represented. He would go to his daughter as she stayed afield herding cattle, to teach her the names of grasses and wild flowers, or to sit by her side when it thundered. Distance to strangers, deep family tenderness, love of knowledge, a narrow, precise, and formal reading of theology – everything we learn of him hangs well together, and builds up a popular Scotch type. If I mention the name of Andrew Fairservice, it is only as I might couple for an instant Dugald Dalgetty with old Marshal London, to help out the reader's comprehension by a popular but unworthy instance of a class. Such was the influence of this good and wise man that his household became a school to itself, and neighbours who came into the farm at meal-time would find the whole family, father, brothers, and sisters, helping themselves with one hand, and holding a book in the other. We are surprised at the prose style of Robert; that of Gilbert need surprise us no less; even William writes a remarkable letter for a young man of such slender opportunities. One anecdote marks the taste of the family. Murdoch brought *Titus Andronicus*, and, with such dominie elocution as we may suppose, began to read it aloud before this rustic audience; but when he had reached the passage where Tamora insults Lavinia, with one voice and 'in an agony of distress' they refused to hear it to an end. In such a father and with such a home, Robert had already the making of an excellent education; and what Murdoch added, although it may not have been much in amount, was in character the very essence of a literary training. Schools and colleges, for one great man whom they complete, perhaps unmake a dozen; the strong spirit can do well upon more scanty fare.

Robert steps before us, almost from the first, in his complete character – a proud, headstrong, impetuous lad, greedy of pleasure, greedy of notice; in his own phrase 'panting after distinction,' and in his brother's 'cherishing a particular jealousy of people who were richer or of more consequence than himself:' with all this, he was emphatically of the artist nature. Already he made a conspicuous figure in Tarbolton church, with the only tied hair in the parish, 'and his plaid, which was of a particular colour, wrapped in a particular manner round his shoulders.' Ten years later, when a married man, the father of a family, a farmer, and an officer of Excise, we shall find him out fishing in masquerade, with fox-skin cap, belted great-coat, and great Highland broadsword. He liked dressing up, in fact, for its own sake. This is the spirit which leads to the extravagant array of Latin Quarter students, and the proverbial velveteen of the English landscape-painter; and, though the pleasure derived is in itself merely personal, it shows a man who is, to say the least of it, not pained by general attention and remark. His father wrote the family name *Burnes*; Robert early adopted the orthography *Burness* from his cousin in the Mearns; and in his twenty-eighth year changed it once more to *Burns*. It is plain that the last transformation was not made without some qualm; for in addressing his cousin he adheres, in at least one more letter, to spelling number two. And this, again, shows a man preoccupied about the manner of his apearance even down to the name, and little willing to follow custom. Again, he was proud, and justly proud, of his powers in conversation. To no other man's have we the same conclusive testimony from different sources and from every rank of life. It is almost a commonplace that the best of his works was what he said in talk. Robertson the historian 'scarcely ever met any man whose conversation displayed greater vigour;' the Duchess of Gordon declared that he 'carried her off her feet;' and, when he came late to an inn, the servants would get out of bed to hear him talk. But, in these early days at least, he was determined to shine by any means. He made himself feared in the village for his tongue. He would crush weaker men to their faces, or even perhaps – for the statement of Sillar is not absolute – say cutting things of his acquaintances behind their back. At the church door, between sermons, he would parade his religious views amid hisses. These details stamp the man. He had no genteel timidities in the conduct of his life. He loved to force his personality upon the world. He would please himself, and shine. Had he lived in the Paris of 1830, and joined his lot with the Romantics, we can conceive him writing *Jehan* for *Jean*, swaggering in Gautier's red waistcoat, and horrifying Bourgeois in a public café with paradox and gasconnade.

A leading trait throughout his whole career was his desire to be in love. *Ne fait pas ce tour qui veut.* His affections were often enough touched, but perhaps never engaged. He was all his life on a voyage of discovery, but it does not appear conclusively that he ever touched the happy isle. A man brings to love a deal of ready-made sentiment, and even from childhood obscurely prognosticates the symptoms of this vital malady. Burns was formed for love; he had passion, tenderness, and a singular bent in the direction; he could foresee, with the intuition of an artist, what love ought to be; and he could not conceive a worthy life without it. But he had ill-fortune, and was besides so greedy after every shadow of the true divinity, and so much the slave of a strong temperament, that perhaps his nerve was relaxed and his heart had lost the power of self-devotion before an opportunity occurred. The circumstances of his youth doubtless counted for something in the result. For the lads of Ayrshire, as soon as the day's work was over and the beasts were stabled, would take the road, it might be in a winter tempest, and travel perhaps miles by moss and moorland to spend an hour or two in courtship. Rule 10 of the Bachelors' Club at Tarbolton provides that 'every man proper for a member of this Society must be a professed lover of *one or more* of the female sex.' The rich, as Burns himself points out, may have a choice of pleasurable occupations, but these lads had nothing but their 'cannie hour at e'en.' It was upon love and flirtation that this rustic society was built; gallantry was the essence of life among the Ayrshire hills as well as in the Court of Versailles; and the days were distinguished from each other by love-letters, meetings, tiffs, reconciliations, and expansions to the chosen confidant, as in a comedy of Marivaux. Here was a field for a man of Burns's indiscriminate personal ambition, where he might pursue his voyage of discovery in quest of true love, and enjoy temporary triumphs by the way. He was 'constantly the victim of some fair enslaver' – at least, when it was not the other way about; and there were often underplots and secondary fair enslavers in the background. Many – or may we not say most? – of these affairs were entirely artificial. One, he tells us, he began out of 'a vanity of showing his parts in courtship,' for he piqued himself on his ability at a love-letter. But, however they began, these flames of his were fanned into a passion ere the end; and he stands unsurpassed in his power of self-deception, and positively without a competitor in the art, to use his own words, of 'battering himself into a warm affection,' – a debilitating and futile exercise. Once he had worked himself into the vein, 'the agitations of his mind and body' were an astonishment to all who knew him. Such a course as this, however pleasant to a thirsty vanity, was lowering to his nature. He sank more and more towards the professional Don Juan. With a leer of what the French call fatuity, he bids the belles of Mauchline beware of his seductions; and the same cheap self-satisfaction finds a yet uglier vent when he plumes himself on the scandal at the birth of his first bastard. We can well believe what we hear of his facility in striking up an acquaintance with women: he would have conquering manners; he would bear down upon his rustic game with the grace that comes of absolute assurance – the Richelieu of Lochlea or Mossgiel. In yet another manner did these quaint ways of courtship help him into fame. If he were great as principal, he was unrivalled as confidant. He could enter into a passion; he could counsel wary moves, being, in his own phrase, so old a hawk; nay, he could turn a letter for some unlucky swain, or even string a few lines of verse that should clinch the business and fetch the hesitating fair one to the ground. Nor, perhaps, was it only his 'curiosity, zeal, and intrepid dexterity' that recommended him for a second in such affairs; it must have been a distinction to have the assistance and advice of *Rab the Ranter*; and one who was in no way formidable by himself might grow dangerous and attractive through the fame of his associate.

I think we can conceive him, in these early years, in that rough moorland country, poor among the poor with his seven pounds a year, looked upon with doubt by respectable elders, but for all that the best talker, the best letter-writer, the most famous lover and confidant, the laureate poet, and the only man who wore his hair tied in the parish. He says he had then as high a notion of himself as ever after; and I can well believe it. Among the youth he walked *facile princeps*, an apparent god; and even if, from time to time, the Reverend Mr Auld should swoop upon him with the thunders of the Church, and, in company with seven others, Rab the Ranter must figure some fine Sunday on the stool of repentance, would there not be a sort of glory, an infernal apotheosis, in so conspicuous a shame? Was not Richelieu in disgrace more idolised than ever by the dames of Paris? and when was the highwayman most acclaimed but on his way to Tyburn? Or, to take a simile from nearer home, and still more exactly to the point, what could even corporal punishment avail, administered by a cold, abstract, unearthly schoolmaster, against the influence and fame of the school's hero?

And now we come to the culminating point of Burns's early period. He began to be received into the unknown upper world. His fame soon spread from among his fellow-rebels on the benches, and began to reach the ushers and monitors of this great Ayrshire academy. This arose in part from his lax views about religion; for at this time that old war of the creeds and confessors, which is always grumbling from end to end of our poor Scotland, brisked up in these parts into a hot and virulent skirmish; and Burns found himself identified with the opposition party – a clique of roaring lawyers and half-heretical divines, with wit enough to appreciate the value of the poet's help, and not sufficient taste to moderate his grossness and personality. We may judge of their surprise when *Holy Willie* was put into their hand; like the amorous lads of Tarbolton, they recognised in him the best of seconds. His satires began to go the round in manuscript; Mr Aiken, one of the lawyers, 'read him into fame;' he himself was soon welcome in many houses of a better sort, where his admirable talk, and his manners, which he had direct from his Maker, except for a brush he gave them at a country dancing school, completed what his poems had begun. We have a sight of him at his first visit to Adamhill, in his ploughman's shoes, coasting around the carpet as though that were sacred ground. But he soon grew used to carpets and their owners; and he was still the superior of all whom he encountered, and ruled the roost in conversation. Such was the impression made, that a young clergyman, himself a man of ability, trembled and became confused when he saw Robert enter the church in which he was to preach. It is not surprising that the poet determined to publish: he had now stood the test of some publicity, and under this hopeful impulse he composed in six winter months the bulk of his more important poems. Here was a young man who, from a very humble place, was mounting rapidly; from the cynosure of a parish, he had become the talk of a county; once the bard of rural courtships, he was now about to appear as a bound and printed poet in the world's bookshops.

A few more intimate strokes are necessary to complete the sketch. This strong young ploughman, who feared no competitor with the flail, suffered like a fine lady from sleeplessness and vapours; he would fall into the blackest melancholies, and be filled with remorse for the past and terror for the future. He was still not perhaps devoted to religion, but haunted by it; and at a touch of sickness prostrated himself before God in what I can only call unmanly penitence. As he had aspirations beyond his place in the world, so he had tastes, thoughts, and weaknesses to match. He loved to walk under a wood to the sound of a winter tempest; he had a singular tenderness for animals; he carried a book with him in his pocket when he went abroad, and wore out in this service two copies of the *Man of Feeling*. With young people in the field at work he was very long-suffering; and when his brother Gilbert spoke sharply to them – 'O man, ye are no for young folk,' he would say, and give the defaulter a helping hand and a smile. In the hearts of the men whom he met, he read as in a book; and, what is yet more rare, his knowledge of himself equalled his knowledge of others. There are no truer things said of Burns than what is to be found in his own letters. Country Don Juan as he was, he had none of that blind vanity which values itself on what it is not; he knew his own strength and weakness to a hair: he took himself boldly for what he was, and, except in moments of hypochondria, declared himself content.

THE LOVE STORIES

On the night of Mauchline races, 1785, the young men and women of the place joined in a penny ball, according to their custom. In the same set danced Jean Armour, the master-mason's daughter, and our dark-eyed Don Juan. His dog (not the immortal Luath, but a successor unknown to fame, *caret quia vate sacro*), apparently sensible of some neglect, followed his master to and fro, to the confusion of the dancers. Some mirthful comments followed; and Jean heard the poet say to his partner – or, as I should imagine, laughingly launch the remark to the company at large – that 'he wished he could get any of the lasses to like him as well as his dog.' Some time after, as the girl was bleaching clothes on Mauchline green, Robert chanced to go by, still accompanied by his dog; and the dog, 'scouring in long excursion,' scampered with four black paws across the linen. This brought the two into conversation; when Jean, with a somewhat hoydenish advance, inquired if 'he had yet got any of the lasses to like him as well as his dog?' It is one of the misfortunes of the professional Don Juan that his honour forbids him to refuse battle; he is in life like the Roman soldier upon duty, or like the sworn physician who must attend on all diseases. Burns accepted the provocation; hungry hope reawakened in his heart; here was a girl – pretty, simple at least, if not honestly stupid, and plainly not averse to his attentions; it seemed to him once more as if love might here be waiting him. Had he but known the truth! for this facile and empty-headed girl had nothing more in view than a flirtation; and her heart, from the first and on to the end of her story, was engaged by another man. Burns once more commenced the celebrated process of 'battering himself into a warm affection;' and the proofs of his success are to be found in many verses of the period. Nor did he succeed with himself only; Jean, with her heart still elsewhere, succumbed to his fascination, and early in the next year the natural consequence became manifest. It was a heavy stroke for this unfortunate couple. They had trifled with life, and were now rudely reminded of life's serious issues. Jean awoke to the ruin of her hopes; the best she had now to expect was marriage with a man who was a stranger to her dearest thoughts; she might now be glad if she could get what she would never have chosen. As for Burns, at the stroke of the calamity he recognised that his voyage of discovery had led him into a wrong hemisphere – that he was not, and never had been, really in love with Jean. Hear him in the pressure of the hour. 'Against two things,' he writes, 'I am as fixed as fate – staying at home, and owning her conjugally. The first, by heaven, I will not do! – the last, by hell, I will never do!' And then he adds, perhaps already in a more relenting temper: 'If you see Jean, tell her I will meet her, so God help me in my hour of need.' They met accordingly; and Burns, touched with her misery, came down from these heights of independence, and gave her a written acknowledgement of marriage. It is the punishment of Don Juanism to create continually false positions – relations in life which are wrong in themselves, and which it is equally wrong to break or to perpetuate. This was such a case. Worldly Wiseman would have laughed and gone his way; let us be glad that Burns was better counselled by his heart. When we discover that we can be no longer true, the next best is to be kind. I daresay he came away from that interview not very content, but with a glorious conscience; and as he went homeward, he would sing his favourite, 'How are Thy servants blest, O Lord!' Jean, on the other hand, armed with her 'lines,' confided her position to the master-mason, her father, and his wife. Burns and his brother were then in a fair way to ruin themselves in their farm; the poet was an execrable match for any well-to-do country lass; and perhaps old Armour had an inkling of a previous attachment on his daughter's part. At least, he was not so much incensed by her slip from virtue as by the marriage which had been designed to cover it. Of this he would not hear a word. Jean, who had besought the acknowledgement only to appease her parents, and not at all from any violent inclination to the poet, readily gave up the paper for destruction; and all parties imagined, although wrongly, that the marriage was thus dissolved. To a proud man like Burns here was a crushing blow. The concession which had been wrung from his pity was now publicly thrown back in his teeth. The Armour family preferred disgrace to his connection. Since the promise, besides, he had doubtless been busy 'battering himself' back again into his affection for the girl; and the blow would not only take him in his vanity, but wound him at the heart.

He relieved himself in verse; but for such a smarting affront manuscript poetry was insufficient to console him. He must find a more powerful remedy in good flesh and blood, and after this discomfiture, set forth again at once upon his voyage of discovery in quest of love. It is perhaps one of the most touching things in human nature, as it is a commonplace of psychology, that when a man has just lost hope or confidence in one love, he is then most eager to find and lean upon another. The universe could not be yet exhausted; there must be hope and love waiting for him somewhere; and so, with his head down, this poor, insulted poet ran once more upon his fate. There was an innocent and gentle Highland nursery-maid at service in a neighbouring family; and he had soon battered himself and her into a warm affection and a secret engagement. Jean's marriage lines had not been destroyed till March 13, 1786; yet all was settled between Burns and Mary Campbell by Sunday, May 14, when they met for the last time, and said farewell with rustic solemnities upon the banks of Ayr. They each wet their hands in a stream, and, standing one on either bank, held a Bible between them as they vowed eternal faith. Then they exchanged Bibles, on one of which Burns, for greater security, had inscribed texts as to the binding nature of an oath; and surely, if ceremony can do aught to fix the wandering affections, here were two people united for life. Mary came of a superstitious family, so that she perhaps insisted on these rites; but they must have been eminently to the taste of Burns at this period; for nothing would seem superfluous, and no oath great enough, to stay his tottering constancy.

Events of consequence now happened thickly in the poet's life. His book was announced; the Armours sought to summon him at law for the aliment of the child; he lay here and there in hiding to correct the sheets; he was under an engagement for Jamaica, where Mary was to join him as his wife; now, he had 'orders within three weeks at latest to repair aboard the *Nancy*, Captain Smith;' now his chest was already on the road to Greenock; and now, in the wild autumn weather on the moorland, he measures verses of farewell: —

> The bursting tears my heart declare;
> Farewell the bonny banks of Ayr!

But the great master dramatist had secretly another intention for the piece; by the most violent and complicated solution, in which death and birth and sudden fame all play a part as interposing deities, the act-drop fell upon a scene of transformation. Jean was brought to bed of twins, and, by an amicable arrangement, the Burnses took the boy to bring up by hand, while the girl remained with her mother. The success of the book was immediate and emphatic; it put £20 at once into the author's purse; and he was encouraged upon all hands to go to Edinburgh and push his success in a second and larger edition. Third and last in these series of interpositions, a letter came one day to Mossgiel Farm for Robert. He went to the window to read it; a sudden change came over his face, and he left the room without a word. Years afterwards, when the story began to leak out, his family understood that he had then learned the death of Highland Mary. Except in a few poems and a few dry indications purposely misleading as to date, Burns himself made no reference to this passage of his life; it was an adventure of which, for I think sufficient reasons, he desired to bury the details. Of one thing we may be glad: in after years he visited the poor girl's mother, and left her with the impression that he was 'a real warm-hearted chield.'

Perhaps a month after he received this intelligence, he set out for Edinburgh on a pony he had borrowed from a friend. The town that winter was 'agog with the ploughman poet.' Robertson, Dugald Stewart, Blair, 'Duchess Gordon and all the gay world,' were of his acquaintance. Such a revolution is not to be found in literary history. He was now, it must be remembered, twenty-seven years of age; he had fought since his early boyhood an obstinate battle against poor soil, bad seed, and inclement seasons, wading deep in Ayrshire mosses, guiding the plough in the furrow, wielding 'the thresher's weary flingin'-tree;' and his education, his diet, and his pleasures, had been those of a Scotch countryman. Now he stepped forth suddenly among the polite and learned. We can see him as he then was, in his boots and buckskins, his blue coat and waistcoat striped with buff and blue, like a farmer in his Sunday best; the heavy ploughman's figure firmly planted on its burly legs; his face full of sense and shrewdness, and with a somewhat melancholy air of thought, and his large dark eye 'literally glowing' as he spoke. 'I never saw such another eye in a human head,' says Walter Scott, 'though I have seen the most distinguished men of my time.' With men, whether they were lords or omnipotent critics, his manner was plain, dignified, and free from bashfulness or affectation. If he made a slip, he had the social courage to pass on and refrain from explanation. He was not embarrassed in this society, because he read and judged the men; he could spy snobbery in a titled lord; and, as for the critics, he dismissed their system in an epigram. 'These gentlemen,' said he, 'remind me of some spinsters in my country who spin their thread so fine that it is neither fit for weft nor woof.' Ladies, on the other hand, surprised him; he was scarce commander of himself in their society; he was disqualified by his acquired nature as a Don Juan; and he, who had been so much at his ease with country lasses, treated the town dames to an extreme of deference. One lady, who met him at a ball, gave Chambers a speaking sketch of his demeanour. 'His manner was not prepossessing – scarcely, she thinks, manly or natural. It seemed as if he affected a rusticity or *landertness*, so that when he said the music was "bonnie, bonnie," it was like the expression of a child.' These would be company manners; and doubtless on a slight degree of intimacy the affectation would grow less. And his talk to women had always 'a turn either to the pathetic or humorous, which engaged the attention particularly.'

The Edinburgh magnates (to conclude this episode at once) behaved well to Burns from first to last. Were heaven-born genius to revisit us in similar guise, I am not venturing too far when I say that he need expect neither so warm a welcome nor such solid help. Although Burns was only a peasant, and one of no very elegant reputation as to morals, he was made welcome to their homes. They gave him a great deal of good advice, helped him to some five hundred pounds of ready money, and got him, as soon as he asked it, a place in the Excise. Burns, on his part, bore the elevation with perfect dignity; and with perfect dignity returned, when the time had come, into a country privacy of life. His powerful sense never deserted him, and from the first he recognised that his Edinburgh popularity was but an ovation and the affair of a day. He wrote a few letters in a high-flown, bombastic vein of gratitude; but in practice he suffered no man to intrude upon his self-respect. On the other hand, he never turned his back, even for a moment, on his old associates; and he was always ready to sacrifice an acquaintance to a friend, although the acquaintance were a duke. He would be a bold man who should promise similar conduct in equally exacting circumstances. It was, in short, an admirable appearance on the stage of life – socially successful, intimately self-respecting, and like a gentleman from first to last.

In the present study, this must only be taken by the way, while we return to Burns's love affairs. Even on the road to Edinburgh he had seized upon the opportunity of a flirtation, and had carried the 'battering' so far that when next he moved from town, it was to steal two days with this anonymous fair one. The exact importance to Burns of this affair may be gathered from the song in which he commemorated its occurrence. 'I love the dear lassie,' he sings, 'because she loves me;' or, in the tongue of prose: 'Finding an opportunity, I did not hesitate to profit by it; and even now, if it returned, I should not hesitate to profit by it again.' A love thus founded has no interest for mortal man. Meantime, early in the winter, and only once, we find him regretting Jean in his correspondence. 'Because' – such is his reason – 'because he does not think he will ever meet so delicious an armful again;' and then, after a brief excursion into verse, he goes straight on to describe a new episode in the voyage of discovery with the daughter of a Lothian farmer for a heroine. I must ask the reader to follow all these references to his future wife; they are essential to the comprehension of Burns's character and fate. In June, we find him back at Mauchline, a famous man. There, the Armour family greeted him with a 'mean, servile compliance,' which increased his former disgust. Jean was not less compliant; a second time the poor girl submitted to the fascination of the man whom she did not love, and whom she had so cruelly insulted little more than a year ago; and, though Burns took advantage of her weakness, it was in the ugliest and most cynical spirit, and with a heart absolutely indifferent. Judge of this by a letter written some twenty days after his return – a letter to my mind among the most degrading in the whole collection – a letter which seems to have been inspired by a boastful, libertine bagman. 'I am afraid,' it goes, 'I have almost ruined one source, the principal one, indeed, of my former happiness – the eternal propensity I always had to fall in love. My heart no more glows with feverish rapture; I have no paradisiacal evening interviews.' Even the process of 'battering' has failed him, you perceive. Still he had someone in his eye – a lady, if you please, with a fine figure and elegant manners, and who had 'seen the politest quarters in Europe.' 'I frequently visited her,' he writes, 'and after passing regularly the intermediate degrees between the distant formal bow and the familiar grasp round the waist, I ventured, in my careless way, to talk of friendship in rather ambiguous terms; and after her return to ———, I wrote her in the same terms. Miss, construing my remarks further than even I intended, flew off in a tangent of female dignity and reserve, like a mounting lark in an April morning; and wrote me an answer which measured out very completely what an immense way I had to travel before I could reach the climate of her favours. But I am an old hawk at the sport, and wrote her such a cool, deliberate, prudent reply, as brought my bird from her aerial towerings, pop, down to my foot, like Corporal Trim's hat.' I avow a carnal longing, after this transcription, to buffet the Old Hawk about the ears. There is little question that to this lady he must have repeated his addresses, and that he was by her (Miss Chalmers) eventually, though not at all unkindly, rejected. One more detail to characterise the period. Six months after the date of this letter, Burns, back in Edinburgh, is served with a writ *in meditatione fugæ*, on behalf of some Edinburgh fair one, probably of humble rank, who declared an intention of adding to his family.

About the beginning of December (1787), a new period opens in the story of the poet's random affections. He met at a tea party one Mrs Agnes M'Lehose, a married woman of about his own age, who, with her two children, had been deserted by an unworthy husband. She had wit, could use her pen, and had read *Werther* with attention. Sociable, and even somewhat frisky, there was a good, sound, human kernel in the woman; a warmth of love, strong dogmatic religious feeling, and a considerable, but not authoritative, sense of the proprieties. Of what biographers refer to daintily as 'her somewhat voluptuous style of beauty,' judging from the silhouette in Mr Scott Douglas's invaluable edition, the reader will be fastidious if he does not approve. Take her for all in all, I believe she was the best woman Burns encountered. The pair took a fancy for each other on the spot; Mrs M'Lehose, in her turn, invited him to tea; but the poet, in his character of the Old Hawk, preferred a *tête-à-tête*, excused himself at the last moment, and offered a visit instead. An accident confined him to his room for nearly a month, and this led to the famous Clarinda and Sylvander correspondence. It was begun in simple sport; they are already at their fifth or sixth exchange, when Clarinda writes: 'It is really curious so much *fun* passing between two persons who saw each other only *once*;' but it is hardly safe for a man and woman in the flower of their years to write almost daily, and sometimes in terms too ambiguous, sometimes in terms too plain, and generally in terms too warm, for mere acquaintance. The exercise partakes a little of the nature of battering, and danger may be apprehended when next they meet. It is difficult to give any account of this remarkable correspondence; it is too far away from us, and perhaps, not yet far enough, in point of time and manner; the imagination is baffled by these stilted literary utterances, warming, in bravura passages, into downright truculent nonsense. Clarinda has one famous sentence in which she bids Sylvander connect the thought of his mistress with the changing phases of the year; it was enthusiastically admired by the swain, but on the modern mind produces mild amazement and alarm. 'Oh, Clarinda,' writes Burns, 'shall we not meet in a state – some yet unknown state – of being, where the lavish hand of Plenty shall minister to the highest wish of Benevolence, and where the chill north wind of Prudence shall never blow over the flowery field of Enjoyment?' The design may be that of an Old Hawk, but the style is more suggestive of a Bird of Paradise. It is sometimes hard to fancy they are not gravely making fun of each other as they write. Religion, poetry, love, and charming sensibility, are the current topics. 'I am delighted, charming Clarinda, with your honest enthusiasm for religion,' writes Burns; and the pair entertained a fiction that this was their 'favourite subject.' 'This is Sunday,' writes the lady, 'and not a word on our favourite subject. O fy! "divine Clarinda!"' I suspect, although quite unconsciously on the part of the lady, who was bent on his redemption, they but used the favourite subject as a stalking-horse. In the meantime, the sportive acquaintance was ripening steadily into a genuine passion. Visits took place, and then became frequent. Clarinda's friends were hurt and suspicious; her clergyman interfered; she herself had smart attacks of conscience; but her heart had gone from her control; it was altogether his, and she 'counted all things but loss – heaven excepted – that she might win and keep him.' Burns himself was transported while in her neighbourhood, but his transports somewhat rapidly declined during an absence. I am tempted to imagine that, womanlike, he took on the colour of his mistress's feeling; that he could not but heat himself at the fire of her unaffected passion; but that, like one who should leave the hearth upon a winter's night, his temperature soon fell when he was out of sight, and in a word, though he could share the symptoms, that he had never shared the disease. At the same time, amid the fustian of the letters there are forcible and true expressions, and the love verses that he wrote upon Clarinda are among the most moving in the language.

We are approaching the solution. In mid-winter, Jean, once more in the family way, was turned out of doors by her family; and Burns had her received and cared for in the house of a friend. For he remained to the last imperfect in his character of Don Juan, and lacked the sinister courage to desert his victim. About the middle of February (1788), he had to tear himself from his Clarinda and make a journey into the south-west on business. Clarinda gave him two shirts for his little son. They were daily to meet in prayer at an appointed hour. Burns, too late for the post at Glasgow, sent her a letter by parcel that she might not have to wait. Clarinda on her part writes, this time with a beautiful simplicity: 'I think the streets look deserted-like since Monday; and there's a certain insipidity in good kind folks I once enjoyed not a little. Miss Wardrobe supped here on Monday. She once named you, which kept me from falling asleep. I drank your health in a glass of ale – as the lasses do at Hallowe'en – "in to mysel".' Arrived at Mauchline, Burns installed Jean Armour in a lodging, and prevailed on Mrs Armour to promise her help and countenance in the approaching confinement. This was kind at least; but hear his expressions: 'I have taken her a room; I have taken her to my arms; I have given her a mahogany bed; I have given her a guinea . . . I swore her privately and solemnly never to attempt any claim on me as a husband, even though anybody should persuade her she had such a claim – which she has not, neither during my life nor after my death. She did all this like a good girl.' And then he took advantage of the situation. To Clarinda he wrote: 'I this morning called for a certain woman. I am disgusted with her; I cannot endure her;' and he accused her of 'tasteless insipidity, vulgarity of soul, and mercenary fawning.' This was already in March; by the thirteenth of that month he was back in Edinburgh. On the 17th, he wrote to Clarinda: 'Your hopes, your fears, your cares, my love, are mine; so don't mind them. I will take you in my hand through the dreary wilds of this world, and scare away the ravening bird or beast that would annoy you.' Again, on the 21st: 'Will you open, with satisfaction and delight, a letter from a man who loves you, who has loved you, and who will love you, to death, through death, and for ever. . . How rich am I to have such a treasure as you! . . . "The Lord God knoweth," and, perhaps, "Israel he shall know," my love and your merit. Adieu, Clarinda! I am going to remember you in my prayers.' By the 7th of April, seventeen days later, he had already decided to make Jean Armour publicly his wife.

A more astonishing stage-trick is not to be found. And yet his conduct is seen, upon a nearer examination, to be grounded both in reason and in kindness. He was now about to embark on a solid worldly career; he had taken a farm; the affair with Clarinda, however gratifying to his heart, was too contingent to offer any great consolation to a man like Burns, to whom marriage must have seemed the very dawn of hope and self-respect. This is to regard the question from its lowest aspect; but there is no doubt that he entered on this new period of his life with a sincere determination to do right. He had just helped his brother with a loan of a hundred and eighty pounds; should he do nothing for the poor girl whom he had ruined? It was true he could not do as he did without brutally wounding Clarinda; that was the punishment of his bygone fault; he was, as he truly says, 'damned with a choice only of different species of error and misconduct.' To be professional Don Juan, to accept the provocation of any lively lass upon the village green, may thus lead a man through a series of detestable words and actions, and land him at last in an undesired and most unsuitable union for life. If he had been strong enough to refrain or bad enough to persevere in evil; if he had only not been Don Juan at all, or been Don Juan altogether, there had been some possible road for him throughout this troublesome world; but a man, alas! who is equally at the call of his worse and better instincts, stands among changing events without foundation or resource.[1]

DOWNWARD COURSE

It may be questionable whether any marriage could have tamed Burns; but it is at least certain that there was no hope for him in the marriage he contracted. He did right, but then he had done wrong before; it was, as I said, one of those relations in life which it seems equally wrong to break or to perpetuate. He neither loved nor respected his wife. 'God knows,' he writes, 'my choice was as random as blind man's buff.' He consoles himself by the thought that he has acted kindly to her; that she 'has the most sacred enthusiasm of attachment to him;' that she has a good figure; that she has a 'wood-note wild,' 'her voice rising with ease to B natural,' no less. The effect on the reader is one of unmingled pity for both parties concerned. This was not the wife who (in his own words)

[1]For the love affairs see, in particular, Mr Scott Douglas's edition under the different dates.

could 'enter into his favourite studies or relish his favourite authors;' this was not even a wife, after the affair of the marriage lines, in whom a husband could joy to place his trust. Let her manage a farm with sense, let her voice rise to B natural all day long, she would still be a peasant to her lettered lord, and an object of pity rather than of equal affection. She could now be faithful, she could now be forgiving, she could now be generous even to a pathetic and touching degree; but coming from one who was unloved, and who had scarce shown herself worthy of the sentiment, these were all virtues thrown away, which could neither change her husband's heart nor affect the inherent destiny of their relation. From the outset, it was a marriage that had no root in nature; and we find him, ere long, lyrically regretting Highland Mary, renewing correspondence with Clarinda in the warmest language, on doubtful terms with Mrs Riddel, and on terms unfortunately beyond any question with Anne Park.

Alas! this was not the only ill circumstance in his future. He had been idle for some eighteen months, superintending his new edition, hanging on to settle with the publisher, travelling in the Highlands with Willie Nichol, or philandering with Mrs M'Lehose; and in this period the radical part of the man had suffered irremediable hurt. He had lost his habits of industry, and formed the habit of pleasure. Apologetical biographers assure us of the contrary; but from the first, he saw and recognised the danger for himself; his mind, he writes, is 'enervated to an alarming degree' by idleness and dissipation; and again, 'my mind has been vitiated with idleness.' It never fairly recovered. To business he could bring the required diligence and attention without difficulty; but he was thenceforward incapable, except in rare instances, of that superior effort of concentration which is required for serious literary work. He may be said, indeed, to have worked no more, and only amused himself with letters. The man who had written a volume of masterpieces in six months, during the remainder of his life rarely found courage for any more sustained effort than a song. And the nature of the songs is itself characteristic of these idle later years; for they are often as polished and elaborate as his earlier works were frank, and headlong, and colloquial; and this sort of verbal elaboration in short flights is, for a man of literary turn, simply the most agreeable of pastimes. The change in manner coincides exactly with the Edinburgh visit. In 1786 he had written the *Address to a Louse*, which may be taken as an extreme instance of the first manner; and already, in 1787, we come upon the rosebud pieces to Miss Cruikshank, which are extreme examples of the second. The change was, therefore, the direct and very natural consequence of his great change in life; but it is not the less typical of his loss of moral courage that he should have given up all larger ventures, nor the less melancholy that a man who first attacked literature with a hand that seemed capable of moving mountains, should have spent his later years in whittling cherry-stones.

Meanwhile, the farm did not prosper; he had to join to it the salary of an exciseman; at last he had to give it up, and rely altogether on the latter resource. He was an active officer; and, though he sometimes tempered severity with mercy, we have local testimony oddly representing the public feeling of the period, that, while 'in everything else he was a perfect gentleman, when he met with anything seizable he was no better than any other gauger.'

There is but one manifestation of the man in these last years which need delay us: and that was the sudden interest in politics which arose from his sympathy with the great French Revolution. His only political feeling had been hitherto a sentimental Jacobitism, not more or less respectable than that of Scott, Aytoun, and the rest of what George Borrow has nicknamed the 'Charlie over the water' Scotchmen. It was a sentiment almost entirely literary and picturesque in its origin, built on ballads and the adventures of the Young Chevalier; and in Burns it is the more excusable, because he lay out of the way of active politics in his youth. With the great French Revolution, something living, practical, and feasible appeared to him for the first time in this realm of human action. The young ploughman who had desired so earnestly to rise, now reached out his sympathies to a whole nation animated with the same desire. Already in 1788 we find the old Jacobitism hand in hand with the new popular doctrine, when, in a letter of indignation against the zeal of a Whig clergyman, he writes: 'I daresay the American Congress in 1776 will be allowed to be as able and as enlightened as the English Convention was in 1688; and that their posterity will celebrate the centenary of their deliverance from us, as duly and sincerely as we do ours from the oppressive measures of the wrong-headed house of Stuart.' As time wore on, his sentiments grew more pronounced and even violent; but there was a basis of sense and generous feeling to his hottest excess. What he asked was a fair chance for the individual in life; an open road to success and distinction for all classes of men. It was in the same spirit that he had helped to found a public library in the parish where his farm was situated, and that he sang his fervent snatches against tyranny and tyrants. Witness, were it alone, this verse: –

> Here's freedom to him that wad read,
> Here's freedom to him that wad write;
> There's nane ever feared that the truth should be heard
> But them wham the truth wad indite.

Yet his enthusiasm for the cause was scarce guided by wisdom. Many stories are preserved of the bitter and unwise words he used in country coteries; how he proposed Washington's health as an amendment to Pitt's, gave as a toast 'the last verse of the last chapter of Kings,' and celebrated Dumouriez in a doggerel impromptu full of ridicule and hate. Now his sympathies would inspire him with *Scots, wha hae*; now involve him in a drunken broil with a loyal officer, and consequent apologies and explanations, hard to offer for a man of Burns's stomach. Nor was this the front of his offending. On February 27, 1792, he took part in the capture of an armed smuggler, bought at the subsequent sale four carronades, and despatched them with a letter to the French Assembly. Letter and guns were stopped at Dover by the English officials; there was trouble for Burns with his superiors; he was reminded firmly, however delicately, that, as a paid official, it was his duty to obey and to be silent; and all the blood of this poor, proud, and falling man must have rushed to his head at the humiliation. His letter to Mr Erskine, subsequently Earl of Mar, testifies, in its turgid, turbulent phrases, to a perfect passion of alarmed self-respect and vanity. He had been muzzled, and muzzled, when all was said, by his paltry salary as an exciseman; alas! had he not a family to keep? Already, he wrote, he looked forward to some such judgement from a hackney scribbler as this: 'Burns, notwithstanding the *fanfaronnade* of independence to be found in his works, and after having been held forth to view and to public estimation as a man of some genius, yet, quite destitute of resources within himself to support his borrowed dignity, he dwindled into a paltry exciseman, and shrunk out the rest of his insignificant existence in the meanest of pursuits, and among the vilest of mankind.' And then on he goes, in a style of rhodomontade, but filled with living indignation, to declare his right to a political opinion, and his willingness to shed his blood for the political birthright of his sons. Poor, perturbed spirit! he was indeed exercised in vain; those who share and those who differ from his sentiments about the Revolution, alike understand and sympathise with him in this painful strait; for poetry and human manhood are lasting like the race, and politics, which are but a wrongful striving after right, pass and change from year to year and age to age. The *Twa Dogs* has already outlasted the constitution of Siéyès and the policy of the Whigs; and Burns is better known among English-speaking races than either Pitt or Fox.

Meanwhile, whether as a man, a husband, or a poet, his steps led downward. He knew, knew bitterly, that the best was out of him; he refused to make another volume, for he felt that it would be a disappointment; he grew petulantly alive to criticism, unless he was sure it reached him from a friend. For his songs, he would take nothing; they were all that he could do; the proposed Scotch play, the proposed series of Scotch tales in verse, all had gone to water; and in a fling of pain and disappointment, which is surely noble with the nobility of a viking, he would rather stoop to borrow than to accept money for these last and inadequate efforts of his muse. And this desperate abnegation rises at times near to the height of madness; as when he pretended that he had not written, but only found and published, his immortal *Auld Lang Syne*. In the same spirit he became more scrupulous as an artist; he was doing so little, he would fain do that little well; and about two months before his death, he asked Thomson to send back all his manuscripts for revisal, saying that he would rather write five songs to his taste than twice that number otherwise. The battle of his life was lost; in forlorn efforts to do well, in desperate submissions to evil, the last years flew by. His temper is dark and explosive, launching epigrams, quarrelling with his friends, jealous of young puppy officers. He tries to be a good father; he boasts himself a libertine. Sick, sad, and jaded, he can refuse no occasion of temporary pleasure, no opportunity to shine; and he who had once refused the invitations of lords and ladies is now whistled to the inn by any curious stranger. His death (July 21, 1796), in his thirty-seventh year, was indeed a kindly dispensation. It is the fashion to say he died of drink; many a man has drunk more and yet lived with reputation, and reached a good age. That drink and debauchery helped to destroy his constitution, and were the means of his unconscious suicide, is doubtless true; but he had failed in life, had lost his power of work, and was already married to the poor, unworthy, patient Jean, before he had shown his inclination to convivial nights, or at least before that inclination had become dangerous either to his health or his self-respect. He had trifled with life, and must pay the penalty. He had chosen to be Don Juan, he had grasped at temporary pleasures, and substantial happiness and solid industry had passed him by. He died of being Robert Burns, and there is no levity in such a statement of the case; for shall we not, one and all, deserve a similar epitaph?

WORKS

The somewhat cruel necessity which has lain upon me throughout this paper only to touch upon those points in the life of Burns where correction or amplification seemed desirable, leaves me little opportunity to speak of the works which have made his name so famous. Yet, even here, a few observations seem necessary.

At the time when the poet made his appearance and great first success, his work was remarkable in two ways. For, first, in an age when poetry had become abstract and conventional, instead of continuing to deal with shepherds, thunderstorms, and personifications, he dealt with the actual circumstances of his life, however matter-of-fact and sordid these might be. And, second, in a time when English versification was particularly stiff, lame, and feeble, and words were used with ultra-academical timidity, he wrote verses that were easy, racy, graphic, and forcible, and used language with absolute tact and courage as it seemed most fit to give a clear impression. If you take even those English authors whom we know Burns to have most admired and studied, you will see at once that he owed them nothing but a warning. Take Shenstone, for instance, and watch that elegant author as he tries to grapple with the facts of life. He has a description, I remember, of a gentleman engaged in sliding or walking on thin ice, which is a little miracle of incompetence. You see my memory fails me, and I positively cannot recollect whether his hero was sliding or walking; as though a writer should describe a skirmish, and the reader, at the end, be still uncertain whether it were a charge of cavalry or a slow and stubborn advance of foot. There could be no such ambiguity in Burns; his work is at the opposite pole from such indefinite and stammering performances; and a whole lifetime passed in the study of Shenstone would only lead a man further and further from writing the *Address to a Louse*. Yet Burns, like most great artists, proceeded from a school and continued a tradition; only the school and tradition were Scotch, and not English. While the English language was becoming daily more pedantic and inflexible, and English letters more colourless and slack, there was another dialect in the sister country, and a different school of poetry tracing its descent, through King James I, from Chaucer. The dialect alone accounts for much; for it was then written colloquially, which kept it fresh and supple; and, although not shaped for heroic flights, it was a direct and vivid medium for all that had to do with social life. Hence, whenever Scotch poets left their laborious imitations of bad English verses, and fell back on their own dialect, their style would kindle, and they would write of their convivial and somewhat gross existences with pith and point. In Ramsay, and far more in the poor lad Fergusson, there was mettle, humour, literary courage, and a power of saying what they wished to say definitely and brightly, which in the latter case should have justified great anticipations. Had Burns died at the same age as Fergusson, he would have left us literally nothing worth remark. To Ramsay and to Fergusson, then, he was indebted in a very uncommon degree, not only following their tradition and using their measures, but directly and avowedly imitating their pieces. The same tendency to borrow a hint, to work on someone else's foundation, is notable in Burns from first to last, in the period of song-writing as well as in that of the early poems; and strikes one oddly in a man of such deep originality, who left so strong a print on all he touched, and whose work is so greatly distinguished by that character of 'inevitability' which Wordsworth denied to Goethe.

When we remember Burns's obligations to his predecessors, we must never forget his immense advances on them. They had already 'discovered' nature; but Burns discovered poetry – a higher and more intense way of thinking of the things that go to make up nature, a higher and more ideal key of words in which to speak of them. Ramsay and Fergusson excelled at making a popular – or shall we say vulgar? – sort of society verses, comical and prosaic, written, you would say, in taverns while a supper party waited for its laureate's word; but on the appearance of Burns, this coarse and laughing literature was touched to finer issues, and learned gravity of thought and natural pathos.

What he had gained from his predecessors was a direct, speaking style, and to walk on his own feet instead of on academical stilts. There was never a man of letters with more absolute command of his means; and we may say of him, without excess, that his style was his slave. Hence that energy of epithet, so concise and telling, that a foreigner is tempted to explain it by some special richness or aptitude in the dialect he wrote. Hence that Homeric justice and completeness of description which gives us the very physiognomy of nature, in body and detail, as nature is. Hence, too, the unbroken literary quality of his best pieces, which keeps him from any slip into the weariful trade of word-painting, and presents everything, as everything should be presented by the art of words, in a clear, continuous medium of thought. Principal Shairp, for instance, gives us a paraphrase of one tough verse of the original; and for those who know the Greek poets only by paraphrase, this has the very quality they are accustomed to look for and admire in Greek. The contemporaries of Burns were surprised that he should visit so many celebrated mountains and waterfalls, and not seize the opportunity to make a poem. Indeed, it is not for those who have a true command of the art of words, but for peddling, professional amateurs, that these pointed occasions are most useful and inspiring. As those who speak French imperfectly are glad to dwell on any topic they may have talked upon or heard others talk upon before, because they know appropriate words for it in French, so the dabbler in verse rejoices to behold a waterfall, because he has learned the sentiment and knows appropriate words for it in poetry. But the dialect of Burns was fitted to deal with any subject; and whether it was a stormy night, a shepherd's collie, a sheep struggling in the snow, the conduct of cowardly soldiers in the field, the gait and cogitations of a drunken man, or only a village cockcrow in the morning, he could find language to give it freshness, body, and relief. He was always ready to borrow the hint of a design, as though he had a difficulty in commencing – a difficulty, let us say, in choosing a subject out of a world which seemed all equally living and significant to him; but once he had the subject chosen, he could cope with nature single-handed, and make every stroke a triumph. Again, his absolute mastery in his art enabled him to express each and all of his different humours, and to pass smoothly and congruously from one to another. Many men invent a dialect for only one side of their nature – perhaps their pathos or their humour, or the delicacy of their senses – and, for lack of a medium, leave all the others unexpressed. You meet such an one, and find him in conversation full of thought, feeling, and experience, which he has lacked the art to employ in his writings. But Burns was not thus hampered in the practice of the literary art; he could throw the whole weight of his nature into his work, and impregnate it from end to end. If Doctor Johnson, that stilted and accomplished stylist, had lacked the sacred Boswell, what should we have known of him? and how should we have delighted in his acquaintance as we do? Those who spoke with Burns tell us how much we have lost who did not. But I think they exaggerate their privilege: I think we have the whole Burns in our possession set forth in his consummate verses.

It was by his style, and not by his matter, that he affected Wordsworth and the world. There is, indeed, only one merit worth considering in a man of letters – that he should write well; and only one damning fault – that he should write ill. We are little the better for the reflections of the sailor's parrot in the story. And so, if Burns helped to change the course of literary history, it was by his frank, direct, and masterly utterance, and not by his homely choice of subjects. That was imposed upon him, not chosen upon a principle. He wrote from his own experience, because it was his nature so to do, and the tradition of the school from which he proceeded was fortunately not opposed to homely subjects. But to these homely subjects he communicated the rich commentary of his nature; they were all steeped in Burns; and they interest us not in themselves, but because they have been passed through the spirit of so genuine and vigorous a man. Such is the stamp of living literature; and there was never any more alive than that of Burns.

What a gust of sympathy there is in him sometimes flowing out in byways hitherto unused, upon mice, and flowers, and the devil himself; sometimes speaking plainly between human hearts; sometimes ringing out in exultation like a peal of bells! When we compare the *Farmer's Salutation to his Auld Mare Maggie*, with the clever and inhumane production of half a century earlier, *The Auld Man's Mare's dead*, we see in a nutshell the spirit of the change introduced by Burns. And as to its manner, who that has read it can forget how the collie, Luath, in the *Twa Dogs*, describes and enters into the merry-making in the cottage?

> The luntin' pipe an' sneeshin' mill,
> Are handed round wi' richt guid will;
> The canty auld folks crackin' crouse,
> The young anes rantin' through the house –
> My heart has been sae fain to see them
> That I for joy hae barkit wi' them.

It was this ardent power of sympathy that was fatal to so many women, and, through Jean Armour, to himself at last. His humour comes from him in a stream so deep and easy that I will venture to call him the best of humorous poets. He turns about in the midst to utter a noble sentiment or a trenchant remark on human life, and the style changes and rises to the occasion. I think it is Principal Shairp who says, happily, that Burns would have been no Scotchman if he had not loved to moralise; neither, may we add, would he have been his father's son; but (what is worthy of note) his moralisings are to a large extent the moral of his own career. He was among the least impersonal of artists. Except in the *Jolly Beggars*, he shows no gleam of dramatic instinct. Mr Carlyle has complained that *Tam o' Shanter* is, from the absence of this quality, only a picturesque and external piece of work; and I may add that in the *Twa Dogs* it is precisely in the infringement of dramatic propriety that a great deal of the humour of the speeches depends for its existence and effect. Indeed, Burns was so full of his identity that it breaks forth on every page; and there is scarce an appropriate remark either in praise or blame of his own conduct, but he has put it himself into verse. Alas! for the tenor of these remarks! They are, indeed, his own pitiful apology for such a marred existence and talents so misused and stunted; and they seem to prove for ever how small a part is played by reason in the conduct of man's affairs. Here was one, at least, who with unfailing judgement predicted his own fate; yet his knowledge could not avail him, and with open eyes he must fulfil his tragic destiny. Ten years before the end he had written his epitaph; and neither subsequent events, nor the critical eyes of posterity, have shown us a word in it to alter. And, lastly, has he not put in for himself the last unanswerable plea? –

> Then gently scan your brother man,
>   Still gentler sister woman;
> Though they may gang a kennin wrang,
>   To step aside is human;
> One point must still be greatly dark –

THE OLD PACIFIC CAPITAL

THE WOODS AND THE PACIFIC

The Bay of Monterey has been compared by no less a person than General Sherman to a bent fishing-hook; and the comparison, if less important than the march through Georgia, still shows the eye of a soldier for topography. Santa Cruz sits exposed at the shank; the mouth of the Salinas river is at the middle of the bend; and Monterey itself is cosily ensconced beside the barb. Thus the ancient capital of California faces across the bay, while the Pacific Ocean, though hidden by low hills and forest, bombards her left flank and rear with never-dying surf. In front of the town, the long line of sea-beach trends north and north-west, and then westward to enclose the bay. The waves which lap so quietly about the jetties of Monterey grow louder and larger in the distance; you can see the breakers leaping high and white by day; at night, the outline of the shore is traced in transparent silver by the moonlight and the flying foam; and from all round, even in quiet weather, the low, distant, thrilling roar of the Pacific hangs over the coast and the adjacent country like smoke above a battle.

These long beaches are enticing to the idle man. It would be hard to find a walk more solitary and at the same time more exciting to the mind. Crowds of ducks and sea-gulls hover over the sea. Sandpipers trot in and out by troops after the retiring waves, trilling together in a chorus of infinitesimal song. Strange sea-tangles, new to the European eye, the bones of whales, or sometimes a whole whale's carcase, white with carrion-gulls and poisoning the wind, lie scattered here and there along the sands. The waves come in slowly, vast and green, curve their translucent necks, and burst with a surprising uproar, that runs, waxing and waning, up and down the long key-board of the beach. The foam of these great ruins mounts in an instant to the ridge of the sand glacis, swiftly fleets back again, and is met and buried by the next breaker. The interest is perpetually fresh. On no other coast that I know shall you enjoy, in calm, sunny weather, such a spectacle of Ocean's greatness, such beauty of changing colour, or such degrees of thunder in the sound. The very air is more than usually salt by this Homeric deep.

Inshore, a tract of sand-hills borders on the beach. Here and there a lagoon, more or less brackish, attracts the birds and hunters. A rough, spotty undergrowth partially conceals the sand. The crouching, hardy, live-oaks flourish singly or in thickets – the kind of wood for murderers to crawl among – and here and there the skirts of the forest extend downward from the hills with a floor of turf and long aisles of pine-trees hung with Spaniard's Beard. Through this quaint desert the railway cars drew near to Monterey from the junction at Salinas City – though that and so many other things are now for ever altered – and it was from here that you had the first view of the old township lying in the sands, its white windmills bickering in the chill, perpetual wind, and the first fogs of the evening drawing drearily around it from the sea.

The one common note of all this country is the haunting presence of the ocean. A great faint sound of breakers follows you high up into the inland cañons; the roar of water dwells in the clean, empty rooms of Monterey as in a shell upon the chimney; go where you will, you have but to pause and listen to hear the voice of the Pacific. You pass out of the town to the south-west, and mount the hill among pine woods. Glade, thicket, and grove surround you. You follow winding sandy tracks that lead nowhither. You see a deer; a multitude of quail arises. But the sound of the sea still follows you as you advance, like that of wind among the trees, only harsher and stranger to the ear; and when at length you gain the summit, out breaks on every hand and with freshened vigour that same unending distant, whispering rumble of the ocean; for now you are on the top of Monterey peninsula, and the noise no longer only mounts to you from behind along the beach towards Santa Cruz, but from your right also, round by Chinatown and Pinos lighthouse, and from down before you to the mouth of the Carmello river. The whole woodland is begirt with thundering surges. The silence that immediately surrounds you where you stand is not so much broken as it is haunted by this distant, circling rumour. It sets your senses upon edge; you strain your attention; you are clearly and unusually conscious of small sounds near at hand; you walk listening like an Indian hunter; and that voice of the Pacific is a sort of disquieting company to you in your walk.

When once I was in these woods I found it difficult to turn homeward. All woods lure a rambler onward; but in those of Monterey it was the surf that particularly invited me to prolong my walks. I would push straight for the shore where I thought it to be nearest. Indeed, there was scarce a direction that would not, sooner or later, have brought me forth on the Pacific. The emptiness of the woods gave me a sense of freedom and discovery in these excursions. I never in all my visits met but one man. He was a Mexican, very dark of hue, but smiling and fat, and he carried an axe, though his true business at that moment was to seek for straying cattle. I asked him what o'clock it was, but he seemed neither to know nor care; and when he in his turn asked me for news of his cattle, I showed myself equally indifferent. We stood and smiled upon each other for a few seconds, and then turned without a word and took our several ways across the forest.

One day – I shall never forget it – I had taken a trail that was new to me. After a while the woods began to open, the sea to sound nearer hand. I came upon a road, and, to my surprise, a stile. A step or two farther, and, without leaving the woods, I found myself among trim houses. I walked through street after street, parallel and at right angles, paved with sward and dotted with trees, but still undeniable streets, and each with its name posted at the corner, as in a real town. Facing down the main thoroughfare – 'Central Avenue,' as it was ticketed – I saw an open-air temple, with benches and sounding-board, as though for an orchestra. The houses were all tightly shuttered; there was no smoke, no sound but of the waves, no moving thing. I have never been in any place that seemed so dreamlike. Pompeii is all in a bustle with visitors, and its antiquity and strangeness deceive the imagination; but this town had plainly not been built above a year or two, and perhaps had been deserted overnight. Indeed, it was not so much like a deserted town as like a scene upon the stage by daylight, and with no one on the boards. The barking of a dog led me at last to the only house still occupied, where a Scotch pastor and his wife pass the winter alone in this empty theatre. The place was 'The Pacific Camp Grounds, the Christian Seaside Resort.' Thither, in the warm season, crowds come to enjoy a life of teetotalism, religion, and flirtation, which I am willing to think blameless and agreeable. The neighbourhood at least is well selected. The Pacific booms in front. Westward is Point Pinos, with the lighthouse in a wilderness of sand, where you will find the lightkeeper playing the piano, making models and bows and arrows, studying dawn and sunrise in amateur oil-painting, and with a dozen other elegant pursuits and interests to surprise his brave, old-country rivals. To the east, and still nearer, you will come upon a space of open down, a hamlet, a haven among rocks, a world of surge and screaming seagulls. Such scenes are very similar in different climates; they appear homely to the eyes of all; to me this was like a dozen spots in Scotland. And yet the boats that ride in the haven are of strange outlandish design; and, if you walk into the hamlet, you will behold costumes and faces and hear a tongue that are unfamiliar to the memory. The joss-stick burns, the opium pipe is smoked, the floors are strewn with slips of coloured paper – prayers, you would say, that had somehow missed their destination – and a man guiding his upright pencil from right to left across the sheet, writes home the news of Monterey to the Celestial Empire.

The woods and the Pacific rule between them the climate of this seaboard region. On the streets of Monterey, when the air does not smell salt from the one, it will be blowing perfumed from the resinous tree-tops of the other. For days together a hot, dry air will overhang the town, close as from an oven, yet healthful and aromatic in the nostrils. The cause is not far to seek, for the woods are afire, and the hot wind is blowing from the hills. These fires are one of the great dangers of California. I have seen from Monterey as many as three at the same time, by day a cloud of smoke, by night a red coal of conflagration in the distance. A little thing will start them, and, if the wind be favourable, they gallop over miles of country faster than a horse. The inhabitants must turn out and work like demons, for it is not only the pleasant groves that are destroyed; the climate and the soil are equally at stake, and these fires prevent the rains of the next winter and dry up perennial fountains. California has been a land of promise in its time, like Palestine; but if the woods continue so swiftly to perish, it may become, like Palestine, a land of desolation.

To visit the woods while they are languidly burning is a strange piece of experience. The fire passes through the underbrush at a run. Every here and there a tree flares up instantaneously from root to summit, scattering tufts of flame, and is quenched, it seems, as quickly. But this last is only in semblance. For after this first squib-like conflagration of the dry moss and twigs, there remains behind a deep-rooted and consuming fire in the very entrails of the tree. The resin of the pitch-pine is principally condensed at the base of the bole and in the spreading roots. Thus, after the light, showy, skirmishing flames, which are only as the match to the explosion, have already scampered down the wind into the distance, the true harm is but beginning for this giant of the woods. You may approach the tree from one side, and see it, scorched indeed from top to bottom, but apparently survivor of the peril. Make the circuit, and there, on the other side of the column, is a clear mass of living coal, spreading like an ulcer; while underground, to their most extended fibre, the roots are being eaten out by fire, and the smoke is rising through the fissures to the surface. A little while, and, without a nod of warning, the huge pine-tree snaps off short across the ground and falls prostrate with a crash. Meanwhile the fire continues its silent business; the roots are reduced to a fine ash; and long afterwards, if you pass by, you will find the earth pierced with radiating galleries, and preserving the design of all these subterranean spurs, as though it were the mould for a new tree instead of the print of an old one. These pitch-pines of Monterey are, with the single exception of the Monterey cypress, the most fantastic of forest trees. No words can give an idea of the contortion of their growth; they might figure without change in a circle of the nether hell as Dante pictured it; and at the rate at which trees grow, and at which forest fires spring up and gallop through the hills of California, we may look forward to a time when there will not be one of them left standing in that land of their nativity. At least they have not so much to fear from the axe, but perish by what may be called a natural although a violent death; while it is man in his short-sighted greed that robs the country of the nobler redwood. Yet a little while and perhaps all the hills of seaboard California may be as bald as Tamalpais.

I have an interest of my own in these forest fires, for I came so near to lynching on one occasion, that a braver man might have retained a thrill from the experience. I wished to be certain whether it was the moss, that quaint funereal ornament of Californian forests, which blazed up so rapidly when the flame first touched the tree. I suppose I must have been under the influence of Satan, for instead of plucking off a piece for my experiment, what should I do but walk up to a great pine-tree in a portion of the wood which had escaped so much as scorching, strike a match, and apply the flame gingerly to one of the tassels. The tree went off simply like a rocket; in three seconds it was a roaring pillar of fire. Close by I could hear the shouts of those who were at work combating the original conflagration. I could see the waggon that had brought them tied to a live oak in a piece of open; I could even catch the flash of an axe as it swung up through the underwood into the sunlight. Had anyone observed the result of my experiment my neck was literally not worth a pinch of snuff; after a few minutes of passionate expostulation I should have been run up to a convenient bough.

To die for faction is a common evil;
But to be hanged for nonsense is the devil.

I have run repeatedly, but never as I ran that day. At night I went out of town, and there was my own particular fire, quite distinct from the other, and burning as I thought with even greater vigour.

But it is the Pacific that exercises the most direct and obvious power upon the climate. At sunset, for months together, vast, wet, melancholy fogs arise and come shoreward from the ocean. From the hill-top above Monterey the scene is often noble, although it is always sad. The upper air is still bright with sunlight; a glow still rests upon the Gabelano Peak; but the fogs are in possession of the lower levels; they crawl in scarves among the sandhills; they float, a little higher, in clouds of a gigantic size and often of a wild configuration; to the south, where they have struck the seaward shoulder of the mountains of Santa Lucia, they double back and spire up skyward like smoke. Where their shadow touches, colour dies out of the world. The air grows chill and deadly as they advance. The trade-wind freshens, the trees begin to sigh, and all the windmills in Monterey are whirling and creaking and filling their cisterns with the brackish water of the sands. It takes but a little while till the invasion is complete. The sea, in its lighter order, has submerged the earth. Monterey is curtained in for the night in thick, wet, salt, and frigid clouds, so to remain till day returns; and before the sun's rays they slowly disperse and retreat in broken squadrons to the bosom of the sea. And yet often when the fog is thickest and most chill, a few steps out of the town and up the slope, the night will be dry and warm and full of inland perfume.

MEXICANS, AMERICANS, AND INDIANS

The history of Monterey has yet to be written. Founded by Catholic missionaries, a place of wise beneficence to Indians, a place of arms, a Mexican capital continually wrested by one faction from another, an American capital when the first House of Representatives held its deliberations, and then falling lower and lower from the capital of the State to the capital of a county, and from that again, by the loss of its charter and town lands, to a mere bankrupt village, its rise and decline is typical of that of all Mexican institutions and even Mexican families in California.

Nothing is stranger in that strange State than the rapidity with which the soil has changed hands. The Mexicans, you may say, are all poor and landless, like their former capital; and yet both it and they hold themselves apart and preserve their ancient customs and something of their ancient air.

The town, when I was there, was a place of two or three streets, economically paved with sea-sand, and two or three lanes, which were watercourses in the rainy season, and were, at all times, rent up by fissures four or five feet deep. There were no street lights. Short sections of wooden sidewalk only added to the dangers of the night, for they were often high above the level of the roadway, and no one could tell where they would be likely to begin or end. The houses were, for the most part, built of unbaked adobe brick, many of them old for so new a country, some of very elegant proportions, with low, spacious, shapely rooms, and walls so thick that the heat of summer never dried them to the heart. At the approach of the rainy season a deathly chill and a graveyard smell began to hang about the lower floors; and diseases of the chest are common and fatal among house-keeping people of either sex.

There was no activity but in and around the saloons, where people sat almost all day long playing cards. The smallest excursion was made on horseback. You would scarcely ever see the main street without a horse or two tied to posts, and making a fine figure with their Mexican housings. It struck me oddly to come across some of the *Cornhill* illustrations to Mr Blackmore's *Erema*, and see all the characters astride on English saddles. As a matter of fact, an English saddle is a rarity even in San Francisco, and, you may say, a thing unknown in all the rest of California. In a place so exclusively Mexican as Monterey, you saw not only Mexican saddles but true Vaquero riding – men always at the hand-gallop up hill and down dale, and round the sharpest corner, urging their horses with cries and gesticulations and cruel rotatory spurs, checking them dead with a touch, or wheeling them right-about-face in a square yard. The type of face and character of bearing are surprisingly un-American. The first ranged from something like the pure Spanish, to something, in its sad fixity, not unlike the pure Indian, although I do not suppose there was one pure blood of either race in all the country. As for the second, it was a matter of perpetual surprise to find, in that world of absolutely mannerless Americans, a people full of deportment, solemnly courteous, and doing all things with grace and decorum. In dress they ran to colour and bright sashes. Not even the most Americanised could always resist the temptation to stick a red rose into his hatband. Not even the most Americanised would descend to wear the vile dress hat of civilisation. Spanish was the language of the streets. It was difficult to get along without a word or two of that language for an occasion. The only communications in which the population joined were with a view to amusement. A weekly public ball took place with great etiquette, in addition to the numerous fandangoes in private houses. There was a really fair amateur brass band. Night after night serenaders would be going about the street, sometimes in a company and with several instruments and voices together, sometimes severally, each guitar before a different window. It was a strange thing to lie awake in nineteenth-century America, and hear the guitar accompany, and one of these old, heart-breaking Spanish love songs mount into the night air, perhaps in a deep baritone, perhaps in that high-pitched, pathetic, womanish alto which is so common among Mexican men, and which strikes on the unaccustomed ear as something not entirely human but altogether sad.

The town, then, was essentially and wholly Mexican; and yet almost all the land in the neighbourhood was held by Americans, and it was from the same class, numerically so small, that the principal officials were selected. This Mexican and that Mexican would describe to you his old family estates, not one rood of which remained to him. You would ask him how that came about, and elicit some tangled story back-foremost, from which you gathered that the Americans had been greedy like designing men, and the Mexicans greedy like children, but no other certain fact. Their merits and their faults contributed alike to the ruin of the former landholders. It is true they were improvident, and easily dazzled with the sight of ready money; but they were gentlefolk besides, and that in a way which curiously unfitted them to combat Yankee craft. Suppose they have a paper to sign, they would think it a reflection on the other party to examine the terms with any great minuteness; nay, suppose them to observe some doubtful clause, it is ten to one they would refuse from delicacy to object to it. I know I am speaking within the mark, for I have seen such a case occur, and the Mexican, in spite of the advice of his lawyer, has signed the imperfect paper like a lamb. To have spoken in the matter, he said, above all to have let the other party guess that he had seen a lawyer, would have 'been like doubting his word.' The scruple sounds oddly to one of ourselves, who have been brought up to understand all business as a competition in fraud, and honesty itself to be a virtue which regards the carrying out but not the creation of agreements. This single unworldly trait will account for much of that revolution of which we are speaking. The Mexicans have the name of being great swindlers, but certainly the accusation cuts both ways. In a contest of this sort, the entire booty would scarcely have passed into the hands of the more scrupulous race.

Physically the Americans have triumphed; but it is not entirely seen how far they have themselves been morally conquered. This is, of course, but a part of a part of an extraordinary problem now in the course of being solved in the various States of the American Union. I am reminded of an anecdote. Some years ago, at a great sale of wine, all the odd lots were purchased by a grocer in a small way in the old town of Edinburgh. The agent had the curiosity to visit him some time after and inquire what possible use he could have for such material. He was shown, by way of answer, a huge vat where all the liquors, from humble Gladstone to imperial Tokay, were fermenting together. 'And what,' he asked, 'do you propose to call this?' 'I'm no very sure,' replied the grocer, 'but I think it's going to turn out port.' In the older Eastern States, I think we may say that this hotch-potch of races is going to turn out English, or thereabout. But the problem is indefinitely varied in other zones. The elements are differently mingled in the south, in what we may call the Territorial belt, and in the group of States on the Pacific coast. Above all, in these last, we may look to see some monstrous hybrid – whether good or evil, who shall forecast? but certainly original and all their own. In my little restaurant at Monterey, we have sat down to table day after day, a Frenchman, two Portuguese, an Italian, a Mexican, and a Scotchman: we had for common visitors an American from Illinois, a nearly pure blood Indian woman, and a naturalised Chinese; and from time to time a Switzer and a German came down from country ranches for the night. No wonder that the Pacific coast is a foreign land to visitors from the Eastern States, for each race contributes something of its own. Even the despised Chinese have taught the youth of California, none indeed of their virtues, but the debasing use of opium. And chief among these influences is that of the Mexicans.

The Mexicans although in the State are out of it. They still preserve a sort of international independence, and keep their affairs snug to themselves. Only four or five years ago Vasquez, the bandit, his troops being dispersed and the hunt too hot for him in other parts of California, returned to his native Monterey, and was seen publicly in her streets and saloons, fearing no man. The year that I was there there occurred two reputed murders. As the Montereyans are exceptionally vile speakers of each other and of everyone behind his back, it is not possible for me to judge how much truth there may have been in these reports; but in the one case everyone believed, and in the other some suspected, that there had been foul play; and nobody dreamed for an instant of taking the authorities into their counsel. Now this is, of course, characteristic enough of the Mexicans; but it is a noteworthy feature that all the Americans in Monterey acquiesced without a word in this inaction. Even when I spoke to them upon the subject, they seemed not to understand my surprise; they had forgotten the traditions of their own race and upbringing, and become, in a word, wholly Mexicanised.

Again, the Mexicans, having no ready money to speak of, rely almost entirely in their business transactions upon each other's worthless paper. Pedro the penniless pays you with an IOU from the equally penniless Miguel. It is a sort of local currency by courtesy. Credit in these parts has passed into a superstition. I have seen a strong, violent man struggling for months to recover a debt, and getting nothing but an exchange of waste paper. The very storekeepers are averse to asking for cash payments, and are more surprised than pleased when they are offered. They fear there must be something under it, and that you mean to withdraw your custom from them. I have seen the enterprising chemist and stationer begging me with fervour to let my account run on, although I had my purse open in my hand; and partly from the commonness of the case, partly from some remains of that generous old Mexican tradition which made all men welcome to their tables, a person may be notoriously both unwilling and unable to pay, and still find credit for the necessaries of life in the stores of Monterey. Now this villainous habit of living upon 'tick' has grown into Californian nature. I do not mean that the American and European storekeepers of Monterey are as lax as Mexicans; I mean that American farmers in many parts of the State expect unlimited credit, and profit by it in the meanwhile, without a thought for consequences. Jew storekeepers have already learned the advantage to be gained from this; they lead on the farmer into irretrievable indebtedness, and keep him ever after as their bond-slave hopelessly grinding in the mill. So the whirligig of time brings in its revenges, and except that the Jew knows better than to foreclose, you may see Americans bound in the same chains with which they themselves had formerly bound the Mexican. It seems as if certain sorts of follies, like certain sorts of grain, were natural to the soil rather than to the race that holds and tills it for the moment.

In the meantime, however, the Americans rule in Monterey County. The new county seat, Salinas City, in the bald, corn-bearing plain under the Gabelano Peak, is a town of a purely American character. The land is held, for the most part, in those enormous tracts which are another legacy of Mexican days, and form the present chief danger and disgrace of California; and the holders are mostly of American or British birth. We have here in England no idea of the troubles and inconveniences which flow from the existence of these large landholders – land-thieves, land-sharks, or land-grabbers, they are more commonly and plainly called. Thus the townlands of Monterey are all in the hands of a single man. How they came there is an obscure, vexatious question, and, rightly or wrongly, the man is hated with a great hatred. His life has been repeatedly in danger. Not very long ago, I was told, the stage was stopped and examined three evenings in succession by disguised horsemen thirsting for his blood. A certain house on the Salinas road, they say, he always passes in his buggy at full speed, for the squatter sent him warning long ago. But a year since he was publicly pointed out for death by no less a man than Mr Dennis Kearney. Kearney is a man too well known in California, but a word of explanation is required for English readers. Originally an Irish drayman, he rose, by his command of bad language, to almost dictatorial authority in the State; throned it there for six months or so, his mouth full of oaths, gallowses, and conflagrations; was first snuffed out last winter by Mr Coleman, backed by his San Francisco Vigilantes and three gatling guns; completed his own ruin by throwing in his lot with the grotesque Greenbacker party; and had at last to be rescued by his old enemies, the police, out of the hands of his rebellious followers. It was while he was at the top of his fortune that Kearney visited Monterey with his battle-cry against Chinese labour, the railroad monopolists, and the land-thieves; and his one articulate counsel to the Montereyans was to 'hang David Jacks.' Had the town been American, in my private opinion, this would have been done years ago. Land is a subject on which there is no jesting in the West, and I have seen my friend the lawyer drive out of Monterey to adjust a competition of titles with the face of a captain going into battle and his Smith-and-Wesson convenient to his hand.

On the ranche of another of these landholders you may find our old friend, the truck system, in full operation. Men live there, year in year out, to cut timber for a nominal wage, which is all consumed in supplies. The longer they remain in this desirable service the deeper they will fall in debt – a burlesque injustice in a new country, where labour should be precious, and one of those typical instances which explains the prevailing discontent and the success of the demagogue Kearney.

In a comparison between what was and what is in California, the praisers of times past will fix upon the Indians of Carmel. The valley drained by the river so named is a true Californian valley, bare, dotted with chaparal, overlooked by quaint, unfinished hills. The Carmel runs by many pleasant farms, a clear and shallow river, loved by wading kine; and at last, as it is falling towards a quicksand and the great Pacific, passes a ruined mission on a hill. From the mission church the eye embraces a great field of ocean, and the ear is filled with a continuous sound of distant breakers on the shore. But the day of the Jesuit has gone by, the day of the Yankee has succeeded, and there is no one left to care for the converted savage. The church is roofless and ruinous, sea-breezes and sea-fogs, and the alternation of the rain and sunshine, daily widening the breaches and casting the crockets from the wall. As an antiquity in this new land, a quaint specimen of missionary architecture, and a memorial of good deeds, it had a triple claim to preservation from all thinking people; but neglect and abuse have been its portion. There is no sign of American interference, save where a headboard has been torn from a grave to be a mark for pistol bullets. So it is with the Indians for whom it was erected. Their lands, I was told, are being yearly encroached upon by the neighbouring American proprietor, and with that exception no man troubles his head for the Indians of Carmel. Only one day in the year, the day before our Guy Fawkes, the *padre* drives over the hill from Monterey; the little sacristy, which is the only covered portion of the church, is filled with seats and decorated for the service; the Indians troop together, their bright dresses contrasting with their dark and melancholy faces; and there, among a crowd of somewhat unsympathetic holiday-makers, you may hear God served with perhaps more touching circumstances than in any other temple under heaven. An Indian, stone-blind and about eighty years of age, conducts the singing; other Indians compose the choir; yet they have the Gregorian music at their finger ends, and pronounce the Latin so correctly that I could follow the meaning as they sang. The pronunciation was odd and nasal, the singing hurried and staccato. 'In sæcula sæculo-ho-horum,' they went, with a vigorous aspirate to every additional syllable. I have never seen faces more vividly lit up with joy than the faces of these Indian singers. It was to them not only the worship of God, nor an act by which they recalled and commemorated better days, but was besides an exercise of culture, where all they knew of art and letters was united and expressed. And it made a man's heart sorry for the good fathers of yore who had taught them to dig and to reap, to read and to sing, who had given them European mass-books which they still preserve and study in their cottages, and who had now passed away from all authority and influence in that land – to be succeeded by greedy land-thieves and sacrilegious pistol-shots. So ugly a thing may our Anglo-Saxon Protestantism appear beside the doings of the Society of Jesus.

But revolution in this world succeeds to revolution. All that I say in this paper is in a paulo-past tense. The Monterey of last year exists no longer. A huge hotel has sprung up in the desert by the railway. Three sets of diners sit down successively to table. Invaluable toilettes figure along the beach and between the live oaks; and Monterey is advertised in the newspapers, and posted in the waiting-rooms at railway stations, as a resort for wealth and fashion. Alas for the little town! it is not strong enough to resist the influence of the flaunting caravanserai, and the poor, quaint, penniless native gentlemen of Monterey must perish, like a lower race, before the millionaire vulgarians of the Big Bonanza.

SAMUEL PEPYS

In two books a fresh light has recently been thrown on the character and position of Samuel Pepys. Mr Mynors Bright has given us a new transcription of the Diary, increasing it in bulk by near a third, correcting many errors, and completing our knowledge of the man in some curious and important points. We can only regret that he has taken liberties with the author and the public. It is no part of the duties of the editor of an established classic to decide what may or may not be 'tedious to the reader.' The book is either an historical document or not, and in condemning Lord Braybrooke Mr Bright condemns himself. As for the time-honoured phrase, 'unfit for publication,' without being cynical, we may regard it as the sign of a precaution more or less commercial; and we may think, without being sordid, that when we purchase six huge and distressingly expensive volumes, we are entitled to be treated rather more like scholars and rather less like children. But Mr Bright may rest assured: while we complain, we are still grateful. Mr Wheatley, to divide our obligation, brings together, clearly and with no lost words, a body of illustrative material. Sometimes we might ask a little more; never, I think, less. And as a matter of fact, a great part of Mr Wheatley's volume might be transferred, by a good editor of Pepys, to the margin of the text, for it is precisely what the reader wants.

In the light of these two books, at least, we have now to read our author. Between them they contain all we can expect to learn for, it may be, many years. Now, if ever, we should be able to form some notion of that unparalleled figure in the annals of mankind – unparalleled for three good reasons: first, because he was a man known to his contemporaries in a halo of almost historical pomp, and to his remote descendants with an indecent familiarity, like a tap-room comrade; second, because he has outstripped all competitors in the art or virtue of a conscious honesty about oneself; and, third, because, being in many ways a very ordinary person, he has yet placed himself before the public eye with such a fulness and such an intimacy of detail as might be envied by a genius like Montaigne. Not then for his own sake only, but as a character in a unique position, endowed with a unique talent, and shedding a unique light upon the lives of the mass of mankind, he is surely worthy of prolonged and patient study.

THE DIARY

That there should be such a book as Pepys's Diary is incomparably strange. Pepys, in a corrupt and idle period, played the man in public employments, toiling hard and keeping his honour bright. Much of the little good that is set down to James the Second comes by right to Pepys; and if it were little for a king, it is much for a subordinate. To his clear, capable head was owing somewhat of the greatness of England on the seas. In the exploits of Hawke, Rodney, or Nelson, this dead Mr Pepys of the Navy Office had some considerable share. He stood well by his business in the appalling plague of 1666. He was loved and respected by some of the best and wisest men in England. He was President of the Royal Society; and when he came to die, people said of his conduct in that solemn hour – thinking it needless to say more – that it was answerable to the greatness of his life. Thus he walked in dignity, guards of soldiers sometimes attending him in his walks, subalterns bowing before his periwig; and when he uttered his thoughts they were suitable to his state and services. On February 8, 1668, we find him writing to Evelyn, his mind bitterly occupied with the late Dutch war, and some thoughts of the different story of the repulse of the Great Armada:

Sir, you will not wonder at the backwardness of my thanks for the present you made me, so many days since, of the Prospect of the Medway, while the Hollander rode master in it, when I have told you that the sight of it hath led me to such reflections on my particular interest, by my employment, in the reproach due to that miscarriage, as have given me little less disquiet than he is fancied to have who found his face in Michael Angelo's hell. The same should serve me also in excuse for my silence in celebrating your mastery shown in the design and draught, did not indignation rather than courtship urge me so far to commend them, as to wish the furniture of our House of Lords changed from the story of '88 to that of '67 (of Evelyn's designing), till the pravity of this were reformed to the temper of that age, wherein God Almighty found his blessings more operative than, I fear, he doth in ours his judgments.

This is a letter honourable to the writer, where the meaning rather than the words is eloquent. Such was the account he gave of himself to his contemporaries; such thoughts he chose to utter, and in such language: giving himself out for a grave and patriotic public servant. We turn to the same date in the Diary by which he is known, after two centuries, to his descendants. The entry begins in the same key with the letter, blaming the 'madness of the House of Commons' and 'the base proceedings, just the epitome of all our public proceedings in this age, of the House of Lords;' and then, without the least transition, this is how our diarist proceeds:

To the Strand, to my bookseller's, and there bought an idle, rogueish French book, *L'escholle des Filles*, which I have bought in plain binding, avoiding the buying of it better bound, because I resolve, as soon as I have read it, to burn it, that it may not stand in the list of books, nor among them, to disgrace them, if it should be found.

Even in our day, when responsibility is so much more clearly apprehended, the man who wrote the letter would be notable; but what about the man, I do not say who bought a roguish book, but who was ashamed of doing so, yet did it, and recorded both the doing and the shame in the pages of his daily journal?

We all, whether we write or speak, must somewhat drape ourselves when we address our fellows; at a given moment we apprehend our character and acts by some particular side; we are merry with one, grave with another, as befits the nature and demands of the relation. Pepys's letter to Evelyn would have little in common with that other one to Mrs Knipp which he signed by the pseudonym of *Dapper Dicky*; yet each would be suitable to the character of his correspondent. There is no untruth in this, for man, being a Protean animal, swiftly shares and changes with his company and surroundings; and these changes are the better part of his education in the world. To strike a posture once for all, and to march through life like a drum-major, is to be highly disagreeable to others and a fool for oneself into the bargain. To Evelyn and to Knipp we understand the double facing; but to whom was he posing in the Diary, and what, in the name of astonishment, was the nature of the pose? Had he suppressed all mention of the book, or had he bought it, gloried in the act, and cheerfully recorded his glorification, in either case we should have made him out. But no; he is full of precautions to conceal the 'disgrace' of the purchase, and yet speeds to chronicle the whole affair in pen and ink. It is a sort of anomaly in human action, which we can exactly parallel from another part of the Diary.

Mrs Pepys had written a paper of her too just complaints against her husband, and written it in plain and very pungent English. Pepys, in an agony lest the world should come to see it, brutally seizes and destroys the tell-tale document; and then – you disbelieve your eyes – down goes the whole story with unsparing truth and in the cruellest detail. It seems he has no design but to appear respectable, and here he keeps a private book to prove he was not. You are at first faintly reminded of some of the vagaries of the morbid religious diarist; but at a moment's thought the resemblance disappears. The design of Pepys is not at all to edify; it is not from repentance that he chronicles his peccadilloes, for he tells us when he does repent, and, to be just to him, there often follows some improvement. Again, the sins of the religious diarist are of a very formal pattern, and are told with an elaborate whine. But in Pepys you come upon good, substantive misdemeanours; beams in his eye of which he alone remains unconscious; healthy outbreaks of the animal nature, and laughable subterfuges to himself that always command belief and often engage the sympathies.

Pepys was a young man for his age, came slowly to himself in the world, sowed his wild oats late, took late to industry, and preserved till nearly forty the headlong gusto of a boy. So, to come rightly at the spirit in which the Diary was written, we must recall a class of sentiments which with most of us are over and done before the age of twelve. In our tender years we still preserve a freshness of surprise at our prolonged existence; events make an impression out of all proportion to their consequence; we are unspeakably touched by our own past adventures, and look forward to our future personality with sentimental interest. It was something of this, I think, that clung to Pepys. Although not sentimental in the abstract, he was sweetly sentimental about himself. His own past clung about his heart, an evergreen. He was the slave of an association. He could not pass by Islington, where his father used to carry him to cakes and ale, but he must light at the 'King's Head' and eat and drink 'for remembrance of the old house sake.' He counted it good fortune to lie a night at Epsom to renew his old walks, 'where Mrs Hely and I did use to walk and talk, with whom I had the first sentiments of love and pleasure in a woman's company, discourse and taking her by the hand, she being a pretty woman.' He goes about weighing up the *Assurance*, which lay near Woolwich under water, and cries in a parenthesis, 'Poor ship, that I have been twice merry in, in Captain Holland's time;' and after revisiting the *Naseby*, now changed into the *Charles*, he confesses 'it was a great pleasure to myself to see the ship that I began my good fortune in.' The stone that he was cut for he preserved in a case; and to the Turners he kept alive such gratitude for their assistance that for years, and after he had begun to mount himself into higher zones, he continued to have that family to dinner on the anniversary of the operation. Not Hazlitt nor Rousseau had a more romantic passion for their past, although at times they might express it more romantically; and if Pepys shared with them this childish fondness, did not Rousseau, who left behind him the *Confessions*, or Hazlitt, who wrote the *Liber Amoris*, and loaded his essays with loving personal detail, share with Pepys in his unwearied egotism? For the two things go hand in hand; or, to be more exact, it is the first that makes the second either possible or pleasing.

But, to be quite in sympathy with Pepys, we must return once more to the experience of children. I can remember to have written, in the fly-leaf of more than one book, the date and the place where I then was – if, for instance, I was ill in bed or sitting in a certain garden; these were jottings for my future self; if I should chance on such a note in after years, I thought it would cause me a particular thrill to recognise myself across the intervening distance. Indeed, I might come upon them now, and not be moved one tittle – which shows that I have comparatively failed in life, and grown older than Samuel Pepys. For in the Diary we can find more than one such note of perfect childish egotism; as when he explains that his candle is going out, 'which makes me write thus slobberingly;' or as in this incredible particularity, 'To my study, where I only wrote thus much of this day's passages to this *, and so out again;' or lastly, as here, with more of circumstance: 'I staid up till the bellman came by with his bell under my window, *as I was writing of this very line*, and cried, "Past one of the clock, and a cold, frosty, windy morning."' Such passages are not to be misunderstood. The appeal to Samuel Pepys years hence is unmistakable. He desires that dear, though unknown, gentleman keenly to realise his predecessor; to remember why a passage was uncleanly written; to recall (let us fancy, with a sigh) the tones of the bellman, the chill of the early, windy morning, and the very line his own romantic self was scribing at the moment. The man, you will perceive, was making reminiscences – a sort of pleasure by ricochet, which comforts many in distress, and turns some others into sentimental libertines: and the whole book, if you will but look at it in that way, is seen to be a work of art to Pepys's own address.

Here, then, we have the key to that remarkable attitude preserved by him throughout his Diary, to that unflinching – I had almost said, that unintelligent – sincerity which makes it a miracle among human books.

He was not unconscious of his errors – far from it; he was often startled
into shame, often reformed, often made and broke his vows of change.
But whether he did ill or well, he was still his own unequalled self; still
that entrancing *ego* of whom alone he cared to write; and still sure of his
own affectionate indulgence, when the parts should be changed, and the
writer come to read what he had written. Whatever he did, or said, or
thought, or suffered, it was still a trait of Pepys, a character of his
career; and as, to himself, he was more interesting than Moses or than
Alexander, so all should be faithfully set down. I have called his Diary a
work of art. Now when the artist has found something, word or deed,
exactly proper to a favourite character in play or novel, he will neither
suppress nor diminish it, though the remark be silly or the act mean. The
hesitation of Hamlet, the credulity of Othello, the baseness of Emma
Bovary, or the irregularities of Mr Swiveller, caused neither disappointment nor disgust to their creators. And so with Pepys and his adored
protagonist; adored not blindly, but with trenchant insight and
enduring, human toleration. I have gone over and over the greater part
of the Diary; and the points where, to the most suspicious scrutiny, he
has seemed not perfectly sincere, are so few, so doubtful, and so petty,
that I am ashamed to name them. It may be said that we all of us write
such a diary in airy characters upon our brain; but I fear there is a
distinction to be made; I fear that as we render to our consciousness an
account of our daily fortunes and behaviour, we too often weave a tissue
of romantic compliments and dull excuses; and even if Pepys were the
ass and coward that men call him, we must take rank as sillier and more
cowardly than he. The bald truth about oneself, what we are all too
timid to admit when we are not too dull to see it, that was what he saw
clearly and set down unsparingly.

It is improbable that the Diary can have been carried on in the same
single spirit in which it was begun. Pepys was not such an ass, but he
must have perceived, as he went on, the extraordinary nature of the
work he was producing. He was a great reader, and he knew what other
books were like. It must, at least, have crossed his mind that someone
might ultimately decipher the manuscript, and he himself, with all his
pains and pleasures, be resuscitated in some later day; and the thought,
although discouraged, must have warmed his heart. He was not such an
ass, besides, but he must have been conscious of the deadly explosives,
the gun-cotton and the giant powder, he was hoarding in his drawer. Let
some contemporary light upon the Journal, and Pepys was plunged for

ever in social and political disgrace. We can trace the growth of his terrors by two facts. In 1660, while the Diary was still in its youth, he tells about it, as a matter of course, to a lieutenant in the navy; but in 1669, when it was already near an end, he could have bitten his tongue out, as the saying is, because he had let slip his secret to one so grave and friendly as Sir William Coventry. And from two other facts I think we may infer that he had entertained, even if he had not acquiesced in, the thought of a far-distant publicity. The first is of capital importance: the Diary was not destroyed. The second – that he took unusual precautions to confound the cipher in 'rogueish' passages – proves, beyond question, that he was thinking of some other reader besides himself. Perhaps while his friends were admiring the 'greatness of his behaviour' at the approach of death, he may have had a twinkling hope of immortality. *Mens cujusque is est quisque*, said his chosen motto; and, as he had stamped his mind with every crook and foible in the pages of the Diary, he might feel that what he left behind him was indeed himself. There is perhaps no other instance so remarkable of the desire of man for publicity and an enduring name. The greatness of his life was open, yet he longed to communicate its smallness also; and, while contemporaries bowed before him, he must buttonhole posterity with the news that his periwig was once alive with nits. But this thought, although I cannot doubt he had it, was neither his first nor his deepest; it did not colour one word that he wrote; and the Diary, for as long as he kept it, remained what it was when he began, a private pleasure for himself. It was his bosom secret; it added a zest to all his pleasures; he lived in and for it, and might well write these solemn words, when he closed that confidant for ever:

And so I betake myself to that course which is almost as much as to see myself go into the grave; for which, and all the discomforts that will accompany my being blind, the good God prepare me.

A LIBERAL GENIUS

Pepys spent part of a certain winter Sunday, when he had taken physic, composing 'a song in praise of a liberal genius (such as I take my own to be) to all studies and pleasures.' The song was unsuccessful, but the Diary is, in a sense, the very song that he was seeking; and his portrait by Hales, so admirably reproduced in Mynors Bright's edition, is a confirmation of the Diary. Hales, it would appear, had known his business; and though he put his sitter to a deal of trouble, almost breaking his neck 'to have the portrait full of shadows,' and draping him in an Indian gown hired expressly for the purpose, he was preoccupied about no merely picturesque effects, but to portray the essence of the man. Whether we read the picture by the Diary or the Diary by the picture, we shall at least agree that Hales was among the number of those who can 'surprise the manners in the face.' Here we have a mouth pouting, moist with desires; eyes greedy, protuberant, and yet apt for weeping too; a nose great alike in character and dimensions; and altogether a most fleshly, melting countenance. The face is attractive by its promise of reciprocity. I have used the word *greedy*, but the reader must not suppose that he can change it for that closely kindred one of *hungry*, for there is here no aspiration, no waiting for better things, but an animal joy in all that comes. It could never be the face of an artist; it is the face of a *viveur* – kindly, pleased and pleasing, protected from excess and upheld in contentment by the shifting versatility of his desires. For a single desire is more rightly to be called a lust; but there is health in a variety, where one may balance and control another.

The whole world, town or country, was to Pepys a garden of Armida. Wherever he went his steps were winged with the most eager expectation; whatever he did, it was done with the most lively pleasure. An insatiable curiosity in all the shows of the world and all the secrets of knowledge, filled him brimful of the longing to travel, and supported him in the toils of study. Rome was the dream of his life; he was never happier than when he read or talked of the Eternal City. When he was in Holland, he was 'with child' to see any strange thing. Meeting some friends and singing with them in a palace near the Hague, his pen fails him to express his passion of delight, 'the more so because in a heaven of pleasure and in a strange country.' He must go to see all famous executions. He must needs visit the body of a murdered man, defaced 'with a broad wound,' he says, 'that makes my hand now shake to write of it.' He learned to dance, and was 'like to make a dancer.' He learned to sing, and walked about Gray's Inn Fields 'humming to myself (which is now my constant practice) the trillo.' He learned to play the lute, the flute, the flageolet, and the theorbo, and it was not the fault of his intention if he did not learn the harpsichord or the spinet. He learned to compose songs, and burned to give forth 'a scheme and theory of music not yet ever made in the world.' When he heard 'a fellow whistle like a bird exceeding well,' he promised to return another day and give an angel for a lesson in the art. Once, he writes, 'I took the Bezan back with me, and with a brave gale and tide reached up that night to the Hope, taking great pleasure in learning the seamen's manner of singing when they sound the depths.' If he found himself rusty in his Latin grammar, he must fall to it like a schoolboy. He was a member of Harrington's Club till its dissolution, and of the Royal Society before it had received the name. Boyle's *Hydrostatics* was 'of infinite delight' to him, walking in Barnes Elms. We find him comparing Bible concordances, a captious judge of sermons, deep in Descartes and Aristotle. We find him, in a single year, studying timber and the measurement of timber; tar and oil, hemp, and the process of preparing cordage; mathematics and accounting; the hull and the rigging of ships from a model; and 'looking and improving himself of the (naval) stores with' — hark to the fellow! — 'great delight.' His familiar spirit of delight was not the same with Shelley's; but how true it was to him through life! He is only copying something, and behold, he 'takes great pleasure to rule the lines, and have the capital words wrote with red ink;' he has only had his coal-cellar emptied and cleaned, and behold, 'it do please him exceedingly.' A hog's harslett is 'a piece of meat he loves.' He cannot ride home in my Lord Sandwich's coach, but he must exclaim, with breathless gusto, 'his noble, rich coach.' When he is bound for a supper party, he anticipates a 'glut of pleasure.' When he has a new watch, 'to see my childishness,' says he, 'I could not forbear carrying it in my hand and seeing what o'clock it was an hundred times.' To go to Vauxhall, he says, and 'to hear the nightingales and other birds, hear fiddles, and there a harp and here a Jew's trump, and here laughing, and there fine people walking, is mighty divertising.' And the nightingales, I take it, were particularly dear to him; and it was again 'with great pleasure' that he paused to hear them as he walked to Woolwich, while the fog was rising and the April sun broke through.

He must always be doing something agreeable, and, by preference, two agreeable things at once. In his house he had a box of carpenter's tools, two dogs, an eagle, a canary, and a blackbird that whistled tunes, lest, even in that full life, he should chance upon an empty moment. If he had to wait for a dish of poached eggs, he must put in the time by playing on the flageolet; if a sermon were dull, he must read in the book of Tobit or divert his mind with sly advances on the nearest women. When he walked, it must be with a book in his pocket to beguile the way in case the nightingales were silent; and even along the streets of London, with so many pretty faces to be spied for and dignitaries to be saluted, his trail was marked by little debts 'for wine, pictures, etc.,' the true headmark of a life intolerant of any joyless passage. He had a kind of idealism in pleasure; like the princess in the fairy story, he was conscious of a rose-leaf out of place. Dearly as he loved to talk, he could not enjoy nor shine in a conversation when he thought himself unsuitably dressed. Dearly as he loved eating, he 'knew not how to eat alone;' pleasure for him must heighten pleasure; and the eye and ear must be flattered like the palate ere he avow himself content. He had no zest in a good dinner when it fell to be eaten 'in a bad street and in a periwig-maker's house;' and a collation was spoiled for him by indifferent music. His body was indefatigable, doing him yeoman's service in this breathless chase of pleasures. On April 11, 1662, he mentions that he went to bed 'weary, *which I seldom am*;' and already over thirty, he would sit up all night cheerfully to see a comet. But it is never pleasure that exhausts the pleasure-seeker; for in that career, as in all others, it is failure that kills. The man who enjoys so wholly and bears so impatiently the slightest widowhood from joy, is just the man to lose a night's rest over some paltry question of his right to fiddle on the leads, or to be 'vexed to the blood' by a solecism in his wife's attire; and we find in consequence that he was always peevish when he was hungry, and that his head 'aked mightily' after a dispute. But nothing could divert him from his aim in life; his remedy in care was the same as his delight in prosperity; it was with pleasure, and with pleasure only, that he sought to drive out sorrow; and, whether he was jealous of his wife or skulking from a bailiff, he would equally take refuge in the theatre. There, if the house be full and the company noble, if the songs be tunable, the actors perfect, and the play diverting, this odd hero of the secret Diary, this private self-adorer, will speedily be healed of his distresses.

Equally pleased with a watch, a coach, a piece of meat, a tune upon the fiddle, or a fact in hydrostatics, Pepys was pleased yet more by the beauty, the worth, the mirth, or the mere scenic attitude in life of his fellow-creatures. He shows himself throughout a sterling humanist. Indeed, he who loves himself, not in idle vanity, but with a plenitude of knowledge, is the best equipped of all to love his neighbours. And perhaps it is in this sense that charity may be most properly said to begin at home. It does not matter what quality a person has: Pepys can appreciate and love him for it. He 'fills his eyes' with the beauty of Lady Castlemaine; indeed, he may be said to dote upon the thought of her for years; if a woman be good-looking and not painted, he will walk miles to have another sight of her; and even when a lady by a mischance spat upon his clothes, he was immediately consoled when he had observed that she was pretty. But, on the other hand, he is delighted to see Mrs Pett upon her knees, and speaks thus of his Aunt James: 'a poor, religious, well-meaning, good soul, talking of nothing but God Almighty, and that with so much innocence that mightily pleased me.' He is taken with Pen's merriment and loose songs, but not less taken with the sterling worth of Coventry. He is jolly with a drunken sailor, but listens with interest and patience, as he rides the Essex roads, to the story of a Quaker's spiritual trials and convictions. He lends a critical ear to the discourse of kings and royal dukes. He spends an evening at Vauxhall with 'Killigrew and young Newport – loose company,' says he, 'but worth a man's being in for once, to know the nature of it, and their manner of talk and lives.' And when a rag-boy lights him home, he examines him about his business and other ways of livelihood for destitute children. This is almost half-way to the beginning of philanthropy; had it only been the fashion, as it is at present, Pepys had perhaps been a man famous for good deeds. And it is through this quality that he rises, at times, superior to his surprising egotism; his interest in the love affairs of others is, indeed, impersonal; he is filled with concern for my Lady Castlemaine, whom he only knows by sight, shares in her very jealousies, joys with her in her successes; and it is not untrue, however strange it seems in his abrupt presentment, that he loved his maid Jane because she was in love with his man Tom.

Let us hear him, for once, at length:

So the women and W. Hewer and I walked upon the Downes, where a flock of sheep was; and the most pleasant and innocent sight that ever I saw in my life. We found a shepherd and his little boy reading, far from any houses or sight of people, the Bible to him; so I made the boy read to me, which he did with the forced tone that children do usually read, that was mighty pretty; and then I did give him something, and went to the father, and talked with him. He did content himself mightily in my liking his boy's reading, and did bless God for him, the most like one of the old patriarchs that ever I saw in my life, and it brought those thoughts of the old age of the world in my mind for two or three days after. We took notice of his woolen knit stockings of two colours mixed, and of his shoes shod with iron, both at the toe and heels, and with great nails in the soles of his feet, which was mighty pretty; and taking notice of them, 'Why,' says the poor man, 'the downes, you see, are full of stones, and we are faine to shoe ourselves thus; and these,' says he, 'will make the stones fly till they ring before me.' I did give the poor man something, for which he was mighty thankful, and I tried to cast stones with his horne crooke. He values his dog mightily, that would turn a sheep any way which he would have him, when he goes to fold them; told me there was about eighteen score sheep in his flock, and that he hath four shillings a week the year round for keeping of them; and Mrs. Turner, in the common fields here, did gather one of the prettiest nosegays that ever I saw in my life.

And so the story rambles on to the end of that day's pleasuring; with cups of milk, and glowworms, and people walking at sundown with their wives and children, and all the way home Pepys still dreaming 'of the old age of the world' and the early innocence of man. This was how he walked through life, his eyes and ears wide open, and his hand, you will observe, not shut; and thus he observed the lives, the speech, and the manners of his fellow-men, with prose fidelity of detail and yet a lingering glamour of romance.

It was 'two or three days after' that he extended this passage in the pages of his Journal, and the style has thus the benefit of some reflection. It is generally supposed that, as a writer, Pepys must rank at the bottom of the scale of merit. But a style which is indefatigably lively, telling, and picturesque through six large volumes of everyday experience, which deals with the whole matter of a life, and yet is rarely wearisome, which condescends to the most fastidious particulars, and yet sweeps all away in the forthright current of the narrative, – such a style may be ungrammatical, it may be inelegant, it may be one tissue of mistakes, but it can never be devoid of merit. The first and the true function of the writer has been thoroughly performed throughout; and though the manner of his utterance may be childishly awkward, the matter has been transformed and assimilated by his unfeigned interest and delight. The gusto of the man speaks out fierily after all these years. For the difference between Pepys and Shelley, to return to that half-whimsical approxima-tion, is one of quality but not one of degree; in his sphere, Pepys felt as keenly, and his is the true prose of poetry – prose because the spirit of the man was narrow and earthly, but poetry because he was delightedly alive. Hence, in such a passage as this about the Epsom shepherd, the result upon the reader's mind is entire conviction and unmingled pleasure. So, you feel, the thing fell out, not otherwise; and you would no more change it than you would change a sublimity of Shakespeare's, a homely touch of Bunyan's, or a favoured reminiscence of your own.

There never was a man nearer being an artist, who yet was not one. The tang was in the family; while he was writing the journal for our enjoyment in his comely house in Navy Gardens, no fewer than two of his cousins were tramping the fens, kit under arm, to make music to the country girls. But he himself, though he could play so many instruments and pass judgement in so many fields of art, remained an amateur. It is not given to anyone so keenly to enjoy, without some greater power to understand. That he did not like Shakespeare as an artist for the stage may be a fault, but it is not without either parallel or excuse. He certainly admired him as a poet; he was the first beyond mere actors on the rolls of that innumerable army who have got 'To be or not to be' by heart. Nor was he content with that; it haunted his mind; he quoted it to himself in the pages of the Diary, and, rushing in where angels fear to tread, he set it to music. Nothing, indeed, is more notable than the heroic quality of the verses that our little sensualist in a periwig chose out to marry with his own mortal strains. Some gust from brave Elizabethan times must have warmed his spirit, as he sat tuning his sublime theorbo. 'To be or not to be. Whether 'tis nobler' – 'Beauty retire, thou dost my pity move' – 'It is decreed, nor shall thy fate, O Rome;' – open and dignified in the sound, various and majestic in the sentiment, it was no inapt, as it was certainly no timid, spirit that selected such a range of themes. Of 'Gaze not on Swans,' I know no more than these four words; yet that also seems to promise well. It was, however, on a probable suspicion, the work of his master, Mr Berkenshaw – as the drawings that figure at the breaking up of a young ladies' seminary are the work of the professor attached to the establishment. Mr Berkenshaw was not altogether happy in his pupil. The amateur cannot usually rise into the artist, some leaven of the world still clogging him; and we find Pepys behaving like a pickthank to the man who taught him composition. In relation to the stage, which he so warmly loved and understood, he was not only more hearty, but more generous to others. Thus he encounters Colonel Reames, 'a man,' says he, 'who understands and loves a play as well as I, and I love him for it.' And again, when he and his wife had seen a most ridiculous insipid piece, 'Glad we were,' he writes, 'that Betterton had no part in it.' It is by such a zeal and loyalty to those who labour for his delight that the amateur grows worthy of the artist. And it should be kept in mind that, not only in art, but in morals, Pepys rejoiced to recognise his betters. There was not one speck of envy in the whole human-hearted egotist.

RESPECTABILITY

When writers inveigh against respectability, in the present degraded meaning of the word, they are usually suspected of a taste for clay pipes and beer cellars; and their performances are thought to hail from the *Owl's Nest* of the comedy. They have something more, however, in their eye than the dulness of a round million dinner parties that sit down yearly in old England. For to do anything because others do it, and not because the thing is good, or kind, or honest in its own right, is to resign all moral control and captaincy upon yourself, and go post-haste to the devil with the greater number. We smile over the ascendency of priests; but I had rather follow a priest than what they call the leaders of society. No life can better than that of Pepys illustrate the dangers of this respectable theory of living. For what can be more untoward than the occurrence, at a critical period and while the habits are still pliable, of such a sweeping transformation as the return of Charles the Second? Round went the whole fleet of England on the other tack; and while a few tall pintas, Milton or Pen, still sailed a lonely course by the stars and their own private compass, the cock-boat, Pepys, must go about with the majority among 'the stupid starers and the loud huzzas.'

The respectable are not led so much by any desire of applause as by a positive need for countenance. The weaker and the tamer the man, the more will he require this support; and any positive quality relieves him, by just so much, of this dependence. In a dozen ways, Pepys was quite strong enough to please himself without regard for others; but his positive qualities were not co-extensive with the field of conduct; and in many parts of life he followed, with gleeful precision, in the footprints of the contemporary Mrs Grundy. In morals, particularly, he lived by the countenance of others; felt a slight from another more keenly than a meanness in himself; and then first repented when he was found out. You could talk of religion or morality to such a man; and by the artist side of him, by his lively sympathy and apprehension, he could rise, as it were dramatically, to the significance of what you said. All that matter in religion which has been nicknamed other-worldliness was strictly in his gamut; but a rule of life that should make a man rudely virtuous, following right in good report and ill report, was foolishness and a stumbling-block to Pepys. He was much thrown across the Friends; and nothing can be more instructive than his attitude towards these most interesting people of that age. I have mentioned how he conversed with one as he rode; when he saw some brought from a meeting under arrest, 'I would to God,' said he, 'they would either conform, or be more wise and not be catched;' and to a Quaker in his own office he extended a timid though effectual protection. Meanwhile there was growing up next door to him that beautiful nature, William Pen. It is odd that Pepys condemned him for a fop; odd, though natural enough when you see Pen's portrait, that Pepys was jealous of him with his wife. But the cream of the story is when Pen publishes his *Sandy Foundation Shaken*, and Pepys has it read aloud by his wife. 'I find it,' he says, 'so well writ as, I think, it is too good for him ever to have writ it; and it is a serious sort of book, and *not fit for everybody to read*.' Nothing is more galling to the merely respectable than to be brought in contact with religious ardour. Pepys had his own foundation, sandy enough, but dear to him from practical considerations, and he would read the book with true uneasiness of spirit; for conceive the blow if, by some plaguy accident, this Pen were to convert him! It was a different kind of doctrine that he judged profitable for himself and others.

A good sermon of Mr. Gifford's at our church, upon 'Seek ye first the kingdom of heaven.' A very excellent and persuasive, good and moral sermon. He showed, like a wise man, that righteousness is a surer moral way of being rich than sin and villainy.

It is thus that respectable people desire to have their Greathearts address them, telling, in mild accents, how you may make the best of both worlds, and be a moral hero without courage, kindness, or troublesome reflection; and thus the Gospel, cleared of Eastern metaphor, becomes a manual of worldly prudence, and a handybook for Pepys and the successful merchant.

The respectability of Pepys was deeply grained. He has no idea of truth except for the Diary. He has no care that a thing shall be, if it but appear; gives out that he has inherited a good estate, when he has seemingly got nothing but a lawsuit; and is pleased to be thought liberal when he knows he has been mean. He is conscientiously ostentatious. I say conscientiously, with reason. He could never have been taken for a fop, like Pen, but arrayed himself in a manner nicely suitable to his position. For long he hesitated to assume the famous periwig; for a public man should travel gravely with the fashions, not foppishly before, nor dowdily behind, the central movement of his age. For long he durst not keep a carriage; that, in his circumstances, would have been improper; but a time comes, with the growth of his fortune, when the impropriety has shifted to the other side, and he is 'ashamed to be seen in a hackney.' Pepys talked about being 'a Quaker or some very melancholy thing;' for my part, I can imagine nothing so melancholy, because nothing half so silly, as to be concerned about such problems.

But so respectability and the duties of society haunt and burden their poor devotees; and what seems at first the very primrose path of life, proves difficult and thorny like the rest. And the time comes to Pepys, as to all the merely respectable, when he must not only order his pleasures, but even clip his virtuous movements, to the public pattern of the age. There was some juggling among officials to avoid direct taxation; and Pepys, with a noble impulse, growing ashamed of this dishonesty, designed to charge himself with £1000; but finding none to set him an example, 'nobody of our ablest merchants' with this moderate liking for clean hands, he judged it 'not decent;' he feared it would 'be thought vain glory;' and, rather than appear singular, cheerfully remained a thief. One able merchant's countenance, and Pepys had dared to do an honest act! Had he found one brave spirit, properly recognised by society, he might have gone far as a disciple. Mrs Turner, it is true, can fill him full of sordid scandal, and make him believe, against the testimony of his senses, that Pen's venison pasty stank like the devil; but, on the other hand, Sir William Coventry can raise him by a word into another being. Pepys, when he is with Coventry, talks in the vein of an old Roman. What does he care for office or emolument? 'Thank God, I have enough of my own,' says he, 'to buy me a good book and a good fiddle, and I have a good wife.' And again, we find this pair projecting an old age when an ungrateful country shall have dismissed them from the field of public service; Coventry living retired in a fine house, and Pepys dropping in, 'it may be, to read a chapter of Seneca.'

Under this influence, the only good one in his life, Pepys continued zealous and, for the period, pure in his employment. He would not be 'bribed to be unjust,' he says, though he was 'not so squeamish as to refuse a present after,' suppose the king to have received no wrong. His new arrangement for the victualling of Tangier, he tells us with honest complacency, will save the king a thousand and gain Pepys three hundred pounds a year, – a statement which exactly fixes the degree of the age's enlightenment. But for his industry and capacity no praise can be too high. It was an unending struggle for the man to stick to his business in such a garden of Armida as he found this life; and the story of his oaths, so often broken, so courageously renewed, is worthy rather of admiration that the contempt it has received.

Elsewhere, and beyond the sphere of Coventry's influence, we find him losing scruples and daily complying further with the age. When he began the Journal, he was a trifle prim and puritanic; merry enough, to be sure, over his private cups, and still remembering Magdalene ale and his acquaintance with Mrs Ainsworth of Cambridge. But youth is a hot season with all; when a man smells April and May he is apt at times to stumble; and in spite of a disordered practice, Pepys's theory, the better things that he approved and followed after, we may even say were strict. Where there was 'tag, rag, and bobtail, dancing, singing, and drinking,' he felt 'ashamed, and went away;' and when he slept in church, he prayed God forgive him. In but a little while we find him with some ladies keeping each other awake 'from spite,' as though not to sleep in church were an obvious hardship; and yet later he calmly passes the time of service, looking about him, with a perspective glass, on all the pretty women. His favourite ejaculation, 'Lord!' occurs but once that I have observed in 1660, never in '61, twice in '62, and at least five times in '63; after which the 'Lords' may be said to pullulate like herrings, with here and there a solitary 'damned,' as it were a whale among the shoal. He and his wife, once filled with dudgeon by some innocent freedoms at a marriage, are soon content to go pleasuring with my Lord Brouncker's mistress, who was not even, by his own account, the most discreet of mistresses. Tag, rag, and bobtail, dancing, singing, and drinking, become his natural element; actors and actresses and drunken, roaring courtiers are to be found in his society; until the man grew so involved with Saturnalian manners and companions that he was shot almost unconsciously into the grand domestic crash of 1668.

That was the legitimate issue and punishment of years of staggering walk and conversation. The man who has smoked his pipe for half a century in a powder magazine finds himself at last the author and the victim of a hideous disaster. So with our pleasant-minded Pepys and his peccadilloes. All of a sudden, as he still trips dexterously enough among the dangers of a double-faced career, thinking no great evil, humming to himself the trillo, Fate takes the further conduct of that matter from his hands, and brings him face to face with the consequences of his acts. For a man still, after so many years, the lover, although not the constant lover, of his wife, – for a man, besides, who was so greatly careful of appearances, – the revelation of his infidelities was a crushing blow. The tears that he shed, the indignities that he endured, are not to be measured. A vulgar woman, and now justly incensed, Mrs Pepys spared him no detail of suffering. She was violent, threatening him with the tongs; she was careless of his honour, driving him to insult the mistress whom she had driven him to betray and to discard; worst of all, she was hopelessly inconsequent, in word and thought and deed, now lulling him with reconciliations, and anon flaming forth again with the original anger. Pepys had not used his wife well; he had wearied her with jealousies, even while himself unfaithful; he had grudged her clothes and pleasures, while lavishing both upon himself; he had abused her in words; he had bent his fist at her in anger; he had once blacked her eye; and it is one of the oddest particulars in that odd Diary of his, that, while the injury is referred to once in passing, there is no hint as to the occasion or the manner of the blow. But now, when he is in the wrong, nothing can exceed the long-suffering affection of this impatient husband. While he was still sinning and still undiscovered, he seems not to have known a touch of penitence stronger than what might lead him to take his wife to the theatre, or for an airing, or to give her a new dress, by way of compensation. Once found out, however, and he seems to himself to have lost all claim to decent usage. It is perhaps the strongest instance of his externality. His wife may do what she pleases, and though he may groan, it will never occur to him to blame her; he has no weapon left but tears and the most abject submission. We should perhaps have respected him more had he not given way so utterly – above all, had he refused to write, under his wife's dictation, an insulting letter to his unhappy fellow-culprit, Miss Willet; but somehow I believe we like him better as he was.

The death of his wife, following so shortly after, must have stamped the impression of this episode upon his mind. For the remaining years of his long life we have no Diary to help us, and we have seen already how little stress is to be laid upon the tenor of his correspondence; but what with the recollection of the catastrophe of his married life, what with the natural influence of his advancing years and reputation, it seems not unlikely that the period of gallantry was at an end for Pepys; and it is beyond a doubt that he sat down at last to an honoured and agreeable old age among his books and music, the correspondent of Sir Isaac Newton, and, in one instance at least, the poetical counsellor of Dryden. Through all this period, that Diary which contained the secret memoirs of his life, with all its inconsistencies and escapades, had been religiously preserved; nor, when he came to die, does he appear to have provided for its destruction. So we may conceive him faithful to the end to all his dear and early memories; still mindful of Mrs Hely in the woods at Epsom; still lighting at Islington for a cup of kindness to the dead; still, if he heard again that air that once so much disturbed him, thrilling at the recollection of the love that bound him to his wife.

DAVOS IN WINTER

A mountain valley has, at the best, a certain prison-like effect on the imagination; but a mountain valley, an Alpine winter, and an invalid's weakness make up among them a prison of the most effective kind. The roads indeed are cleared, and at least one footpath dodging up the hill; but to these the health-seeker is rigidly confined. There are for him no cross cuts over the field, no following of streams, no unguided rambles in the wood. His walks are cut and dry. In five or six different directions he can push as far, and no farther, than his strength permits; never deviating from the line laid down for him and beholding at each repetition the same field of wood and snow from the same corner of the road. This, of itself, would be a little trying to the patience in the course of months; but to this is added, by the heaped mantle of the snow, an almost utter absence of detail and an almost unbroken identity of colour. Snow, it is true, is not merely white. The sun touches it with roseate and golden lights. Its own crushed infinity of crystals, its own richness of tiny sculpture, fills it, when regarded near at hand, with wonderful depths of coloured shadow, and, though wintrily transformed, it is still water, and has watery tones of blue. But, when all is said, these fields of white and blots of crude black forest are but a trite and staring substitute for the infinite variety and pleasantness of the earth's face. Even a boulder, whose front is too precipitous to have retained the snow, seems, if you come upon it in your walk, a perfect gem of colour, reminds you almost painfully of other places, and brings into your head the delights of more Arcadian days – the path across the meadow, the hazel dell, the lilies on the stream, and the scents, the colours, and the whisper of the woods. And scents here are as rare as colours. Unless you get a gust of kitchen in passing some hotel, you shall smell nothing all day long but the faint and choking odour of frost. Sounds, too, are absent: not a bird pipes, not a bough waves, in the dead, windless atmosphere. If a sleigh goes by, the sleigh bells ring, and that is all; you work all winter through to no other accompaniment but the crunching of your steps upon the frozen snow.

It is the curse of Alpine valleys to be each one village from one end to the other. Go where you please, houses will still be in sight, before and behind you, and to the right and left. Climb as high as an invalid is able, and it is only to spy new habitations nested in the wood. Nor is that all; for about the health resort the walks are besieged by single people walking rapidly with plaids about their shoulders, by sudden troops of German boys trying to learn to *jodel*, and by German couples silently and, as you venture to fancy, not quite happily, pursuing love's young dream. You may perhaps be an invalid who likes to make bad verses as he walks abroad. Alas! no muse will suffer this imminence of interruption – and at the second stampede of jodellers you find your modest inspiration fled. Or you may only have a taste for solitude: it may try your nerves to have someone always in front whom you are visibly overtaking, and someone always behind who is audibly overtaking you, to say nothing of a score or so who brush past you in an opposite direction. It may annoy you to take your walks and seats in public view. Alas! there is no help for it among the Alps. There are no recesses, as in Gorbio Valley by the oil-mill; no sacred solitude of olive gardens on the Roccabruna-road; no nook upon Saint Martin's Cape, haunted by the voice of breakers, and fragrant with the threefold sweetness of the rosemary and the sea-pines and the sea.

For this publicity there is no cure and no alleviation; but the storms, of which you will complain so bitterly while they endure, chequer and by their contrast brighten the sameness of fair-weather scenes. When sun and storm contend together – when the thick clouds are broken up and pierced by arrows of golden daylight – there will be startling rearrangements and transfigurations of the mountain summits. A sun-dazzling spire of alp hangs suspended in mid-sky among awful glooms and blackness; or perhaps the edge of some great mountain shoulder will be designed in living gold, and appear for the duration of a glance bright like a constellation, and alone 'in the unapparent.' You may think you know the figure of these hills; but when they are thus revealed, they belong no longer to the things of earth – meteors we should rather call them, appearances of sun and air that endure but for a moment and return no more. Other variations are more lasting, as when, for instance, heavy and wet snow has fallen through some windless hours, and the thin, spiry, mountain pine-trees stand each stock-still and loaded with a shining burthen. You may drive through a forest so disguised, the tongue-tied torrent struggling silently in the cleft of the ravine, and all still except the jingle of the sleigh bells and you shall fancy yourself in some untrodden northern territory – Lapland, Labrador, or Alaska.

Or, possibly, you arise very early in the morning; totter downstairs in a state of somnambulism; take the simulacrum of a meal by the glimmer of one lamp in the deserted coffee-room; and find yourself by seven o'clock outside in a belated moonlight and a freezing chill. The mail-sleigh takes you up and carries you on, and you reach the top of the ascent in the first hour of the day. To trace the fires of the sunrise as they pass from peak to peak, to see the unlit tree-tops stand out soberly against the lighted sky, to be for twenty minutes in a wonderland of clear, fading shadows, disappearing vapours, solemn blooms of dawn, hills half-glorified already with the day and still half-confounded with the greyness of the western heaven – these will seem to repay you for the discomforts of that early start; but as the hour proceeds, and these enchantments vanish, you will find yourself upon the further side in yet another Alpine valley, snow-white and coal-black, with such another long-drawn congeries of hamlets and such another senseless water-course bickering along the foot. You have had your moment; but you have not changed the scene. The mountains are about you like a trap; you cannot foot it up a hillside and behold the sea as a great plain, but live in holes and corners, and can change only one for another.

THE MISGIVINGS OF CONVALESCENCE

There is no problem more difficult, in view of modern thought upon morality, than to make a decent and human-hearted convalescence. Many elements are questionable. It may be open to doubt whether the man will or will not make an ultimate recovery, or whether it might or might not be better for humanity that he should die. A little while ago, and such inquiries would have been fantastic; but the weathercock has gone about; opinion tends to lie, if not in the direction of more modesty, at least in that of more self-consciousness; and between wisdom and folly, any young man, not yet riveted to life by years and complications, comes to regard the question of the importance of his own survival with a critical eye. In all this mass of rights and duties in which we find ourselves involved no right and no duty seem more doubtful, in hours of sickness and depression, than those that have to do with our own continued existence. A question, perhaps essentially impertinent, but yet continually recurring and almost as old as the art of logical speech – it is hardly imperative to state it: *cui bono?* – haunts any phthisical young man like his own shadow, and, in many instances, steps between him and the beginning of recovery. The world is too much with us, not only in getting and spending, but in our dank and downhearted speculations. Truths of social complexity and instant, personal obligation, which we may be proud to call noble, have yet their sickly and sophisticated side. A considerable body of lugubrious prose and some verses, worthy at best of a tooth-comb for *obbligato*, teach a proportion of the human race to feel a pride in self-abasement; and even political economy, read with a generous spirit, leads the same class of people to grudge perhaps too bitterly the expenses of their sickness. If you asked them the highest purpose to which humanity might apply its hoarded treasures, they would tell you to alleviate the pains and combat the dangers of sickness. But in their own case they cannot see the application. Yet a few natural tears, and they will lay them down with dignity to die. Existences that have not yet begun to be efficient among men, names that have not been writ even in water, who is to mourn, who to suffer by their loss? And ten to one, there is some old parent to whom the world will be clean darkened by that death.

There is a mixture of the hero and of Mawworm in this attitude, which makes it neither beautiful nor ugly; only superlatively young. The true heroic lies the other way. The man who has father, mother, wife, sister, friend, an honourable work to live for, cannot tamely die without, one need not say dishonour, but defeat. It is an uphill work to fight the sapping malady with one hand, the failing courage with the other; its difficulty alone would lend it some nobility; but when we reflect upon the prize of that contention, and how the man holds up against outward assaults and inward failings, not for the love of life, which is a feeble passion, but that he may bear and forbear, help and serve, and love and let himself be loved for some years longer in this rugged world, it will be clear there are few fights more worthy to be fought and few victories more to be lauded, than what are fought and won against disease. To those who fall, we say Farewell! theirs is the better part. From all our dangers and dissensions they escape; they leave us, when our time shall come, to follow through the same unknown and agonising pass; and to those who love them they bequeath no portion of their part in this world's happiness, only a continual blank and slowly diminishing pang. There is sense in pity for the dying: pity for the dead is false to nature and reason. We have spoken of the true heroic; the true pathetic, at least, is to conquer; to return again into the strife among our fellows, and take our share, with a sound spirit, in giving and receiving charities. There are many, it is more than possible, who will do no good, but only harm, in what remains to them of a career; but to recognise yourself for one of these is to do your utmost to ensure the fact that it shall be so. Perpetual previous failure should make a man, who is a man at all, nigh desperate to retrieve some part of such a past.

To keep up the braver, to encourage the feebler of these spirits, is a great end in medicine as well as in morality. Whatever tends to do so makes in the first place for recovery, and in the second supports and improves the tone of the recovering invalid. Never to have despaired is ground for a just satisfaction with oneself, and is second best to never having lost one's health. Hence, even if the directly medical effect were equal, that health resort would still be preferable where the moral influence is stronger and more brisk.

Now, if anywhere there was an emasculated air and an effeminate loveliness in nature that unstrung and dispirited the sick for vigorous resistance, it was to that place they would be sent in the old days of treatment. We cannot say that it was bad, since they avoided many obvious dangers and had an opportunity to heal them of their wounds; yet there is certainly a sense in which the influence of such a climate and surroundings was not good. A swoon descended on the mind. Tender and dreamy not enterprising thoughts, resignation not rebellion, the quiet of peace not the ardour and glory of exercise, were the suggestions of that languorous land. Active memories came to the invalid only at long intervals, and veiled in a poetic haze; not otherwise than, from time to time about sundown, Corsica would swim for a little into view – farther, it would seem, and softer than a star, fainter and more immaterial than a cloud. Flowers and scents and phantom islands, delicate, tearful fancies, and deliquescence of the radical man, beauty over all, and nowhere any strength – such was the discipline in the older kind of sanitarium; and when suddenly a mistral struck along the hills and sent a living shiver through the olive gardens, there would be such a panic among the sunshades and the respirators as though fleet-foot Achilles had burst in panoply upon the lotus-eaters' island.

For each case, of course, there is a different rule. But *similia similibus*; a man who puts his pleasure in activity, who desires a stirring life or none at all, will be certain to do better in the Alps. The continual, almost painful bracing, the boisterous inclemencies, the rough pleasure of tobogganing, the doctor exciting him to be up and walking, and to walk daily further, the glittering, unhomely landscape, the glare of day, the solemn splendours of the night, spur him to the gallop in his quest of health. He takes a risk; he makes an effort; action is in all his thoughts. The very sameness of his prison valley bids him make a push to recover and escape. The ground is deep with snow; and he cannot lounge on violets. The frost flutters his heart and tingles in his nerves; today, if not yesterday, he will gain the summit of that hill. And, in a word, if pluck, vigour, and the desire of living at all help or speed the invalid in his recovery, it is here upon the Alps, and not among the perfumed valleys of Liguria, that he will find the stimulus required. Cold he may dismiss from his consideration; he will rarely feel it. Dulness at first he must endure; his eagerness will be so vastly greater than his strength. And it is never pleasant to be ill nor easy to recover. But here he will be free from morbid weakness on his own part; he will be eager, human, decently mirthful, at least rationally hopeful; he will work briskly at his own recovery like a piece of business; and, even if he shall not succeed, he makes a better figure in defeat and is a shorter time a-dying.

THE FOREIGNER AT HOME

This is no my ain house;
I ken by the biggin' o't.

Two recent books, one by Mr Grant White on England, one on France by the diabolically clever Mr Hillebrand, may well have set people thinking on the divisions of races and nations. Such thoughts should arise with particular congruity and force to inhabitants of that United Kingdom, peopled from so many different stocks, babbling so many different dialects, and offering in its extent such singular contrasts, from the busiest over-population to the unkindliest desert, from the Black Country to the Moor of Rannoch. It is not only when we cross the seas that we go abroad; there are foreign parts of England; and the race that has conquered so wide an empire has not yet managed to assimilate the islands whence she sprang. Ireland, Wales, and the Scottish mountains still cling, in part, to their old Gaelic speech. It was but the other day that English triumphed in Cornwall, and they still show in Mousehole, on St Michael's Bay, the house of the last Cornish-speaking woman. English itself, which will now frank the traveller through the most of North America, through the greater South Sea Islands, in India, along much of the coast of Africa, and in the ports of China and Japan, is still to be heard, in its home country, in half a hundred varying stages of transition. You may go all over the States, and – setting aside the actual intrusion and influence of foreigners, negro, French, or Chinese – you shall scarce meet with so marked a difference of accent as in the forty miles between Edinburgh and Glasgow, or of dialect as in the hundred miles between Edinburgh and Aberdeen. Book English has gone round the world, but at home we still preserve the racy idioms of our fathers, and every county, in some parts every dale, has its own quality of speech, vocal or verbal. In like manner, local custom and prejudice, even local religion and local law, linger on into the latter end of the nineteenth century – *imperia in imperio*, foreign things at home.

In spite of these promptings to reflection, ignorance of his neighbours is the character of the typical John Bull. His is a domineering nature, steady in fight, imperious to command, but neither curious nor quick about the life of others. In French colonies, and still more in the Dutch, I have read that there is an immediate and lively contact between the dominant and the dominated race, that a certain sympathy is begotten, or at the least a transfusion of prejudices, making life easier for both. But the Englishman sits apart, bursting with pride and ignorance. He figures among his vassals in the hour of peace with the same disdainful air that led him on to victory. A passing enthusiasm for some foreign art or fashion may deceive the world, it cannot impose upon his intimates. He may be amused by a foreigner as by a monkey, but he will never condescend to study him with any patience. Miss Bird, an authoress with whom I profess myself in love, declares all the viands of Japan to be uneatable – a staggering pretension. So, when the Prince of Wales's marriage was celebrated at Mentone by a dinner to the Mentonese, it was proposed to give them solid English fare – roast beef and plum pudding, and no tomfoolery. Here we have either pole of the Britannic folly. We will not eat the food of any foreigner; nor, when we have the chance, will we suffer him to eat of it himself. The same spirit inspired Miss Bird's American missionaries, who had come thousands of miles to change the faith of Japan, and openly professed their ignorance of the religions they were trying to supplant.

I quote an American in this connection without scruple. Uncle Sam is better than John Bull, but he is tarred with the English stick. For Mr Grant White the States are the New England States and nothing more. He wonders at the amount of drinking in London; let him try San Francisco. He wittily reproves English ignorance as to the status of women in America; but has he not himself forgotten Wyoming? The name Yankee, of which he is so tenacious, is used over the most of the great Union as a term of reproach. The Yankee States, of which he is so staunch a subject, are but a drop in the bucket. And we find in his book a vast virgin ignorance of the life and prospects of America; every view partial, parochial, not raised to the horizon; the moral feeling proper, at the largest, to a clique of States; and the whole scope and atmosphere not American, but merely Yankee. I will go far beyond him in repro-bating the assumption and the incivility of my countryfolk to their cousins from beyond the sea; I grill in my blood over the silly rudeness of our newspaper articles; and I do not know where to look when I find myself in company with an American and see my countrymen unbending to him as to a performing dog. But in the case of Mr Grant White example were better than precept. Wyoming is, after all, more readily accessible to Mr White than Boston to the English, and the New England self-sufficiency no better justified than the Britannic.

It is so, perhaps, in all countries; perhaps in all, men are most ignorant of the foreigners at home. John Bull is ignorant of the States; he is probably ignorant of India; but considering his opportunities, he is far more ignorant of countries nearer his own door. There is one country, for instance – its frontier not so far from London, its people closely akin, its language the same in all essentials with the English – of which I will go bail he knows nothing. His ignorance of the sister kingdom cannot be described; it can only be illustrated by anecdote. I once travelled with a man of plausible manners and good intelligence, – a University man, as the phrase goes, – a man, besides, who had taken his degree in life and knew a thing or two about the age we live in. We were deep in talk, whirling between Peterborough and London; among other things, he began to describe some piece of legal injustice he had recently encountered, and I observed in my innocence that things were not so in Scotland. 'I beg your pardon,' said he, 'this is a matter of law.' He had never heard of the Scots law; nor did he choose to be informed. The law was the same for the whole country, he told me roundly; every child knew that. At last, to settle matters, I explained to him that I was a member of a Scottish legal body, and had stood the brunt of an examination in the very law in question. Thereupon he looked me for a moment full in the face and dropped the conversation. This is a monstrous instance, if you like, but it does not stand alone in the experience of Scots.

England and Scotland differ, indeed, in law, in history, in religion, in education, and in the very look of nature and men's faces, not always widely, but always trenchantly. Many particulars that struck Mr Grant White, a Yankee, struck me, a Scot, no less forcibly; he and I felt ourselves foreigners on many common provocations. A Scotchman may tramp the better part of Europe and the United States, and never again receive so vivid an impression of foreign travel and strange lands and manners as on his first excursion into England. The change from a hilly to a level country strikes him with delighted wonder. Along the flat horizon there arise the frequent venerable towers of churches. He sees at the end of airy vistas the revolution of the windmill sails. He may go where he pleases in the future; he may see Alps, and Pyramids, and lions; but it will be hard to beat the pleasure of that moment. There are, indeed, few merrier spectacles than that of many windmills bickering together in a fresh breeze over a woody country; their halting alacrity of movement, their pleasant business, making bread all day with uncouth gesticulations, their air, gigantically human, as of a creature half alive, put a spirit of romance into the tamest landscape. When the Scotch child sees them first he falls immediately in love; and from that time forward windmills keep turning in his dreams. And so, in their degree, with every feature of the life and landscape. The warm, habitable age of towns and hamlets, the green, settled, ancient look of the country; the lush hedgerows, stiles, and privy pathways in the fields; the sluggish, brimming rivers; chalk and smock-frocks; chimes of bells and the rapid, pertly-sounding English speech – they are all new to the curiosity; they are all set to English airs in the child's story that he tells himself at night. The sharp edge of novelty wears off; the feeling is scotched, but I doubt whether it is ever killed. Rather it keeps returning, ever the more rarely and strangely, and even in scenes to which you have been long accustomed suddenly awakes and gives a relish to enjoyment or heightens the sense of isolation.

One thing especially continues unfamiliar to the Scotchman's eye – the domestic architecture, the look of streets and buildings; the quaint, venerable age of many, and the thin walls and warm colouring of all. We have, in Scotland, far fewer ancient buildings, above all in country places; and those that we have are all of hewn or harled masonry. Wood has been sparingly used in their construction; the window-frames are sunken in the wall, not flat to the front, as in England; the roofs are steeper-pitched; even a hill farm will have a massy, square, cold and permanent appearance. English houses, in comparison, have the look of cardboard toys, such as a puff might shatter. And to this the Scotchman never becomes used. His eye can never rest consciously on one of these brick houses – rickles of brick, as he might call them – or on one of these flat-chested streets, but he is instantly reminded where he is, and instantly travels back in fancy to his home. 'This is no my ain house; I ken by the biggin' o't.' And yet perhaps it is his own, bought with his own money, the key of it long polished in his pocket; but it has not yet been, and never will be, thoroughly adopted by his imagination; nor does he cease to remember that, in the whole length and breadth of his native country, there was no building even distantly resembling it.

But it is not alone in scenery and architecture that we count England foreign. The constitution of society, the very pillars of the empire, surprise and even pain us. The dull, neglected peasant, sunk in matter, insolent, gross and servile, makes a startling contrast with our own long-legged, long-headed, thoughtful, Bible-quoting ploughman. A week or two in such a place as Suffolk leaves the Scotchman gasping. It seems incredible that within the boundaries of his own island a class should have been thus forgotten. Even the educated and intelligent, who hold our own opinions and speak in our own words, yet seem to hold them with a difference or from another reason, and to speak on all things with less interest and conviction. The first shock of English society is like a cold plunge. It is possible that the Scot comes looking for too much, and to be sure his first experiment will be in the wrong direction. Yet surely his complaint is grounded; surely the speech of Englishmen is too often lacking in generous ardour, the better part of the man too often withheld from the social commerce, and the contact of mind with mind evaded as with terror. A Scotch peasant will talk more liberally out of his own experience. He will not put you by with conversational counters and small jests; he will give you the best of himself, like one interested in life and man's chief end. A Scotchman is vain, interested in himself and others, eager for sympathy, setting forth his thoughts and experience in the best light. The egotism of the Englishman is self-contained. He does not seek to proselytise. He takes no interest in Scotland or the Scotch, and, what is the unkindest cut of all, he does not care to justify his indifference. Give him the wages of going on and being an Englishman, that is all he asks; and in the meantime, while you continue to associate, he would rather not be reminded of your baser origin. Compared with the grand, tree-like self-sufficiency of his demeanour, the vanity and curiosity of the Scot seem uneasy, vulgar and immodest. That you should continually try to establish human and serious relations, that you should actually feel an interest in John Bull, and desire and invite a return of interest from him, may argue something more awake and lively in your mind, but it still puts you in the attitude of a suitor and a poor relation. Thus even the lowest class of the educated English towers over a Scotchman by the head and shoulders.

Different indeed is the atmosphere in which Scotch and English youth begin to look about them, come to themselves in life, and gather up those first apprehensions which are the material of future thought and, to a great extent, the rule of future conduct. I have been to school in both countries, and I found, in the boys of the North, something at once rougher and more tender, at once more reserve and more expansion, a greater habitual distance chequered by glimpses of a nearer intimacy, and on the whole wider extremes of temperament and sensibility. The boy of the South seems more wholesome, but less thoughtful; he gives himself to games as to a business, striving to excel, but is not readily transported by imagination; the type remains with me as cleaner in mind and body, more active, fonder of eating, endowed with a lesser and a less romantic sense of life and of the future, and more immersed in present circumstances. And certainly, for one thing, English boys are younger for their age. Sabbath observance makes a series of grim, and perhaps serviceable, pauses in the tenor of Scotch boyhood – days of great stillness and solitude for the rebellious mind, when in the dearth of books and play, and in the intervals of studying the Shorter Catechism, the intellect and senses prey upon and test each other. The typical English Sunday, with the huge midday dinner and the plethoric afternoon, leads perhaps to different results. About the very cradle of the Scot there goes a hum of metaphysical divinity; and the whole of two divergent systems is summed up, not merely speciously, in the two first questions of the rival catechisms, the English tritely inquiring, 'What is your name?' the Scottish striking at the very roots of life with, 'What is the chief end of man?' and answering nobly, if obscurely, 'To glorify God and to enjoy Him for ever.' I do not wish to make an idol of the Shorter Catechism; but the fact of such a question being asked opens to us Scotch a great field of speculation; and the fact that it is asked of all of us, from the peer to the ploughboy, binds us more nearly together. No Englishman of Byron's age, character and history, would have had patience for long theological discussions on the way to fight for Greece; but the daft Gordon blood and the Aberdonian schooldays kept their influence to the end. We have spoken of the material conditions; nor need much more be said of these: of the land lying everywhere more exposed, of the wind always louder and bleaker, of the black, roaring winters, of the gloom of high-lying, old stone cities, imminent on the windy seaboard; compared with the level streets, the warm colouring of the brick, the domestic quaintness of the architecture, among which English children begin to grow up and come to themselves in life. As the stage of the University approaches, the contrast becomes more express. The English lad goes to Oxford or Cambridge; there, in an ideal world of gardens, to lead a semi-scenic life, costumed, disciplined and drilled by proctors. Nor is this to be regarded merely as a stage of education; it is a piece of privilege besides, and a step that separates him further from the bulk of his compatriots. At an earlier age the Scottish lad begins his greatly different experience of crowded class-rooms, of a gaunt quadrangle, of a bell hourly booming over the traffic of the city to recall him from the public-house where he has been lunching, or the streets where he has been wandering fancy-free. His college life has little of restraint, and nothing of necessary gentility. He will find no quiet clique of the exclusive, studious and cultured; no rotten borough of the arts. All classes rub shoulders on the greasy benches. The raffish young gentleman in gloves must measure his scholarship with the plain, clownish laddie from the parish school. They separate, at the session's end, one to smoke cigars about a watering-place, the other to resume the labours of the field beside his peasant family. The first muster of a college class in Scotland is a scene of curious and painful interest; so many lads, fresh from the heather, hang round the stove in cloddish embarrassment, ruffled by the presence of their smarter comrades, and afraid of the sound of their own rustic voices. It was in these early days, I think, that Professor Blackie won the affection of his pupils, putting these uncouth, umbrageous students at their ease with ready human geniality. Thus, at least, we have a healthy democratic atmosphere to breathe in while at work; even when there is no cordiality there is always a juxtaposition of the different classes, and in the competition of study the intellectual power of each is plainly demonstrated to the other. Our tasks ended, we of the North go forth as freemen into the humming, lamplit city. At five o'clock you may see the last of us hiving from the college gates, in the glare of the shop windows, under the green glimmer of the winter sunset. The frost tingles in our blood; no proctor lies in wait to intercept us; till the bell sounds again, we are the masters of the world; and some portion of our lives is always Saturday, *la trêve de Dieu.*

Nor must we omit the sense of the nature of his country and his country's history gradually growing in the child's mind from story and from observation. A Scottish child hears much of shipwreck, outlying iron skerries, pitiless breakers, and great sea-lights; much of heathery mountains, wild clans, and hunted Covenanters. Breaths come to him in song of the distant Cheviots and the ring of foraying hoofs. He glories in his hard-fisted forefathers, of the iron girdle and the handful of oatmeal, who rode so swiftly and lived so sparely on their raids. Poverty, ill-luck, enterprise, and constant resolution are the fibres of the legend of his country's history. The heroes and kings of Scotland have been tragically fated; the most marking incidents in Scottish history – Flodden, Darien, or the Forty-five – were still either failures or defeats; and the fall of Wallace and the repeated reverses of the Bruce combine with the very smallness of the country to teach rather a moral than a material criterion for life. Britain is altogether small, the mere taproot of her extended empire; Scotland, again, which alone the Scottish boy adopts in his imagination, is but a little part of that, and avowedly cold, sterile and unpopulous. It is not so for nothing. I once seemed to have perceived in an American boy a greater readiness of sympathy for lands that are great, and rich, and growing, like his own. It proved to be quite otherwise: a mere dumb piece of boyish romance, that I had lacked penetration to divine. But the error serves the purpose of my argument; for I am sure, at least, that the heart of young Scotland will be always touched more nearly by paucity of number and Spartan poverty of life.

So we may argue, and yet the difference is not explained. That Shorter Catechism which I took as being so typical of Scotland, was yet composed in the city of Westminster. The division of races is more sharply marked within the borders of Scotland itself than between the countries. Galloway and Buchan, Lothian and Lochaber, are like foreign parts; yet you may choose a man from any of them, and, ten to one, he shall prove to have the headmark of a Scot. A century and a half ago, the Highlander wore a different costume, spoke a different language, worshipped in another church, held different morals, and obeyed a different social constitution from his fellow-countrymen either of the south or north. Even the English, it is recorded, did not loathe the Highlander and the Highland costume as they were loathed by the remainder of the Scotch. Yet the Highlander felt himself a Scot. He would willingly raid into the Scotch lowlands; but his courage failed him at the border, and he regarded England as a perilous, unhomely land. When the Black Watch, after years of foreign service, returned to Scotland, veterans leaped out and kissed the earth at Port Patrick. They had been in Ireland, stationed among men of their own race and language, where they were well liked and treated with affection; but it was the soil of Galloway that they kissed at the extreme end of the hostile lowlands, among a people who did not understand their speech, and who had hated, harried, and hanged them since the dawn of history. Last, and perhaps most curious, the sons of chieftains were often educated on the continent of Europe. They went abroad speaking Gaelic; they returned speaking, not English, but the broad dialect of Scotland. Now, what idea had they in their minds when they thus, in thought, identified themselves with their ancestral enemies? What was the sense in which they were Scotch and not English, or Scotch and not Irish? Can a bare name be thus influential on the minds and affections of men, and a political aggregation blind them to the nature of facts? The story of the Austrian Empire would seem to answer, No; the far more galling business of Ireland clenches the negative from nearer home. Is it common education, common morals, a common language or a common faith, that join men into nations? There were practically none of these in the case we are considering.

The fact remains: in spite of the difference of blood and language, the Lowlander feels himself the sentimental countryman of the Highlander. When they meet abroad, they fall upon each other's necks in spirit; even at home there is a kind of clannish intimacy in their talk. But from his compatriot in the south the Lowlander stands consciously apart. He has had a different training; he obeys different laws; he makes his will in other terms, is otherwise divorced and married; his eyes are not at home in an English landscape or with English houses; his ear continues to remark the English speech; and even though his tongue acquire the Southern knack, he will still have a strong Scotch accent of the mind.

A GOSSIP ON ROMANCE

In anything fit to be called by the name of reading, the process itself should be absorbing and voluptuous; we should gloat over a book, be rapt clean out of ourselves, and rise from the perusal, our mind filled with the busiest, kaleidoscopic dance of images, incapable of sleep or of continuous thought. The words, if the book be eloquent, should run thenceforward in our ears like the noise of breakers, and the story, if it be a story, repeat itself in a thousand coloured pictures to the eye. It was for this last pleasure that we read so closely, and loved our books so dearly, in the bright, troubled period of boyhood. Eloquence and thought, character and conversation, were but obstacles to brush aside as we dug blithely after a certain sort of incident, like a pig for truffles. For my part, I liked a story to begin with an old wayside inn where, 'towards the close of the year 17—,' several gentlemen in three-cocked hats were playing bowls. A friend of mine preferred the Malabar coast in a storm, with a ship beating to windward, and a scowling fellow of Herculean proportions striding along the beach; he, to be sure, was a pirate. This was further afield than my home-keeping fancy loved to travel, and designed altogether for a larger canvas than the tales that I affected. Give me a highwayman and I was full to the brim; a Jacobite would do, but the highwayman was my favourite dish. I can still hear that merry clatter of the hoofs along the moonlit lane; night and the coming of day are still related in my mind with the doings of John Rann or Jerry Abershaw; and the words 'post-chaise,' the 'great North road,' 'ostler,' and 'nag' still sound in my ears like poetry. One and all, at least, and each with his particular fancy, we read story-books in childhood, not for eloquence or character or thought, but for some quality of the brute incident. That quality was not mere bloodshed or wonder. Although each of these was welcome in its place, the charm for the sake of which we read depended on something different from either. My elders used to read novels aloud; and I can still remember four different passages which I heard, before I was ten, with the same keen and lasting pleasure. One I discovered long afterwards to be the admirable opening of *What will he Do with It*: it was no wonder I was pleased with that. The other three still remain unidentified. One is a little vague; it was about a dark, tall house at night, and people groping on the stairs by the light that escaped from the open door of a sick-room. In another, a lover left a ball, and went walking in a cool, dewy park, whence he could watch the lighted windows and the figures of the dancers as they moved. This was the most sentimental impression I think I had yet received, for a child is somewhat deaf to the sentimental. In the last, a poet, who had been tragically wrangling with his wife, walked forth on the sea-beach on a tempestuous night and witnessed the horrors of a wreck.[1] Different as they are, all these early favourites have a common note – they have all a touch of the romantic.

Drama is the poetry of conduct, romance the poetry of circumstance. The pleasure that we take in life is of two sorts – the active and the passive. Now we are conscious of a great command over our destiny; anon we are lifted up by circumstance, as by a breaking wave, and dashed we know not how into the future. Now we are pleased by our conduct, anon merely pleased by our surroundings. It would be hard to say which of these modes of satisfaction is the more effective, but the latter is surely the more constant. Conduct is three parts of life, they say; but I think they put it high. There is a vast deal in life and letters both which is not immoral, but simply a-moral; which either does not regard the human will at all, or deals with it in obvious and healthy relations; where the interest turns, not upon what a man shall choose to do, but on how he manages to do it; not on the passionate slips and hesitations of the conscience, but on the problems of the body and of the practical intelligence, in clean, open-air adventure, the shock of arms or the diplomacy of life. With such material as this it is impossible to build a play, for the serious theatre exists solely on moral grounds, and is a standing proof of the dissemination of the human conscience. But it is possible to build, upon this ground, the most joyous of verses, and the most lively, beautiful, and buoyant tales.

One thing in life calls for another; there is a fitness in events and places. The sight of a pleasant arbour puts it in our mind to sit there. One place suggests work, another idleness, a third early rising and long rambles in the dew. The effect of night, of any flowing water, of lighted cities, of the peep of day, of ships, of the open ocean, calls up in the mind

---

[1] Since traced by many obliging correspondents to the gallery of Charles Kingsley.

an army of anonymous desires and pleasures. Something, we feel, should happen; we know not what, yet we proceed in quest of it. And many of the happiest hours of life fleet by us in this vain attendance on the genius of the place and moment. It is thus that tracts of young fir, and low rocks that reach into deep soundings, particularly torture and delight me. Something must have happened in such places, and perhaps ages back, to members of my race; and when I was a child I tried in vain to invent appropriate games for them, as I still try, just as vainly, to fit them with the proper story. Some places speak distinctly. Certain dank gardens cry aloud for a murder; certain old houses demand to be haunted; certain coasts are set apart for shipwreck. Other spots again seem to abide their destiny, suggestive and impenetrable, 'miching mallecho.' The inn at Burford Bridge, with its arbours and green garden and silent, eddying river – though it is known already as the place where Keats wrote some of his *Endymion* and Nelson parted from his Emma – still seems to wait the coming of the appropriate legend. Within these ivied walls, behind these old green shutters, some further business smoulders, waiting for its hour. The old Hawes Inn at the Queen's Ferry makes a similar call upon my fancy. There it stands, apart from the town, beside the pier, in a climate of its own, half inland, half marine – in front, the ferry bubbling with the tide and the guard-ship swinging to her anchor; behind, the old garden with the trees. Americans seek it already for the sake of Lovel and Oldbuck, who dined there at the beginning of the *Antiquary*. But you need not tell me – that is not all; there is some story, unrecorded or not yet complete, which must express the meaning of that inn more fully. So it is with names and faces; so it is with incidents that are idle and inconclusive in themselves, and yet seem like the beginning of some quaint romance, which the all-careless author leaves untold. 'How many of these romances have we not seen determine at their birth; how many people have met us with a look of meaning in their eye, and sunk at once into trivial acquaintances; to how many places have we not drawn near, with express intimations – 'here my destiny awaits me' – and we have but dined there and passed on! I have lived both at the Hawes and Burford in a perpetual flutter, on the heels, as it seemed, of some adventure that should justify the place; but though the feeling had me to bed at night and called me again at morning in one unbroken round of pleasure and suspense, nothing befell me in either worth remark. The man or the hour had not yet come; but some day, I think, a boat shall put off from the Queen's Ferry, fraught with a dear cargo, and some frosty night a horseman, on a tragic errand, rattle with his whip upon the green shutters of the inn at Burford.[1]

Now, this is one of the natural appetites with which any lively literature has to count. The desire for knowledge, I had almost added the desire for meat, is not more deeply seated than this demand for fit and striking incident. The dullest of clowns tells, or tries to tell, himself a story, as the feeblest of children uses invention in his play; and even as the imaginative grown person, joining in the game, at once enriches it with many delightful circumstances, the great creative writer shows us the realisation and the apotheosis of the day-dreams of common men. His stories may be nourished with the realities of life, but their true mark is to satisfy the nameless longings of the reader, and to obey the ideal laws of the day-dream. The right kind of thing should fall out in the right kind of place; the right kind of thing should follow; and not only the characters talk aptly and think naturally, but all the circumstances in a tale answer one to another like notes in music. The threads of a story come from time to time together and make a picture in the web; the characters fall from time to time into some attitude to each other or to nature, which stamps the story home like an illustration. Crusoe recoiling from the footprint, Achilles shouting over against the Trojans, Ulysses bending the great bow, Christian running with his fingers in his ears, these are each culminating moments in the legend, and each has been printed on the mind's eye for ever. Other things we may forget; we may forget the words, although they are beautiful; we may forget the author's comment, although perhaps it was ingenious and true; but these epoch-making scenes, which put the last mark of truth upon a story and fill up, at one blow, our capacity for sympathetic pleasure, we so adopt into the very bosom of our mind that neither time nor tide can efface or weaken the impression. This, then, is the plastic part of literature: to embody character, thought, or emotion in some act or attitude that shall be remarkably striking to the mind's eye. This is the highest and hardest thing to do in words; the thing which, once accomplished, equally delights the schoolboy and the sage, and makes, in its own right, the quality of epics. Compared with this, all other purposes in literature, except the purely lyrical or the purely philosophic, are bastard in nature, facile of execution, and feeble in result. It is one thing to write about the inn at Burford, or to describe scenery with

---

[1]Since the above was written I have tried to launch the boat with my own hands in *Kidnapped*. Some day, perhaps, I may try a rattle at the shutters.

the word-painters; it is quite another to seize on the heart of the suggestion and make a country famous with a legend. It is one thing to remark and to dissect, with the most cutting logic, the complications of life, and of the human spirit; it is quite another to give them body and blood in the story of Ajax or of Hamlet. The first is literature, but the second is something besides, for it is likewise art.

English people of the present day are apt, I know not why, to look somewhat down on incident, and reserve their admiration for the clink of teaspoons and the accents of the curate. It is thought clever to write a novel with no story at all, or at least with a very dull one. Reduced even to the lowest terms, a certain interest can be communicated by the art of narrative; a sense of human kinship stirred; and a kind of monotonous fitness, comparable to the words and air of *Sandy's Mull*, preserved among the infinitesimal occurrences recorded. Some people work, in this manner, with even a strong touch. Mr Trollope's inimitable clergymen naturally arise to the mind in this connection. But even Mr Trollope does not confine himself to chronicling small beer. Mr Crawley's collision with the Bishop's wife, Mr Melnotte dallying in the deserted banquet-room, are typical incidents, epically conceived, fitly embodying a crisis. Or again look at Thackeray. If Rawdon Crawley's blow were not delivered, *Vanity Fair* would cease to be a work of art. That scene is the chief ganglion of the tale; and the discharge of energy from Rawdon's fist is the reward and consolation of the reader. The end of *Esmond* is a yet wider excursion from the author's customary fields; the scene at Castlewood is pure Dumas; the great and wily English borrower has here borrowed from the great, unblushing French thief; as usual, he has borrowed admirably well, and the breaking of the sword rounds off the best of all his books with a manly, martial note. But perhaps nothing can more strongly illustrate the necessity for marking incident than to compare the living fame of *Robinson Crusoe* with the discredit of *Clarissa Harlowe*. *Clarissa* is a book of a far more startling import, worked out, on a great canvas, with inimitable courage and unflagging art. It contains wit, character, passion, plot, conversations full of spirit and insight, letters sparkling with unstrained humanity; and if the death of the heroine be somewhat frigid and artificial, the last days of the hero strike the only note of what we now call Byronism, between the Elizabethans and Byron himself. And yet a little story of a shipwrecked sailor, with not a tenth part of the style nor a thousandth part of the wisdom, exploring none of the arcana of humanity and deprived of the perennial interest of love, goes on from edition to edition, ever young, while *Clarissa* lies upon the shelves unread. A friend of mine, a Welsh blacksmith, was twenty-five years old and could neither read nor write, when he heard a chapter of *Robinson* read aloud in a farm kitchen. Up to that moment he had sat content, huddled in his ignorance, but he left that farm another man. There were day-dreams, it appeared, divine day-dreams, written and printed and bound, and to be bought for money and enjoyed at pleasure. Down he sat that day, painfully learned to read Welsh, and returned to borrow the book. It had been lost, nor could he find another copy but one that was in English. Down he sat once more, learned English, and at length, and with entire delight, read *Robinson*. It is like the story of a love-chase. If he had heard a letter from *Clarissa*, would he have been fired with the same chivalrous ardour? I wonder. Yet *Clarissa* has every quality that can be shown in prose, one alone excepted – pictorial or picture-making romance. While *Robinson* depends, for the most part and with the overwhelming majority of its readers, on the charm of circumstance.

In the highest achievements of the art of words, the dramatic and the pictorial, the moral and romantic interest, rise and fall together by a common and organic law. Situation is animated with passion, passion clothed upon with situation. Neither exists for itself, but each inheres indissolubly with the other. This is high art; and not only the highest art possible in words, but the highest art of all, since it combines the greatest mass and diversity of the elements of truth and pleasure. Such are epics, and the few prose tales that have the epic weight. But as from a school of works, aping the creative, incident and romance are ruthlessly discarded, so may character and drama be omitted or subordinated to romance. There is one book, for example, more generally loved than Shakespeare, that captivates in childhood, and still delights in age – I mean the *Arabian Nights* – where you shall look in vain for moral or for intellectual interest. No human face or voice greets us among that wooden crowd of kings and genies, sorcerers and beggarmen. Adventure, on the most naked terms, furnishes forth the entertainment and is found enough. Dumas approaches perhaps nearest of any modern to these Arabian authors in the purely material charm of some of his romances. The early part of *Monte Cristo*, down to the finding of the treasure, is a piece of perfect story-telling; the man never breathed who shared these moving incidents without a tremor; and yet Faria is a thing of packthread and Dantès little more than a name. The sequel is one long-drawn error, gloomy, bloody, unnatural and dull; but as for these early chapters, I do not believe there is another volume extant where you can breathe the same unmingled atmosphere of romance. It is very thin and light, to be sure, as on a high mountain; but it is brisk and clear and sunny in proportion. I saw the other day, with envy, an old and a very clever lady setting forth on a second or third voyage into *Monte Cristo*. Here are stories which powerfully affect the reader, which can be reperused at any age, and where the characters are no more than puppets. The bony fist of the showman visibly propels them; their springs are an open secret; their faces are of wood, their bellies filled with bran; and yet we thrillingly partake of their adventures. And the point may be illustrated still further. The last interview between Lucy and Richard Feverel is pure drama; more than that, it is the strongest scene, since Shakespeare, in the English tongue. Their first meeting by the river, on the other hand, is pure romance; it has nothing to do with character; it might happen to any other boy and maiden, and be none the less delightful for the change. And yet I think he would be a bold man who should choose between these passages. Thus, in the same book, we may have two scenes, each capital in its order: in the one, human passion, deep calling unto deep, shall utter its genuine voice; in the second, according circumstances, like instruments in tune, shall build up a trivial but desirable incident, such as we love to prefigure for ourselves; and in the end, in spite of the critics, we may hesitate to give the preference to either. The one may ask more genius – I do not say it does; but at least the other dwells as clearly in the memory.

True romantic art, again, makes a romance of all things. It reaches into the highest abstraction of the ideal; it does not refuse the most pedestrian realism. *Robinson Crusoe* is as realistic as it is romantic; both qualities are pushed to an extreme, and neither suffers. Nor does romance depend upon the material importance of the incidents. To deal with strong and deadly elements, banditti, pirates, war and murder, is to conjure with great names, and, in the event of failure, to double the disgrace. The arrival of Haydn and Consuelo at the Canon's villa is a very trifling incident; yet we may read a dozen boisterous stories from beginning to end, and not receive so fresh and stirring an impression of adventure. It was the scene of Crusoe at the wreck, if I remember rightly, that so bewitched my blacksmith. Nor is the fact surprising. Every single article the castaway recovers from the hulk is 'a joy for ever' to the man who reads of them. They are the things that should be found, and the bare enumeration stirs the blood. I found a glimmer of the same interest the other day in a new book, *The Sailor's Sweetheart*, by Mr Clark Russell. The whole business of the brig *Morning Star* is very rightly felt and spiritedly written; but the clothes, the books and the money satisfy the reader's mind like things to eat. We are dealing here with the old cut-and-dry, legitimate interest of treasure trove. But even treasure trove can be made dull. There are few people who have not groaned under the plethora of goods that fell to the lot of the *Swiss Family Robinson*, that dreary family. They found article after article, creature after creature, from milk kine to pieces of ordnance, a whole consignment; but no informing taste had presided over the selection, there was no smack or relish in the invoice; and these riches left the fancy cold. The box of goods in Verne's *Mysterious Island* is another case in point: there was no gusto and no glamour about that; it might have come from a shop. But the two hundred and seventy-eight Australian sovereigns on board the *Morning Star* fell upon me like a surprise that I had expected; whole vistas of secondary stories, besides the one in hand, radiated forth from that discovery, as they radiate from a striking particular in life; and I was made for the moment as happy as a reader has the right to be.

To come at all at the nature of this quality of romance, we must bear in mind the peculiarity of our attitude to any art. No art produces illusion; in the theatre we never forget that we are in the theatre; and while we read a story, we sit wavering between two minds, now merely clapping our hands at the merit of the performance, now condescending to take an active part in fancy with the characters. This last is the triumph of romantic story-telling: when the reader consciously plays at being the hero, the scene is a good scene. Now in character-studies the pleasure that we take is critical; we watch, we approve, we smile at incongruities, we are moved to sudden heats of sympathy with courage, suffering or virtue. But the characters are still themselves, they are not us; the more clearly they are depicted, the more widely do they stand away from us, the more imperiously do they thrust us back into our place as a spectator. I cannot identify myself with Rawdon Crawley or with Eugène de Rastignac, for I have scarce a hope or fear in common with them. It is not character but incident that woos us out of our reserve. Something happens as we desire to have it happen to ourselves; some situation, that we have long dallied with in fancy, is realised in the story with enticing and appropriate details. Then we forget the characters; then we push the hero aside; then we plunge into the tale in our own person and bathe in fresh experience; and then, and then only, do we say we have been reading a romance. It is not only pleasurable things that we imagine in our day-dreams; there are lights in which we are willing to contemplate even the idea of our own death; ways in which it seems as if it would amuse us to be cheated, wounded or calumniated. It is thus possible to construct a story, even of tragic import, in which every incident, detail and trick of circumstance shall be welcome to the reader's thoughts. Fiction is to the grown man what play is to the child; it is there that he changes the atmosphere and tenor of his life; and when the game so chimes with his fancy that he can join in it with all his heart, when it pleases him with every turn, when he loves to recall it and dwells upon its recollection with entire delight, fiction is called romance.

Walter Scott is out and away the king of the romantics. *The Lady of the Lake* has no indisputable claim to be a poem beyond the inherent fitness and desirability of the tale. It is just such a story as a man would make up for himself, walking, in the best health and temper, through just such scenes as it is laid in. Hence it is that a charm dwells undefinable among these slovenly verses, as the unseen cuckoo fills the mountains with his note; hence, even after we have flung the book aside, the scenery and adventures remain present to the mind, a new and green possession, not unworthy of that beautiful name, *The Lady of the Lake*, or that direct, romantic opening – one of the most spirited and poetical in literature – 'The stag at eve had drunk his fill.' The same strength and the same weaknesses adorn and disfigure the novels. In that ill-written, ragged book, *The Pirate*, the figure of Cleveland – cast up by the sea on the resounding foreland of Dunrossness – moving, with the blood on his hands and the Spanish words on his tongue, among the simple islanders – singing a serenade under the window of his Shetland mistress – is conceived in the very highest manner of romantic invention. The words of his song, 'Through groves of palm,' sung in such a scene and by such a lover, clench, as in a nutshell, the emphatic contrast upon which the tale is built. In *Guy Mannering*, again, every incident is delightful to the imagination; and the scene when Harry Bertram lands at Ellangowan is a model instance of romantic method.

'I remember the tune well,' he says, 'though I cannot guess what should at present so strongly recall it to my memory.' He took his flageolet from his pocket and played a simple melody. Apparently the tune awoke the corresponding associations of a damsel . . . She immediately took up the song –
    'Are these the links of Forth, she said;

Or are they the crooks of Dee,
Or the bonny woods of Warroch Head
That I so fain would see?'
'By heaven!' said Bertram, 'it is the very ballad.'

On this quotation two remarks fall to be made. First, as an instance of modern feeling for romance, this famous touch of the flageolet and the old song is selected by Miss Braddon for omission. Miss Braddon's idea of a story, like Mrs Todgers's idea of a wooden leg, were something strange to have expounded. As a matter of personal experience, Meg's appearance to old Mr Bertram on the road, the ruins of Derncleugh, the scene of the flageolet, and the Dominie's recognition of Harry, are the four strong notes that continue to ring in the mind after the book is laid aside. The second point is still more curious. The reader will observe a mark of excision in the passage as quoted by me. Well, here is how it runs in the original: 'a damsel, who, close behind a fine spring about half-way down the descent, and which had once supplied the castle with water, was engaged in bleaching linen.' A man who gave in such copy would be discharged from the staff of a daily paper. Scott has forgotten to prepare the reader for the presence of the 'damsel'; he has forgotten to mention the spring and its relation to the ruin; and now, face to face with his omission, instead of trying back and starting fair, crams all this matter, tail foremost, into a single shambling sentence. It is not merely bad English, or bad style; it is abominably bad narrative besides.

Certainly the contrast is remarkable; and it is one that throws a strong light upon the subject of this paper. For here we have a man of the finest creative instinct touching with perfect certainty and charm the romantic junctures of his story; and we find him utterly careless, almost, it would seem, incapable, in the technical matter of style, and not only frequently weak, but frequently wrong in points of drama. In character parts, indeed, and particularly in the Scotch, he was delicate, strong and truthful; but the trite, obliterated features of too many of his heroes have already wearied two generations of readers. At times his characters will speak with something far beyond propriety, with a true heroic note; but on the next page they will be wading wearily forward with an ungrammatical and undramatic rigmarole of words. The man who could conceive and write the character of Elspeth of the Craigburnfoot, as Scott has conceived and written it, had not only splendid romantic, but splendid tragic gifts. How comes it, then, that he could so often fob us off with languid, inarticulate twaddle?

It seems to me that the explanation is to be found in the very quality of his surprising merits. As his books are play to the reader, so were they play to him. He conjured up the romantic with delight, but he had hardly patience to describe it. He was a great day-dreamer, a seer of fit and beautiful and humorous visions, but hardly a great artist; hardly, in the manful sense, an artist at all. He pleased himself, and so he pleases us. Of the pleasures of his art he tasted fully; but of its toils and vigils and distresses never man knew less. A great romantic – an idle child.

THE CHARACTER OF DOGS

The civilisation, the manners, and the morals of dog-kind are to a great extent subordinated to those of his ancestral master, man. This animal, in many ways so superior, has accepted a position of inferiority, shares the domestic life, and humours the caprices of the tyrant. But the potentate, like the British in India, pays small regard to the character of his willing client, judges him with listless glances, and condemns him in a byword. Listless have been the looks of his admirers, who have exhausted idle terms of praise, and buried the poor soul below exaggerations. And yet more idle and, if possible, more unintelligent has been the attitude of his express detractors; those who are very fond of dogs 'but in their proper place'; who say 'poo' fellow, poo' fellow,' and are themselves far poorer; who whet the knife of the vivisectionist or heat his oven; who are not ashamed to admire 'the creature's instinct'; and flying far beyond folly, have dared to resuscitate the theory of animal machines. The 'dog's instinct' and the 'automaton-dog,' in this age of psychology and science, sound like strange anachronisms. An automaton he certainly is; a machine working independently of his control, the heart like the mill-wheel, keeping all in motion, and the consciousness, like a person shut in the mill garret, enjoying the view out of the window and shaken by the thunder of the stones; an automaton in one corner of which a living spirit is confined: an automaton like man. Instinct again he certainly possesses. Inherited aptitudes are his, inherited frailties. Some things he at once views and understands, as though he were awakened from a sleep, as though he came 'trailing clouds of glory.' But with him, as with man, the field of instinct is limited; its utterances are obscure and occasional; and about the far larger part of life both the dog and his master must conduct their steps by deduction and observation.

The leading distinction between dog and man, after and perhaps before the different duration of their lives, is that the one can speak and that the other cannot. The absence of the power of speech confines the dog in the development of his intellect. It hinders him from many speculations, for words are the beginning of metaphysic. At the same blow it saves him from many superstitions, and his silence has won for him a higher name for virtue than his conduct justifies. The faults of the dog are many. He is vainer than man, singularly greedy of notice, singularly intolerant of ridicule, suspicious like the deaf, jealous to the degree of frenzy, and radically devoid of truth. The day of an intelligent small dog is passed in the manufacture and the laborious communication of falsehood; he lies with his tail, he lies with his eye, he lies with his protesting paw; and when he rattles his dish or scratches at the door his purpose is other than appears. But he has some apology to offer for the vice. Many of the signs which form his dialect have come to bear an arbitrary meaning, clearly understood both by his master and himself; yet when a new want arises he must either invent a new vehicle of meaning or wrest an old one to a different purpose; and this necessity frequently recurring must tend to lessen his idea of the sanctity of symbols. Meanwhile the dog is clear in his own conscience, and draws, with a human nicety, the distinction between formal and essential truth. Of his punning perversions, his legitimate dexterity with symbols, he is even vain; but when he has told and been detected in a lie, there is not a hair upon his body but confesses guilt. To a dog of gentlemanly feeling theft and falsehood are disgraceful vices. The canine, like the human, gentleman demands in his misdemeanours Montaigne's '*je ne sais quoi de généreux.*' He is never more than half ashamed of having barked or bitten; and for those faults into which he has been led by the desire to shine before a lady of his race, he retains, even under physical correction, a share of pride. But to be caught lying, if he understands it, instantly uncurls his fleece.

Just as among dull observers he preserves a name for truth, the dog has been credited with modesty. It is amazing how the use of language blunts the faculties of man – that because vainglory finds no vent in words, creatures supplied with eyes have been unable to detect a fault so gross and obvious. If a small spoiled dog were suddenly to be endowed with speech, he would prate interminably, and still about himself; when we had friends, we should be forced to lock him in a garret; and what with his whining jealousies and his foible for falsehood, in a year's time he would have gone far to weary out our love. I was about to compare him to Sir Willoughby Patterne, but the Patternes have a manlier sense of their own merits; and the parallel, besides, is ready. Hans Christian Andersen, as we behold him in his startling memoirs, thrilling from top to toe with an excruciating vanity, and scouting even along the street for shadows of offence – here was the talking dog.

It is just this rage for consideration that has betrayed the dog into his satellite position as the friend of man. The cat, an animal of franker appetites, preserves his independence. But the dog, with one eye ever on the audience, has been wheedled into slavery, and praised and patted into the renunciation of his nature. Once he ceased hunting and became man's plate-licker, the Rubicon was crossed. Thenceforth he was a gentleman of leisure; and except the few whom we keep working, the whole race grew more and more self-conscious, mannered and affected. The number of things that a small dog does naturally is strangely small. Enjoying better spirits and not crushed under material cares, he is far more theatrical than average man. His whole life, if he be a dog of any pretension to gallantry, is spent in a vain show, and in the hot pursuit of admiration. Take out your puppy for a walk, and you will find the little ball of fur clumsy, stupid, bewildered, but natural. Let but a few months pass, and when you repeat the process you will find nature buried in convention. He will do nothing plainly; but the simplest processes of our material life will all be bent into the forms of an elaborate and mysterious etiquette. Instinct, says the fool, has awakened. But it is not so. Some dogs – some, at the very least – if they be kept separate from others, remain quite natural; and these, when at length they meet with a companion of experience, and have the game explained to them, distinguish themselves by the severity of their devotion to its rules. I wish I were allowed to tell a story which would radiantly illuminate the point; but men, like dogs, have an elaborate and mysterious etiquette. It is their bond of sympathy that both are the children of convention.

The person, man or dog, who has a conscience is eternally condemned to some degree of humbug; the sense of the law in their members fatally precipitates either towards a frozen and affected bearing. And the converse is true; and in the elaborate and conscious manners of the dog, moral opinions and the love of the ideal stand confessed. To follow for ten minutes in the street some swaggering, canine cavalier, is to receive a lesson in dramatic art and the cultured conduct of the body; in every act and gesture you see him true to a refined conception; and the dullest cur, beholding him, pricks up his ear and proceeds to imitate and parody that charming ease. For to be a high-mannered and high-minded gentleman, careless, affable, and gay, is the inborn pretension of the dog. The large dog, so much lazier, so much more weighed upon with matter, so majestic in repose, so beautiful in effort, is born with the dramatic means to wholly represent the part. And it is more pathetic and perhaps more instructive to consider the small dog in his conscientious and imperfect efforts to outdo Sir Philip Sidney. For the ideal of the dog is feudal and religious; the ever-present polytheism, the whip-bearing Olympus of mankind, rules them on the one hand; on the other, their singular difference of size and strength among themselves effectually prevents the appearance of the democratic notion. Or we might more exactly compare their society to the curious spectacle presented by a school – ushers, monitors, and big and little boys – qualified by one circumstance, the introduction of the other sex. In each, we should observe a somewhat similar tension of manner, and somewhat similar points of honour. In each the larger animal keeps a contemptuous good humour; in each the smaller annoys him with wasp-like impudence, certain of practical immunity; in each we shall find a double life producing double characters, and an excursive and noisy heroism combined with a fair amount of practical timidity. I have known dogs, and I have known school heroes that, set aside the fur, could hardly have been told apart; and if we desire to understand the chivalry of old, we must turn to the school playfields or the dungheap where the dogs are trooping.

Woman, with the dog, has been long enfranchised. Incessant massacre of female innocents has changed the proportions of the sexes and perverted their relations. Thus, when we regard the manners of the dog, we see a romantic and monogamous animal, once perhaps as delicate as the cat, at war with impossible conditions. Man has much to answer for; and the part he plays is yet more damnable and parlous than Corin's in the eyes of Touchstone. But his intervention has at least created an imperial situation for the rare surviving ladies. In that society they reign without a rival: conscious queens; and in the only instance of a canine wife-beater that has ever fallen under my notice, the criminal was somewhat excused by the circumstances of his story. He is a little, very alert, well-bred, intelligent Skye, as black as a hat, with a wet bramble for a nose and two cairngorms for eyes. To the human observer, he is decidedly well-looking; but to the ladies of his race he seems abhorrent. A thorough elaborate gentleman, of the plume and sword-knot order, he was born with a nice sense of gallantry to women. He took at their hands the most outrageous treatment; I have heard him bleating like a sheep, I have seen him streaming blood, and his ear tattered like a regimental banner; and yet he would scorn to make reprisals. Nay more, when a human lady upraised the contumelious whip against the very dame who had been so cruelly misusing him, my little great-heart gave but one hoarse cry and fell upon the tyrant tooth and nail. This is the tale of a soul's tragedy. After three years of unavailing chivalry, he suddenly, in one hour, threw off the yoke of obligation; had he been Shakespeare he would then have written *Troilus and Cressida* to brand the offending sex; but being only a little dog, he began to bite them. The surprise of the ladies whom he attacked indicated the monstrosity of his offence; but he had fairly beaten off his better angel, fairly committed moral suicide; for almost in the same hour, throwing aside the last rags of decency, he proceeded to attack the aged also. The fact is worth remark, showing, as it does, that ethical laws are common both to dogs and men; and that with both a single deliberate violation of the conscience loosens all. 'But while the lamp holds on to burn,' says the paraphrase, 'the greatest sinner may return.' I have been cheered to see symptoms of effectual penitence in my sweet ruffian; and by the handling that he accepted uncomplainingly the other day from an indignant fair one, I begin to hope the period of *Sturm und Drang* is closed.

All these little gentlemen are subtle casuists. The duty to the female dog is plain; but where competing duties rise, down they will sit and study them out, like Jesuit confessors. I knew another little Skye, somewhat plain in manner and appearance, but a creature compact of amiability and solid wisdom. His family going abroad for a winter, he was received for that period by an uncle in the same city. The winter over, his own family home again, and his own house (of which he was very proud) reopened, he found himself in a dilemma between two conflicting duties of loyalty and gratitude. His old friends were not to be neglected, but it seemed hardly decent to desert the new. This was how he solved the problem. Every morning, as soon as the door was opened, off posted Coolin to his uncle's, visited the children in the nursery, saluted the whole family, and was back at home in time for breakfast and his bit of fish. Nor was this done without a sacrifice on his part, sharply felt; for he had to forego the particular honour and jewel of his day – his morning's walk with my father. And, perhaps from this cause, he gradually wearied of and relaxed the practice, and at length returned entirely to his ancient habits. But the same decision served him in another and more distressing case of divided duty, which happened not long after. He was not at all a kitchen dog, but the cook had nursed him with unusual kindness during the distemper; and though he did not adore her as he adored my father – although (born snob) he was critically conscious of her position as 'only a servant' – he still cherished for her a special gratitude. Well, the cook left, and retired some streets away to lodgings of her own; and there was Coolin in precisely the same situation with any young gentleman who has had the inestimable benefit of a faithful nurse. The canine conscience did not solve the problem with a pound of tea at Christmas. No longer content to pay a flying visit, it was the whole forenoon that he dedicated to his solitary friend. And so, day by day, he continued to comfort her solitude until (for some reason which I could never understand and cannot approve) he was kept locked up to break him of the graceful habit. Here, it is not the similarity, it is the difference, that is worthy of remark; the clearly marked degrees of gratitude and the proportional duration of his visits. Anything further removed from instinct it were hard to fancy; and one is even stirred to a certain impatience with a character so destitute of spontaneity, so passionless in justice, and so priggishly obedient to the voice of reason.

There are not many dogs like this good Coolin, and not many people. But the type is one well marked, both in the human and the canine family. Gallantry was not his aim, but a solid and somewhat oppressive respectability. He was a sworn foe to the unusual and the conspicuous, a praiser of the golden mean, a kind of city uncle modified by Cheeryble. And as he was precise and conscientious in all the steps of his own blameless course, he looked for the same precision and an even greater gravity in the bearing of his deity, my father. It was no sinecure to be Coolin's idol: he was exacting like a rigid parent; and at every sign of levity in the man whom he respected, he announced loudly the death of virtue and the proximate fall of the pillars of the earth.

I have called him a snob; but all dogs are so, though in varying degrees. It is hard to follow their snobbery among themselves; for though I think we can perceive distinctions of rank, we cannot grasp what is the criterion. Thus in Edinburgh, in a good part of the town, there were several distinct societies or clubs that met in the morning to – the phrase is technical – to 'rake the backets' in a troop. A friend of mine, the master of three dogs, was one day surprised to observe that they had left one club and joined another; but whether it was a rise or a fall, and the result of an invitation or an expulsion, was more than he could guess. And this illustrates pointedly our ignorance of the real life of dogs, their social ambitions and their social hierarchies. At least, in their dealings with men they are not only conscious of sex, but of the difference of station. And that in the most snobbish manner; for the poor man's dog is not offended by the notice of the rich, and keeps all his ugly feeling for those poorer or more ragged than his master. And again, for every station they have an ideal of behaviour, to which the master, under pain of derogation, will do wisely to conform. How often has not a cold glance of an eye informed me that my dog was disappointed; and how much more gladly would he not have taken a beating than to be thus wounded in the seat of piety!

I knew one disrespectable dog. He was far liker a cat; cared little or nothing for men, with whom he merely co-existed as we do with cattle, and was entirely devoted to the art of poaching. A house would not hold him, and to live in a town was what he refused. He led, I believe, a life of troubled but genuine pleasure, and perished beyond all question in a trap. But this was an exception, a marked reversion to the ancestral type; like the hairy human infant. The true dog of the nineteenth century, to judge by the remainder of my fairly large acquaintance, is in love with respectability. A street-dog was once adopted by a lady. While still an Arab, he had done as Arabs do, gambolling in the mud, charging into butchers' stalls, a cat-hunter, a sturdy beggar, a common rogue and vagabond; but with his rise into society he laid aside these inconsistent pleasures. He stole no more, he hunted no more cats; and conscious of his collar, he ignored his old companions. Yet the canine upper class was never brought to recognise the upstart, and from that hour, except for human countenance, he was alone. Friendless, shorn of his sports and the habits of a lifetime, he still lived in a glory of happiness, content with his acquired respectability, and with no care but to support it solemnly. Are we to condemn or praise this self-made dog? We praise his human brother. And thus to conquer vicious habits is as rare with dogs as with men. With the more part, for all their scruple-mongering and moral thought, the vices that are born with them remain invincible throughout; and they live all their years, glorying in their virtues, but still the slaves of their defects. Thus the sage Coolin was a thief to the last; among a thousand peccadilloes, a whole goose and a whole cold leg of mutton lay upon his conscience; but Woggs,[1] whose soul's shipwreck in

---

[1] Walter, Watty, Woggy, Woggs, Wogg, and lastly Bogue; under which last name he fell in battle some twelve months ago. Glory was his aim and he attained it; for his icon, by the hand of Caldecott, now lies among the treasures of the nation.

the matter of gallantry I have recounted above, has only twice been known to steal, and has often nobly conquered the temptation. The eighth is his favourite commandment. There is something painfully human in these unequal virtues and mortal frailties of the best. Still more painful is the bearing of those 'stammering professors' in the house of sickness and under the terror of death. It is beyond a doubt to me that, somehow or other, the dog connects together, or confounds, the uneasiness of sickness and the consciousness of guilt. To the pains of the body he often adds the tortures of the conscience; and at these times his haggard protestations form, in regard to the human deathbed, a dreadful parody or parallel.

I once supposed that I had found an inverse relation between the double etiquette which dogs obey; and that those who were most addicted to the showy street life among other dogs were less careful in the practice of home virtues for the tyrant man. But the female dog, that mass of carneying affectations, shines equally in either sphere; rules her rough posse of attendant swains with unwearying tact and gusto; and with her master and mistress pushes the arts of insinuation to their crowning point. The attention of man and the regard of other dogs flatter (it would thus appear) the same sensibility; but perhaps, if we could read the canine heart, they would be found to flatter it in very different degrees. Dogs live with man as courtiers round a monarch, steeped in the flattery of his notice and enriched with sinecures. To push their favour in this world of pickings and caresses is, perhaps, the business of their lives; and their joys may lie outside. I am in despair at our persistent ignorance. I read in the lives of our companions the same processes of reason, the same antique and fatal conflicts of the right against the wrong, and of unbitted nature with too rigid custom; I see them with our weaknesses, vain, false, inconstant against appetite, and with our one stalk of virtue, devoted to the dream of an ideal; and yet, as they hurry by me on the street with tail in air, or come singly to solicit my regard, I must own the secret purport of their lives is still inscrutable to man. Is man the friend, or is he the patron only? Have they indeed forgotten nature's voice? or are those moments snatched from courtiership when they touch noses with the tinker's mongrel, the brief reward and pleasure of their artificial lives? Doubtless, when man shares with his dog the toils of a profession and the pleasures of an art, as with the shepherd or the poacher, the affection warms and strengthens till it fills the soul. But doubtless, also, the masters are, in many cases, the object of a merely interested cultus, sitting aloft like Louis Quatorze, giving and receiving flattery and favour; and the dogs, like the majority of men, have but foregone their true existence and become the dupes of their ambition.

A HUMBLE REMONSTRANCE

I

We have recently enjoyed a quite peculiar pleasure: hearing, in some detail, the opinions, about the art they practise, of Mr Walter Besant and Mr Henry James; two men certainly of very different calibre: Mr James so precise of outline, so cunning of fence, so scrupulous of finish, and Mr Besant so genial, so friendly, with so persuasive and humorous a vein of whim: Mr James the very type of the deliberate artist, Mr Besant the impersonation of good nature. That such doctors should differ will excite no great surprise; but one point in which they seem to agree fills me, I confess, with wonder. For they are both content to talk about the 'art of fiction;' and Mr Besant, waxing exceedingly bold, goes on to oppose this so-called 'art of fiction' to the 'art of poetry.' By the art of poetry he can mean nothing but the art of verse, an art of handicraft, and only comparable with the art of prose. For that heat and height of sane emotion which we agree to call by the name of poetry, is but a libertine and vagrant quality; present, at times, in any art, more often absent from them all; too seldom present in the prose novel, too frequently absent from the ode and epic. Fiction is in the same case; it is no substantive art, but an element which enters largely into all the arts but architecture. Homer, Wordsworth, Phidias, Hogarth, and Salvini, all deal in fiction; and yet I do not suppose that either Hogarth or Salvini, to mention but these two, entered in any degree into the scope of Mr Besant's interesting lecture or Mr James's charming essay. The art of fiction, then, regarded as a definition, is both too ample and too scanty. Let me suggest another; let me suggest that what both Mr James and Mr Besant had in view was neither more nor less than the art of narrative.

But Mr Besant is anxious to speak solely of 'the modern English novel,' the stay and bread-winner of Mr Mudie; and in the author of the most pleasing novel on that roll, *All Sorts and Conditions of Men*, the desire is natural enough. I can conceive then, that he would hasten to propose two additions, and read thus: the art of *fictitious* narrative *in prose.*

Now the fact of the existence of the modern English novel is not to be denied; materially, with its three volumes, leaded type, and gilded lettering, it is easily distinguishable from other forms of literature; but to talk at all fruitfully of any branch of art, it is needful to build our definitions on some more fundamental ground than binding. Why, then, are we to add 'in prose?' *The Odyssey* appears to me the best of romances; *The Lady of the Lake* to stand high in the second order; and Chaucer's tales and prologues to contain more of the matter and art of the modern English novel than the whole treasury of Mr Mudie. Whether a narrative be written in blank verse or the Spenserian stanza, in the long period of Gibbon or the clipped phrase of Charles Reade, the principles of the art of narrative must be equally observed. The choice of a noble and swelling style in prose affects the problem of narration in the same way, if not to the same degree, as the choice of measured verse; for both imply a closer synthesis of events, a higher key of dialogue, and a more picked and stately strain of words. If you are to refuse *Don Juan*, it is hard to see why you should include *Zanoni* or (to bracket works of very different value) *The Scarlet Letter*; and by what discrimination are you to open your doors to *The Pilgrim's Progress* and close them on *The Faery Queen*? To bring things closer home, I will here propound to Mr Besant a conundrum. A narrative called *Paradise Lost* was written in English verse by one John Milton; what was it then? It was next translated by Chateaubriand into French prose; and what was it then? Lastly, the French translation was, by some inspired compatriot of George Gilfillan (and of mine) turned bodily into an English novel; and, in the name of clearness, what was it then?

But, once more, why should we add 'fictitious'? The reason why is obvious. The reason why not, if something more recondite, does not want for weight. The art of narrative, in fact, is the same, whether it is applied to the selection and illustration of a real series of events or of an imaginary series. Boswell's *Life of Johnson* (a work of cunning and inimitable art) owes its success to the same technical manœuvres as (let us say) *Tom Jones*: the clear conception of certain characters of man, the choice and presentation of certain incidents out of a great number that offered, and the invention (yes, invention) and preservation of a certain key in dialogue. In which these things are done with the more art – in which with the greater air of nature – readers will differently judge. Boswell's is, indeed, a very special case, and almost a generic; but it is not only in Boswell, it is in every biography with any salt of life, it is in every history where events and men, rather than ideas, are presented – in Tacitus, in Carlyle, in Michelet, in Macaulay – that the novelist will find many of his own methods most conspicuously and adroitly handled. He will find besides that he, who is free – who has the right to invent or steal a missing incident, who has the right, more precious still, of wholesale omission – is frequently defeated, and, with all his advantages, leaves a less strong impression of reality and passion. Mr James utters his mind with a becoming fervour on the sanctity of truth to the novelist; on a more careful examination truth will seem a word of very debateable propriety, not only for the labours of the novelist, but for those of the historian. No art – to use the daring phrase of Mr James – can successfully 'compete with life;' and the art that seeks to do so is condemned to perish *montibus aviis*. Life goes before us, infinite in complication; attended by the most various and surprising meteors; appealing at once to the eye, to the ear, to the mind – the seat of wonder, to the touch – so thrillingly delicate, and to the belly – so imperious when starved. It combines and employs in its manifestation the method and material, not of one art only, but of all the arts. Music is but an arbitrary trifling with a few of life's majestic chords; painting is but a shadow of its pageantry of light and colour; literature does but drily indicate that wealth of incident, of moral obligation, of virtue, vice, action, rapture and agony, with which it teems. To 'compete with life,' whose sun we cannot look upon, whose passions and diseases waste and slay us – to compete with the flavour of wine, the beauty of the dawn, the scorching of fire, the bitterness of death and separation – here is, indeed, a projected escalade of heaven; here are, indeed, labours for a Hercules in a dress coat, armed with a pen and a dictionary to depict the passions, armed with a tube of superior flake-white to paint the portrait of the insufferable sun. No art is true in this sense: none can 'compete with life:' not even history, built indeed of indisputable facts, but these facts robbed of their vivacity and sting; so that even when we read of the sack of a city or the fall of an empire, we are surprised, and justly commend the author's talent, if our pulse be quickened. And mark, for a last differentia, that this quickening of the pulse is, in almost every case, purely agreeable; that these phantom reproductions of experience, even at their most acute, convey decided pleasure; while experience itself, in the cockpit of life, can torture and slay.

What, then, is the object, what the method, of an art, and what the source of its power? The whole secret is that no art does 'compete with life.' Man's one method, whether he reasons or creates, is to half-shut his eyes against the dazzle and confusion of reality. The arts, like arithmetic and geometry, turn away their eyes from the gross, coloured and mobile nature at our feet, and regard instead a certain figmentary abstraction. Geometry will tell us of a circle, a thing never seen in nature; asked about a green circle or an iron circle, it lays its hand upon its mouth. So with the arts. Painting, ruefully comparing sunshine and flake-white, gives up truth of colour, as it had already given up relief and movement; and instead of vying with nature, arranges a scheme of harmonious tints. Literature, above all in its most typical mood, the mood of narrative, similarly flees the direct challenge and pursues instead an independent and creative aim. So far as it imitates at all, it imitates not life but speech: not the facts of human destiny, but the emphasis and the suppressions with which the human actor tells of them. The real art that dealt with life directly was that of the first men who told their stories round the savage camp-fire. Our art is occupied, and bound to be occupied, not so much in making stories true as in making them typical; not so much in capturing the lineaments of each fact, as in marshalling all of them towards a common end. For the welter of impressions, all forcible but all discrete, which life presents, it substitutes a certain artificial series of impressions, all indeed most feebly represented, but all aiming at the same effect, all eloquent of the same idea, all chiming together like consonant notes in music or like the graduated tints in a good picture. From all its chapters, from all its pages, from all its sentences, the well-written novel echoes and re-echoes its one creative and controlling thought; to this must every incident and character contribute; the style must have been pitched in unison with this; and if there is anywhere a word that looks another way, the book would be stronger, clearer, and (I had almost said) fuller without it. Life is monstrous, infinite, illogical, abrupt and poignant; a work of art, in comparison, is neat, finite, self-contained, rational, flowing and emasculate. Life imposes by brute energy, like inarticulate thunder; art catches the ear, among the far louder noises of experience, like an air artificially made by a discreet musician. A proposition of geometry does not compete with life; and a proposition of geometry is a fair and luminous parallel for a work of art. Both are reasonable, both untrue to the crude fact; both inhere in nature, neither represents it. The novel, which is a work of art, exists, not by its resemblances to life, which are forced and material, as a shoe must still consist of leather, but by its immeasurable difference from life, which is designed and significant, and is both the method and the meaning of the work.

The life of man is not the subject of novels, but the inexhaustible magazine from which subjects are to be selected; the name of these is legion; and with each new subject – for here again I must differ by the whole width of heaven from Mr James – the true artist will vary his method and change the point of attack. That which was in one case an excellence, will become a defect in another; what was the making of one book, will in the next be impertinent or dull. First each novel, and then each class of novels, exists by and for itself. I will take, for instance, three main classes, which are fairly distinct: first, the novel of adventure, which appeals to certain almost sensual and quite illogical tendencies in man; second, the novel of character, which appeals to our intellectual appreciation of man's foibles and mingled and inconstant motives; and third, the dramatic novel, which deals with the same stuff as the serious theatre, and appeals to our emotional nature and moral judgment.

And first for the novel of adventure. Mr James refers, with singular generosity of praise, to a little book about a quest for hidden treasure; but he lets fall, by the way, some rather startling words. In this book he misses what he calls the 'immense luxury' of being able to quarrel with his author. The luxury, to most of us, is to lay by our judgment, to be submerged by the tale as by a billow, and only to awake, and begin to distinguish and find fault, when the piece is over and the volume laid aside. Still more remarkable is Mr James's reason. He cannot criticise the author, as he goes, 'because,' says he, comparing it with another work, *'I have been a child, but I have never been on a quest for buried treasure.'* Here is, indeed, a wilful paradox; for if he has never been on a quest for buried treasure, it can be demonstrated that he has never been a child. There never was a child (unless Master James) but has hunted gold, and been a pirate, and a military commander, and a bandit of the mountains; but has fought, and suffered shipwreck and prison, and imbrued its little hands in gore, and gallantly retrieved the lost battle, and triumphantly protected innocence and beauty. Elsewhere in his essay Mr James has protested with excellent reason against too narrow a conception of experience; for the born artist, he contends, the 'faintest hints of life' are converted into revelations; and it will be found true, I believe, in a majority of cases, that the artist writes with more gusto and effect of those things which he has only wished to do, than of those which he has done. Desire is a wonderful telescope, and Pisgah the best observatory. Now, while it is true that neither Mr James nor the author of the work in question has ever, in the fleshly sense, gone questing after gold, it is probable that both have ardently desired and fondly imagined the details of such a life in youthful day-dreams; and the author, counting upon that, and well aware (cunning and low-minded man!) that this class of interest, having been frequently treated, finds a readily accessible and beaten road to the sympathies of the reader, addressed himself throughout to the building up and circumstantiation of this boyish dream. Character to the boy is a sealed book; for him, a pirate is a beard, a pair of wide trousers and a liberal complement of pistols. The author, for the sake of circumstantiation and because he was himself more or less grown up, admitted character, within certain limits, into his design; but only within certain limits. Had the same puppets figured in a scheme of another sort, they had been drawn to very different purpose; for in this elementary novel of adventure, the characters need to be presented with but one class of qualities – the warlike and formidable. So as they appear insidious in deceit and fatal in the combat, they have served their end. Danger is the matter with which this class of novel deals; fear, the passion with which it idly trifles; and the characters are portrayed only so far as they realise the sense of danger and provoke the sympathy of fear. To add more traits, to be too clever, to start the hare of moral or intellectual interest while we are running the fox of material interest, is not to enrich but to stultify your tale. The stupid reader will only be offended, and the clever reader lose the scent.

The novel of character has this difference from all others: that it requires no coherency of plot, and for this reason, as in the case of *Gil Blas*, it is sometimes called the novel of adventure. It turns on the humours of the persons represented; these are, to be sure, embodied in incidents, but the incidents themselves, being tributary, need not march in a progression; and the characters may be statically shown. As they enter, so they may go out; they must be consistent, but they need not grow. Here Mr James will recognise the note of much of his own work: he treats, for the most part, the statics of character, studying it at rest or only gently moved; and, with his usual delicate and just artistic instinct, he avoids those stronger passions which would deform the attitudes he loves to study, and change his sitters from the humorists of ordinary life to the brute forces and bare types of more emotional moments. In his recent *Author of Beltraffio*, so just in conception, so nimble and neat in workmanship, strong passion is indeed employed; but observe that it is not displayed. Even in the heroine the working of the passion is suppressed; and the great struggle, the true tragedy, the *scène-à-faire*, passes unseen behind the panels of a locked door. The delectable invention of the young visitor is introduced, consciously or not, to this end: that Mr James, true to his method, might avoid the scene of passion. I trust no reader will suppose me guilty of undervaluing this little masterpiece. I mean merely that it belongs to one marked class of novel, and that it would have been very differently conceived and treated had it belonged to that other marked class, of which I now proceed to speak.

I take pleasure in calling the dramatic novel by that name, because it enables me to point out by the way a strange and peculiarly English misconception. It is sometimes supposed that the drama consists of incident. It consists of passion, which gives the actor his opportunity; and that passion must progressively increase, or the actor, as the piece proceeded, would be unable to carry the audience from a lower to a higher pitch of interest and emotion. A good serious play must therefore be founded on one of the passionate *cruces* of life, where duty and inclination come nobly to the grapple; and the same is true of what I call, for that reason, the dramatic novel. I will instance a few worthy specimens, all of our own day and language; Meredith's *Rhoda Fleming*, that wonderful and painful book, long out of print,[1] and hunted for at bookstalls like an Aldine; Hardy's *Pair of Blue Eyes*; and two of Charles Reade's, *Griffith Gaunt* and *The Double Marriage*, originally called *White Lies*, and founded (by an accident quaintly favourable to my nomenclature) on a play by Maquet, the partner of the great Dumas. In this kind of novel the closed door of *The Author of Beltraffio* must be broken open; passion must appear upon the scene and utter its last word; passion is the be-all and the end-all, the plot and the solution, the protagonist and the *deus ex machina* in one. The characters may come anyhow upon the stage: we do not care; the point is, that, before they leave it, they shall become transfigured and raised out of themselves by passion. It may be part of the design to draw them with detail; to depict a full-length character, and then behold it melt and change in the furnace of emotion. But there is no obligation of the sort; nice portraiture is not required; and we are content to accept mere abstract types, so they be strongly and sincerely moved. A novel of this class may be even great, and yet contain no individual figure; it may be great, because it displays the workings of the perturbed heart and the impersonal utterance of

[1] Now no longer so, thank Heaven!

passion; and with an artist of the second class it is, indeed, even more likely to be great, when the issue has thus been narrowed and the whole force of the writer's mind directed to passion alone. Cleverness again, which has its fair field in the novel of character, is debarred all entry upon this more solemn theatre. A far-fetched motive, an ingenious evasion of the issue, a witty instead of a passionate turn, offend us like an insincerity. All should be plain, all straightforward to the end. Hence it is that, in *Rhoda Fleming*, Mrs Lovel raises such resentment in the reader; her motives are too flimsy, her ways are too equivocal, for the weight and strength of her surroundings. Hence the hot indignation of the reader when Balzac, after having begun the *Duchesse de Langeais* in terms of strong if somewhat swollen passion, cuts the knot by the derangement of the hero's clock. Such personages and incidents belong to the novel of character; they are out of place in the high society of the passions; when the passions are introduced in art at their full height, we look to see them, not baffled and impotently striving, as in life, but towering above circumstance and acting substitutes for fate.

And here I can imagine Mr James, with his lucid sense, to intervene. To much of what I have said he would apparently demur; in much he would, somewhat impatiently, acquiesce. It may be true; but it is not what he desired to say or to hear said. He spoke of the finished picture and its worth when done; I, of the brushes, the palette, and the north light. He uttered his views in the tone and for the ear of good society; I, with the emphasis and technicalities of the obtrusive student. But the point, I may reply, is not merely to amuse the public, but to offer helpful advice to the young writer. And the young writer will not so much be helped by genial pictures of what an art may aspire to at its highest, as by a true idea of what it must be on the lowest terms. The best that we can say to him is this: Let him choose a motive, whether of character or passion; carefully construct his plot so that every incident is an illustration of the motive, and every property employed shall bear to it a near relation of congruity or contrast; avoid a sub-plot, unless, as sometimes in Shakespeare, the sub-plot be a reversion or complement of the main intrigue; suffer not his style to flag below the level of the argument; pitch the key of conversation, not with any thought of how men talk in parlours, but with a single eye to the degree of passion he may be called on to express; and allow neither himself in the narrative nor any character in the course of the dialogue, to utter one sentence that is not part and parcel of the business of the story or the discussion of the problem involved. Let him not regret if this shortens his book; it will be better so; for to add irrelevant matter is not to lengthen but to bury. Let him not mind if he miss a thousand qualities, so that he keeps unflaggingly in pursuit of the one he has chosen. Let him not care particularly if he miss the tone of conversation, the pungent material detail of the day's manners, the reproduction of the atmosphere and the environment. These elements are not essential: a novel may be excellent, and yet have none of them; a passion or a character is so much the better depicted as it rises clearer from material circumstance. In this age of the particular, let him remember the ages of the abstract, the great books of the past, the brave men that lived before Shakespeare and before Balzac. And as the root of the whole matter, let him bear in mind that his novel is not a transcript of life, to be judged by its exactitude; but a simplification of some side or point of life, to stand or fall by its significant simplicity. For although, in great men, working upon great motives, what we observe and admire is often their complexity, yet underneath appearances the truth remains unchanged: that simplification was their method, and that simplicity is their excellence.

II

Since the above was written another novelist has entered repeatedly the lists of theory: one well worthy of mention, Mr W. D. Howells; and none ever couched a lance with narrower convictions. His own work and those of his pupils and masters singly occupy his mind; he is the bondslave, the zealot of his school; he dreams of an advance in art like what there is in science; he thinks of past things as radically dead; he thinks a form can be outlived: a strange immersion in his own history; a strange forgetfulness of the history of the race! Meanwhile, by a glance at his own works (could he see them with the eager eyes of his readers) much of this illusion would be dispelled. For while he holds all the poor little orthodoxies of the day – no poorer and no smaller than those of yesterday or tomorrow, poor and small, indeed, only so far as they are exclusive – the living quality of much that he has done is of a contrary, I had almost said of a heretical, complexion. A man, as I read him, of an originally strong romantic bent – a certain glow of romance still resides in many of his books, and lends them their distinction. As by accident he runs out and revels in the exceptional; and it is then, as often as not, that his reader rejoices – justly, as I contend. For in all this excessive eagerness to be centrally human, is there not one central human thing that Mr Howells is too often tempted to neglect: I mean himself? A poet, a finished artist, a man in love with the appearances of life, a cunning reader of the mind, he has other passions and aspirations than those he loves to draw. And why should he suppress himself and do such reverence to the Lemuel Barkers? The obvious is not of necessity the normal; fashion rules and deforms; the majority fall tamely into the contemporary shape, and thus attain, in the eyes of the true observer, only a higher power of insignificance; and the danger is lest, in seeking to draw the normal, a man should draw the null, and write the novel of society instead of the romance of man.

THE DAY AFTER TOMORROW

History is much decried; it is a tissue of errors, we are told, no doubt correctly; and rival historians expose each other's blunders with gratification. Yet the worst historian has a clearer view of the period he studies than the best of us can hope to form of that in which we live. The obscurest epoch is today; and that for a thousand reasons of inchoate tendency, conflicting report, and sheer mass and multiplicity of experience; but chiefly, perhaps, by reason of an insidious shifting of landmarks. Parties and ideas continually move, but not by measurable marches on a stable course; the political soil itself steals forth by imperceptible degrees, like a travelling glacier, carrying on its bosom not only political parties but their flag-posts and cantonments; so that what appears to be an eternal city founded on hills is but a flying island of Laputa. It is for this reason in particular that we are all becoming Socialists without knowing it; by which I would not in the least refer to the acute case of Mr Hyndman and his horn-blowing supporters, sounding their trumps of a Sunday within the walls of our individualist Jericho – but to the stealthy change that has come over the spirit of Englishmen and English legislation. A little while ago, and we were still for liberty; 'crowd a few more thousands on the bench of Government,' we seemed to cry; 'keep her head direct on liberty, and we cannot help but come to port.' This is over; *laissez-faire* declines in favour; our legislation grows authoritative, grows philanthropical, bristles with new duties and new penalties, and casts a spawn of inspectors, who now begin, note-book in hand, to darken the face of England. It may be right or wrong, we are not trying that; but one thing it is beyond doubt: it is Socialism in action, and the strange thing is that we scarcely know it.

Liberty has served us a long while, and it may be time to seek new altars. Like all other principles, she has been proved to be self-exclusive in the long run. She has taken wages besides (like all other virtues) and dutifully served Mammon; so that many things we were accustomed to admire as the benefits of freedom and common to all, were truly benefits of wealth, and took their value from our neighbours' poverty. A few shocks of logic, a few disclosures (in the journalistic phrase) of what the freedom of manufacturers, landlords, or shipowners may imply for operatives, tenants or seamen, and we not unnaturally begin to turn to that other pole of hope, beneficent tyranny. Freedom, to be desirable, involves kindness, wisdom, and all the virtues of the free; but the free man as we have seen him in action has been, as of yore, only the master of many helots; and the slaves are still ill-fed, ill-clad, ill-taught, ill-housed, insolently entreated, and driven to their mines and workshops by the lash of famine. So much, in other men's affairs, we have begun to see clearly; we have begun to despair of virtue in these other men, and from our seat in Parliament begin to discharge upon them, thick as arrows, the host of our inspectors. The landlord has long shaken his head over the manufacturer; those who do business on land have lost all trust in the virtues of the shipowner; the professions look askance upon the retail traders and have even started their co-operative stores to ruin them; and from out the smoke-wreaths of Birmingham a finger has begun to write upon the wall the condemnation of the landlord. Thus, piece by piece, do we condemn each other, and yet not perceive the conclusion, that our whole estate is somewhat damnable. Thus, piece by piece, each acting against his neighbour, each sawing away the branch on which some other interest is seated, do we apply in detail our Socialistic remedies, and yet not perceive that we are all labouring together to bring in Socialism at large. A tendency so stupid and so selfish is like to prove invincible; and if Socialism be at all a practicable rule of life, there is every chance that our grandchildren will see the day and taste the pleasures of existence in something far liker an ant-heap than any previous human polity. And this not in the least because of the voice of Mr Hyndman or the horns of his followers; but by the mere glacier movement of the political soil, bearing forward on its bosom, apparently undisturbed, the proud camps of Whig and Tory. If Mr Hyndman were a man of keen humour, which is far from my conception of his character, he might rest from his troubling and look on: the walls of Jericho begin already to crumble and dissolve. That great servile war, the Armageddon of money and numbers, to which we looked forward when young, becomes more and more unlikely; and we may rather look to see a peaceable and blindfold evolution, the work of dull men immersed in political tactics and dead to political results.

The principal scene of this comedy lies, of course, in the House of Commons; it is there, besides, that the details of this new evolution (if it proceed) will fall to be decided; so that the state of Parliament is not only diagnostic of the present but fatefully prophetic of the future. Well, we all know what Parliament is, and we are all ashamed of it. We may pardon it some faults, indeed, on the ground of Irish obstruction – a bitter trial, which it supports with notable good humour. But the excuse is merely local; it cannot apply to similar bodies in America and France; and what are we to say of these? President Cleveland's letter may serve as a picture of the one; a glance at almost any paper will convince us of the weakness of the other. Decay appears to have seized on the organ of popular government in every land; and this just at the moment when we begin to bring to it, as to an oracle of justice, the whole skein of our private affairs to be unravelled, and ask it, like a new Messiah, to take upon itself our frailties and play for us the part that should be played by our own virtues. For that, in few words, is the case. We cannot trust ourselves to behave with decency; we cannot trust our consciences; and the remedy proposed is to elect a round number of our neighbours, pretty much at random, and say to these: 'Be ye our conscience; make laws so wise, and continue from year to year to administer them so wisely, that they shall save us from ourselves and make us righteous and happy, world without end. Amen.' And who can look twice at the British Parliament and then seriously bring it such a task? I am not advancing this as an argument against Socialism: once again, nothing is further from my mind. There are great truths in Socialism, or no one, not even Mr Hyndman, would be found to hold it; and if it came, and did one-tenth part of what it offers, I for one should make it welcome. But if it is to come, we may as well have some notion of what it will be like; and the first thing to grasp is that our new polity will be designed and administered (to put it courteously) with something short of inspiration. It will be made, or will grow, in a human parliament; and the one thing that will not very hugely change is human nature. The Anarchists think otherwise, from which it is only plain that they have not carried to the study of history the lamp of human sympathy.

Given, then, our new polity, with its new waggon-load of laws, what headmarks must we look for in the life? We chafe a good deal at that excellent thing, the income-tax, because it brings into our affairs the prying fingers, and exposes us to the tart words, of the official. The official, in all degrees, is already something of a terror to many of us. I would not willingly have to do with even a police-constable in any other spirit than that of kindness. I still remember in my dreams the eye-glass of a certain *attaché* at a certain embassy – an eye-glass that was a standing indignity to all on whom it looked; and my next most disagreeable remembrance is of a bracing, Republican postman in the city of San Francisco. I lived in that city among working folk, and what my neighbours accepted at the postman's hands – nay, what I took from him myself – it is still distasteful to recall. The bourgeois, residing in the upper parts of society, has but few opportunities of tasting this peculiar bowl; but about the income-tax, as I have said, or perhaps about a patent, or in the halls of an embassy at the hands of my friend of the eye-glass, he occasionally sets his lips to it; and he may thus imagine (if he has that faculty of imagination, without which most faculties are void) how it tastes to his poorer neighbours, who must drain it to the dregs. In every contact with authority, with their employer, with the police, with the School Board officer, in the hospital, or in the workhouse, they have equally the occasion to appreciate the light-hearted civility of the man in office; and as an experimentalist in several out-of-the-way provinces of life, I may say it has but to be felt to be appreciated. Well, this golden age of which we are speaking will be the golden age of officials. In all our concerns it will be their beloved duty to meddle, with what tact, with what obliging words, analogy will aid us to imagine. It is likely these gentlemen will be periodically elected; they will therefore have their turn of being underneath, which does not always sweeten men's conditions. The laws they will have to administer will be no clearer than those we know today, and the body which is to regulate their administration no wiser than the British Parliament. So that upon all hands we may look for a form of servitude most galling to the blood – servitude to many and changing masters, and for all the slights that accompany the rule of jack-in-office. And if the Socialistic programme be carried out with the least fulness, we shall have lost a thing, in most respects not much to be regretted, but as a moderator of oppression, a thing nearly invaluable – the newspaper. For the independent journal is a creature of capital and competition; it stands and falls with millionaires and railway-bonds and all the abuses and glories of today; and as soon as the State has fairly taken its bent to authority and philanthropy, and laid the least touch on private property, the days of the independent journal are numbered. State railways may be good things and so may State bakeries; but a State newspaper will never be a very trenchant critic of the State officials.

But again, these officials would have no sinecure. Crime would perhaps be less, for some of the motives of crime we may suppose would pass away. But if Socialism were carried out with any fulness, there would be more contraventions. We see already new sins springing up like mustard – School Board sins, factory sins, Merchant Shipping Act sins – none of which I would be thought to except against in particular, but all of which, taken together, show us that Socialism can be a hard master even in the beginning. If it go on to such heights as we hear proposed and lauded, if it come actually to its ideal of the ant-heap, ruled with iron justice, the number of new contraventions will be out of all proportion multiplied. Take the case of work alone. Man is an idle animal. He is at least as intelligent as the ant; but generations of advisers have in vain recommended him the ant's example. Of those who are found truly indefatigable in business, some are misers; some are the practisers of delightful industries, like gardening; some are students, artists, inventors, or discoverers, men lured forward by successive hopes; and the rest are those who live by games of skill or hazard – financiers, billiard-players, gamblers, and the like. But in unloved toils, even under the prick of necessity, no man is continually sedulous. Once eliminate the fear of starvation, once eliminate or bound the hope of riches, and we shall see plenty of skulking and malingering. Society will then be something not wholly unlike a cotton plantation in the old days; with cheerful, careless, demoralised slaves, with elected overseers, and, instead of the planter, a chaotic popular assembly. If the blood be purposeful and the soil strong, such a plantation may succeed, and be, indeed, a busy ant-heap, with full granaries and long hours of leisure. But even then I think the whip will be in the overseer's hands, and not in vain. For, when it comes to be a question of each man doing his own share or the rest doing more, prettiness of sentiment will be forgotten. To dock the skulker's food is not enough; many will rather eat haws and starve on petty pilferings than put their shoulder to the wheel for one hour daily. For such as these, then, the whip will be in the overseer's hand; and his own sense of justice and the superintendence of a chaotic popular assembly will be the only checks on its employment. Now, you may be an industrious man and a good citizen, and yet not love, nor yet be loved by, Dr Fell the inspector. It is admitted by private soldiers that the disfavour of a sergeant is an evil not to be combated; offend the sergeant, they say, and in a brief while you will either be disgraced or have deserted. And the sergeant can no longer appeal to the lash. But if these things go on, we shall see, or our sons shall see, what it is to have offended an inspector.

This for the unfortunate. But with the fortunate also, even those whom the inspector loves, it may not be altogether well. It is concluded that in such a state of society, supposing it to be financially sound, the level of comfort will be high. It does not follow: there are strange depths of idleness in man, a too-easily-got sufficiency, as in the case of the sago-eaters, often quenching the desire for all besides; and it is possible that the men of the richest ant-heaps may sink even into squalor. But suppose they do not; suppose our tricksy instrument of human nature, when we play upon it this new tune, should respond kindly; suppose no one to be damped and none exasperated by the new conditions, the whole enterprise to be financially sound – a vaulting supposition – and all the inhabitants to dwell together in a golden mean of comfort: we have yet to ask ourselves if this be what man desire, or if it be what man will even deign to accept for a continuance. It is certain that man loves to eat, it is not certain that he loves that only or that best. He is supposed to love comfort; it is not a love, at least, that he is faithful to. He is supposed to love happiness; it is my contention that he rather loves excitement. Danger, enterprise, hope, the novel, the aleatory are dearer to man than regular meals. He does not think so when he is hungry, but he thinks so again as soon as he is fed; and on the hypothesis of a successful ant-heap, he would never go hungry. It would be always after dinner in that society, as, in the land of the Lotos-eaters, it was always afternoon; and food, which, when we have it not, seems all-important, drops in our esteem, as soon as we have it, to a mere pre-requisite of living. That for which man lives is not the same thing for all individuals nor in all ages; yet it has a common base; what he seeks and what he must have is that which will seize and hold his attention. Regular meals and weatherproof lodgings will not do this long. Play in its wide sense, as the artificial induction of sensation, including all games and all arts, will, indeed, go far to keep him conscious of himself; but in the end he wearies for realities. Study or experiment, to some rare natures, are the unbroken pastime of a life. These are enviable natures; people shut in the house by sickness often bitterly envy them; but the commoner man cannot continue to exist upon such altitudes: his feet itch for physical adventure; his blood boils for physical dangers, pleasures, and triumphs; his fancy, the looker after new things, cannot continue to look for them in books and crucibles, but must seek them on the breathing stage of life. Pinches, buffets, the glow of hope, the shock of disappoint-ment, furious contention with obstacles: these are the true elixir for all vital spirits, these are what they seek alike in their romantic enterprises and their unromantic dissipations. When they are taken in some pinch closer than the common, they cry 'Catch me here again!' and sure enough you catch them there again – perhaps before the week is out. It is as old as *Robinson Crusoe*; as old as man. Our race has not been strained for all these ages through that sieve of dangers that we call Natural Selection, to sit down with patience in the tedium of safety; the voices of its fathers call it forth. Already in our society as it exists, the *bourgeois* is too much cottoned about for any zest in living; he sits in his parlour out of reach of any danger, often out of reach of any vicissitude but one of health; and there he yawns. If the people in the next villa took pot-shots at him, he might be killed indeed, but, so long as he escaped, he would find his blood oxygenated and his views of the world brighter. If Mr Mallock, on his way to the publishers, should have his skirts pinned to the wall by a javelin, it would not occur to him – at least for several hours – to ask if life were worth living; and if such peril were a daily matter, he would ask it never more; he would have other things to think about, he would be living indeed – not lying in a box with cotton safe, but immeasurably dull. The aleatory, whether it touch life, or fortune, or renown – whether we explore Africa or only toss for half-pence – that is what I conceive men to love best, and that is what we are seeking to exclude from men's existences. Of all forms of the aleatory, that which most commonly attends our working men – the danger of misery from want of work – is the least inspiriting: it does not whip the blood, it does not evoke the glory of contest; it is tragic, but it is passive; and yet, in so far as it is aleatory, and a peril sensibly touching them, it does truly season the men's lives. Of those who fail, I do not speak – despair should be sacred; but to those who even modestly succeed, the changes of their life bring interest: a job found, a shilling saved, a dainty earned, all these are wells of pleasure springing afresh for the successful poor; and it is not from these but from the villa dweller that we hear complaints of the unworthiness of life. Much, then, as the average of the proletariate would gain in this new state of life, they would also lose a certain something, which would not be missed in the beginning, but would be missed progressively and progressively lamented. Soon there would be a looking back: there would be tales of the old world humming in young men's ears, tales of the tramp and the pedlar, and the hopeful emigrant. And in the stall-fed life of the successful ant-heap – with its regular meals, regular duties, regular pleasures, an even course of life, and fear excluded – the vicissitudes, delights, and havens of today will seem of epic breadth. This may seem a shallow observation; but the springs by which men are moved lie much on the surface. Bread, I believe, has always been considered first, but the circus comes close upon its heels. Bread we suppose to be given amply; the cry for circuses will be the louder, and if the life of our descendants be such as we have conceived, there are two beloved pleasures on which they will be likely to fall back: the pleasures of intrigue and of sedition.

In all this I have supposed the ant-heap to be financially sound. I am no economist, only a writer of fiction; but even as such, I know one thing that bears on the economic question – I know the imperfection of man's faculty for business. The Anarchists, who count some rugged elements of common-sense among what seems to me their tragic errors, have said upon this matter all that I could wish to say, and condemned beforehand great economical polities. So far it is obvious that they are right; they may be right also in predicting a period of communal independence, and they may even be right in thinking that desirable. But the rise of communes is none the less the end of economic equality, just when we were told it was beginning. Communes will not be all equal in extent, nor in quality of soil, nor in growth of population; nor will the surplus produce of all be equally marketable. It will be the old story of competing interests, only with a new unit; and as it appears to me, a new, inevitable danger. For the merchant and the manufacturer, in this new world, will be a sovereign commune; it is a sovereign power that will see its crops undersold, and its manufactures worsted in the market. And all the more dangerous that the sovereign power should be small. Great powers are slow to stir; national affronts, even with the aid of newspapers, filter slowly into popular consciousness; national losses are so unequally shared, that one part of the population will be counting its gains while another sits by a cold hearth. But in the sovereign commune all will be centralised and sensitive. When jealousy springs up, when (let us say) the commune of Poole has overreached the commune of Dorchester, irritation will run like quicksilver throughout the body politic; each man in Dorchester will have to suffer directly in his diet and his dress; even the secretary, who drafts the official correspondence, will sit down to his task embittered, as a man who has dined ill and may expect to dine worse; and thus a business difference between communes will take on much the same colour as a dispute between diggers in the lawless West, and will lead as directly to the arbitrament of blows. So that the establishment of the communal system will not only reintroduce all the injustices and heart-burnings of economic inequality, but will, in all human likelihood, inaugurate a world of hedgerow warfare.

Dorchester will march on Poole, Sherborne on Dorchester, Wimborne on both; the waggons will be fired on as they follow the highway, the trains wrecked on the lines, the ploughman will go armed into the field of tillage; and if we have not a return of ballad literature, the local press at least will celebrate in a high vein the victory of Cerne Abbas or the reverse of Toller Porcorum. At least this will not be dull; when I was younger, I could have welcomed such a world with relief; but it is the New-Old with a vengeance, and irresistibly suggests the growth of military powers and the foundation of new empires.

THOMAS STEVENSON,
CIVIL ENGINEER

The death of Thomas Stevenson will mean not very much to the general reader. His service to mankind took on forms of which the public knows little and understands less. He came seldom to London, and then only as a task, remaining always a stranger and a convinced provincial; putting up for years at the same hotel where his father had gone before him; faithful for long to the same restaurant, the same church, and the same theatre, chosen simply for propinquity: steadfastly refusing to dine out. He had a circle of his own, indeed, at home; few men were more beloved in Edinburgh, where he breathed an air that pleased him; and wherever he went, in railway carriages or hotel smoking-rooms, his strange, humorous vein of talk, and his transparent honesty, raised him up friends and admirers. But to the general public and the world of London, except about the parliamentary committee-rooms, he remained unknown. All the time, his lights were in every part of the world, guiding the mariner; his firm were consulting engineers to the Indian, the New Zealand, and the Japanese Lighthouse Boards, so that Edinburgh was a world centre for that branch of applied science; in Germany, he had been called 'the Nestor of lighthouse illumination;' even in France, where his claims were long denied, he was at last, on the occasion of the late Exposition, recognised and medalled. And to show by one instance the inverted nature of his reputation, comparatively small at home, yet filling the world, a friend of mine was this winter on a visit to the Spanish main, and was asked by a Peruvian if he 'knew Mr Stevenson the author, because his works were much esteemed in Peru?' My friend supposed the reference was to the writer of tales; but the Peruvian had never heard of *Dr Jekyll*; what he had in his eye, what was esteemed in Peru, were the volumes of the engineer.

Thomas Stevenson was born at Edinburgh in the year 1818, the grandson of Thomas Smith, first engineer to the Board of Northern Lights, son of Robert Stevenson, brother of Alan and David; so that his nephew, David Alan Stevenson, joined with him at the time of his death in the engineership, is the sixth of the family who has held, successively or conjointly, that office. The Bell Rock, his father's great triumph, was finished before he was born; but he served under his brother Alan in the building of Skerryvore, the noblest of all extant deep-sea lights; and, in conjunction with his brother David, he added two – the Chickens and Dhu Heartach – to that small number of man's extreme outposts in the ocean. Of shore lights, the two brothers last named erected no fewer than twenty-seven; of beacons,[1] about twenty-five. Many harbours were successfully carried out: one, the harbour of Wick, the chief disaster of my father's life, was a failure; the sea proved too strong for man's arts; and after expedients hitherto unthought of, and on a scale hyper-cyclopean, the work must be deserted, and now stands a ruin in that bleak, God-forsaken bay, ten miles from John-o'-Groat's. In the improvement of rivers the brothers were likewise in a large way of practice over both England and Scotland, nor had any British engineer anything approaching their experience.

It was about this nucleus of his professional labours that all my father's scientific inquiries and inventions centred; these proceeded from, and acted back upon, his daily business. Thus it was as a harbour engineer that he became interested in the propagation and reduction of waves; a difficult subject in regard to which he has left behind him much suggestive matter and some valuable approximate results. Storms were his sworn adversaries, and it was through the study of storms that he approached that of meteorology at large. Many who knew him not otherwise, knew – perhaps have in their gardens – his louvre-boarded screen for instruments. But the great achievement of his life was, of course, in optics as applied to lighthouse illumination. Fresnel had done much; Fresnel had settled the fixed light apparatus on a principle that still seems unimprovable; and when Thomas Stevenson stepped in and brought to a comparable perfection the revolving light, a not unnatural jealousy and much painful controversy rose in France. It had its hour; and, as I have told already, even in France it has blown by. Had it not, it would have mattered the less, since all through his life my father continued to justify his claim by fresh advances. New apparatus for lights in new situations was continually being designed with the same unwearied search after perfection, the same nice ingenuity of means; and though the holophotal revolving light perhaps still remains his most

[1]In Dr Murray's admirable new dictionary, I have remarked a flaw *sub voce* Beacon. In its express, technical sense, a beacon may be defined as 'a founded, artificial sea-mark, not lighted.'

elegant contrivance, it is difficult to give it the palm over the much later condensing system, with its thousand possible modifications. The number and the value of these improvements entitle their author to the name of one of mankind's benefactors. In all parts of the world a safer landfall awaits the mariner. Two things must be said: and, first, that Thomas Stevenson was no mathematician. Natural shrewdness, a sentiment of optical laws, and a great intensity of consideration led him to just conclusions; but to calculate the necessary formulæ for the instruments he had conceived was often beyond him, and he must fall back on the help of others, notably on that of his cousin and lifelong intimate friend, *emeritus* Professor Swan, of St Andrews, and his later friend, Professor P. G. Tait. It is a curious enough circumstance, and a great encouragement to others, that a man so ill equipped should have succeeded in one of the most abstract and arduous walks of applied science. The second remark is one that applies to the whole family, and only particularly to Thomas Stevenson from the great number and importance of his inventions: holding as the Stevensons did a Government appointment, they regarded their original work as something due already to the nation, and none of them has ever taken out a patent. It is another cause of the comparative obscurity of the name: for a patent not only brings in money, it infallibly spreads reputation; and my father's instruments enter anonymously into a hundred light-rooms, and are passed anonymously over in a hundred reports, where the least considerable patent would stand out and tell its author's story.

But the life-work of Thomas Stevenson remains; what we have lost, what we now rather try to recall, is the friend and companion. He was a man of a somewhat antique strain: with a blended sternness and softness that was wholly Scottish and at first somewhat bewildering; with a profound essential melancholy of disposition and (what often accompanies it) the most humorous geniality in company; shrewd and childish; passionately attached, passionately prejudiced; a man of many extremes, many faults of temper, and no very stable foothold for himself among life's troubles. Yet he was a wise adviser; many men, and these not inconsiderable, took counsel with him habitually. 'I sat at his feet,' writes one of these, 'when I asked his advice, and when the broad brow was set in thought and the firm mouth said his say, I always knew that no man could add to the worth of the conclusion.' He had excellent taste, though whimsical and partial; collected old furniture and delighted specially in sunflowers long before the days of Mr Wilde; took a lasting pleasure in prints and pictures; was a devout admirer of Thomson of Duddingston at a time when few shared the taste; and though he read little, was constant to his favourite books. He had never any Greek; Latin he happily re-taught himself after he had left school, where he was a mere consistent idler: happily, I say, for Lactantius, Vossius, and Cardinal Bona were his chief authors. The first he must have read for twenty years uninterruptedly, keeping it near him in his study, and carrying it in his bag on journeys. Another old theologian, Brown of Wamphray, was often in his hands. When he was indisposed, he had two books, *Guy Mannering* and *The Parent's Assistant*, of which he never wearied. He was a strong Conservative, or, as he preferred to call himself, a Tory; except in so far as his views were modified by a hot-headed chivalrous sentiment for women. He was actually in favour of a marriage law under which any woman might have a divorce for the asking, and no man on any ground whatever; and the same sentiment found another expression in a Magdalen Mission in Edinburgh, founded and largely supported by himself. This was but one of the many channels of his public generosity; his private was equally unstrained. The Church of Scotland, of which he held the doctrines (though in a sense of his own) and to which he bore a clansman's loyalty, profited often by his time and money; and though, from a morbid sense of his own unworthiness, he would never consent to be an office-bearer, his advice was often sought, and he served the Church on many committees. What he perhaps valued highest in his work were his contributions to the defence of Christianity; one of which, in particular, was praised by Hutchinson Stirling and reprinted at the request of Professor Crawford.

His sense of his own unworthiness I have called morbid; morbid, too, were his sense of the fleetingness of life and his concern for death. He had never accepted the conditions of man's life or his own character; and his inmost thoughts were ever tinged with the Celtic melancholy. Cases of conscience were sometimes grievous to him, and that delicate employment of a scientific witness cost him many qualms. But he found respite from these troublesome humours in his work, in his lifelong study of natural science, in the society of those he loved, and in his daily walks, which now would carry him far into the country with some congenial friend, and now keep him dangling about the town from one old bookshop to another, and scraping romantic acquaintance with every dog that passed. His talk, compounded of so much sterling sense and so much freakish humour, and clothed in language so apt, droll, and emphatic, was a perpetual delight to all who knew him before the clouds began to settle on his mind. His use of language was both just and picturesque; and when at the beginning of his illness he began to feel the ebbing of this power, it was strange and painful to hear him reject one word after another as inadequate, and at length desist from the search and leave his phrase unfinished rather than finish it without propriety. It was perhaps another Celtic trait that his affections and emotions, passionate as these were, and liable to passionate ups and downs, found the most eloquent expression both in words and gestures. Love, anger, and indignation shone through him and broke forth in imagery, like what we read of Southern races. For all these emotional extremes, and in spite of the melancholy ground of his character, he had upon the whole a happy life; nor was he less fortunate in his death, which at the last came to him unaware.

A CHAPTER ON DREAMS

The past is all of one texture—whether feigned or suffered—whether acted out in three dimensions, or only witnessed in that small theatre of the brain which we keep brightly lighted all night long, after the jets are down, and darkness and sleep reign undisturbed in the remainder of the body. There is no distinction on the face of our experiences; one is vivid indeed, and one dull, and one pleasant, and another agonising to remember; but which of them is what we call true, and which a dream, there is not one hair to prove. The past stands on a precarious footing; another straw split in the field of metaphysic, and behold us robbed of it. There is scarce a family that can count four generations but lays a claim to some dormant title or some castle and estate: a claim not prosecutable in any court of law, but flattering to the fancy and a great alleviation of idle hours. A man's claim to his own past is yet less valid. A paper might turn up (in proper story-book fashion) in the secret drawer of an old ebony secretary, and restore your family to its ancient honours, and reinstate mine in a certain West Indian islet (not far from St Kitt's, as beloved tradition hummed in my young ears) which was once ours, and is now unjustly someone else's, and for that matter (in the state of the sugar trade) is not worth anything to anybody. I do not say that these revolutions are likely; only no man can deny that they are possible; and the past, on the other hand, is lost for ever: our old days and deeds, our old selves, too, and the very world in which these scenes were acted, all brought down to the same faint residuum as a last night's dream, to some incontinuous images, and an echo in the chambers of the brain. Not an hour, not a mood, not a glance of the eye, can we revoke; it is all gone, past conjuring. And yet conceive us robbed of it, conceive that little thread of memory that we trail behind us broken at the pocket's edge; and in what naked nullity should we be left! for we only guide ourselves, and only know ourselves, by these air-painted pictures of the past.

Upon these grounds, there are some among us who claim to have lived longer and more richly than their neighbours; when they lay asleep they claim they were still active; and among the treasures of memory that all men review for their amusement, these count in no second place the harvests of their dreams. There is one of this kind whom I have in my eye, and whose case is perhaps unusual enough to be described. He was from a child an ardent and uncomfortable dreamer. When he had a touch of fever at night, and the room swelled and shrank, and his clothes, hanging on a nail, now loomed up instant to the bigness of a church, and now drew away into a horror of infinite distance and infinite littleness, the poor soul was very well aware of what must follow, and struggled hard against the approaches of that slumber which was the beginning of sorrows. But his struggles were in vain; sooner or later the night-hag would have him by the throat, and pluck him, strangling and screaming, from his sleep. His dreams were at times commonplace enough, at times very strange: at times they were almost formless, he would be haunted, for instance, by nothing more definite than a certain hue of brown, which he did not mind in the least while he was awake, but feared and loathed while he was dreaming; at times, again, they took on every detail of circumstance, as when once he supposed he must swallow the populous world, and awoke screaming with the horror of the thought. The two chief troubles of his very narrow existence – the practical and everyday trouble of school tasks and the ultimate and airy one of hell and judgment – were often confounded together into one appalling nightmare. He seemed to himself to stand before the Great White Throne; he was called on, poor little devil, to recite some form of words, on which his destiny depended; his tongue stuck, his memory was blank, hell gaped for him; and he would awake, clinging to the curtain-rod with his knees to his chin.

These were extremely poor experiences, on the whole; and at that time of life my dreamer would have very willingly parted with his power of dreams. But presently, in the course of his growth, the cries and physical contortions passed away, seemingly for ever; his visions were still for the most part miserable, but they were more constantly supported; and he would awake with no more extreme symptom than a flying heart, a freezing scalp, cold sweats, and the speechless midnight fear. His dreams, too, as befitted a mind better stocked with particulars, became more circumstantial, and had more the air and continuity of life. The look of the world beginning to take hold on his attention, scenery came to play a part in his sleeping as well as in his waking thoughts, so that he would take long, uneventful journeys and see strange towns and beautiful places as he lay in bed. And, what is more significant, an odd taste that he had for the Georgian costume and for stories laid in that period of English history, began to rule the features of his dreams; so that he masqueraded there in a three-cornered hat, and was much engaged with Jacobite conspiracy between the hour for bed and that for breakfast. About the same time, he began to read in his dreams – tales, for the most part, and for the most part after the manner of G. P. R. James, but so incredibly more vivid and moving than any printed book, that he has ever since been malcontent with literature.

And then, while he was yet a student, there came to him a dream-adventure which he has no anxiety to repeat; he began, that is to say, to dream in sequence and thus to lead a double life – one of the day, one of the night – one that he had every reason to believe was the true one, another that he had no means of proving to be false. I should have said he studied, or was by way of studying, at Edinburgh College, which (it may be supposed) was how I came to know him. Well, in his dream-life, he passed a long day in the surgical theatre, his heart in his mouth, his teeth on edge, seeing monstrous malformations and the abhorred dexterity of surgeons. In a heavy, rainy, foggy evening he came forth into the South Bridge, turned up the High Street, and entered the door of a tall *land*, at the top of which he supposed himself to lodge. All night long, in his wet clothes, he climbed the stairs, stair after stair in endless series, and at every second flight a flaring lamp with a reflector. All night long, he brushed by single persons passing downward – beggarly women of the street, great, weary, muddy labourers, poor scarecrows of men, pale parodies of women – but all drowsy and weary like himself, and all single, and all brushing against him as they passed. In the end, out of a northern window, he would see day beginning to whiten over the Firth, give up the ascent, turn to descend, and in a breath be back again upon the streets, in his wet clothes, in the wet, haggard dawn, trudging to another day of monstrosities and operations. Time went quicker in the life of dreams, some seven hours (as near as he can guess) to one; and it went, besides, more intensely, so that the gloom of these fancied experiences clouded the day, and he had not shaken off their shadow ere it was time to lie down and to renew them. I cannot tell how long it was that he endured this discipline; but it was long enough to leave a great black blot upon his memory, long enough to send him, trembling for his reason, to the doors of a certain doctor; whereupon with a simple draught he was restored to the common lot of man.

The poor gentleman has since been troubled by nothing of the sort; indeed, his nights were for some while like other men's, now blank, now chequered with dreams, and these sometimes charming, sometimes appalling, but except for an occasional vividness, of no extraordinary kind. I will just note one of these occasions, ere I pass on to what makes my dreamer truly interesting. It seemed to him that he was in the first floor of a rough hill-farm. The room showed some poor efforts at gentility, a carpet on the floor, a piano, I think, against the wall; but, for all these refinements, there was no mistaking he was in a moorland place, among hillside people, and set in miles of heather. He looked down from the window upon a bare farmyard, that seemed to have been long disused. A great, uneasy stillness lay upon the world. There was no sign of the farm-folk or of any livestock, save for an old, brown, curly dog of the retriever breed, who sat close in against the wall of the house and seemed to be dozing. Something about this dog disquieted the dreamer; it was quite a nameless feeling, for the beast looked right enough – indeed, he was so old and dull and dusty and broken-down, that he should rather have awakened pity; and yet the conviction came and grew upon the dreamer that this was no proper dog at all, but something hellish. A great many dozing summer flies hummed about the yard; and presently the dog thrust forth his paw, caught a fly in his open palm, carried it to his mouth like an ape, and looking suddenly up at the dreamer in the window, winked to him with one eye. The dream went on, it matters not how it went; it was a good dream as dreams go; but there was nothing in the sequel worthy of that devilish brown dog. And the point of interest for me lies partly in that very fact: that having found so singular an incident, my imperfect dreamer should prove unable to carry the tale to a fit end and fall back on indescribable noises and indiscriminate horrors. It would be different now; he knows his business better!

For, to approach at last the point: This honest fellow had long been in the custom of setting himself to sleep with tales, and so had his father before him; but these were irresponsible inventions, told for the teller's pleasure, with no eye to the crass public or the thwart reviewer: tales where a thread might be dropped, or one adventure quitted for another, on fancy's least suggestion. So that the little people who manage man's internal theatre had not as yet received a very rigorous training; and played upon their stage like children who should have slipped into the house and found it empty, rather than like drilled actors performing a set piece to a huge hall of faces. But presently my dreamer began to turn his former amusement of story-telling to (what is called) account; by which I mean that he began to write and sell his tales. Here was he, and here were the little people who did that part of his business, in quite new conditions. The stories must now be trimmed and pared and set upon all fours, they must run from a beginning to an end and fit (after a manner) with the laws of life; the pleasure, in one word, had become a business; and that not only for the dreamer, but for the little people of his theatre. These understood the change as well as he. When he lay down to prepare himself for sleep, he no longer sought amusement, but printable and profitable tales; and after he had dozed off in his box-seat, his little people continued their evolutions with the same mercantile designs. All other forms of dream deserted him but two: he still occasionally reads the most delightful books, he still visits at times the most delightful places; and it is perhaps worthy of note that to these same places, and to one in particular, he returns at intervals of months and years, finding new field-paths, visiting new neighbours, beholding that happy valley under new effects of noon and dawn and sunset. But all the rest of the family of visions is quite lost to him: the common, mangled version of yesterday's affairs, the raw-head-and-bloody-bones nightmare, rumoured to be the child of toasted cheese – these and their like are gone; and, for the most part, whether awake or asleep, he is simply occupied – he or his little people – in consciously making stories for the market. This dreamer (like many other persons) has encountered some trifling vicissitudes of fortune. When the bank begins to send letters and the butcher to linger at the back gate, he sets to belabouring his brains after a story, for that is his readiest money-winner; and, behold! at once the little people begin to bestir themselves in the same quest, and labour all night long, and all night long set before him truncheons of tales upon their lighted theatre. No fear of his being frightened now; the flying heart and the frozen scalp are things bygone; applause, growing applause, growing interest, growing exultation in his own cleverness (for he takes all the credit), and at last a jubilant leap to wakefulness, with the cry, 'I have it, that'll do!' upon his lips: with such and similar emotions he sits at these nocturnal dramas, with such outbreaks, like Claudius in the play, he scatters the performance in the midst. Often enough the waking is a disappointment: he has been too deep asleep, as I explain the thing; drowsiness has gained his little people, they have gone stumbling and maundering through their parts; and the play, to the awakened mind, is seen to be a tissue of absurdities. And yet how often have these sleepless Brownies done him honest service, and given him, as he sat idly taking his pleasure in the boxes, better tales than he could fashion for himself.

Here is one, exactly as it came to him. It seemed he was the son of a very rich and wicked man, the owner of broad acres and a most damnable temper. The dreamer (and that was the son) had lived much abroad, on purpose to avoid his parent; and when at length he returned to England, it was to find him married again to a young wife, who was supposed to suffer cruelly and to loathe her yoke. Because of this marriage (as the dreamer indistinctly understood) it was desirable for father and son to have a meeting; and yet both being proud and both angry, neither would condescend upon a visit. Meet they did accordingly, in a desolate, sandy country by the sea; and there they quarrelled, and the son, stung by some intolerable insult, struck down the father dead. No suspicion was aroused; the dead man was found and buried, and the dreamer succeeded to the broad estates, and found himself installed under the same roof with his father's widow, for whom no provision had been made. These two lived very much alone, as people may after a bereavement, sat down to table together, shared the long evenings, and grew daily better friends; until it seemed to him of a sudden that she was prying about dangerous matters, that she had conceived a notion of his guilt, that she watched him and tried him with questions. He drew back from her company as men draw back from a precipice suddenly discovered; and yet so strong was the attraction that he would drift again and again into the old intimacy, and again and again be startled back by some suggestive question or some inexplicable meaning in her eye. So they lived at cross purposes, a life full of broken dialogue, challenging glances, and suppressed passion; until, one day, he saw the woman slipping from the house in a veil, followed her to the station, followed her in the train to the seaside country, and out over the sandhills to the very place where the murder was done. There she began to grope among the bents, he watching her, flat upon his face; and presently she had something in her hand – I cannot remember what it was, but it was deadly evidence against the dreamer – and as she held it up to look at it, perhaps from the shock of the discovery, her foot slipped, and she hung at some peril on the brink of the tall sand-wreaths. He had no thought but to spring up and rescue her; and there they stood face to face, she with that deadly matter openly in her hand – his very presence on the spot another link of proof. It was plain she was about to speak, but this was more than he could bear – he could bear to be lost, but not to talk of it with his destroyer; and he cut her short with trivial conversation. Arm in arm, they returned together to the train, talking he knew not what, made the journey back in the same carriage, sat down to dinner, and passed the evening in the drawing-room as in the past. But suspense and fear drummed in the dreamer's bosom. 'She has not denounced me yet' – so his thoughts ran – 'when will she denounce me? Will it be tomorrow?' And it was not tomorrow, nor the next day, nor the next; and their life settled back on the old terms, only that she seemed kinder than before, and that, as for him, the burthen of his suspense and wonder grew daily more unbearable, so that he wasted away like a man with a disease. Once, indeed, he broke all bounds of decency, seized an occasion when she was abroad, ransacked her room, and at last, hidden away among her jewels, found the damning evidence. There he stood, holding this thing, which was his life, in the hollow of his hand, and marvelling at her inconsequent behaviour, that she should seek, and keep, and yet not use it; and then the door opened, and behold herself. So, once more, they stood, eye to eye, with the evidence between them; and once more she raised to him a face brimming with some communication; and once more he shied away from speech and cut her off. But before he left the room, which he had turned upside down, he laid back his death-warrant where he had found it; and at that, her face lighted up. The next thing he heard, she was explaining to her maid, with some ingenious falsehood, the disorder of her things. Flesh and blood could bear the strain no longer; and I think it was the next morning (though chronology is always hazy in the theatre of the mind) that he burst from his reserve. They had been breakfasting together in one corner of a great, parqueted, sparely-furnished room of many windows; all the time of the meal she had tortured him with sly allusions; and no sooner were the servants gone, and these two protagonists alone together, than he leaped to his feet. She too sprang up, with a pale face; with a pale face, she heard him as he raved out his complaint: Why did she torture him so? she knew all, she knew he was no enemy to her; why did she not denounce him at once? what signified her whole behaviour? why did she torture him? and yet again, why did she torture him? And when he had done, she fell upon her knees, and with outstretched hands: 'Do you not understand?' she cried. 'I love you!'

Hereupon, with a pang of wonder and mercantile delight, the dreamer awoke. His mercantile delight was not of long endurance; for it soon became plain that in this spirited tale there were unmarketable elements; which is just the reason why you have it here so briefly told. But his wonder has still kept growing; and I think the reader's will also, if he consider it ripely. For now he sees why I speak of the little people as of substantive inventors and performers. To the end they had kept their secret. I will go bail for the dreamer (having excellent grounds for valuing his candour) that he had no guess whatever at the motive of the woman – the hinge of the whole well-invented plot – until the instant of that highly dramatic declaration. It was not his tale; it was the little people's! And observe: not only was the secret kept, the story was told with really guileful craftsmanship. The conduct of both actors is (in the cant phrase) psychologically correct, and the emotion aptly graduated up to the surprising climax. I am awake now, and I know this trade; and yet I cannot better it. I am awake, and I live by this business; and yet I could not outdo – could not perhaps equal – that crafty artifice (as of some old, experienced carpenter of plays, some Dennery or Sardou) by which the same situation is twice presented and the two actors twice brought face to face over the evidence, only once it is in her hand, once in his – and these in their due order, the least dramatic first. The more I think of it, the more I am moved to press upon the world my question: Who are the Little People? They are near connections of the dreamer's, beyond doubt; they share in his financial worries and have an eye to the bank-book; they share plainly in his training; they have plainly learned like him to build the scheme of a considerate story and to arrange emotion in progressive order; only I think they have more talent; and one thing is beyond doubt, they can tell him a story piece by piece, like a serial, and keep him all the while in ignorance of where they aim. Who are they, then? and who is the dreamer?

Well, as regards the dreamer, I can answer that, for he is no less a person than myself; – as I might have told you from the beginning, only that the critics murmur over my consistent egotism; – and as I am positively forced to tell you now, or I could advance but little farther with my story. And for the Little People, what shall I say they are but just my Brownies, God bless them! who do one-half my work for me while I am fast asleep, and in all human likelihood, do the rest for me as well, when I am wide awake and fondly suppose I do it for myself. That part which is done while I am sleeping is the Brownies' part beyond contention; but that which is done when I am up and about is by no means necessarily mine, since all goes to show the Brownies have a hand in it even then. Here is a doubt that much concerns my conscience. For myself – what I call I, my conscious ego, the denizen of the pineal gland unless he has changed his residence since Descartes, the man with the conscience and the variable bank-account, the man with the hat and the boots, and the privilege of voting and not carrying his candidate at the general elections – I am sometimes tempted to suppose he is no story-teller at all, but a creature as matter of fact as any cheesemonger or any cheese, and a realist bemired up to the ears in actuality; so that, by that account, the whole of my published fiction should be the single-handed product of some Brownie, some Familiar, some unseen collaborator, whom I keep locked in a back garret, while I get all the praise and he but a share (which I cannot prevent him getting) of the pudding. I am an excellent adviser, something like Molière's servant; I pull back and I cut down; and I dress the whole in the best words and sentences that I can find and make; I hold the pen, too; and I do the sitting at the table, which is about the worst of it; and when all is done, I make up the manuscript and pay for the registration; so that, on the whole, I have some claim to share, though not so largely as I do, in the profits of our common enterprise.

I can but give an instance or so of what part is done sleeping and what part awake, and leave the reader to share what laurels there are, at his own nod, between myself and my collaborators; and to do this I will first take a book that a number of persons have been polite enough to read, the *Strange Case of Dr Jekyll and Mr Hyde*. I had long been trying to write a story on this subject, to find a body, a vehicle, for that strong sense of man's double being which must at times come in upon and overwhelm the mind of every thinking creature. I had even written one, *The Travelling Companion*, which was returned by an editor on the plea that it was a work of genius and indecent, and which I burned the other day on the ground that it was not a work of genius, and that *Jekyll* had supplanted it. Then came one of those financial fluctuations to which (with an elegant modesty) I have hitherto referred in the third person. For two days I went about racking my brains for a plot of any sort; and on the second night I dreamed the scene at the window, and a scene afterward split in two, in which Hyde, pursued for some crime, took the powder and underwent the change in the presence of his pursuers. All the rest was made awake, and consciously, although I think I can trace in much of it the manner of my Brownies. The meaning of the tale is therefore mine, and had long pre-existed in my garden of Adonis, and tried one body after another in vain; indeed, I do most of the morality, worse luck! and my Brownies have not a rudiment of what we call a conscience. Mine, too, is the setting, mine the characters. All that was given me was the matter of three scenes, and the central idea of a voluntary change becoming involuntary. Will it be thought ungenerous, after I have been so liberally ladling out praise to my unseen collaborators, if I here toss them over, bound hand and foot, into the arena of the critics? For the business of the powders, which so many have censured, is, I am relieved to say, not mine at all but the Brownies'. Of another tale, in case the reader should have glanced at it, I may say a word: the not very defensible story of *Olalla*. Here the court, the mother, the mother's niche, Olalla, Olalla's chamber, the meetings on the stair, the broken window, the ugly scene of the bite, were all given me in bulk and detail as I have tried to write them; to this I added only the external scenery (for in my dream I never was beyond the court), the portrait, the characters of Felipe and the priest, the moral, such as it is, and the last pages, such as, alas! they are. And I may even say that in this case the moral itself was given me; for it arose immediately on a comparison of the mother and the daughter, and from the hideous trick of atavism in the first. Sometimes a parabolic sense is still more undeniably present in a dream; sometimes I cannot but suppose my Brownies have been aping Bunyan, and yet in no case with what would possibly be called a moral in a tract; never with the ethical narrowness; conveying hints instead of life's larger limitations and that sort of sense which we seem to perceive in the arabesque of time and space.

For the most part, it will be seen, my Brownies are somewhat fantastic, like their stories hot and hot, full of passion and the picturesque, alive with animating incident; and they have no prejudice against the supernatural. But the other day they gave me a surprise, entertaining me with a love-story, a little April comedy, which I ought certainly to hand over to the author of *A Chance Acquaintance*, for he could write it as it should be written, and I am sure (although I mean to try) that I cannot. – But who would have supposed that a Brownie of mine should invent a tale for Mr Howells?

THE LANTERN-BEARERS

I

These boys congregated every autumn about a certain easterly fisher-village, where they tasted in a high degree the glory of existence. The place was created seemingly on purpose for the diversion of young gentlemen. A street or two of houses, mostly red and many of them tiled; a number of fine trees clustered about the manse and the kirkyard, and turning the chief street into a shady alley; many little gardens more than usually bright with flowers; nets a-drying, and fisher-wives scolding in the backward parts; a smell of fish, a genial smell of seaweed; whiffs of blowing sand at the street-corners; shops with golf-balls and bottled lollipops; another shop with penny pickwicks (that remarkable cigar) and the *London Journal*, dear to me for its startling pictures, and a few novels, dear for their suggestive names: such, as well as memory serves me, were the ingredients of the town. These, you are to conceive posted on a spit between two sandy bays, and sparsely flanked with villas – enough for the boys to lodge in with their subsidiary parents, not enough (not yet enough) to cocknify the scene: a haven in the rocks in front: in front of that, a file of gray islets: to the left, endless links and sand wreaths, a wilderness of hiding-holes, alive with popping rabbits and soaring gulls: to the right, a range of seaward crags, one rugged brow beyond another; the ruins of a mighty and ancient fortress on the brink of one; coves between – now charmed into sunshine quiet, now whistling with wind and clamorous with bursting surges; the dens and sheltered hollows redolent of thyme and southernwood, the air at the cliff's edge brisk and clean and pungent of the sea – in front of all, the Bass Rock, tilted seaward like a doubtful bather, the surf ringing it with white, the solan-geese hanging round its summit like a great and glittering smoke. This choice piece of seaboard was sacred, besides, to the wrecker; and the Bass, in the eye of fancy, still flew the colours of King James; and in the ear of fancy the arches of Tantallon still rang with horse-shoe iron, and echoed to the commands of Bell-the-Cat.

There was nothing to mar your days, if you were a boy summering in that part, but the embarrassment of pleasure. You might golf if you wanted; but I seem to have been better employed. You might secrete yourself in the Lady's Walk, a certain sunless dingle of elders, all mossed over by the damp as green as grass, and dotted here and there by the stream-side with roofless walls, the cold homes of anchorites. To fit themselves for life, and with a special eye to acquire the art of smoking, it was even common for the boys to harbour there; and you might have seen a single penny pickwick, honestly shared in lengths with a blunt knife, bestrew the glen with these apprentices. Again, you might join our fishing parties, where we sat perched as thick as solan-geese, a covey of little anglers, boy and girl, angling over each other's heads, to the much entanglement of lines and loss of podleys and consequent shrill recrimination – shrill as the geese themselves. Indeed, had that been all, you might have done this often; but though fishing be a fine pastime, the podley is scarce to be regarded as a dainty for the table; and it was a point of honour that a boy should eat all that he had taken. Or again, you might climb the Law, where the whale's jawbone stood landmark in the buzzing wind, and behold the face of many counties, and the smoke and spires of many towns, and the sails of distant ships. You might bathe, now in the flaws of fine weather, that we pathetically call our summer, now in a gale of wind, with the sand scouring your bare hide, your clothes thrashing abroad from underneath their guardian stone, the froth of the great breakers casting you headlong ere it had drowned your knees. Or you might explore the tidal rocks, above all in the ebb of springs, when the very roots of the hills were for the nonce discovered; following my leader from one group to another, groping in slippery tangle for the wreck of ships, wading in pools after the abominable creatures of the sea, and ever with an eye cast backward on the march of the tide and the menaced line of your retreat. And then you might go Crusoeing, a word that covers all extempore eating in the open air: digging perhaps a house under the margin of the links, kindling a fire of the sea-ware, and cooking apples there – if they were truly apples, for I sometimes suppose the merchant must have played us off with some inferior and quite local fruit, capable of resolving, in the neighbourhood of fire, into mere sand and smoke and iodine; or perhaps pushing to Tantallon, you might lunch on sandwiches and visions in the grassy court, while the wind hummed in the crumbling turrets; or clambering along the coast, eat geans[1] (the worst, I must

[1]Wild cherries.

[227]

suppose, in Christendom) from an adventurous gean tree that had taken
root under a cliff, where it was shaken with an ague of east wind, and
silvered after gales with salt, and grew so foreign among its bleak
surroundings that to eat of its produce was an adventure in itself.

There are mingled some dismal memories with so many that were
joyous. Of the fisher-wife, for instance, who had cut her throat at Canty
Bay; and of how I ran with the other children to the top of the Quadrant,
and beheld a posse of silent people escorting a cart, and on the cart,
bound in a chair, her throat bandaged, and the bandage all bloody –
horror! – the fisher-wife herself, who continued thenceforth to hag-ride
my thoughts, and even today (as I recall the scene) darkens daylight. She
was lodged in the little old jail in the chief street; but whether or no she
died there, with a wise terror of the worst, I never inquired. She had been
tippling; it was but a dingy tragedy; and it seems strange and hard that,
after all these years, the poor crazy sinner should be still pilloried on her
cart in the scrap-book of my memory. Nor shall I readily forget a certain
house in the Quadrant where a visitor died, and a dark old woman
continued to dwell alone with the dead body; nor how this old woman
conceived a hatred to myself and one of my cousins, and in the dread
hour of the dusk, as we were clambering on the garden-walls, opened a
window in that house of mortality and cursed us in a shrill voice and
with a marrowy choice of language. It was a pair of very colourless
urchins that fled down the lane from this remarkable experience! But I
recall with a more doubtful sentiment, compounded out of fear and
exultation, the coil of equinoctial tempests; trumpeting squalls,
scouring flaws of rain; the boats with their reefed lugsails scudding for
the harbour mouth, where danger lay, for it was hard to make when the
wind had any east in it; the wives clustered with blowing shawls at the
pier-head, where (if fate was against them) they might see boat and
husband and sons – their whole wealth and their whole family –
engulfed under their eyes; and (what I saw but once) a troop of
neighbours forcing such an unfortunate homeward, and she squalling
and battling in their midst, a figure scarcely human, a tragic Mænad.

These are things that I recall with interest; but what my memory
dwells upon the most, I have been all this while withholding. It was a
sport peculiar to the place, and indeed to a week or so of our two
months' holiday there. Maybe it still flourishes in its native spot; for
boys and their pastimes are swayed by periodic forces inscrutable to
man; so that tops and marbles reappear in their due season, regular like

the sun and moon; and the harmless art of knucklebones has seen the fall of the Roman empire and the rise of the United States. It may still flourish in its native spot, but nowhere else, I am persuaded; for I tried myself to introduce it on Tweedside, and was defeated lamentably; its charm being quite local, like a country wine that cannot be exported.

The idle manner of it was this: –

Toward the end of September, when school-time was drawing near and the nights were already black, we would begin to sally from our respective villas, each equipped with a tin bull's-eye lantern. The thing was so well known that it had worn a rut in the commerce of Great Britain; and the grocers, about the due time, began to garnish their windows with our particular brand of luminary. We wore them buckled to the waist upon a cricket belt, and over them, such was the rigour of the game, a buttoned top-coat. They smelled noisomely of blistered tin; they never burned aright, though they would always burn our fingers; their use was naught; the pleasure of them merely fanciful; and yet a boy with a bull's-eye under his top-coat asked for nothing more. The fishermen used lanterns about their boats, and it was from them, I suppose, that we had got the hint; but theirs were not bull's-eyes, nor did we ever play at being fishermen. The police carried them at their belts, and we had plainly copied them in that; yet we did not pretend to be policemen. Burglars, indeed, we may have had some haunting thoughts of; and we had certainly an eye to past ages when lanterns were more common, and to certain story-books in which we had found them to figure very largely. But take it for all in all, the pleasure of the thing was substantive; and to be a boy with a bull's-eye under his top-coat was good enough for us.

When two of these asses met, there would be an anxious 'Have you got your lantern?' and a gratified 'Yes!' That was the shibboleth, and very needful too; for, as it was the rule to keep our glory contained, none could recognise a lantern-bearer, unless (like the polecat) by the smell. Four or five would sometimes climb into the belly of a ten-man lugger, with nothing but the thwarts above them – for the cabin was usually locked, or choose out some hollow of the links where the wind might whistle overhead. There the coats would be unbuttoned and the bull's-eyes discovered; and in the chequering glimmer, under the huge windy hall of the night, and cheered by a rich steam of toasting tinware, these fortunate young gentlemen would crouch together in the cold sand of the links or on the scaly bilges of the fishing-boat, and delight themselves with inappropriate talk. Woe is me that I may not give some specimens – some of their foresights of life, or deep inquiries into the rudiments of man and nature, these were so fiery and so innocent, they were so richly silly, so romantically young. But the talk, at any rate, was but a condiment; and these gatherings themselves only accidents in the career of the lantern-bearer. The essence of this bliss was to walk by yourself in the black night; the slide shut, the top-coat buttoned; not a ray escaping, whether to conduct your footsteps or to make your glory public: a mere pillar of darkness in the dark; and all the while, deep down in the privacy of your fool's heart, to know you had a bull's-eye at your belt, and to exult and sing over the knowledge.

II

It is said that a poet has died young in the breast of the most stolid. It may be contended, rather, that this (somewhat minor) bard in almost every case survives, and is the spice of life to his possessor. Justice is not done to the versatility and the unplumbed childishness of man's imagination. His life from without may seem but a rude mound of mud; there will be some golden chamber at the heart of it, in which he dwells delighted; and for as dark as his pathway seems to the observer, he will have some kind of a bull's-eye at his belt.

It would be hard to pick out a career more cheerless than that of Dancer, the miser, as he figures in the 'Old Bailey Reports,' a prey to the most sordid persecutions, the butt of his neighbourhood, betrayed by his hired man, his house beleaguered by the impish school-boy, and he himself grinding and fuming and impotently fleeing to the law against these pin-pricks. You marvel at first that anyone should willingly prolong a life so destitute of charm and dignity; and then you call to memory that had he chosen, had he ceased to be a miser, he could have been freed at once from these trials, and might have built himself a castle and gone escorted by a squadron. For the love of more recondite joys, which we cannot estimate, which, it may be, we should envy, the man had willingly forgone both comfort and consideration. 'His mind to him a kingdom was'; and sure enough, digging into that mind, which seems at first a dust-heap, we unearth some priceless jewels. For Dancer must have had the love of power and the disdain of using it, a noble character in itself; disdain of many pleasures, a chief part of what is commonly called wisdom; disdain of the inevitable end, that finest trait of mankind; scorn of men's opinions, another element of virtue; and at the back of all, a conscience just like yours and mine, whining like a cur, swindling like a thimble-rigger, but still pointing (there or thereabout) to some conventional standard. Here were a cabinet portrait to which Hawthorne perhaps had done justice; and yet not Hawthorne either, for he was mildly minded, and it lay not in him to create for us that throb of the miser's pulse, his fretful energy of gusto, his vast arms of ambition clutching in he knows not what: insatiable, insane, a god with a muck-rake. Thus, at least, looking in the bosom of the miser, consideration detects the poet in the full tide of life, with more, indeed, of the poetic fire than usually goes to epics; and tracing that mean man about his cold hearth, and to and fro in his discomfortable house, spies within him a blazing bonfire of delight. And so with others, who do not live by bread alone, but by some cherished and perhaps fantastic pleasure; who are meat salesmen to the external eye, and possibly to themselves are Shakespeares, Napoleons, or Beethovens; who have not one virtue to rub against another in the field of active life, and yet perhaps, in the life of contemplation, sit with the saints. We see them on the street, and we can count their buttons; but heaven knows in what they pride themselves! heaven knows where they have set their treasure!

There is one fable that touches very near the quick of life: the fable of the monk who passed into the woods, heard a bird break into song, hearkened for a trill or two, and found himself on his return a stranger at his convent gates; for he had been absent fifty years, and of all his comrades there survived but one to recognise him. It is not only in the woods that this enchanter carols, though perhaps he is native there. He sings in the most doleful places. The miser hears him and chuckles, and the days are moments. With no more apparatus than an ill-smelling lantern I have evoked him on the naked links. All life that is not merely mechanical is spun out of two strands: seeking for that bird and hearing him. And it is just this that makes life so hard to value, and the delight of each so incommunicable. And just a knowledge of this, and a remembrance of those fortunate hours in which the bird has sung to us, that fills us with such wonder when we turn the pages of the realist. There, to be sure, we find a picture of life in so far as it consists of mud and of old iron, cheap desires and cheap fears, that which we are ashamed to remember and that which we are careless whether we forget; but of the note of that time-devouring nightingale we hear no news.

The case of these writers of romance is most obscure. They have been boys and youths; they have lingered outside the window of the beloved, who was then most probably writing to someone else; they have sat before a sheet of paper, and felt themselves mere continents of congested poetry, not one line of which would flow; they have walked alone in the woods, they have walked in cities under the countless lamps; they have been to sea, they have hated, they have feared, they have longed to knife a man, and maybe done it; the wild taste of life has stung their palate. Or, if you deny them all the rest, one pleasure at least they have tasted to the full – their books are there to prove it – the keen pleasure of successful literary composition. And yet they fill the globe with volumes, whose cleverness inspires me with despairing admiration, and whose consistent falsity to all I care to call existence, with despairing wrath. If I had no better hope than to continue to revolve among the dreary and petty businesses, and to be moved by the paltry hopes and fears with which they surround and animate their heroes, I declare I would die now. But there has never an hour of mine gone quite so dully yet; if it were spent waiting at a railway junction, I would have some scattering thoughts, I could count some grains of memory, compared to which the whole of one of these romances seems but dross.

These writers would retort (if I take them properly) that this was very true; that it was the same with themselves and other persons of (what they call) the artistic temperament; that in this we were exceptional, and should apparently be ashamed of ourselves; but that our works must deal exclusively with (what they call) the average man, who was a prodigious dull fellow, and quite dead to all but the paltriest consider-ations. I accept the issue. We can only know others by ourselves. The artistic temperament (a plague on the expression!) does not make us different from our fellow-men, or it would make us incapable of writing novels; and the average man (a murrain on the word!) is just like you and me, or he would not be average. It was Whitman who stamped a kind of Birmingham sacredness upon the latter phrase; but Whitman knew very well, and showed very nobly, that the average man was full of joys and full of a poetry of his own. And this harping on life's dulness and man's meanness is a loud profession of incompetence; it is one of two things: the cry of the blind eye, *I cannot see*, or the complaint of the dumb tongue, *I cannot utter*. To draw a life without delights is to prove I have not realised it. To picture a man without some sort of poetry – well, it goes near to prove my case, for it shows an author may have little enough. To see Dancer only as a dirty, old, small-minded, impotently fuming man, in a dirty house, besieged by Harrow boys, and probably beset by small attorneys, is to show myself as keen an observer as . . . the Harrow boys. But these young gentlemen (with a more becoming modesty) were content to pluck Dancer by the coat-tails; they did not suppose they had surprised his secret or could put him living in a book: and it is there my error would have lain. Or say that in the same romance – I continue to call these books romances, in the hope of giving pain – say that in the same romance, which now begins really to take shape, I should leave to speak of Dancer, and follow instead the Harrow boys; and say that I came on some such business as that of my lantern-bearers on the links; and described the boys as very cold, spat upon by flurries of rain, and drearily surrounded, all of which they were; and their talk as silly and indecent, which it certainly was. I might upon these lines, and had I Zola's genius, turn out, in a page or so, a gem of literary art, render the lantern-light with the touches of a master, and lay on the indecency with the ungrudging hand of love; and when all was done, what a triumph would my picture be of shallowness and dulness! how it would have missed the point! how it would have belied the boys! To the ear of the stenographer, the talk is merely silly and indecent; but ask the boys themselves, and they are discussing (as it is highly proper they should) the possibilities of existence. To the eye of the observer they are wet and cold and drearily surrounded; but ask themselves, and they are in the heaven of a recondite pleasure, the ground of which is an ill-smelling lantern.

III

For, to repeat, the ground of a man's joy is often hard to hit. It may hinge at times upon a mere accessory, like the lantern, it may reside, like Dancer's, in the mysterious inwards of psychology. It may consist with perpetual failure, and find exercise in the continued chase. It has so little bond with externals (such as the observer scribbles in his note-book) that it may even touch them not; and the man's true life, for which he consents to live, lie altogether in the field of fancy. The clergyman, in his spare hours, may be winning battles, the farmer sailing ships, the banker reaping triumph in the arts: all leading another life, plying another trade from that they chose; like the poet's housebuilder, who, after all is cased in stone.

> By his fireside, as impotent fancy prompts,
> Rebuilds it to his liking.

In such a case the poetry runs underground. The observer (poor soul, with his documents!) is all abroad. For to look at the man is but to court deception. We shall see the trunk from which he draws his nourishment; but he himself is above and abroad in the green dome of foliage, hummed through by winds and nested in by nightingales. And the true realism were that of the poets, to climb up after him like a squirrel, and catch some glimpse of the heaven for which he lives. And the true realism, always and everywhere, is that of the poets: to find out where joy resides, and give it a voice far beyond singing.

For to miss the joy is to miss all. In the joy of the actors lies the sense of any action. That is the explanation, that the excuse. To one who has not the secret of the lanterns, the scene upon the links is meaningless. And hence the haunting and truly spectral unreality of realistic books. Hence, when we read the English realists, the incredulous wonder with which we observe the hero's constancy under the submerging tide of dulness, and how he bears up with his jibbing sweetheart, and endures the chatter of idiot girls, and stands by his whole unfeatured wilderness of an existence, instead of seeking relief in drink or foreign travel. Hence in the French, in that meat-market of middle-aged sensuality, the disgusted surprise with which we see the hero drift sidelong, and practically quite untempted, into every description of misconduct and dishonour. In each, we miss the personal poetry, the enchanted atmosphere, that rainbow work of fancy that clothes what is naked and seems to ennoble what is base; in each, life falls dead like dough, instead of soaring away like a balloon into the colours of the sunset; each is true, each inconceivable; for no man lives in the external truth, among salts and acids, but in the warm, phantasmagoric chamber of his brain, with the painted windows and the storied walls.

Of this falsity we have had a recent example from a man who knows far better – Tolstoi's *Powers of Darkness*. Here is a piece full of force and truth, yet quite untrue. For before Mikita was led into so dire a situation he was tempted, and temptations are beautiful at least in part; and a work which dwells on the ugliness of crime and gives no hint of any loveliness in the temptation, sins against the modesty of life, and even when a Tolstoi writes it, sinks to melodrama. The peasants are not understood; they saw their life in fairer colours; even the deaf girl was clothed in poetry for Mikita, or he had never fallen. And so, once again, even an Old Bailey melodrama, without some brightness of poetry and lustre of existence, falls into the inconceivable and ranks with fairy tales.

IV

In nobler books we are moved with something like the emotions of life; and this emotion is very variously provoked. We are so moved when Levine labours in the field, when André sinks beyond emotion, when Richard Feverel and Lucy Desborough meet beside the river, when Antony, 'not cowardly, puts off his helmet,' when Kent has infinite pity on the dying Lear, when, in Dostoieffky's *Despised and Rejected*, the uncomplaining hero drains his cup of suffering and virtue. These are notes that please the great heart of man. Not only love, and the fields, and the bright face of danger, but sacrifice and death and unmerited suffering humbly supported, touch in us the vein of the poetic. We love to think of them, we long to try them, we are humbly hopeful that we may prove heroes also.

We have heard, perhaps, too much of lesser matters. Here is the door, here is the open air. *Itur in antiquam silvam.*

CONFESSIONS OF A UNIONIST

I find the newspapers in the United States much occupied with the doings and sufferings, the appearance, speech and even apparel of a person in whom I take an interest and who is quite unused to such publicity. In a single article I have seen solemnly chronicled the hour at which he was supposed to rise and the disposition of his whole morning, accompanied by remarks upon his 'fleshiness' and the lustre of his eye. On these last, I am not qualified to speak; he might be as corpulent as a hog and his eyes as brilliant as a deep-sea light, and I should be the last to know it in any critical spirit: But as to the other particulars, it is noteworthy that they were all false at the time, although some have proved to be prophetic. Let me suppose the public to care for information of this sort and to peruse with really unaffected joy this court circular of the obscure; and then it will seem strange the want should be so ill supplied – it will seem strange the article should have been entirely false, and yet published not so many hundred miles from the poor dignitary it purported to describe, and he dwelling quite open to inspection, without body-guard or chamberlain or so much as a single sentry at his palace door. And the thought slips into my head unbidden: if the papers are unfaithful in the microscopically small, if they cannot find out when a gentleman gets up in the morning, when he takes a walk, when he receives his mail or with what appetite he sits to breakfast, how shall we believe them on affairs of public policy or public morals?

The newspaper exists to give us news, most of which is very unnecessary; and it is by glancing through the columns, and gleaning here and there a random fact, that we are supposed to build up the image of our epoch and correct and fortify our thought. That is the ground on which it claims its license: the public, it says, must be informed; no matter what injustice falls on private parties, the larger public justice must prevail. It is an argument of some authority, not lightly to be set aside. Even rumours may be worth commemorating; they may be true on the one hand; on the other, even if they are false, they may indicate the current of men's thought; and the newspaper, holding up a mirror to the day's doings, small and great, should possibly reflect these also. Poor Mr Ferry may read with amazement of his peculations, poor General Butler may weary of the story of the teaspoons, poor Mr Stevenson may start back in amazement from the image of himself as a devotee of Wagner's music; but they have no true ground of quarrel: in the course of the day's business these rumours floated up, and the impartial mirror reflects, the irresponsible echo re-enounces them. By this course of reasoning, the mirror ought to be impartial; as the *Standard*, for instance, tries to be in England and the *Evening Post* here in the States: black swans in the world of journalism. Still more, by this course of reasoning, there is one sin unpardonable: that of suppression. On the ground that everything must be repeated, whether true or false, men try to bear up as best they can under a hundred indiscretions and a hundred calumnies. On the same ground, when they find material facts omitted, they do well to be angry.

Now the newspapers in the States, even my *Evening Post*, have long struck me by the quality of their Irish news. I do not mean simply that the news is given with the prepossession of a partisan, for that I fear is not avoidable. I mean that a large class of facts (to me, the most material of all) receive, as far as I have read, no illustration whatever. As I read and waited and wondered, there occurred to me a recent utterance of M. Rochefort's. 'Public Opinion?' he is reported to have said. 'O, we know how that is manufactured.' And I began at last to see why the Americans, who have had their own share of suffering from Irish lawlessness and are (in their own land) so prompt in its suppression, should yet be all upon the side of anarchy in the Emerald Isle. According to the Irish news published in this country, I began to reflect that the position of the present majority of British subjects was merely unthinkable. No grounds were given on which a man could possibly be what we call a Unionist. I asked the question of a very clever and fair man; and he owned he had been puzzled, but seeing no tenable excuse in the American papers, had been driven to suppose it was some 'job about landlords.' It was what I had supposed; and yet I thought it noteworthy, that one country should be led to think so meanly of another, and that even a newspaper should suppose the right to be entirely on one side of any possible dispute. There must be some illusory shadow of argument for a party that has carried the polls. The honest man whom you probably knew under his Irish nickname of Buckshot Forster, was a federationist in principle: yet he had earned that nickname, or earned at least the detestation that supplied it. Many of us have been in favour of home rule for Ireland ten or a dozen years before Mr Gladstone; we have no Irish land, we know no Irish landlords; and yet here we are today in the camp of Union. Once more, there must be some colour of pretext for this attitude.

I wish to try to say to the Americans, what that attitude really is, and why some of us hold it. And first, for a confession: the state of Ireland is a perpetual and crying blot upon the fame of England. England went there, as every nation in the world has gone where you now find it, because it consisted with her interest. She conquered it, as the Normans had conquered herself not so long before; and she has ever since majestically proved her incapacity to rule it. It is not an easy country to rule; its economical condition is perplexing, its ethical state much like that of the Scots Highlands before the pacification, its people still much behind the age. But this backwardness is the fault of English indifference, English sentimentality, and the wavering of English party government. To and fro has the majority rolled, and now repressed and now relaxed; and now made a transitory show of sternness, and anon stuffed our naughty child with flattery and indulgence; until if the Irish people had been angels, they must still have been corrupted. I once knew a superlatively wicked billygoat whom, in indignation at a score of treacheries, I determined to punish. The plan adopted was to feed, cajole, pet, abuse, kick, feed and cajole him, for a whole long summer's day, in an unbroken series. By about four in the afternoon, the billy-goat (as you say) 'left hold.' He would no longer eat, he would no longer butt; he gave up life as quite insoluble, and went and lay down in a ditch, whence nothing could dislodge him. Well, the treatment of the billy-goat is very like the treatment Ireland has received.

But second, it must not be supposed (in our day at least) that the excess has ever been upon the side of harshness. The Irish may have been treated harshly by their landlords; the case is not peculiar to the Emerald Isle; they may, owing to economic conditions and their own inertia, lie specially helpless against such treatment; I do not know. It is more important to observe how far the government has gone and is still going in its attempt to modify these burthens: so far as to stultify the whole of the rest of the home policy, and to commit England at large to many sweeping measures which a day may bring forth. For I believe it will be found we are indeed committed to a doctrine, harmless enough in itself if it went by its right name of *the land for the peasants*, but harmful, perhaps very harmful, since it masquerades under the *alias* of *the land for the people*. But if the word 'people' were only used when the people is really meant, how very small a modicum of our political prating would remain! It must be owned these concessions, so alien to what was then the English sentiment, smack not at all of harshness. And not only harshness has been absent, but even common firmness and the respect of our own laws. The harshness is upon the other side. These coercion acts, which should be called protection acts, are directed simply against crime: the crime over which your journals love to pass so lightly; unmanly murders, the harshest extreme of boycotting, and that applied to the poorest and most pitiable persons: murders like the Joyce murder or the Curtin murder: boycottings like that of the Curtin family: crimes which, if any government permit and do not sternly suppress, it has ceased to be a government at all. And observe, these are not ordinary crimes of greed, revenge or guilty love. They are part of a system; they are subsidised with money openly collected; they are applied to stifle the voice of a minority, and that minority, the law observers; and they are suggested and protected by the leaders of the party, speaking openly from the platform. To no student of the French Revolution will this state of matters appear strange: it is the Jacobin system. Used today for one end and to stifle the voice of the minority, it will be used tomorrow for another; tomorrow it is the majority that will sit trembling by its hearths; and the day after, the scum of a nation will hold it by the reins and drive it, through blood and pillage into slavery.

Let us, for the moment, waive this point and look upon these crimes as ordinary crimes; and I repeat they are such as, if any government permit, it shall have ceased to be a government. For a nation is constituted with two ends: to prevent external violence by defensive arms, to stay internal violence by rigid law. Rigid, not just: none can be just – that is a dream; law is a compromise. The law is in constant flux and progress; but in the nature of things it must lag behind opinion. Hence our true distinction between morality and law. Morality is the sense of a nation; law is an attempt to apply that sense to the thousand complications of life, and to express it in clear words. And again morality is the sense of the public at this moment, *hic et nunc*; and law is only so much of that as has been overtaken and perpetuated by enactment. Law will therefore generally embody the greater part of the morality of any age and nation, but never its more lively part; for our new sensations (witness the fine old school-boy story of the negro and the Jew) are still the most exquisitely felt. In short, it is in the very nature of law to be always as a whole behind the age, and to be invariably not quite just in the particular instance. It offers not abstract justice; upon which I wonder how many of us are agreed? It offers instead specific terms of compromise, and a stern regularity in their application; so that a man shall know what he should do, how he should do it, and what he must expect if he shall fail. The end of a nation is therefore perfectly served, when she is strong enough abroad to keep her borders unassailed, and strong enough at home to make her laws respected – until they shall be changed, if needful.

This is where we have failed in Ireland. Through sentimentality, through the craven vagaries of a popular assembly, we have suffered the law to tumble in the muck.

Violence surrounds us, the Jacobin is abroad, the Kingdom of the Bully at hand; and we still palter with this staring duty, we still leave our brother in the respect of law naked of protection! And here in one word, is the heart of the Unionist position. We will not, at this moment, so much as discuss the question of home rule. With all the lessons of history at our back, we will grant nothing that shall even appear to be extorted by brutality and murder. We shall see the law paramount, before we talk of its reform.

An English journal and my friend Mr Grant Allen (*et tu brute!*) inform me I know nothing of morality, because I take the side of the police against the dynamiter. They will have to find another name for morals, or a new derivation for the old one – if they care anything for the history of words; but I fear they care nothing for any history whatever, whether of words or things.

To be on the side of the weak, they think, is not to be far wrong; and I hope all are of the same opinion. The point is, which is which? I will not be so illogical as to taunt them with the Joyce children, or the Curtin girls, or the poor little sight-seers at the Tower; for this were to argue in their own manner, from particular instances. The justification of our attitude has nothing to say to these; we stand firm on our belief that, in the long run and on a scale of generations, the cause of the law is the cause of the weak. We think it the one bond of man, the one bulwark of progress and of such happiness as men taste. If it protect us, we willingly forgive its incident injustices; but we feel these as well as our neighbours: and if it fail to protect us, we desire to see an end of it, and to fight for our own hands on equal terms. We think law the best thing; we prefer it (that is) with all its defects, to a mere barbarous scramble. But if we cannot have law effectual, we want none of it. Drop the farce, give us an equal chance, and do not bind the honest man and set the bully free. In other words, give us law, or let us have open war; there is no tenable halting point between. – Well, in all this, we may be quite wrong, and Mr Allen and the *Pall Mall* quite right. And I hazard the guess they will find any article stimulant. I hazard the guess because such effects are usually opposite and equal; and it is from their views and utterances, and the views and utterances of those whom they admire, that the Unionist draws resolutions. Ireland might be filled with disorder, and that would be bad enough; it would shame, it would *not* startle us.

It is bad enough to have crime, and crime unpunished. But crime committed for a political end, and upon that very ground unpunished and minimised by journalists and politicians? O, this is a very different matter; this is the Girondin playing once more (as though history had never been written) with the Jacobin tiger; this is the sentimentalist once more preparing the pathway of the brute. And it would be difficult to say with what resolution this inspires us. We think that Ireland has been wronged, it is hard to say how much, for it is all dusted over with the nonsense of the public platform. On the other hand we believe its chief wrong, in all our time, to have been the want of firm authority. And however that may be, and however the crying woes of that distressful island, we are persuaded (in view of the attitude of our sentimentalists and the course of history) that far graver and far wider sorrows – sorrows perhaps as wide as humanity – would be the consequence of any fresh capitulation to political crime.

And suppose this fear to be chimerical, we have yet another and a present reason. For in a country ruled by violence, by tumultuary movements, the fear of midnight murder and the pressure of boycotting, votes have no significance. A large proportion of citizens are very quick to swim with the tide, a still larger are before all things cowardly. In France, as the Terror drew near, these gradually refrained from voting; until the enormous majority of the nation, more than six-sevenths, had desisted from the least control of its own fate. Something of the same sort prevails today in South American republics. And if in Ireland people still come to the polls, they do so under conditions highly peculiar: threading an Irish mob, seeing on this hand the moonlighter, on that the boycotter, and hearing from the candidate menacing doctrines. How are we to know they come there willingly? How are we to know if the majority polled be a majority of sentiments? or only a majority of fists?

And as long as there shall remain the least shadow of doubt on such a point, and until the whole machinery of terrorism is destroyed, and coercive political crime a thing of the past, we refuse to begin to consider an organic change.

And now for a particular word to the Americans. If Ireland had been in the hands of the States, there would be none of this: not because the Irish would have been contented, but because you would have put them down. It is one of the fortunate circumstances of my wandering career that I was present in San Francisco during the sand-lot troubles. Here was our poor Ireland over again: the Irish lawlessness, the Irish helplessness, the Irish appeal to violence. They have ground at home in Ireland, they had ground as good in California. Landlordism is nowhere that I have seen so indefensible as in the land of gold; men at up-country ranches were working and falling in debt on the truck system; Chinese immigration had taken the bread from thousands; and there were the squatters on the brink of open revolt along the line of a new railway; and there in the midst of the city, rose the spire of San Francisco stock exchange, the very temple of the Spoliation of the Weak by the Strong. But when it came to a talk of lawlessness the San Franciscans (who knew what lawlessness implies) did not hesitate one moment; and the weapons were burnished in the armouries, and the gatling guns rattled on the street.

How much I have envied this promptitude for France in 1792, when it would have changed the face of history; How much I am sometimes tempted to envy it today for Ireland! A vigilance committee, an appearance of Judge Lynch, are things to be deplored; but there are worse alternatives. They tell of the defeat of the law; but they represent the victory of the class of law-observers. It was by similar means that law first triumphed; and even today, when the bully takes to his club, it may be the best and shortest way to meet him upon equal terms. But this dispute is by the way. My point is simpler: had Ireland been a part of the United States, you would long ago (if I know anything of Americans) have formed a vigilance committee, and the whole movement (if I know anything of the Irish) would have subsided at the very name. When boycotting began the other day in New York, I was delighted to observe the attitude and the triumph of decent people. Had the attractions of moonlighting and midnight murder been added to the programme, you would have been none less prompt and much more sweeping in your measures. This is not the mark of a country where the law is strong (and it seems to be especially weak against the rich); but it is the mark of a people with some lively and enviable virtues.

With your border experiences, with the pulse of the law beating so feebly in the huge body of your continent, a certain semi-barbarous self-reliance remains to you. You have no idea what sheep the middle class tends to become, what sheep they are in England, how difficult to rouse to any masculine resolve, how prone to maudlin sentiment and (what flows from it) easy generosity at the expense of others. You have no idea in what disarmed, unwieldy helplessness we lie at the mercy of parliamentary obstruction and agrarian brutality. It is a strange frame of mind, not cowed, not frightened, not sulky, not angry, not even angry enough: a form of sentimental paralysis, in which we love to coquette with the wolf while the sheep are scattered, in which we love to dangle in our Girondin lap the Jacobin tiger. We cannot ask you to admire us, for the picture is contemptible enough; but we do ask you not to be led away by your newspapers and the stump oratory of the Irish; to wipe from your minds the talk of tyranny and the epithet Bloody, so delicately applied to Mr Balfour; and to conceive of Ireland as a country groaning for a vigilance committee and of the English government as a government false to its trust through maudlin sentiment and party distraction, but not at all through sternness. We ask you to sympathise with that party who are trying, as you would do, although with less decision and by milder means, to put an end to violence and the rule of the bully.

We appeal at much disadvantage; against the bulk of your newspapers; against the prestige of the name of Mr Gladstone, conspicuous by his venerable age, long services and magnificent dramatic talent; against the insidious influence of all the favourite catch-words of the period, 'oppressed nationality,' 'tyranny,' 'the interest of the poor,' – all which may be invoked against us. But there lies at the bottom of our cause so sound a kernel of common sense and common political honesty, that I do not think we shall appeal in vain. To the student of history however careless, I am sure we shall not.

LETTER TO A YOUNG GENTLEMAN
WHO PROPOSES TO EMBRACE
THE CAREER OF ART

With the agreeable frankness of youth, you address me on a point of some practical importance to yourself and (it is even conceivable) of some gravity to the world: Should you or should you not become an artist? It is one which you must decide entirely for yourself; all that I can do is to bring under your notice some of the materials of that decision; and I will begin, as I shall probably conclude also, by assuring you that all depends on the vocation.

To know what you like is the beginning of wisdom and of old age. Youth is wholly experimental. The essence and charm of that unquiet and delightful epoch is ignorance of self as well as ignorance of life. These two unknowns the young man brings together again and again, now in the airiest touch, now with a bitter hug; now with exquisite pleasure, now with cutting pain; but never with indifference, to which he is a total stranger, and never with that near kinsman of indifference, contentment. If he be a youth of dainty senses or a brain easily heated, the interest of this series of experiments grows upon him out of all proportion to the pleasure he receives. It is not beauty that he loves, nor pleasure that he seeks, though he may think so; his design and his sufficient reward is to verify his own existence and taste the variety of human fate. To him, before the razor-edge of curiosity is dulled, all that is not actual living and the hot chase of experience wears a face of a disgusting dryness difficult to recall in later days; or if there be any exception – and here destiny steps in – it is in those moments when, wearied or surfeited of the primary activity of the senses, he calls up before memory the image of transacted pains and pleasures. Thus it is that such an one shies from all cut-and-dry professions, and inclines insensibly toward that career of art which consists only in the tasting and recording of experience.

This, which is not so much a vocation for art as an impatience of all other honest trades, frequently exists alone; and so existing, it will pass gently away in the course of years. Emphatically, it is not to be regarded; it is not a vocation, but a temptation; and when your father the other day so fiercely and (in my view) so properly discouraged your ambition, he was recalling not improbably some similar passage in his own experience. For the temptation is perhaps nearly as common as the vocation is rare. But again we have vocations which are imperfect; we have men whose minds are bound up, not so much in any art, as in the general *ars artium* and common base of all creative work; who will now dip into painting, and now study counterpoint, and anon will be inditing a sonnet: all these with equal interest, all often with genuine knowledge. And of this temper, when it stands alone, I find it difficult to speak; but I should counsel such an one to take to letters, for in literature (which drags with so wide a net) all his information may be found some day useful, and if he should go on as he has begun, and turn at last into the critic, he will have learned to use the necessary tools. Lastly we come to those vocations which are at once decisive and precise; to the men who are born with the love of pigments, the passion of drawing, the gift of music, or the impulse to create with words, just as other and perhaps the same men are born with the love of hunting, or the sea, or horses, or the turning-lathe. These are predestined; if a man love the labour of any trade, apart from any question of success or fame, the gods have called him. He may have the general vocation too: he may have a taste for all the arts, and I think he often has; but the mark of his calling is this laborious partiality for one, this inextinguishable zest in its technical successes, and (perhaps above all) a certain candour of mind, to take his very trifling enterprise with a gravity that would befit the cares of empire, and to think the smallest improvement worth accomplishing at any expense of time and industry. The book, the statue, the sonata, must be gone upon with the unreasoning good faith and the unflagging spirit of children at their play. *Is it worth doing?* – when it shall have occurred to any artist to ask himself that question, it is implicitly answered in the negative. It does not occur to the child as he plays at being a pirate on the dining-room sofa, nor to the hunter as he pursues his quarry; and the candour of the one and the ardour of the other should be united in the bosom of the artist.

If you recognise in yourself some such decisive taste, there is no room for hesitation: follow your bent. And observe (lest I should too much discourage you) that the disposition does not usually burn so brightly at the first, or rather not so constantly. Habit and practice sharpen gifts; the necessity of toil grows less disgusting, grows even welcome, in the course of years; a small taste (if it be only genuine) waxes with indulgence into an exclusive passion. Enough, just now, if you can look back over a fair interval, and see that your chosen art has a little more than held its own among the thronging interests of youth. Time will do the rest, if devotion help it; and soon your every thought will be engrossed in that beloved occupation.

But even with devotion, you may remind me, even with unfaltering and delighted industry, many thousand artists spend their lives, if the result be regarded, utterly in vain; a thousand artists, and never one work of art. But the vast mass of mankind are incapable of doing anything reasonably well, art among the rest. The worthless artist would not improbably have been a quite incompetent baker. And the artist, even if he does not amuse the public, amuses himself; so that there will always be one man the happier for his vigils. This is the practical side of art: its inexpugnable fortress for the true practitioner. The direct returns – the wages of the trade – are small, but the indirect – the wages of the life – are incalculably great. No other business offers a man his daily bread upon such joyful terms. The soldier and the explorer have moments of a worthier excitement, but they are purchased by cruel hardships and periods of tedium that beggar language. In the life of the artist there need be no hour without its pleasure. I take the author, with whose career I am best acquainted; and it is true he works in a rebellious material, and that the act of writing is cramped and trying both to the eyes and the temper; but remark him in his study, when matter crowds upon him and words are not wanting – in what a continual series of small successes time flows by; with what a sense of power as of one moving mountains, he marshals his petty characters; with what pleasures, both of the ear and eye, he sees his airy structure growing on the page; and how he labours in a craft to which the whole material of his life is tributary, and which opens a door to all his tastes, his loves, his hatreds, and his convictions, so that what he writes is only what he longed to utter. He may have enjoyed many things in this big, tragic playground of the world; but what shall he have enjoyed more fully than a morning of successful work? Suppose it ill paid: the wonder is it should be paid at all. Other men pay, and pay dearly, for pleasures less desirable.

Nor will the practice of art afford you pleasure only; it affords besides an admirable training. For the artist works entirely upon honour. The public knows little or nothing of those merits in the quest of which you are condemned to spend the bulk of your endeavours. Merits of design, the merit of first-hand energy, the merit of a certain cheap accomplishment which a man of the artistic temper easily acquires – these they can recognise, and these they value. But to those more exquisite refinements of proficiency and finish, which the artist so ardently desires and so keenly feels, for which (in the vigorous words of Balzac) he must toil 'like a miner buried in a landslip,' for which, day after day, he recasts and revises and rejects – the gross mass of the public must be ever blind. To those lost pains, suppose you attain the highest pitch of merit, posterity may possibly do justice; suppose, as is so probable, you fail by even a hair's breadth of the highest, rest certain they shall never be observed. Under the shadow of this cold thought, alone in his studio, the artist must preserve from day to day his constancy to the ideal. It is this which makes his life noble; it is by this that the practice of his craft strengthens and matures his character; it is for this that even the serious countenance of the great emperor was turned approvingly (if only for a moment) on the followers of Apollo, and that sternly gentle voice bade the artist cherish his art.

And here there fall two warnings to be made. First, if you are to continue to be a law to yourself, you must beware of the first signs of laziness. This idealism in honesty can only be supported by perpetual effort; the standard is easily lowered, the artist who says '*It will do*,' is on the downward path; three or four pot-boilers are enough at times (above all at wrong times) to falsify a talent, and by the practice of journalism a man runs the risk of becoming wedded to cheap finish. This is the danger on the one side; there is not less upon the other. The consciousness of how much the artist is (and must be) a law to himself, debauches the small heads. Perceiving recondite merits very hard to attain, making or swallowing artistic formulæ, or perhaps falling in love with some particular proficiency of his own, many artists forget the end of all art: to please. It is doubtless tempting to exclaim against the ignorant bourgeois; yet it should not be forgotten, it is he who is to pay us, and that (surely on the face of it) for services that he shall desire to have performed. Here also, if properly considered, there is a question of transcendental honesty. To give the public what they do not want, and yet expect to be supported: we have there a strange pretension, and yet not uncommon, above all with painters. The first duty in this world is for a man to pay his way; when that is quite accomplished, he may plunge into what eccentricity he likes; but emphatically not till then. Till then, he must pay assiduous court to the bourgeois who carries the purse. And if in the course of these capitulations he shall falsify his talent, it can never have been a strong one, and he will have preserved a better thing than talent – character. Or if he be of a mind so independent that he cannot stoop to this necessity, one course is yet open: he can desist from art, and follow some more manly way of life.

I speak of a more manly way of life, it is a point on which I must be frank. To live by a pleasure is not a high calling; it involves patronage, however veiled; it numbers the artist, however ambitious, along with dancing girls and billiard markers. The French have a romantic evasion for one employment, and call its practitioners the Daughters of Joy. The artist is of the same family, he is of the Sons of Joy, chose his trade to please himself, gains his livelihood by pleasing others, and has parted with something of the sterner dignity of man. Journals but a little while ago declaimed against the Tennyson peerage; and this Son of Joy was blamed for condescension when he followed the example of Lord Lawrence and Lord Cairns and Lord Clyde. The poet was more happily inspired; with a better modesty he accepted the honour; and anonymous journalists have not yet (if I am to believe them) recovered the vicarious disgrace to their profession. When it comes to their turn, these gentlemen can do themselves more justice; and I shall be glad to think of it; for to my barbarian eyesight, even Lord Tennyson looks somewhat out of place in that assembly. There should be no honours for the artist; he has already, in the practice of his art, more than his share of the rewards of life; the honours are pre-empted for other trades, less agreeable and perhaps more useful.

But the devil in these trades of pleasing is to fail to please. In ordinary occupations, a man offers to do a certain thing or to produce a certain article with a merely conventional accomplishment, a design in which (we may almost say) it is difficult to fail. But the artist steps forth out of the crowd and proposes to delight: an impudent design, in which it is impossible to fail without odious circumstances. The poor Daughter of Joy, carrying her smiles and finery quite unregarded through the crowd, makes a figure which it is impossible to recall without a wounding pity. She is the type of the unsuccessful artist. The actor, the dancer, and the singer must appear like her in person, and drain publicly the cup of failure. But though the rest of us escape this crowning bitterness of the pillory, we all court in essence the same humiliation. We all profess to be able to delight. And how few of us are! We all pledge ourselves to be able to continue to delight. And the day will come to each, and even to the most admired, when the ardour shall have declined and the cunning shall be lost, and he shall sit by his deserted booth ashamed. Then shall he see himself condemned to do work for which he blushes to take payment. Then (as if his lot were not already cruel) he must lie exposed to the gibes of the wreckers of the press, who earn a little bitter bread by the condemnation of trash which they have not read, and the praise of excellence which they cannot understand.

And observe that this seems almost the necessary end at least of writers. *Les Blancs et les Bleus* (for instance) is of an order of merit very different from *Le Vicomte de Bragelonne*; and if any gentleman can bear to spy upon the nakedness of *Castle Dangerous*, his name I think is Ham: let it be enough for the rest of us to read of it (not without tears) in the pages of Lockhart. Thus in old age, when occupation and comfort are most needful, the writer must lay aside at once his pastime and his breadwinner. The painter indeed, if he succeed at all in engaging the attention of the public, gains great sums and can stand to his easel until a great age without dishonourable failure. The writer has the double misfortune to be ill-paid while he can work, and to be incapable of working when he is old. It is thus a way of life which conducts directly to a false position.

For the writer (in spite of notorious examples to the contrary) must look to be ill-paid. Tennyson and Montépin make handsome livelihoods; but we cannot all hope to be Tennyson, and we do not all perhaps desire to be Montépin. If you adopt an art to be your trade, weed your mind at the outset of all desire of money. What you may decently expect, if you have some talent and much industry, is such an income as a clerk will earn with a tenth or perhaps a twentieth of your nervous output. Nor have you the right to look for more; in the wages of the life, not in the wages of the trade, lies your reward; the work is here the wages. It will be seen I have little sympathy with the common lamentations of the artist class. Perhaps they do not remember the hire of the field labourer; or do they think no parallel will lie? Perhaps they have never observed what is the retiring allowance of a field officer; or do they suppose their contributions to the arts of pleasing more important than the services of a colonel? Perhaps they forget on how little Millet was content to live; or do they think, because they have less genius, they stand excused from the display of equal virtues? But upon one point there should be no dubiety: if a man be not frugal, he has no business in the arts. If he be not frugal, he steers directly for that last tragic scene of *le vieux saltimbanque*; if he be not frugal, he will find it hard to continue to be honest. Some day, when the butcher is knocking at the door, he may be tempted, he may be obliged, to turn out and sell a slovenly piece of work. If the obligation shall have arisen through no wantonness of his own, he is even to be commended; for words cannot describe how far more necessary it is that a man should support his family, than that he should attain to – or preserve – distinction in the arts. But if the pressure comes through his own fault, he has stolen, and stolen under trust, and stolen (which is the worst of all) in such a way that no law can reach him.

And now you may perhaps ask me, if the debutant artist is to have no thought of money, and if (as is implied) he is to expect no honours from the State, may he not at least look forward to the delights of popularity? Praise, you will tell me, is a savoury dish. And in so far as you may mean the countenance of other artists, you would put your finger on one of the most essential and enduring pleasures of the career of art. But in so far as you should have an eye to the commendations of the public or the notice of the newspapers, be sure you would but be cherishing a dream. It is true that in certain esoteric journals the author (for instance) is duly criticised, and that he is often praised a great deal more than he deserves, sometimes for qualities which he prided himself on eschewing, and sometimes by ladies and gentlemen who have denied themselves the privilege of reading his work. But if a man be sensitive to this wild praise, we must suppose him equally alive to that which often accompanies and always follows it – wild ridicule. A man may have done well for years, and then he may fail; he will hear of his failure. Or he may have done well for years, and still do well, but the critics may have tired of praising him, or there may have sprung up some new idol of the instant, some 'dust a little gilt,' to whom they now prefer to offer sacrifice. Here is the obverse and the reverse of that empty and ugly thing called popularity. Will any man suppose it worth the gaining?

THE EDUCATION OF AN ENGINEER

Anstruther is a place sacred to the Muse; she inspired (really to a considerable extent) Tennant's vernacular poem *Anst'er Fair*; and I have there waited upon her myself with much devotion. This was when I came as a young man to glean engineering experience from the building of the breakwater. What I gleaned, I am sure I do not know; but indeed I had already my own private determination to be an author; I loved the art of words and the appearances of life; and *travellers*, and *headers*, and *rubble*, and *polished ashlar*, and *pierres perdues*, and even the thrilling question of the *string-course*, interested me only (if they interested me at all) as properties for some possible romance or as words to add to my vocabulary. To grow a little catholic is the compensation of years; youth is one-eyed; and in those days, though I haunted the breakwater by day, and even loved the place for the sake of the sunshine, the thrilling seaside air, the wash of waves on the sea-face, the green glimmer of the divers' helmets far below, and the musical chinking of the masons, my one genuine preoccupation lay elsewhere, and my only industry was in the hours when I was not on duty. I lodged with a certain Bailie Brown, a carpenter by trade; and there, as soon as dinner was despatched, in a chamber scented with dry rose-leaves, drew in my chair to the table and proceeded to pour forth literature, at such a speed, and with such intimations of early death and immortality, as I now look back upon with wonder. Then it was that I wrote *Voces Fidelium*, a series of dramatic monologues in verse; then that I indited the bulk of a covenanting novel – like so many others, never finished. Late I sat into the night, toiling (as I thought) under the very dart of death, toiling to leave a memory behind me. I feel moved to thrust aside the curtain of the years, to hail that poor feverish idiot, to bid him go to bed and clap *Voces Fidelium* on the fire before he goes; so clear does he appear before me, sitting there between his candles in the rose-scented room and the late night; so ridiculous a picture (to my elderly wisdom) does the fool present! But he was driven to his bed at last without miraculous intervention; and the manner of his driving sets the last touch upon this eminently youthful business. The weather was then so warm that I must keep the windows open; the night without was populous with moths. As the late darkness deepened, my literary tapers beaconed forth more brightly; thicker and thicker came the dusty night-fliers, to gyrate for one brilliant instant round the flame and fall in agonies upon my paper. Flesh and blood could not endure the spectacle; to capture immortality was doubtless a noble enterprise, but not to capture it at such a cost of suffering; and out would go the candles, and off would I go to bed in the darkness, raging to think that the blow might fall on the morrow, and there was *Voces Fidelium* still incomplete. Well, the moths are all gone, and *Voces Fidelium* along with them; only the fool is still on hand and practises new follies.

Only one thing in connection with the harbour tempted me, and that was the diving, an experience I burned to taste of. But this was not to be, at least in Anstruther; and the subject involves a change of scene to the sub-arctic town of Wick. You can never have dwelt in a country more unsightly than that part of Caithness, the land faintly swelling, faintly falling, not a tree, not a hedgerow, the fields divided by single slate stones set upon their edge, the wind always singing in your ears and (down the long road that led nowhere) thrumming in the telegraph wires. Only as you approached the coast was there anything to stir the heart. The plateau broke down to the North Sea in formidable cliffs, the tall out-stacks rose like pillars ringed about with surf, the coves were over-brimmed with clamorous froth, the sea-birds screamed, the wind sang in the thyme on the cliff's edge; here and there, small ancient castles toppled on the brim; here and there, it was possible to dip into a dell of shelter, where you might lie and tell yourself you were a little warm, and hear (near at hand) the whin-pods bursting in the afternoon sun, and (farther off) the rumour of the turbulent sea. As for Wick itself, it is one of the meanest of man's towns, and situate certainly on the baldest of God's bays. It lives for herring, and a strange sight it is to see (of an afternoon) the heights of Pulteney blackened by seaward-looking fishers, as when a city crowds to a review – or, as when bees have swarmed, the ground is horrible with lumps and clusters; and a strange sight, and a beautiful, to see the fleet put silently out against a rising moon, the sea-line rough as a wood with sails, and ever and again and one after another, a boat flitting swiftly by the silver disk. This mass of fishers, this great fleet of boats, is out of all proportion to the town itself; and the oars are manned and the nets hauled by immigrants from the

Long Island (as we call the outer Hebrides), who come for that season only, and depart again, if 'the take' be poor, leaving debts behind them. In a bad year, the end of the herring fishery is therefore an exciting time; fights are common, riots often possible; an apple knocked from a child's hand was once the signal for something like a war; and even when I was there, a gunboat lay in the bay to assist the authorities. To contrary interests, it should be observed, the curse of Babel is here added; the Lews men are Gaelic speakers. Caithness has adopted English; an odd circumstance, if you reflect that both must be largely Norsemen by descent. I remember seeing one of the strongest instances of this division: a thing like a Punch-and-Judy box erected on the flat grave-stones of the churchyard; from the hutch or proscenium – I know not what to call it – an eldritch-looking preacher laying down the law in Gaelic about someone of the name of *Powl*, whom I at last divined to be the apostle to the Gentiles; a large congregation of the Lews men very devoutly listening; and on the outskirts of the crowd, some of the town's children (to whom the whole affair was Greek and Hebrew) profanely playing tigg. The same descent, the same country, the same narrow sect of the same religion, and all these bonds made very largely nugatory by an accidental difference of dialect!

Into the bay of Wick stretched the dark length of the unfinished breakwater, in its cage of open staging; the travellers (like frames of churches) over-plumbing all; and away at the extreme end, the divers toiling unseen on the foundation. On a platform of loose planks, the assistants turned their air-mills; a stone might be swinging between wind and water; underneath the swell ran gaily; and from time to time, a mailed dragon with a window-glass snout came dripping up the ladder. Youth is a blessed season after all; my stay at Wick was in the year of *Voces Fidelium* and the rose-leaf room at Bailie Brown's; and already I did not care two straws for literary glory. Posthumous ambition perhaps requires an atmosphere of roses; and the more rugged excitant of Wick east winds had made another boy of me. To go down in the diving-dress, that was my absorbing fancy; and with the countenance of a certain handsome scamp of a diver, Bob Bain by name, I gratified the whim.

It was gray, harsh, easterly weather, the swell ran pretty high, and out in the open there were 'skipper's daughters,' when I found myself at last on the diver's platform, twenty pounds of lead upon each foot and my whole person swollen with ply and ply of woollen underclothing. One moment, the salt wind was whistling round my night-capped head; the next, I was crushed almost double under the weight of the helmet. As that intolerable burthen was laid upon me, I could have found it in my heart (only for shame's sake) to cry off from the whole enterprise. But it was too late. The attendants began to turn the hurdy-gurdy, and the air to whistle through the tube; someone screwed in the barred window of the visor; and I was cut off in a moment from my fellow-men; standing there in their midst, but quite divorced from intercourse: a creature deaf and dumb, pathetically looking forth upon them from a climate of his own. Except that I could move and feel, I was like a man fallen in a catalepsy. But time was scarce given me to realise my isolation; the weights were hung upon my back and breast, the signal rope was thrust into my unresisting hand; and setting a twenty-pound foot upon the ladder, I began ponderously to descend.

Some twenty rounds below the platform, twilight fell. Looking up, I saw a low green heaven mottled with vanishing bells of white; looking around, except for the weedy spokes and shafts of the ladder, nothing but a green gloaming, somewhat opaque but very restful and delicious. Thirty rounds lower, I stepped off on the *pierres perdues* of the foundation; a dumb helmeted figure took me by the hand, and made a gesture (as I read it) of encouragement; and looking in at the creature's window, I beheld the face of Bain. There we were, hand to hand and (when it pleased us) eye to eye; and either might have burst himself with shouting, and not a whisper come to his companion's hearing. Each, in his own little world of air, stood incommunicably separate.

Bob had told me ere this a little tale, a five minutes' drama at the bottom of the sea, which at that moment possibly shot across my mind. He was down with another, settling a stone of the sea-wall. They had it well adjusted; Bob gave the signal, the scissors were slipped, the stone set home; and it was time to turn to something else. But still his companion remained bowed over the block like a mourner on a tomb, or only raised himself to make absurd contortions and mysterious signs unknown to the vocabulary of the diver. There, then, these two stood for awhile, like the dead and the living; till there flashed a fortunate thought into Bob's mind, and he stooped, peered through the window of that other world, and beheld the face of its inhabitant wet with streaming tears. Ah! the man was in pain! And Bob, glancing downward, saw what was the trouble: the block had been lowered on the foot of that unfortunate – he was caught alive at the bottom of the sea under fifteen tons of rock.

That two men should handle a stone so heavy, even swinging in the scissors, may appear strange to the inexpert. These must bear in mind the great density of the water of the sea, and the surprising results of transplantation to that medium. To understand a little what these are, and how a man's weight, so far from being an encumbrance, is the very ground of his agility, was the chief lesson of my submarine experience. The knowledge came upon me by degrees. As I began to go forward with the hand of my estranged companion, a world of tumbled stones was visible, pillared with the weedy uprights of the staging: overhead, a flat roof of green: a little in front, the sea-wall, like an unfinished rampart. And presently in our upward progress, Bob motioned me to leap upon a stone; I looked to see if he were possibly in earnest, and he only signed to me the more imperiously. Now the block stood six feet high; it would have been quite a leap to me unencumbered; with the breast and back weights, and the twenty pounds upon each foot, and the staggering load of the helmet, the thing was out of reason. I laughed aloud in my tomb; and to prove to Bob how far he was astray, I gave a little impulse from my toes. Up I soared like a bird, my companion soaring at my side. As high as to the stone, and then higher, I pursued my impotent and empty flight. Even when the strong arm of Bob had checked my shoulders, my heels continued their ascent; so that I blew out sideways like an autumn leaf, and must be hauled in, hand over hand, as sailors haul in the slack of a sail, and propped upon my feet again like an intoxicated sparrow. Yet a little higher on the foundation, and we began to be affected by the bottom of the swell, running there like a strong breeze of wind. Or so I must suppose; for, safe in my cushion of air, I was conscious of no impact; only swayed idly like a weed, and was now borne helplessly abroad, and now swiftly – and yet with dream-like gentleness – impelled against my guide. So does a child's balloon divagate upon the currents of the air, and touch and slide off again from every obstacle. So must have ineffectually swung, so resented their inefficiency, those light crowds that followed the Star of Hades, and uttered exiguous voices in the land beyond Cocytus.

There was something strangely exasperating, as well as strangely wearying, in these uncommanded evolutions. It is bitter to return to infancy, to be supported, and directed, and perpetually set upon your feet, by the hand of someone else. The air besides, as it is supplied to you by the busy millers on the platform, closes the eustachian tubes and keeps the neophyte perpetually swallowing, till his throat is grown so dry that he can swallow no longer. And for all these reasons – although I had a fine, dizzy, muddle-headed joy in my surroundings, and longed, and tried, and always failed, to lay hands on the fish that darted here and there about me, swift as humming-birds – yet I fancy I was rather relieved than otherwise when Bain brought me back to the ladder and signed to me to mount. And there was one more experience before me even then. Of a sudden, my ascending head passed into the trough of a swell. Out of the green, I shot at once into a glory of rosy, almost of sanguine light – the multitudinous seas incarnadined, the heaven above a vault of crimson. And then the glory faded into the hard, ugly daylight of a Caithness autumn, with a low sky, a gray sea, and a whistling wind.

Bob Bain had five shillings for his trouble, and I had done what I desired. It was one of the best things I got from my education as an engineer: of which however, as a way of life, I wish to speak with sympathy. It takes a man into the open air; it keeps him hanging about harbour-sides, which is the richest form of idling; it carries him to wild islands; it gives him a taste of the genial dangers of the sea; it supplies him with dexterities to exercise; it makes demands upon his ingenuity; it will go far to cure him of any taste (if ever he had one) for the miserable life of cities. And when it has done so, it carries him back and shuts him in an office! From the roaring skerry and the wet thwart of the tossing boat, he passes to the stool and desk; and with a memory full of ships, and seas, and perilous headlands, and the shining pharos, he must apply his long-sighted eyes to the petty niceties of drawing, or measure his inaccurate mind with several pages of consecutive figures. He is a wise youth, to be sure, who can balance one part of genuine life against two parts of drudgery between four walls, and for the sake of the one, manfully accept the other.

Wick was scarce an eligible place of stay. But how much better it was to hang in the cold wind upon the pier, to go down with Bob Bain among the roots of the staging, to be all day in a boat coiling a wet rope and shouting orders – not always very wise – than to be warm and dry, and dull, and dead-alive, in the most comfortable office. And Wick itself had in those days a note of originality. It may have still, but I misdoubt it much. The old minister of Keiss would not preach, in these degenerate times, for an hour and a half upon the clock. The gipsies must be gone from their cavern; where you might see, from the mouth, the women tending their fire, like Meg Merrilies, and the men sleeping off their coarse potations; and where in winter gales, the surf would beleaguer them closely, bursting in their very door. A traveller today upon the Thurso coach would scarce observe a little cloud of smoke among the moorlands, and be told, quite openly, it marked a private still. He would not indeed make that journey, for there is now no Thurso coach. And even if he could, one little thing that happened to me could never happen to him, or not with the same trenchancy of contrast.

We had been upon the road all evening; the coach-top was crowded with Lews fishers going home, scarce anything but Gaelic had sounded in my ears; and our way had lain throughout over a moorish country very northern to behold. Latish at night, though it was still broad day in our subarctic latitude, we came down upon the shores of the roaring Pentland Firth, that grave of mariners; on one hand, the cliffs of Dunnet Head ran seaward; in front was the little bare, white town of Castleton, its streets full of blowing sand; nothing beyond, but the North Islands, the great deep, and the perennial ice-fields of the Pole. And here, in the last imaginable place, there sprang up young outlandish voices and a chatter of some foreign speech; and I saw, pursuing the coach with its load of Hebridean fishers – as they had pursued *vetturini* up the passes of the Apennines or perhaps along the grotto under Virgil's tomb – two little dark-eyed, white-toothed Italian vagabonds, of twelve to fourteen years of age, one with a hurdy-gurdy, the other with a cage of white mice. The coach passed on, and their small Italian chatter died in the distance; and I was left to marvel how they had wandered into that country, and how they fared in it, and what they thought of it, and when (if ever) they should see again the silver wind-breaks run among the olives, and the stone-pine stand guard upon Etruscan sepulchres.

Upon any American, the strangeness of this incident is somewhat lost. For as far back as he goes in his own land, he will find some alien camping there; the Cornish miner, the French or Mexican half-blood, the negro in the South, these are deep in the woods and far among the mountains. But in an old, cold, and rugged country such as mine, the days of immigration are long at an end; and away up there, which was at that time far beyond the northernmost extreme of railways, hard upon the shore of that ill-omened strait of whirlpools, in a land of moors where no stranger came, unless it should be a sportsman to shoot grouse or an antiquary to decipher runes, the presence of these small pedestrians struck the mind as though a bird-of-paradise had risen from the heather or an albatross come fishing in the bay of Wick. They were as strange to their surroundings as my lordly evangelist or the old Spanish grandee on the Fair Isle.

AUTHORS AND PUBLISHERS

An author is usually a man with small capital or none. It takes him a long time to perfect his work, during which he must live and pay his way; his resources are apt to be exhausted, the small bills to be coming round and growing big; and it is then, if there were no publisher, that he would have to meet a fresh and far heavier expense for printing, binding, advertising, and settle down (if his creditors allowed) to a fresh period of waiting and accumulating bills. If his creditors proved impatient, he would pass through the court, his book would leave his hands before it could possibly begin to pay, and he might sit down to begin another work (if he were so inclined) on the compact capital of a bankruptcy certificate. From all this, the publisher saves him. He makes the trade possible for poor men; the rich he relieves of worry, care and risk. All, no doubt, for a consideration. No one supposes the publisher to be a philanthropist. He has a domestic corner of his own, where little publishers bleat daily for sustenance, and he knows, as well as any author, the phenomenon of the little bill.

It is contended, however, that the consideration is too great. The author, it is said, creates the work, his is the sole credit, and he has the least of the return. His is the sole credit, true enough; and observe, he only gets it. But as for the returns, there is more to be said. Some books are successes, for which the publisher has paid very little; and then I am sorry for the author. Some are failures, for which the author has been well paid; and then I am sorry for the publisher. Some bring nothing to either, when we may be allowed to pity both. The trade is a two-sided lottery, and the profit is distributed at random: but what authors are too ready to forget, the loss is still the publisher's, and not only the loss upon one book, but that on his whole business. His position must not be judged as that of a person, or in any single transaction. He is more than a person, he represents a certain capital invested; if the capital show more or less than even shares with the author over the publication of (say) a *Pickwick*, what is that to the question? The publisher's trade is not to publish *Pickwick*s and *She*s and *Robert Elsmere*s; his trade is to keep an open shop, and be ready to make an advance to any young gentleman who appears with a manuscript of promise. It is by this trade as a whole that he must be judged. The only criterion is to take his profit and loss year in, year out, and to inquire whether the return on the capital is vastly greater than in other forms of trade. I have never heard this contention even advanced; and that being so, I will, until further information, assume his trade to be fair, and his percentages, his book-keeping and the whole of his mysterious methods to represent a roughly just division with authors as a whole.

This is far from saying that anyone ought to rejoice in these methods in themselves. They are, on the other hand, profoundly annoying and unnecessary, and cast over transactions, very likely as honest as the day, a grave shadow of suspicion. Under many forms of bargain, the author is simply partner with his publisher. And where in the world will you behold so pitiful a spectacle as this author-partner, who knows nothing whatever of the means, the processes or the profits of the business whereby he lives, who takes what is given him blindfold, who should be called not merely a sleeping but rather an insane or infant partner, from whom figures are kept like edged tools from children? Lately, Mr Besant took up the cudgels; and some firms (all honour to them) begin to send us returns. I like to get them, they please my vanity, they are marks of consideration, I can feel I am getting out of infancy and my guardian now consents to reason with me. But at the same time I smile at what I cannot but think the simplicity of Mr Besant. The late lamented Bully Hayes, the pirate of the Pacific, used to visit islands (where he was sure that nobody could read), the bearer of a letter, which he would obligingly read out himself to the local trader; and that innocent was usually convinced and handed out his oil. I have no curiosity to hear such letters read to me, for I have no idea whether they are read as they were written. And in the same way, I have no curiosity to receive extracts from my publisher's books, or even to see the books themselves; for I have no guess whether they mean what they profess to mean.

To the point, a young author once visited his publisher. It was a Saturday, and the young author's little volume had been out a week. Timidly, he inquired how the publisher was satisfied. 'Delighted, my dear boy – we are delighted,' was the reply. 'But you had better see for yourself.' And so – just what Mr Besant would like – the books were produced, and the young author saw with his own eyes the total of n copies. He went away both sad and puzzled: sad, because n being a very small number, he saw little hope of ever entering upon his postponed royalties; and puzzled, because n being such a very small number, he could not conceive why the publisher should be delighted. His way led him past a bookseller's, with whom he dealt. Here he inquired, and found that a number of copies which we may represent by x had been sold over the counter. Now x was so great a fraction of n that the young author's wonder rather increased; and early the next Monday, chancing to be in another city, he repeated his question of another bookseller. Here he found that y had been sold; and a simple arithmetical calculation yielded the formula $x + y > n$. I do not know if the author was delighted, my dear boy; but he was extremely perplexed. Had the formula given $x + y = n$, the case would have been peculiar. He would then have had to face the coincidence that only two booksellers in England had sold any copies of his work, and these two, in two different cities, the men with whom he dealt: the whole remaining force of the book trade remaining sternly neuter. And even that hypothesis would have left one element unexplained: I mean the delight of the publisher. But $x + y$ was greater than n; not by much indeed, but by some copies; two, I believe. And where had these two copies come from? Perhaps the binder was unfaithful, or possibly the printer, and the circumstance, which would doubtless damp the publisher's delight, had not yet been discovered. Or perhaps the books were kept on a symbolic system, such that n copies sold meant something different from the sale of n copies – meant, for instance (as a guess), that the net profit on the number of copies really sold would equal the gross profit on the sale of n copies.

I cannot tell if the young author was right or not in his deductions; but I know one circumstance that seems to point in that direction. The publishing trade does not stand alone. It is one of three or four interdependent trades: the author, the publisher, the printer, the bookseller, the paper-maker, all hang together, they are fleas upon each other's backs; only the author comes first and is kept outside the ring, and the bookseller comes last, and (I rather believe) has the heavy end of the stick. Now suppose the publisher to give me not only returns but vouchers. One of these will be a receipted bill from a printer, which will legally establish the fact that the publisher has paid over to the printer, on account of our joint venture, the sum of x pounds. I know that the publisher has many other such vouchers, which will be handed round to my brother authors and fill them (as mine fills me) with a sense that all is for the best. Each of these bills is receipted as paid in full. Suppose we had them all together, and added the totals, we should find that the publisher had paid over to the printer, in the course of a year, the sum of n pounds altogether. Now here comes in a habit of the printing trade in England, or in certain parts of it. A printer, when he does steady pieces of work for such an employer as (for instance) a lawyer, sends in at the end of the year a whole series of separate bills for each job charged in full, and a summed bill, reduced (according to the firm) by anything from 10 to 30 per cent. It is only this last that is paid; but all are solemnly receipted. In other words, the lawyer pays 70 to 90, and receives legal vouchers for 100. This is just what I believe of the publisher. He has vouchers for n pounds; I believe he has not paid more than 75 per cent of n; I see with my eyes that he debits me with my share in full; I believe he does the same to all my brother authors; and if that be so it is clear he has put 25 per cent of n clandestinely into his own pocket.

Not dishonestly, mind, or not so in the essence. The supposition is that his profit on the whole is just; the complaint, that these clandestine items are irritating, needless, and in all likelihood formally illegal. In other words, if this is the way the publisher's business is done, it is not a good way to do business. The chance discovery of some such petty misstatement is at the bottom of half of the complaints of authors; and if the same came out before a court of law it might be found illegal, with deplorable results. Doubtless the system arose naturally. It was forced on by the greed of authors, and by their habit of regarding their own particular transaction as the measure of the publisher's profit, whereas the publisher sees in it only a single off-set in a large field of profit and loss. More and more the publisher comes to shroud his operations in shadow; more and more to collect misleading vouchers. And the result, if I am at all right, is a bad set of trade customs, and a dangerous habit of mind in the publisher himself.

I will give an example of what I mean. It is possible that there is nothing illegal in the system of printer's vouchers; it is likely that there is nothing illegal in the system of cross advertisements, with cross cheques and cross receipts, which exists and which alone explains the multiplicity of magazines in England. But I have known this same system of calling operations by other names to lead a respectable publisher into an act that was certainly illegal; I have known him (that is) to hold a book subject to a royalty, to sell the advance sheets in America, and not to account for the proceeds of the sale. We can explain his action thus: he had always meant to reserve this sale of the sheets, he had neglected to express this in the bargain, and he was so used to a system of working in the dark with a hoodwinked author, that he here stepped across the boundary into actual illegality and did not perceive the difference. And observe, most likely it was quite just; he had always meant to do it; the act was needful to put him in a fair position; and perhaps when all was done he lost upon the venture, and the author gained.

Of course, this is all guesswork; which is not my fault, but the fault of publishers. After seventeen years of active authorship, I ought to be far beyond guessing as to the actions of my partners. If my guessing is all wrong, it is therefore no fault of mine. If my guessing is right for some, the rest should clear their feet. If it be right for all, I suggest in our common interest the method should be changed. I do not think in the least they take an unfair advantage; I think they take a fair share in mysterious and shabby ways, and I hope the time has now come when they can afford to be more open. Open altogether? I am the first to admit the difficulty. The author will always continue to regard his venture by itself, the publisher must always continue to think of it as one of many; and the two points of view are hard to bring in focus. A Pacific island King is in the habit of telling traders, 'You cheat me a little, no cheat too much.' I am inclined to parody him, and say, 'I believe you must continue to keep us in blindness, for in the essence of the matter your view of the business is more just than ours; but deceive us not so openly, for we are human and we rage when we find ourselves deceived – even for our own good – even for your necessity.'

It may be asked, why does the publisher require to deceive the author? Why should he not refrain from publishing doubtful and desperate books, and confine his capital on those in which the profit and loss are fairly certain? He has to publish doubtful books for three reasons. 1st, to 'turn over' his capital. 2nd, because the printer and the paper-maker jog him up, in order that they may keep their hands employed and their mills and presses going. 3rd, because it is by this class of books that the big hauls are made and the rising author lassooed and attached. This is the sportsmanlike side of the trade. And it is the one of all others of which the author must not complain, for it is his door of entry.

A smallish class of authors live by their books and help the publisher to live by his capital; another and far larger class may be called the detrimentals. They do not live by their books, the publication of which is a source of some meagre profit, or perhaps none, to themselves, and of loss to the publisher and the established author. To the publisher because he does not recover his outlay; to the established author because there is only a certain amount of money in the market to buy books at all, and every detrimental diverts a small proportion, nothing in itself but (the detrimentals being many) formidable in the sum. I was myself a detrimental for many years, and I am grateful to the publishers for their long-suffering hopefulness, or perhaps I might now be a billiard marker. When I hear Mr Besant come forward with a scheme for the co-operative publication of books by a body of authors, I cannot but recall my years as a detrimental. There is no likelihood that authors (who have something else to do) would manage this branch of business better, or even so well, as a publisher. There would therefore be profit and loss. The loss side of the affair will strike rudely on the authors, so long accustomed to the cushion of the publisher; the detrimental list will steadily be cut down; the established authors will make war upon them root and branch; and we should soon have such a bear-garden as the world can scarcely parallel. The Royal Academicians, the hanging committee of the salon, are complained upon hard enough; it will be nothing to what we shall hear of the Co-operative Authors. The painter is tempted to keep his young rivals off the line, fearing a loss which he can never compute. But the author can compute the loss; he sees it in black and white upon the balance sheet. 'What!' he cries, does he toil all his days producing really saleable works, and curtail his spare hours to run this publishing business, only to find at the year's end that the profits have been reduced by £40 for Brown's novel, and £60 for Jones's poem, and £100 for Robinson's travels in Kurdistan? How will it fare with Brown, Jones and Robinson? And what kind of undignified spectacle should the effete old established authors present to the world, as they held the doors of their monopoly? And what a picture of legitimate anger would be shown by young talent as it beat on these ungenerous portals? If we are artists and scholars, let that be enough. Let us not, for the hope of greater hire, enter upon an arena for which we have no preparation, and where we shall be only tempted to display the worst defects of man and, when age comes, of age.

FATHER DAMIEN: AN OPEN LETTER
TO THE REVEREND DR HYDE
OF HONOLULU

Sydney, February 25, 1890

Sir, – It may probably occur to you that we have met, and visited, and conversed; on my side, with interest. You may remember that you have done me several courtesies, for which I was prepared to be grateful. But there are duties which come before gratitude, and offences which justly divide friends, far more acquaintances. Your letter to the Reverend H. B. Gage is a document which, in my sight, if you had filled me with bread when I was starving, if you had sat up to nurse my father when he lay a-dying, would yet absolve me from the bonds of gratitude. You know enough, doubtless, of the process of canonisation to be aware that, a hundred years after the death of Damien, there will appear a man charged with the painful office of the *devil's advocate*. After that noble brother of mine, and of all frail clay, shall have lain a century at rest, one shall accuse, one defend him. The circumstance is unusual that the devil's advocate should be a volunteer, should be a member of a sect immediately rival, and should make haste to take upon himself his ugly office ere the bones are cold; unusual, and of a taste which I shall leave my readers free to qualify; unusual, and to me inspiring. If I have at all learned the trade of using words to convey truth and to arouse emotion, you have at last furnished me with a subject. For it is in the interest of all mankind and the cause of public decency in every quarter of the world, not only that Damien should be righted, but that you and your letter should be displayed at length, in their true colours, to the public eye.

To do this properly, I must begin by quoting you at large: I shall then proceed to criticise your utterance from several points of view, divine and human, in the course of which I shall attempt to draw again and with more specification the character of the dead saint whom it has pleased you to vilify: so much being done, I shall say farewell to you for ever.

Honolulu, August 2, 1889

'Rev. H. B. Gage.

'Dear Brother, – In answer to your inquiries about Father Damien, I can only reply that we who knew the man are surprised at the extravagant newspaper laudations, as if he was a most saintly philanthropist. The simple truth is, he was a coarse, dirty man, headstrong and bigoted. He was not sent to Molokai, but went there without orders; did not stay at the leper settlement (before he became one himself), but circulated freely over the whole island (less than half the island is devoted to the lepers), and he came often to Honolulu. He had no hand in the reforms and improvements inaugurated, which were the work of our Board of Health, as occasion required and means were provided. He was not a pure man in his relations with women, and the leprosy of which he died should be attributed to his vices and carelessness. Others have done much for the lepers, our own ministers, the government physicians, and so forth, but never with the Catholic idea of meriting eternal life. – Yours, etc.,

'C. M. Hyde.'[1]

To deal fitly with a letter so extraordinary, I must draw at the outset on my private knowledge of the signatory and his sect. It may offend others; scarcely you, who have been so busy to collect, so bold to publish, gossip on your rivals. And this is perhaps the moment when I may best explain to you the character of what you are to read: I conceive you as a man quite beyond and below the reticences of civility: with what measure you mete, with that shall it be measured you again; with you, at last, I rejoice to feel the button off the foil and to plunge home. And if in aught that I shall say I should offend others, your colleagues, whom I respect and remember with affection, I can but offer them my regret; I am not free, I am inspired by the consideration of interests far more large; and such pain as can be inflicted by anything from me must be indeed trifling when compared with the pain with which they read your letter. It is not the hangman, but the criminal, that brings dishonour on the house.

You belong, sir, to a sect – I believe my sect, and that in which my ancestors laboured – which has enjoyed, and partly failed to utilise, an exceptional advantage in the islands of Hawaii. The first missionaries came; they found the land already self-purged of its old and bloody faith; they were embraced, almost on their arrival, with enthusiasm; what troubles they supported came far more from whites than from Hawaiians; and to these last they stood (in a rough figure) in the shoes of

[1]From the Sydney *Presbyterian*, October 26, 1889.

God. This is not the place to enter into the degree or causes of their failure, such as it is. One element alone is pertinent, and must here be plainly dealt with. In the course of their evangelical calling, they – or too many of them – grew rich. It may be news to you that the houses of missionaries are a cause of mocking on the streets of Honolulu. It will at least be news to you, that when I returned your civil visit, the driver of my cab commented on the size, the taste, and the comfort of your home. It would have been news certainly to myself, had anyone told me that afternoon that I should live to drag such matter into print. But you see, sir, how you degrade better men to your own level; and it is needful that those who are to judge betwixt you and me, betwixt Damien and the devil's advocate, should understand your letter to have been penned in a house which could raise, and that very justly, the envy and the comments of the passers-by. I think (to employ a phrase of yours which I admire) it 'should be attributed' to you that you have never visited the scene of Damien's life and death. If you had, and had recalled it, and looked about your pleasant rooms, even your pen perhaps would have been stayed.

Your sect (and remember, as far as any sect avows me, it is mine) has not done ill in a worldly sense in the Hawaiian Kingdom. When calamity befell their innocent parishioners, when leprosy descended and took root in the Eight Islands, a *quid pro quo* was to be looked for. To that prosperous mission, and to you, as one of its adornments, God had sent at last an opportunity. I know I am touching here upon a nerve acutely sensitive. I know that others of your colleagues look back on the inertia of your Church, and the intrusive and decisive heroism of Damien, with something almost to be called remorse. I am sure it is so with yourself; I am persuaded your letter was inspired by a certain envy, not essentially ignoble, and the one human trait to be espied in that performance. You were thinking of the lost chance, the past day; of that which should have been conceived and was not; of the service due and not rendered. *Time was*, said the voice in your ear, in your pleasant room, as you sat raging and writing; and if the words written were base beyond parallel, the rage, I am happy to repeat – it is the only compliment I shall pay you – the rage was almost virtuous. But, sir, when we have failed, and another has succeeded; when we have stood by, and another has stepped in; when we sit and grow bulky in our charming mansions, and a plain, uncouth peasant steps into the battle, under the eyes of God, and succours the afflicted, and consoles the dying, and is himself afflicted in his turn, and dies upon the field of honour – the battle cannot be retrieved as your unhappy irritation has suggested. It is a lost battle, and lost for ever. One thing remained to you in your defeat – some rags of common honour; and these you have made haste to cast away.

Common honour; not the honour of having done anything right, but the honour of not having done aught conspicuously foul; the honour of the inert: that was what remained to you. We are not all expected to be Damiens; a man may conceive his duty more narrowly, he may love his comforts better; and none will cast a stone at him for that. But will a gentleman of your reverend profession allow me an example from the fields of gallantry? When two gentlemen compete for the favour of a lady, and the one succeeds and the other is rejected, and (as will sometimes happen) matter damaging to the successful rival's credit reaches the ear of the defeated, it is held by plain men of no pretensions that his mouth is, in the circumstance, almost necessarily closed. Your Church and Damien's were in Hawaii upon a rivalry to do well: to help, to edify, to set divine examples. You having (in one huge instance) failed, and Damien succeeded, I marvel it should not have occurred to you that you were doomed to silence; that when you had been outstripped in that high rivalry, and sat inglorious in the midst of your well-being, in your pleasant room – and Damien, crowned with glories and horrors, toiled and rotted in that pigstye of his under the cliffs of Kalawao – you, the elect who would not, were the last man on earth to collect and propagate gossip on the volunteer who would and did.

I think I see you – for I try to see you in the flesh as I write these sentences – I think I see you leap at the word pigstye, a hyperbolical expression at the best. 'He had no hand in the reforms,' he was 'a coarse, dirty man'; these were your own words; and you may think it possible that I am come to support you with fresh evidence. In a sense, it is even so. Damien has been too much depicted with a conventional halo and conventional features; so drawn by men who perhaps had not the eye to remark or the pen to express the individual; or who perhaps were only blinded and silenced by generous admiration, such as I partly envy for myself – such as you, if your soul were enlightened, would envy on your bended knees. It is the least defect of such a method of portraiture that it makes the path easy for the devil's advocate, and leaves for the misuse of the slanderer a considerable field of truth. For the truth that is suppressed by friends is the readiest weapon of the enemy. The world, in your despite, may perhaps owe you something, if your letter be the means of substituting once for all a credible likeness for a wax abstraction. For, if that world at all remember you, on the day when Damien of Molokai shall be named Saint, it will be in virtue of one work: your letter to the Reverend H. B. Gage.

You may ask on what authority I speak. It was my inclement destiny to become acquainted, not with Damien, but with Dr Hyde. When I visited the lazaretto Damien was already in his resting grave. But such information as I have, I gathered on the spot in conversation with those who knew him well and long: some indeed who revered his memory; but others who had sparred and wrangled with him, who beheld him with no halo, who perhaps regarded him with small respect, and through whose unprepared and scarcely partial communications the plain, human features of the man shone on me convincingly. These gave me what knowledge I possess; and I learnt it in that scene where it could be most completely and sensitively understood – Kalawao, which you have never visited, about which you have never so much as endeavoured to inform yourself: for, brief as your letter is, you have found the means to stumble into that confession. '*Less than one-half* of the island,' you say, 'is devoted to the lepers.' Molokai – '*Molokai ahina*,' the 'gray,' lofty, and most desolate island – along all its northern side plunges a front of precipice into a sea of unusual profundity. This range of cliff is, from east to west, the true end and frontier of the island. Only in one spot there projects into the ocean a certain triangular and rugged down, grassy, stony, windy, and rising in the midst into a hill with a dead crater: the whole bearing to the cliff that overhangs it somewhat the same relation as a bracket to a wall. With this hint you will now be able to pick out the leper station on a map; you will be able to judge how much of Molokai is thus cut off between the surf and precipice, whether less than a half, or less than a quarter, or a fifth, or a tenth – or say, a twentieth; and the next time you burst into print you will be in a position to share with us the issue of your calculations.

I imagine you to be one of those persons who talk with cheerfulness of that place which oxen and wainropes could not drag you to behold. You, who do not even know its situation on the map, probably denounce sensational descriptions, stretching your limbs the while in your pleasant parlour on Beretania Street. When I was pulled ashore there one early morning, there sat with me in the boat two sisters, bidding farewell (in humble imitation of Damien) to the lights and joys of human life. One of these wept silently; I could not withhold myself

from joining her. Had you been there, it is my belief that nature would
have triumphed even in you; and as the boat drew but a little nearer, and
you beheld the stairs crowded with abominable deformations of our
common manhood, and saw yourself landing in the midst of such a
population as only now and then surrounds us in the horror of a
nightmare – what a haggard eye you would have rolled over your
reluctant shoulder towards the house on Beretania Street! Had you gone
on; had you found every fourth face a blot upon the landscape; had you
visited the hospital and seen the butt-ends of human beings lying there
almost unrecognisable, but still breathing, still thinking, still remembering; you would have understood that life in the lazaretto is an ordeal
from which the nerves of a man's spirit shrink, even as his eye quails
under the brightness of the sun; you would have felt it was (even today) a
pitiful place to visit and a hell to dwell in. It is not the fear of possible
infection. That seems a little thing when compared with the pain, the
pity, and the disgust of the visitor's surroundings, and the atmosphere
of affliction, disease, and physical disgrace in which he breathes. I do
not think I am a man more than usually timid; but I never recall the days
and nights I spent upon that island promontory (eight days and seven
nights), without heartfelt thankfulness that I am somewhere else. I find
in my diary that I speak of my stay as a 'grinding experience': I have once
jotted in the margin, '*Harrowing* is the word'; and when the *Mokolii*
bore me at last towards the outer world, I kept repeating to myself, with
a new conception of their pregnancy, those simple words of the song –

> ''Tis the most distressful country that ever yet was seen.'

And observe: that which I saw and suffered from was a settlement
purged, bettered, beautified; the new village built, the hospital and the
Bishop-Home excellently arranged; the sisters, the doctor, and the
missionaries, all indefatigable in their noble tasks. It was a different
place when Damien came there, and made his great renunciation, and
slept that first night under a tree amidst his rotting brethren: alone with
pestilence; and looking forward (with what courage, with what pitiful
sinkings of dread, God only knows) to a lifetime of dressing sores and
stumps.

You will say, perhaps, I am too sensitive, that sights as painful abound
in cancer hospitals and are confronted daily by doctors and nurses. I
have long learned to admire and envy the doctors and the nurses. But
there is no cancer hospital so large and populous as Kalawao and

Kalaupapa; and in such a matter every fresh case, like every inch of length in the pipe of an organ, deepens the note of the impression; for what daunts the onlooker is that monstrous sum of human suffering by which he stands surrounded. Lastly, no doctor or nurse is called upon to enter once for all the doors of that gehenna; they do not say farewell, they need not abandon hope, on its sad threshold; they but go for a time to their high calling, and can look forward as they go to relief, to recreation, and to rest. But Damien shut to with his own hand the doors of his own sepulchre.

I shall now extract three passages from my diary at Kalawao.

A. Damien is dead and already somewhat ungratefully remembered in the field of his labours and sufferings. 'He was a good man, but very officious,' says one. Another tells me he had fallen (as other priests so easily do) into something of the ways and habits of thought of a Kanaka; but he had the wit to recognise the fact, and the good sense to laugh at [over] it. A plain man it seems he was; I cannot find he was a popular.

B. After Ragsdale's death [Ragsdale was a famous Luna, or overseer, of the unruly settlement] there followed a brief term of office by Father Damien which served only to publish the weakness of that noble man. He was rough in his ways, and he had no control. Authority was relaxed; Damien's life was threatened, and he was soon eager to resign.

C. Of Damien I begin to have an idea. He seems to have been a man of the peasant class, certainly of the peasant type: shrewd; ignorant and bigoted, yet with an open mind, and capable of receiving and digesting a reproof if it were bluntly administered; superbly generous in the least thing as well as in the greatest, and as ready to give his last shirt (although not without human grumbling) as he had been to sacrifice his life; essentially indiscreet and officious, which made him a troublesome colleague; domineering in all his ways, which made him incurably unpopular with the Kanakas, but yet destitute of real authority, so that his boys laughed at him and he must carry out his wishes by the means of bribes. He learned to have a mania for doctoring; and set up the Kanakas against the remedies of his regular rivals: perhaps (if anything matter at all in the treatment of such a disease) the worst thing that he did, and certainly the easiest. The best and worst of the man appear very plainly in his dealings with Mr Chapman's money; he had originally laid it out [intended to lay it out] entirely for the benefit of Catholics, and even so not wisely; but after a long, plain talk, he admitted his error fully and revised the list. The sad state of the boys' home is in part the result of his lack of control; in part, of his own slovenly ways and false ideas of hygiene. Brother officials used to call it 'Damien's Chinatown.' 'Well,' they would say, 'your Chinatown keeps growing.' And he would laugh with perfect good-nature, and adhere to his errors with perfect obstinacy. So much I have gathered of truth about this plain, noble human brother and father of ours; his imperfections are the traits of his face, by which we know him for our fellow; his martyrdom and his example nothing can lessen or annul; and only a person here on the spot can properly appreciate their greatness.

I have set down these private passages, as you perceive, without correction; thanks to you, the public has them in their bluntness. They are almost a list of the man's faults, for it is rather these that I was seeking: with his virtues, with the heroic profile of his life, I and the world were already sufficiently acquainted. I was besides a little suspicious of Catholic testimony; in no ill sense, but merely because Damien's admirers and disciples were the least likely to be critical. I know you will be more suspicious still; and the facts set down above were one and all collected from the lips of Protestants who had opposed the father in his life. Yet I am strangely deceived, or they build up the image of a man, with all his weaknesses, essentially heroic, and alive with rugged honesty, generosity, and mirth.

Take it for what it is, rough private jottings of the worst sides of Damien's character, collected from the lips of those who had laboured with and (in your own phrase) 'knew the man'; – though I question whether Damien would have said that he knew you. Take it, and observe with wonder how well you were served by your gossips, how ill by your intelligence and sympathy; in how many points of fact we are at one, and how widely our appreciations vary. There is something wrong here; either with you or me. It is possible, for instance, that you, who seem to have so many ears in Kalawao, had heard of the affair of Mr Chapman's money, and were singly struck by Damien's intended wrong-doing. I was struck with that also, and set it fairly down; but I was struck much more by the fact that he had the honesty of mind to be convinced. I may here tell you that it was a long business; that one of his colleagues sat with him late into the night, multiplying arguments and accusations; that the father listened as usual with 'perfect good-nature and perfect obstinacy'; but at the last, when he was persuaded – 'Yes,' said he, 'I am very much obliged to you; you have done me a service; it would have been a theft.' There are many (not Catholics merely) who require their heroes and saints to be infallible; to these the story will be painful; not to the true lovers, patrons, and servants of mankind.

And I take it, this is a type of our division; that you are one of those who have an eye for faults and failures; that you take a pleasure to find and publish them; and that, having found them, you make haste to forget the overvailing virtues and the real success which had alone introduced them to your knowledge. It is a dangerous frame of mind.

That you may understand how dangerous, and into what a situation it has already brought you, we will (if you please) go hand-in-hand through the different phrases of your letter, and candidly examine each from the point of view of its truth, its appositeness, and its charity.

Damien was *coarse*.

It is very possible. You make us sorry for the lepers who had only a coarse old peasant for their friend and father. But you, who were so refined, why were you not there, to cheer them with the lights of culture? Or may I remind you that we have some reason to doubt if John the Baptist were genteel; and in the case of Peter, on whose career you doubtless dwell approvingly in the pulpit, no doubt at all he was a 'coarse, headstrong' fisherman! Yet even in our Protestant Bibles Peter is called Saint.

Damien was *dirty*.

He was. Think of the poor lepers annoyed with this dirty comrade! But the clean Dr Hyde was at his food in a fine house.

Damien was *headstrong*.

I believe you are right again; and I thank God for his strong head and heart.

Damien was *bigoted*.

I am not fond of bigots myself, because they are not fond of me. But what is meant by bigotry, that we should regard it as a blemish in a priest? Damien believed his own religion with the simplicity of a peasant or a child; as I would I could suppose that you do. For this, I wonder at him some way off; and had that been his only character, should have avoided him in life. But the point of interest in Damien, which has caused him to be so much talked about and made him at last the subject of your pen and mine, was that, in him, his bigotry, his intense and narrow faith, wrought potently for good, and strengthened him to be one of the world's heroes and exemplars.

Damien *was not sent to Molokai, but went there without orders*.

Is this a misreading? or do you really mean the words for blame? I have heard Christ, in the pulpits of our Church, held up for imitation on the ground that His sacrifice was voluntary. Does Dr Hyde think otherwise?

Damien *did not stay at the settlement, etc.*

It is true he was allowed many indulgences. Am I to understand that you blame the father for profiting by these, or the officers for granting them? In either case, it is a mighty Spartan standard to issue from the house on Beretania Street; and I am convinced you will find yourself with few supporters.

Damien *had no hand in the reforms, etc.*

I think even you will admit that I have already been frank in my description of the man I am defending; but before I take you up upon this head, I will be franker still, and tell you that perhaps nowhere in the world can a man taste a more pleasurable sense of contrast than when he passes from Damien's 'Chinatown' at Kalawao to the beautiful Bishop-Home at Kalaupapa. At this point, in my desire to make all fair for you, I will break my rule and adduce Catholic testimony. Here is a passage from my diary about my visit to the Chinatown, from which you will see how it is (even now) regarded by its own officials:

We went round all the dormitories, refectories, etc. – dark and dingy enough, with a superficial cleanliness, which he [Mr Dutton, the lay brother] did not seek to defend. 'It is almost decent,' said he; 'the sisters will make that all right when we get them here.'

And yet I gathered it was already better since Damien was dead, and far better than when he was there alone and had his own (not always excellent) way. I have now come far enough to meet you on a common ground of fact; and I tell you that, to a mind not prejudiced by jealousy, all the reforms of the lazaretto, and even those which he most vigorously opposed, are properly the work of Damien. They are the evidence of his success; they are what his heroism provoked from the reluctant and the careless. Many were before him in the field; Mr Meyer, for instance, of whose faithful work we hear too little: there have been many since; and some had more worldly wisdom, though none had more devotion, than our saint. Before his day, even you will confess, they had effected little. It was his part, by one striking act of martyrdom, to direct all men's eyes on that distressful country. At a blow, and with the price of his life, he made the place illustrious and public. And that, if you will consider largely, was the one reform needful; pregnant of all that should succeed. It brought money; it brought (best individual addition of them all) the sisters; it brought supervision, for public opinion and public interest landed with the man at Kalawao. If ever any man brought reforms, and died to bring them, it was he. There is not a clean cup or towel in the Bishop-Home, but dirty Damien washed it.

Damien *was not a pure man in his relations with women, etc.*

How do you know that? Is this the nature of the conversation in that house on Beretania Street which the cabman envied, driving past? – racy details of the misconduct of the poor peasant priest, toiling under the cliffs of Molokai?

Many have visited the station before me; they seem not to have heard the rumour. When I was there I heard many shocking tales, for my informants were men speaking with the plainness of the laity; and I heard plenty of complaints of Damien. Why was this never mentioned? and how came it to you in the retirement of your clerical parlour?

But I must not even seem to deceive you. This scandal, when I read it in your letter, was not new to me. I had heard it once before; and I must tell you how. There came to Samoa a man from Honolulu; he, in a public-house on the beach, volunteered the statement that Damien had 'contracted the disease from having connection with the female lepers'; and I find a joy in telling you how the report was welcomed in a public-house. A man sprang to his feet; I am not at liberty to give his name, but from what I heard I doubt if you would care to have him to dinner in Beretania Street. 'You miserable little ———' (here is a word I dare not print, it would so shock your ears). 'You miserable little ———', he cried, 'if the story were a thousand times true, can't you see you are a million times a lower ——— for daring to repeat it?' I wish it could be told of you that when the report reached you in your house, perhaps after family worship, you had found in your soul enough holy anger to receive it with the same expressions; ay, even with that one which I dare not print; it would not need to have been blotted away, like Uncle Toby's oath, by the tears of the recording angel; it would have been counted to you for your brightest righteousness. But you have deliberately chosen the part of the man from Honolulu, and you have played it with improvements of your own. The man from Honolulu – miserable, leering creature – communicated the tale to a rude knot of beach-combing drinkers in a public-house, where (I will so far agree with your temperance opinions) man is not always at his noblest; and the man from Honolulu had himself been drinking – drinking, we may charitably fancy, to excess. It was to your 'Dear Brother, the Reverend H. B. Gage,' that you chose to communicate the sickening story; and the blue ribbon which adorns your portly bosom forbids me to allow you the extenuating plea that you were drunk when it was done. Your 'dear brother' – a brother indeed – made haste to deliver up your letter (as a means of grace, perhaps) to the religious papers; where, after many months, I found and read and wondered at it; and whence I have now reproduced it for the wonder of others. And you and your dear brother have, by this cycle of operations, built up a contrast very edifying to examine in detail. The man whom you would not care to have to dinner, on the one side; on the other, the Reverend Dr Hyde and the Reverend H. B. Gage: the Apia bar-room, the Honolulu manse.

But I fear you scarce appreciate how you appear to your fellow-men; and to bring it home to you, I will suppose your story to be true. I will suppose – and God forgive me for supposing it – that Damien faltered and stumbled in his narrow path of duty; I will suppose that, in the horror of his isolation, perhaps in the fever of incipient disease, he, who was doing so much more than he had sworn, failed in the letter of his priestly oath – he, who was so much a better man than either you or me, who did what we have never dreamed of daring – he too tasted of our common frailty. 'O, Iago, the pity of it!' The least tender should be moved to tears; the most incredulous to prayer. And all that you could do was to pen your letter to the Reverend H. B. Gage!

Is it growing at all clear to you what a picture you have drawn of your own heart? I will try yet once again to make it clearer. You had a father: suppose this tale were about him, and some informant brought it to you, proof in hand: I am not making too high an estimate of your emotional nature when I suppose you would regret the circumstance? that you would feel the tale of frailty the more keenly since it shamed the author of your days? and that the last thing you would do would be to publish it in the religious press? Well, the man who tried to do what Damien did, is my father, and the father of the man in the Apia bar, and the father of all who love goodness; and he was your father too, if God had given you grace to see it.

MY FIRST BOOK
Treasure Island

It was far, indeed, from being my first book, for I am not a novelist alone. But I am well aware that my paymaster, the great public, regards what else I have written with indifference, if not aversion. If it call upon me at all, it calls on me in the familiar and indelible character; and when I am asked to talk of my first book, no question in the world but what is meant is my first novel.

Sooner or later, somehow, anyhow, I was bound I was to write a novel. It seems vain to ask why. Men are born with various manias: from my earliest childhood it was mine to make a plaything of imaginary series of events; and as soon as I was able to write, I became a good friend to the paper-makers. Reams upon reams must have gone to the making of *Rathillet*, the *Pentland Rising*,[1] the *King's Pardon* (otherwise *Park Whitehead*), *Edward Ferren*, *A Country Dance*, and a *Vendetta in the West*; and it is consolatory to remember that these reams are now all ashes, and have been received again into the soil. I have named but a few of my ill-fated efforts: only such, indeed, as came to a fair bulk ere they were desisted from; and even so they cover a long vista of years. *Rathillet* was attemped before fifteen, the *Vendetta* at twenty-nine, and the succession of defeats lasted unbroken till I was thirty-one. By that time I had written little books and little essays and short stories, and had got patted on the back and paid for them – though not enough to live upon. I had quite a reputation. I was the successful man. I passed my days in toil, the futility of which would sometimes make my cheek to burn, – that I should spend a man's energy upon this business, and yet could not earn a livelihood; and still there shone ahead of me an unattained ideal. Although I had attempted the thing with rigour not less than ten or twelve times, I had not yet written a novel. All – all my pretty ones – had gone for a little, and then stopped inexorably, like a schoolboy's watch.

---

[1] *Ne pas confondre.* Not the slim green pamphlet with the imprint of Andrew Elliott, for which (as I see with amazement from the book-lists) the gentlemen of England are willing to pay fancy prices; but its predecessor, a bulky historical romance without a spark of merit, and now deleted from the world.

I might be compared to a cricketer of many years' standing who should never have made a run. Anybody can write a short story – a bad one, I mean – who has industry and paper and time enough; but not everyone may hope to write even a bad novel. It is the length that kills. The accepted novelist may take his novel up and put it down, spend days upon it in vain, and write not any more than he makes haste to blot. Not so the beginner. Human nature has certain rights; instinct – the instinct of self-preservation – forbids that any man (cheered and supported by the consciousness of no previous victory) should endure the miseries of unsuccessful literary toil beyond a period to be measured in weeks. There must be something for hope to feed upon. The beginner must have a slant of wind, a lucky vein must be running, he must be in one of those hours when the words come and the phrases balance of themselves – *even to begin*. And having begun, what a dread looking forward is that until the book shall be accomplished! For so long a time the slant is to continue unchanged, the vein to keep running; for so long a time you must hold at command the same quality of style; for so long a time your puppets are to be always vital, always consistent, always vigorous. I remember I used to look, in those days, upon every three-volume novel with a sort of veneration, as a feat – not possibly of literature – but at least of physical and moral endurance and the courage of Ajax.

In the fated year I came to live with my father and mother at Kinnaird, above Pitlochry. There I walked on the red moors and by the side of the golden burn. The rude, pure air of our mountains inspirited, if it did not inspire us; and my wife and I projected a joint volume of bogie stories, for which she wrote *The Shadow on the Bed*, and I turned out *Thrawn Janet*, and a first draft of the *Merry Men*. I love my native air, but it does not love me; and the end of this delightful period was a cold, a fly blister, and a migration, by Strathairdle and Glenshee, to the Castleton of Braemar. There it blew a good deal and rained in a proportion. My native air was more unkind than man's ingratitude; and I must consent to pass a good deal of my time between four walls in a house lugubriously known as 'the late Miss M'Gregor's cottage.' And now admire the finger of predestination. There was a schoolboy in the late Miss M'Gregor's cottage, home for the holidays, and much in want of 'something craggy to break his mind upon.' He had no thought of literature; it was the art of Raphael that received his fleeting suffrages, and with aid of pen and ink and a shilling box of water-colours, he had soon turned one of the rooms into a picture-gallery. My more immediate duty towards the gallery was to be showman; but I would sometimes unbend a little, join the artist (so to speak) at the easel, and pass the afternoon with him in a generous emulation, making coloured drawings. On one of these occasions I made the map of an island; it was elaborately and (I thought) beautifully coloured; the shape of it took my fancy beyond expression; it contained harbours that pleased me like sonnets; and with the unconsciousness of the predestined, I ticketed my performance *Treasure Island*. I am told there are people who do not care for maps, and find it hard to believe. The names, the shapes of the woodlands, the courses of the roads and rivers, the prehistoric footsteps of man still distinctly traceable up hill and down dale, the mills and the ruins, the ponds and the ferries, perhaps the *Standing Stone* or the *Druidic Circle* on the heath; here is an inexhaustible fund of interest for any man with eyes to see, or tuppenceworth of imagination to understand with. No child but must remember laying his head in the grass, staring into the infinitesimal forest, and seeing it grow populous with fairy armies. Somewhat in this way, as I pored upon my map of *Treasure Island*, the future characters of the book began to appear there visibly among imaginary woods; and their brown faces and bright weapons peeped out upon me from unexpected quarters, as they passed to and fro, fighting and hunting treasure, on these few square inches of a flat projection. The next thing I knew, I had some paper before me and was writing out a list of chapters. How often have I done so, and the thing gone no farther! But there seemed elements of success about this enterprise. It was to be a story for boys; no need of psychology or fine writing; and I had a boy at hand to be a touchstone. Women were excluded. I was unable to handle a brig (which the *Hispaniola* should have been), but I thought I could make shift to sail her as a schooner without public shame. And then I had an idea for John Silver from which I promised myself funds of entertainment: to take an admired friend of mine (whom the reader very likely knows and admires as much as I do), to deprive him of all his finer qualities and higher graces of temperament, to leave him with nothing but his strength, his courage, his quickness, and his magnificent geniality, and to try to express these in terms of the culture of a raw tarpaulin. Such psychical surgery is, I think, a common way of 'making character'; perhaps it is, indeed, the only way. We can put in the quaint figure that spoke a hundred words with us yesterday by the wayside; but do we know him? Our friend, with his infinite variety and flexibility, we know – but can we put him in? Upon the first we must engraft secondary and imaginary qualities, possibly all wrong; from the second, knife in hand, we must cut away and deduct the needless arborescence of his nature; but the trunk and the few branches that remain we may at least be fairly sure of.

On a chill September morning, by the cheek of a brisk fire, and the rain drumming on the window, I began *The Sea Cook*, for that was the original title. I have begun (and finished) a number of other books, but I cannot remember to have sat down to one of them with more complacency. It is not to be wondered at, for stolen waters are proverbially sweet. I am now upon a painful chapter. No doubt the parrot once belonged to Robinson Crusoe. No doubt the skeleton is conveyed from Poe. I think little of these, they are trifles and details: and no man can hope to have a monopoly of skeletons or make a corner in talking birds. The stockade, I am told, is from *Masterman Ready*. It may be, I care not a jot. These useful writers had fulfilled the poet's saying: departing, they had left behind them

<blockquote>
Footprints on the sands of time;
Footprints that perhaps another –
</blockquote>

and I was the other! It is my debt to Washington Irving that exercises my conscience, and justly so, for I believe plagiarism was rarely carried farther. I chanced to pick up the *Tales of a Traveller* some years ago, with a view to an anthology of prose narrative, and the book flew up and struck me; Billy Bones, his chest, the company in the parlour, the whole inner spirit and a good deal of the material detail of my first chapters – all were there, all were the property of Washington Irving. But I had no guess of it then as I sat writing by the fireside, in what seemed the springtide of a somewhat pedestrian inspiration; nor yet day by day, after lunch, as I read aloud my morning's work to the family. It seemed to me original as sin; it seemed to belong to me like my right eye. I had counted on one boy; I found I had two in my audience. My father caught fire at once with all the romance and childishness of his original nature. His own stories, that every night of his life he put himself to sleep with, dealt perpetually with ships, roadside inns, robbers, old sailors, and commercial travellers before the era of steam. He never finished one of these romances: the lucky man did not require to! But in *Treasure Island* he recognised something kindred to his own imagination; it was *his* kind of picturesque; and he not only heard with delight the daily chapter, but set himself actively to collaborate. When the time came for Billy Bones's chest to be ransacked, he must have passed the better part of a day preparing, on the back of a legal envelope, an inventory of its contents, which I exactly followed; and the name of 'Flint's old ship,' the *Walrus*, was given at his particular request. And now, who should come dropping in, *ex machina*, but Doctor Japp, like the disguised prince who is to bring down the curtain upon peace and happiness in the last act, for he carried in his pocket, not a horn or a talisman, but a publisher; had, in fact, been charged by my old friend, Mr Henderson, to unearth new writers for *Young Folks*. Even the ruthlessness of a united family recoiled before the extreme measure of inflicting on our guest the mutilated members of *The Sea Cook*; at the same time we would by no means stop our readings, and accordingly the tale was begun again at the beginning, and solemnly redelivered for the benefit of Doctor Japp. From that moment on I have thought highly of his critical faculty; for when he left us, he carried away the manuscript in his portmanteau.

Here, then, was everything to keep me up – sympathy, help, and now a positive engagement. I had chosen besides a very easy style. Compare it with the almost contemporary *Merry Men*; one would prefer the one style, one the other – 'tis an affair of character, perhaps of mood; but no expert can fail to see that the one is much more difficult, and the other much easier, to maintain. It seems as though a full-grown, experienced man of letters might engage to turn out *Treasure Island* at so many pages a day, and keep his pipe alight. But alas! this was not my case. Fifteen days I stuck to it, and turned out fifteen chapters; and then, in the early paragraphs of the sixteenth, ignominiously lost hold. My mouth was empty; there was not one word more of *Treasure Island* in my bosom; and here were the proofs of the beginning already waiting me at the *Hand and Spear*! There I corrected them, living for the most part alone, walking on the heath at Weybridge on dewy autumn mornings, a good deal pleased with what I had done, and more appalled than I can depict to you in words at what remained for me to do. I was thirty-one; I was the head of a family; I had lost my health; I had never yet paid my way, had never yet made two hundred pounds a year; my father had quite recently bought back and cancelled a book that was judged a failure; was this to be another and last fiasco? I was indeed very close on despair; but I shut my mouth hard, and during the journey to Davos, where I was to pass the winter, had the resolution to think of other things, and bury myself in the novels of M. du Boisgobey. Arrived at my destination, down I sat one morning to the unfinished tale, and behold! it flowed from me like small talk; and in a second tide of delighted industry, and again at the rate of a chapter a day, I finished *Treasure Island*. It had to be transacted almost secretly. My wife was ill, the school-boy remained alone of the faithful, and John Addington Symonds (to whom I timidly mentioned what I was engaged on) looked on me askance. He was at that time very eager I should write on the *Characters* of Theophrastus, so far out may be judgements of the wisest men. But Symonds (to be sure) was scarce the confidant to go to for sympathy in a boy's story. He was large-minded; 'a full man,' if there ever was one; but the very name of my enterprise would suggest to him only capitulations of sincerity and solecisms of style. Well, he was not far wrong.

Treasure Island – it was Mr Henderson who deleted the first title, *The Sea Cook* – appeared duly in the story paper, where it figured in the ignoble midst without woodcuts and attracted not the least attention. I did not care. I liked the tale myself, for much the same reason as my father liked the beginning: it was my kind of picturesque. I was not a little proud of John Silver also, and to this day rather admire that smooth and formidable adventurer. What was infinitely more exhilarating, I had passed a landmark; I had finished a tale, and written 'The End' upon my manuscript, as I had not done since the *Pentland Rising*, when I was a boy of sixteen, not yet at college. In truth it was so by a set of lucky accidents: had not Doctor Japp come on his visit, had not the tale flowed from me with singular ease, it must have been laid aside like its predecessors, and found a circuitous and unlamented way to the fire. Purists may suggest it would have been better so. I am not of that mind. The tale seems to have given much pleasure, and it brought (or was the means of bringing) fire and food and wine to a deserving family in which I took an interest. I need scarce say I mean my own.

But the adventures of *Treasure Island* are not yet quite at an end. I had written it up to the map. The map was the chief part of my plot. For instance, I had called an islet *Skeleton Island*, not knowing what I meant, seeking only for the immediate picturesque; and it was to justify this name that I broke into the gallery of Mr Poe and stole Flint's pointer. And in the same way, it was because I had made two harbours that the *Hispaniola* was sent on her wanderings with Israel Hands. The time came when it was decided to republish, and I sent in my manuscript and the map along with it to Messrs Cassell. The proofs came, they were corrected, but I heard nothing of the map. I wrote and asked; was told it had never been received, and sat aghast. It is one thing to draw a map at random, set a scale in one corner of it at a venture, and write up a story to the measurements. It is quite another to have to examine a whole book, make an inventory of all the allusions contained in it, and with a pair of compasses painfully design a map to suit the data. I did it, and the map was drawn again in my father's office, with embellishments of blowing whales and sailing ships; and my father himself brought into service a knack he had of various writing, and elaborately *forged* the signature of Captain Flint and the sailing directions of Billy Bones. But somehow it was never *Treasure Island* to me.

I have said it was the most of the plot. I might almost say it was the whole. A few reminiscences of Poe, Defoe, and Washington Irving, a copy of Johnson's *Buccaneers*, the name of the Dead Man's Chest from Kingsley's *At Last*, some recollections of canoeing on the high seas, a cruise in a fifteen-ton schooner yacht, and the map itself with its infinite, eloquent suggestion, made up the whole of my materials. It is perhaps not often that a map figures so largely in a tale; yet it is always important. The author must know his countryside whether real or imaginary, like his hand; the distances, the points of the compass, the place of the sun's rising, the behaviour of the moon, should all be beyond cavil. And how troublesome the moon is! I have come to grief over the moon in *Prince Otto*; and, so soon as that was pointed out to me, adopted a precaution which I recommend to other men – I never write now without an almanac. With an almanac, and the map of the country and the plan of every house, either actually plotted on paper or clearly and immediately apprehended in the mind, a man may hope to avoid some of the grossest possible blunders. With the map before him, he will scarce allow the sun to set in the east, as it does in the *Antiquary*. With the almanac at hand, he will scarce allow two horsemen, journeying on the most urgent affair, to employ six days, from three of the Monday morning till late in the Saturday night, upon a journey of, say, ninety or a hundred miles; and before the week is out, and still on the same nags, to cover fifty in one day, as he may read at length in the inimitable novel of *Rob Roy*. And it is certainly well, though far from necessary, to avoid such *croppers*. But it is my contention – my superstition, if you like – that he who is faithful to his map, and consults it, and draws from it his inspiration, daily and hourly, gains positive support, and not mere negative immunity from accident. The tale has a root there: it grows in that soil; it has a spine of its own behind the words. Better if the country be real, and he has walked every foot of it and knows every milestone.

But, even with imaginary places, he will do well in the beginning to provide a map. As he studies it, relations will appear that he had not thought upon. He will discover obvious though unsuspected short cuts and footpaths for his messengers; and even when a map is not all the plot, as it was in *Treasure Island*, it will be found to be a mine of suggestion.

INDEX

NOTE: Works by Robert Louis Stevenson appear under title; other works under the name of the author. Individual essays in the collection are not listed in the index unless referred to in the Introduction.